Open and Clothed

ALSO BY ANDREA SIEGEL

Women in Aikido (*North Atlantic Press*)

Open and Clothed

For the Passionate Clothes Lover

Andrea Siegel

AGAPANTHUS BOOKS

NEW YORK

Published in the United States
by Agapanthus Books, Woodside, New York.
Manufactured in Canada

First Edition

ISBN 0-9672750-0-8
Library of Congress Catalog Number 99-095229
10 9 8 7 6 5 4 3 2 1

For information address
Agapanthus Books
P.O. Box 770103
Woodside New York 11377

Cover design by Jacqueline Thaw
Book design and composition by Julie Murkette

For Ruth Stone and Andrew Gelman
with love and gratitude.

Contents

So I was heading across 96th Street toward a store called Better Your Home (don't ask. . . I mean, is it like, "Better this garbage is in your home than in mine"? Or a directive, as in "Better yourself. Pull yourself up by your bootstraps"? Whatever. They had something I needed, so I went. . .). Anyway, I'm walking up 96th toward Columbus, I've just crossed Amsterdam, and I see this tiny old lady—an old seventy, I'd guess—in this incredible dress. It's a cotton pique floral number with huge flowers on it in a wonderful range of colors (the whole range). And each cloth-covered button down the front is a different color.

I say to her, "Great dress."

She says, "Thank you." Then she comes up close to me and says, "A Saks Fifth Avenue dress. I got it for three dollars. At my age I need to economize. I bought it at a thrift store. I'm not long for this world." She pauses. Some people walk by us. She says, "I'm eighty-eight years old. And when I see a dress like that"—she points to the woman who just passed us wearing a tight, stretchy dress with visible panty line, which clings to her enormous behind— "when I see a dress like that," she continues, "It hastens my end."

I ask her what's her secret, how she found the great dress. She says, "People ask me for advice all the time. But I need to keep it to myself." She pulls her hands to her heart and holds them in fists. She says, "I need it for me."

"To stay alive?" I ask. She nods. I say, "Then don't tell me. I'd rather have you with us and wearing great dresses." She agrees.

A young man walks by. She points him out to me: "He held open a door for me in my building once. I remember that. I remember people who are kind to me." She continues, as if we have known each other a long time, "I can feel my end coming. I'm not myself. I ran into an old friend at the laundromat recently and she said, 'Lil, what's wrong?' I know I don't look like myself. I don't feel myself lately. I've been around here long enough." I tell her I hope that's not so because we need her to wear great dresses in New York. She says, "Thank you for your compliment." I wished her the best of luck and we parted ways. I absolutely loved her.

I walked to the newsstand ten feet away and bought a ballpoint pen for fifty cents and wrote this encounter down on the back of a receipt in my wallet. For some reason I've felt overwhelmed by New York and not kept up my habit of carrying a pen with me everywhere, like it's too intimidating to write here. Maybe writing down stuff like this will help.

Encounters with people like Lil inspired me to write this book. I hope you enjoy reading it as much as I enjoyed writing it.

A. Siegel

Introduction

Thus in this one pregnant subject of clothes, rightly understood,
is included all that men have thought, dreamed, done, and been. . . .
—Thomas Carlyle, *Sartor Resartus*[1]

This is a $52 billion industry and we still don't have the right clothes.
—Olivia Goldsmith, author of *Fashionably Late*[2]

Inner Life Quiz

1. Regarding clothes, I worry:
    a) It's vain to think about clothes.
    b) It's one of my secret pleasures to think about clothes.
    c) I'll never look good in anything.

2. I hate all my clothes:
    a) However, I do have good taste in underwear.
    b) However, I do have good taste in _____.
    c) With no exceptions.

3. I care more about a perfect pair of shoes than world peace:
    a) Often.
    b) Sometimes.
    c) Only if Manolo Blahnik is having a sale.

The clothing tip that most people remember hearing from their mothers is, "Always wear clean underwear." This is often followed by "just in case you're in a car wreck." After a friend was in a car accident, he was cut out of his clothes and underwear by the emergency crew. He reported he was so covered with grease and dirt by the time he reached the emergency room, no one could tell whether his underwear was ever clean. This made me wonder if the things we know about clothes, things we say in our sleep, are completely irrelevant.

Soon after, I was arguing with someone about clothing happiness. She said, "If there is a God, do you think God would want you to be happy or would God want you to be out sacrificing goats?" "Goats, definitely," I said, but upon reflection I reconsidered. This book is the result of that reconsideration.

A greater variety of clothing is available than ever before. Most of our conflicts about clothes aren't about a lack or surplus of clothes, but about a lack of inner clarity. Good judgment about wardrobe may be clouded by a host of factors, among them:

- your mother's opinions
- the state of your closet
- fashion's whirlwind of dictates
- cultural and historical imperatives
- the role you played in your family
- the difference between what you yearn for and what's possible
- the difference between how a garment looks on you and how it feels to you
- and how you feel about your body, your job, your mirror, your life, and even who you shop with.

In addition, society as a whole denies and denigrates the depth of our attachment to clothing. Many of us absorb and parrot those messages without ever exploring what we want. While most of us have been dressing ourselves for years, perhaps we've been doing so with a sense of shame. Maybe there are parts of our clothes or our bodies we hate, or maybe there's nothing we like. One person whom I interviewed, when pressed, said, "Well, my earlobes are OK."

As a result of these influences, gracefully answering the question "What do I wear?" each morning may be a profoundly complicated challenge. How someone feels about even the smallest detail can be intensely personal.

Laurel Fenenga, a hat designer, sees her interest in clothing stemming from her childhood. Laurel's mother had cancer for eight years and died when Laurel was twelve. Her mother taught the kids certain things they could do in the house with her, among them embroidery and origami. Laurel explains:

We all learned how to fold paper. I like pleats. I like crispness, and I like zigzags. I'm always attracted to harlequin patterns or any kind of rickrack, anything with that edge. Origami lends itself well to that kind of thing. And the hats are very paper-like in texture. So is the straw that I work with. Repeat patterns are probably important to a child whose life is kind of chaotic, repeat patterns and the conciseness of the pleats.

Many other people spoke with me about their mothers' attempts to convey loving guidance through dress instruction. These events, however, were often stressful. Clothes lover Daphne Stannard comments about an altercation she and her mother had while Daphne packed for college:

She kept pulling out these ugly things she had bought me, and saying, "Oh, take this." I'd say, "No, Mom, I'm going to take this instead." And I'd pull out, for example, my Army jacket. She cried and said, "I just want you to get everything you want, and I think if you wear the clothes you want to wear, you're going to make mistakes, and you won't get everything you want." And I said, "I have to make those mistakes. You can't protect me from them."

I tell Daphne I feel touched by the idea that something you wear could prevent you from having what you loved. Daphne responds, "It's so true, though, in this culture, because we size people up very quickly. Judgments are made at the drop of a hat."

Laurel's story made me reflect about my own motivations and clothing roots. Daphne's example spoke to me about how mothers' love and dreams for their daughters can play themselves out through clothing conflict.

I am a writer and fabric artist. In my craft, I specialize in customized designs which ornament and enhance individuals' self-expression. Because the stories I heard from clients, friends, and people in the fashion industry were so different from what the media usually bleat about clothes, I wanted to record an alternative. For this book, I took a few years of my life to have conversations with everyone fabulous I could think of, specifically people who work in the rag trade or who simply love clothes. I studied the history of fashion, looked up facts I wasn't sure about, and even read *The Heritage of Cotton* from beginning to end. Throughout the rest of this book, I want to share with you a mosaic of the best of the stories and discussions. I hope these will enable you to ask yourself the deeper questions that lead to wardrobe happiness.

What do clothes do? At their worst, they are an expression of poverty or craziness (the layers of grime and dirt worn by the bag lady), sex-for-sale (the abbreviated, tight, flashy garb of the prostitute), or false dominance in the social status food chain as worn by the shiny set (the ice-perfect designer outfit).

At the most basic level, my friend, the advertising executive and fabu-dresser Lisa Star says choosing clothes is about "Is-it-clean-and-do-I-have-socks-that-match?"

At their best, clothes express something entirely different. Clothing scholar Grace Margaret Morton notes:

> The consumer is a designer in that through assembling a costume she is creating a background for herself as the theme or center of interest, and is expressing her individual personality through use of becoming color, lines, shapes, and textures in accordance with the principles of design. Each completed costume ensemble becomes a new expression and gives satisfaction to the human desire to continually create and conceive a new unity which is beautiful.[3]

On a simpler human level, writer Rhonda Pretlow says, "I know I'm not my body. I know I'm not my skin color. I know I'm not the job I'm doing. I know the essence of me is something that a person can only really see by experiencing me. So the clothes that I wear at different times are just to allow me to get close enough to people so that they can see the real me, basically."

Despite the influence of feminism, in women's traditional arenas such as dress and clothing selection, some of us still wait for the magic wand, diet, or garment to transform us. We moan "What am I going to wear?" as if someone else had the answer. Designer Oscar de la Renta points us in the direction we need to go when he says that being well dressed is "a question of good balance and good common sense, a knowledge of who you are and what you are. There are many kinds of taste. The rules that apply to one person do not hold true for another."[4] For this reason, I wrote *Open and Clothed*.

This is a sourcebook for the clothes lover, a guide through the quagmire of choice. However,

I'm not about to tell you what to wear because, quite simply, that approach does not work. This book focuses on understanding the forces that subvert clarity about dress and, after that, tailoring individual history and personal preference into a vision of wardrobe happiness specific to each person.[5]

Why bother? Maybe it's important to take a stand for what we love. Maybe it's important that we be happy with our clothes, have clarity about how we want to look, and focus our ability to express that. What on earth does a happy centeredness have to do with wardrobe? This idea came to me from watching the pattern of the planets swirling through the star-speckled dark sky of the fabric of a skirt: there is no center to the universe. Or rather, each person, tree or stump has the right to declare her[6] or itself the center.

Too often in the past I have put another at the center of my personal universe. This created an imbalance, an untruth. I ended up dancing around someone else as though I were their satellite, dressing for them, eventually resenting them, because I always felt out of balance, leaning on and looking toward them. I didn't know that I could stand wide-legged and easy, hold out my arms as if to hug the world, and say, "Yes. I sense the weight of my body against the soles of my feet, and the vitality pulsing through my body." I felt this position to be selfish, not seeing that the other option would eventually cause me to coast into that person and crash.

I had understood centeredness to be the same thing as narcissism or big ego. We all know "Big Ego." He struts around the room *as if* he knew everything, and orders people around without knowing what is important. Big Ego ticks people off. Centeredness, coming from a profound experience of joy, comfort, and ease, moves carefully and surely through the world, sensitive to the limits and boundaries of others because she acutely knows her own place in the dance. Her experience is available to people like you and me. With practice. From centeredness comes a whole, unique, integrated person, and a whole person you can dress.

Is this a self-help book? From a glimpse at a random page, it sure looks like one. It might serve those who want that kind of guidance. But if you're seeking miracles, look away. If reading this book helps, the change will be so incremental that no one will notice. Except maybe you, sometimes. No one will applaud you on your cool new look. Lovers will not beat down the doors, fighting for entry with prospective employers begging to pay you seven-figure salaries. Hollywood won't come looking for you. Guaranteed. Change that works occurs subtly. It's hard to create a change that's big enough to matter yet doesn't feel so scary that you react by retrenching deeply into old habits. And we are seeking the keys to the kinds of power that make those changes big enough to matter.

Notes:

1. Carlyle, Thomas. *Sartor Resartus*. Page 67.

2. Bargreen, Melinda. "'Fashionably Late' arrives just in time for summer fun," *Seattle Times*, August 11, 1994. Page M-1.

3. Morton, Grace Margaret. *The Arts of Costume and Personal Appearance*. Page 114.

4. Morris, Bernadine. *The Fashion Makers*. Page 185.

5. A gentle reminder: To have more than one set of clothes is a luxury, and having the time to think about these issues is a privilege in a world where most people are poor and exploited. Many people in the United States and the Western world live in unprecedented ease: hot and cold running water, electricity, free entertainment on call twenty-four hours a day, and the opportunity to have meaningful relationships and work. Any item of food or clothing is available to us almost immediately. Given the speed with which we consume and throw out new goods, it is important to consider our impact and be grateful.

6. While many wonderful men participated in the making of this book, the pronouns address a female reader. For the men in the audience, just change the pronouns as needed for clarity. Also, many of the sex-related examples are heterosexual. By this I do not mean to imply an endorsement of heterosexuality. Please change the pronouns and protuberances as needed to suit yourself.

Part 1
Inner Fundamentals

Fashion and Its Discontents

Does fashion matter? Always—though not quite as much after death.

—Joan Rivers, entertainer[1]

Nine Ways of Looking at the Big Picture

1. Why is there fashion?

The decisively revolutionary machine . . . is the sewing machine.

—Karl Marx, *Capital*[2]

The seeds of the fashion industry can be seen germinating in earlier periods in history; however, the huge growth evident today began in the mid-nineteenth century. The sewing machine was introduced in 1846, the band saw—used to cut patterns atop many layers of fabric—in 1858, and the electric iron in 1882. First used to make uniforms for U.S. Army soldiers, sewing machines became immensely popular after the Civil War, when soldiers returned with clothes of better quality than could be made at home. With these inventions, mass-produced clothing became inexpensive and desirable.

Who would decide what mass-produced clothing to manufacture for women? Logically, manufacturers looked to copy the European couture designers. In this way, manufacturers could dress up (with the air of exclusivity) garments produced by the thousands.

The nineteenth-century invention of photography added a dimension to fashion consumption on a large scale. The mass production of images created a new life for the public imagination, an excited and heightened sense of the variety of choices available to gain stature in American society. In exercising this sense of possibilities, women tried to get clothes that imitated fashion pictures of high society ladies. The advertisements promised the fantasy of clothes providing upward mobility. Advertising also introduced the myth that no alteration would be required for these "ready to wear" garments. Fashion writer Katherine Betts notes, "Ironically, the introduction of the sewing machine . . . didn't improve women's lot—not only did it put them in sweatshops, but it also complicated their clothes with miles of superfluous frills and flounces."[3]

Considering the enormous amount of high fashion seen in the media today, women wear little of fashion in real life. Designers make couture for those few whose art form is wearing exquisite custom-made clothes. The number of couture's fans who will pay $20,000 a suit has diminished significantly, from 20,000 in the late 1940s to an estimated 2,000 women today.[4] To get a sense of how small the couture actually is, consider that Christian Lacroix's wedding dresses constitute sixty percent of his couture business; he produces on average only twenty wedding dresses a year.[5]

What is the fashion spectacle for? There's some truth to the idea that fashion's job is to shock us, and that in seeing the extreme change we become willing to make just a little change. It makes the mass-produced stuff sell better. Fashion designer Rudi Gernreich—who first showed miniskirts and became notorious in the 1960s for the topless bathing suit—said, "I would do it again because I think the topless, by overstating and exaggerating a new freedom of the body, will make the moderate, right degree of freedom more acceptable."[6]

What else is fashion for? Why, to sell the clothes, we think. No. Less than one percent of the women's apparel business in the United States is in designer clothing.[7] Superstar designer Bill Blass explains the fashion show as a "giant come-on," but he does it because "it impresses the hell out of the licensees."[8] Licensees are manufacturers who pay designers gobs of money so they can put the designer's name and logo on mass-produced, factory-made goods. This process falsely gives these common objects the mystique of custom-made specialness. Fashion shows result in sales of designer perfume and bedsheets. The fancier or "higher" the fashion garment, the more likely it is simply imaginary. It is made to parade down a runway once and be photographed.

The magazines and media hawk what's hot and glamorous. The fashion show—what the magazines supposedly report on—gives us the glamor by proxy. It isn't all that glamorous in real life. What do haute couturiers really do? Designer Arnold Scaasi fits maybe four hundred dresses a year. Each fitting takes three hours minimum. Often it takes three fittings or more before a client gets the dress she wants. He comments, "That's a lot of time that you spend standing there with your arms up in the air trying to fit that model who's six feet tall."[9] When Forest Whitaker was researching his role as a designer in the movie *Ready to Wear* he spent a day with New York designers Todd Oldham and Isaac Mizrahi for inspiration. "He was so earnest," says Mizrahi. "But he looked sort of bewildered half the time, especially during a meeting we were having about buttons. I kept wanting to tell him we weren't putting him on, this is really what we do all day."[10]

2. What did fashion replace?

What did fashion replace? How did this occur? And at what cost and benefit? The traditional dress, which existed before the fashion system, by repeating the same patterns in weaving, painting, and adorning, encoded the place of the wearer in her society. Psychologist J.C. Flügel noted that these costumes are the opposite of fashionable ones, "whose value lies mostly in their newness, and which are despised at the slightest sign of their becoming 'old-fashioned' or out of date."[11]

Into the traditional Irish fisherman's sweater were knit patterns representing clan and home; into Guatemalan weaving are woven symbols for home village, marital status, social standing, etc. We see the echoes of this desire to belong in the fans wearing L.A. Dodgers caps and Mickey Mouse–imprinted attire. Only now the group identity is frequently a corporation.

The traditional system of clothing design provided a necessary and beautiful function within the culture. Professor Barbara Brodman observes:

> Native dress helps perpetuate divisions of labor, family systems, and hierarchical orders that have stood the test of millennia and that today are threatened.
>
> In the face of genocidal campaigns, planned dislocations, and forced assimilation into a hostile culture and environment, preserving these overt and material vestiges of culture becomes all important. The imposition of Western fashion, within this context, is no less than a subtle form of genocide.[12]

What do indigenous peoples now wear instead? Our out-of-fashion discards shipped by the containerload by charitable organizations, often cycling back to the countries where they were manufactured a decade or two earlier. This explains why, in news broadcasts of Third World famine or war, people always seem to be wearing our fashions from twenty years ago. They are.[13]

Professor Brodman's perspective would seem to point to the power of embracing traditional roots, whatever they may be. Capitalism, however, has permanently upended many of those traditions, and the insistence by coercion in some fundamentalist countries that women continue to respect tradition subjects them to a different kind of tyranny. In many Muslim countries, if women violate the strict dress codes they may be arrested, jailed, and/or flogged. The U.S. media gives us the following perspective on this issue: when Nada, a woman born in Saudi Arabia, reached puberty, like all Saudi girls she had to cover up. She says, "At first, I was excited to wear the veil. I was twelve—it was a sign I was growing up. But soon, it became a symbol of everything a woman is forbidden to do in my culture."

She continued covering her body, but started removing her veil in public: "When I uncovered my face, men on the street threw stones at me or called me a prostitute. The religious police tried to arrest me. And things became a lot worse as the fundamentalists became more powerful."[14]

The world increasingly industrializes. Poor countries seek to emulate the rich countries. A few impose clothing guidelines, by law, based on tradition. More frequently, the crafted products of the culture, often exquisitely beautiful and unique, become jettisoned in a sometimes involuntary push to assimilate the new, to catch on to this wild ride known as the Industrial Revolution.

In some way I agree with the optimists who call fashion a global unifier because it creates a common visual language of dress: Despite your different skin color and body type, we know you are one of us because you dress like we do. Anyone who watches television perceives this.[15] Sociologist Fred Davis also notes that fashion introduces us to new ideas. Perhaps we can attribute this to the fact that designers are often "in close contact with leading creative and progressive elements in the arts, sciences, politics, and culture generally."[16] Davis goes on to propose that "sharing of significant symbols among diverse groups and peoples could in time bring about an enlightened democratic world order."[17](!)

The degree to which one chooses to embrace or discard aspects of one's own heritage and traditions through dress is a political act. What are your family's traditions? What clothes go with them? To what extent do you wish to honor and preserve those roots? Expression can be problematic. Davis notes that one problem hinges on whether the identity sustained by some distinctive dress style results in others "keeping their distance," thus denying the wearer equality of access, recognition, and recompense. He observes that for others the problem is overcoming social distance and "strangeness" implied by another's distinctive ethnic dress and interacting with him or her "as an equal."[18]

Alison Lurie, author of *The Language of Clothes*, discusses relative degrees of dress emphasis in tribal self-expression, pointing out that,

The London-bred Scot in Highland garb, or the American Black in a dashiki, are determined that no one shall forget who they are for a moment. . . . [T]hey can also be a rebuke to other minority group members who are still rambling around town in the garb of the majority. . . . The Scot whose only sign of his ancestry is a plaid clan tie, or the Black who wears a modest Afro with his or her business suit, do not threaten the rest of us but merely inform us politely if firmly of their sympathies.[19]

What tribe are you from? I'm a Levite, same clan as the Levi's jeans people but not close enough to reap the financial benefits, alas. What pleases you, makes you smile, makes you sit up straighter about the wardrobes of your ancestors? Put the idea of wearing it on the back burner and let it simmer awhile. We'll come back to it later.

Now that we've glanced at tradition, let's return to fashion.

3. What is fashion?[20]

Fashion is Obsolescence.
—Eve Merriam, *Figleaf: The Business of Being in Fashion*[21]

Fashion is the word used to describe new clothes with variation in color, style, theme, proportion, and fabrics which are designed, created, shown to the media, and sold to the public on a time cycle which varies from twice to eight times yearly, depending on the designer/ producer. Fashion is defined by the designers' ads, the media, and what is seen on the street. Depending on your perspective, these people may be 1) the majority, 2) the cool people, or 3) some weird people in Manhattan. The fashion disseminates itself by repeatedly referring visually to the new fashionable details, and by dismissing and not showing the old.

While designers and the media keep asserting that fashion reflects the times, no one can ever draw a straight line, or provide a coherent way to predict how fashion will continue to reflect those times. Successful designers have their hunches proven profitably right repeatedly. It's part of how they stay in business.

For jewelry designer Lisa Graves, seeing fashion trends coming up is easy. "I pride myself at being able to predict things and be ahead of it. What's going to happen next is obvious." Where does that kind of information come from?

Whatever hasn't been done in the last *x* amount of years and whatever you can get really cheap in thrift stores. That's where it all starts. I laughed at one of the recent issues of *Vogue* which showed the grunge look. [This interview took place in May 1993.] Eight years ago, me and my girlfriends were wearing old dresses and boots. And people used to laugh at us. People have been dressing like this for a long time. I couldn't believe that anyone thought it was new. And the prices attached to it were even more hilarious. I saw it happen with punk, with grunge, with the 1960s retro look . . . .

How does she choose what to make next for her business?

Partly whatever I can think of next and partly, because I make jewelry, it's always behind clothing, seasonal. It goes in a cycle. It's been really muted colors. So I know that this fall, it'll go back to jewel tones. And this spring it might go bright again. Spring is either bright or pastel.

Who taught her this?

You just figure it out. You see the patterns. People want something new, but it's always the same. Every three or four years, plaid comes back in. Every three or four years polka dots, or florals. There are only so many different things. If it's last on the list, then it's next to come back. Since I've been doing jewelry, in the last eight years, plaid's been really big twice, and then florals, or sometimes it's fruit.

A challenging aspect of the cyclical nature of fashion for the consumer is seeing one's past as a nightmarish present. I attribute to bell bottoms the anguish and anxiety of adolescence. As fashion moved into a narrower hem, I matured into adulthood. When bell bottoms appeared again in the early 1990s, I felt, "Oh God, my youth haunting me." Lisa comments, "It is true. Youth is haunting you. I wore a bell bottom outfit in pinks and chartreuses, big swirly design, to my senior party."

Some hold with the more mystical theories of fashion origination. Coco Chanel said, "Fashion is not something that exists in dresses only; fashion is something in the air. It's in the wind that blows in the new fashion; you feel it coming, you smell it."[22] Milliner and store owner Chandra Cho has a similar theory to Coco's. Tongue-in-chic she explains:

It's like musical composition. You ask, "Where does the music come from?" If you're a good practicing artist, then whatever you're designing is in touch with the higher realms of arts. It's almost as if a cloud or a misty zone comes out of the earth. In this cloud are all the current fashions and trends. And if you're in touch with yourself, you can pull this information from these ethers. All the good artists who set trends tap this source.

Chandra also looks to politics to understand what's going on in fashion:

Before we went to war and bombed Iraq, I was talking to a friend who's a store owner, buyer, and designer I've known for fifteen years. She was talking about colors and palettes for the coming season. I said, "Oh, you have to do army green. And you have to do Indian prints and madras and ikat—all the other-side-of-the-world-type things. Beads. Like from that place, not from here."

She asked why and I said, "Because it feels to me like there's going to be a war." She became really angry with me. "How can you say that, Chandra?" I said, "Well, I believe it's true."

She said, "I can't do that. I'm not going to capitalize on that." I said, "Well, you've got to give the people what they want. It's not capitalizing on anything. It's what the people want."

Before she got upset, I tried to explain to her. She asked, "How can you do army? What are you trying to say?" I said, "Well, the way you do army is you do epaulets and brass—like navy buttons. It's a playful theme way of expressing what's serious. You have to raise the hemlines. We're going up-to-your-ass short."

She said, "I don't know if I want to go that short." I said, "Do you know what happens before a war? Subconsciously the women show their legs to the men to try to keep them here."

The traditional view of fashion as trickle-down, that the great designers in Paris and maybe in New York design things and that are disseminated outward, is contrary to her view: "The information is available to those who are sensitive, who can pull through." If designers are giving the public what they want, who are we to complain? I'm not complaining about fashion, I'm complaining that the proportion that makes it to the fashion-oriented media doesn't present much of the real spectrum.

Fashion trickles down, trickles up, trickles across. There's a whole lot of trickling going on. This issue of fashion leadership is murky. Where does it begin? It used to begin with royalty. To protect himself from stabbings, James I of England made padding fashionable. Shoes with long points came in during William Rufus's reign because a court favorite, Count Fulk of Anjou, wanted to disguise his bunion-covered feet. Long skirts came in because of the misshapen legs and feet of the daughters of Louis XI of France. Queen Elizabeth I adopted a neck ruff to cover her long, thin, and unshapely neck.[23]

Researchers into modern fashion insist it sometimes starts locally. George Sproles notes, "Instead of looking to higher-status persons for leadership, people look to certain individuals from their own station in life."[24] And, continues Sproles, it starts places we might not want to examine too closely: "Some fashion leadership might even be ascribed to prostitutes, to whom we owe high heels, rouge, and lipstick."[25] Other trends bubble up. Men's mass-produced clothing was first accepted by the lower classes. Work clothes, jeans, boots, and sleeveless undershirts were lower-class styles that became fashion trends. For women, the miniskirt and blue jeans started with the lower classes. Why would trends come from this source? Probably because these styles are, of necessity, less expensive.[26]

As Quentin Bell observed, "Fashion, whose laws are imposed without formal sanctions, is obeyed with wonderful docility, and this despite the fact that her demands are unreasonable, arbitrary, and not infrequently cruel."[27] There are standard ways fashion reportage and advertising manipulate the consumer.

Despite the American slogan of "rugged individualism," we are a nation of lemmings. As the fashion press dictates "This is what you should wear," we look on with a sense of growing dismay, aware that "this" doesn't fit us and makes us look ridiculous, but we don't know another way. The multinational corporations, whose profits depend on Americans blindly spending our way into debt by buying their "goods" and using their credit cards, like it this way. As fashion scholar Joanne Finkelstein summarizes, "Fashionability . . . enables a commodity to be sold and resold in slightly different form many times over, and it is the constant reselling of the chameleonic object that generates much of the wealth of an industrialized economy."[28] Do any of the following shticks get to you?

1. One way to keep a person off balance is to change the rules so fast she can never orient herself. Fashion silhouettes and colors can change as fast as every six to eight weeks for some major retailers—the Gap gets a completely new set of clothes at least every two months—a pace that would be impossible for a body to follow, let alone afford, unless fashion were the woman's sole pursuit and she had an impressive trust fund. The "fashionable body" of the moment changes with the rapidly shifting silhouette. "Her" height varies from 6'+ Claudia Schiffer, as the model du jour, down to 5'7" Kate Moss, and then back up to 5'10"+ Nadja Auermann in the space of a typical year (1994). In that same year, she has C+ cup breasts, she has no breasts, and then who cares about her breasts—her legs are longer than many women's entire bodies. These fashion changes condition us to feel inadequate despite the constancy of our own shapes. Our bodies have a fixed-in-genetics sense of what is possible, and absolutely no interest in the pretty pictures presented as "possibilities." Start to consider what is constant about your own shape.

   • Where does it curve?
   • What lines in garments would be pleasing on your silhouette?
   • Which colors consistently make you look good and which don't?

   Contrast this information with the ever-changing messages you get from the fashion media.

2. The fashion press uses the same twenty words year after year. In any other group of humans, this behavior would be diagnosed as retarded. These masters of the visual (iconographic) language of clothing often have no imagination when it comes to verbalizing. For women's multi-purpose clothing we see words like "easy," "wearability," "clear," "modern," "relaxed," "contemporary," "spare," "executive," and "simplicity." For the work wardrobe the adjectives go something like this: "an effective, flexible wardrobe that will help you look and feel attractive, yet express your message as a professional."[29] The fashion industry's net verbal contribution to our understanding of how to meaningfully speak of clothes is silence. We need to form and develop our own vocabulary of what makes clothes work for us, and take back the language of clothing.

3. In our "climate controlled" environments and in climates that vary little from season to season, the urge to dress for the seasons has become emotional rather than necessary, with the exception of outerwear for rough weather and light clothing for hottest summer. Shaking myself out of this old habit, I found it useful to look at how many basic staples of wardrobe I needed, as opposed to special-weather clothes.

   • For economy's sake, adopt the "seasonless dressing" concept, jazzed up with an occasional inexpensive accessory to tie clothes into the spirit of the season.
   • Note how the idea of seasonal clothing is shown in the stores through color, cut, and fabric.
   • Notice throughout the year what you actually prefer to wear and how that compares with what they would like you to buy.

4. Also mitigating against good sense is the American consumer's expectation of "new and better products every year."[30] While there has been major clothing progress in our lifetime—down jackets, Gore-Tex, microfiber, better sneakers, sport bras, etc.—the new offers such a lively attraction because "it is experienced as an instrument of personal liberation, as an experiment to be undertaken, an experience to be lived, a little adventure of the self."[31] So year after year, consumers rush out to buy this year's version of the "new polyester," touted by the media as being "just like silk," only to find that it self-destructs after a few wearings or a washing. If you're lured by some garment or make-up touted as "new and improved," wait a few years until it's perfected. More likely than not, the product will disappear from the marketplace due to unforeseen problems, like those spontaneously combusting rayon broomstick skirts which were so popular a few years ago.[32]

5. Fashion of the last three decades has demanded the impossible: that we stay young. This demand is made as if the request were reasonable, and all that would be required is a little discipline (and dollars) to make time stop for us.

The blankness of models' yet-to-be-lived lives shows in the expressions painted on their faces, making a striking counterpoint to the drama of the clothes, providing a void for the fantasy of your choice. The beauty of youthful fertility, the virgin sacrificed to the gods, shows up in these garments, in the "kinderwhore" look. The rest of us feel abused if we forget that for the fashions shown in the mass media, "youth" is part of the look. Few of us can master such an inexperienced look, and few of us, if we really thought about it, would want to. Photographers attempting to get the appropriate expression from models ask them to look "dumb" or "bored." "Think, 'Duh!' " suggested one photographer.[33]

Imagine an ancient crone looking beautiful in exquisite garments. Imagine yourself, as you are right now, looking wonderful in beautiful clothes.

To avoid the pull of the waste of fashion, the individual needs to stabilize a sense of self. Remember that human development takes place at an organic rate, slowly. So, since clothes often last a long time, the actual need for changes in wardrobe, if they are to reflect changes in self, takes place slowly as well. Amy Gross, former editor of *Elle* magazine, notes:

> Real change takes place in the smallest increments, invisibly—it's hard to see the progress. I used to work for a magazine that specialized in makeovers, and inevitably the subject of the makeover would revert to her original look. The change was violent, not an evolution but a violation of her way of expressing herself.[34]

4. Why it works: The vulnerability of modern life

We are, most of us, anonymous cogs in a huge city machine. Less than 4% of the U.S. population live on family farms now, down from 30% in 1920.[35] Once, many Americans earned their livings putting their hands in the earth and making it produce and grow; now most don't. Disconnected from the sense of accomplishment that comes from creating something real, people find identifying substance more difficult. Instead they reach for dreamlike alternatives of TV, style, and entertainment, and become vulnerable to the idea that they have to "buy" everything they need, even a sense of self.

Fashion, style, glamor, and advertising appeal to a yearning that knows no rules or boundaries, an endlessly beating heart of wanting. You can become full with glamor, but never satisfied. Why? Glamor is created and fostered by distance, not intimacy, and intimacy nourishes and satisfies. Many feel ambivalence about their voracious fascination with the subject:

> Greta Garbo, New York's most elusive, least photographed celebrity, is window-shopping along the street when she is spotted by a *Women's Wear Daily* photographer. He begins snapping. Garbo runs, into one shop and out of another. The photographer stays in hot pursuit. He confronts her finally; she covers her face with her newspaper; he finishes shooting a roll of film. Next day, pictures of Miss Garbo hiding her face behind a copy of *Women's Wear Daily* run in the newspaper she has been hiding from.[36]

The powerful energy of that hunger, in all of us, can be rechanneled, disciplined, and used. To emerge from the fantasy, we must identify and satisfy our hungers in an enduring and comforting way. It is possible.

We are not trained to look at the media discerningly. We believe in the glamorous image despite the well-documented reports that most models do their jobs on drugs and are sexually abused.[37] Discussing prostitution in the modeling business, former modeling agency owner Jeremy Foster-Fell says, "Any agent who says it doesn't happen is lying."[38] Even the top models, who can remain relatively untouched by the sex-favors trade, acknowledge their work amounts to prostitution. As supermodel Kate Moss said of supermodel Claudia Schiffer: "That's how she made her fortune. . . . She's got an amazing body and big tits. She sold her body like I sold mine."[39] What we see in the pretty pictures usually has little to do with what's actually going on with the human who has been photographed.[40]

We read meanings into photographs that just aren't there.[41] For example, in fashion advertisements, we falsely assume the clothing in ads is for sale. We don't see how clothes are dramatically altered for the photo shoot. Supermodel Lauren Hutton comments that dresses she modeled were cut apart on her, then straight-pinned together and stuffed with toilet paper.[42] Emily Cho notes that "in all too many cases it's the model and her movement that create the excitement and the illusion of glamor,"[43] not the clothes.[44]

Perhaps glamor's effectiveness resides in the power dynamic created by painting over the wounds of abuse. The viewer intuits the tension between the perfectly beautiful surface and the bruised interior. Think about the actual lives of glamor icons Marilyn, Marlon, Elvis, and Madonna. We revere masking—who cares if there is no substance? We make emptiness sacred. Glamor may reflect a kind of hunger for attention, an insatiability on the part of one who projects it. Rock star George Michael agrees: "You don't understand. It's not that there's something extra that makes a superstar. It's that there's something missing."[45]

What does a star get as a result of this glamor? In tell-all biographies they write about bulimia and the blank stares of enthralled people. At a fashion show, Irene Daria observes the "commoners" meeting fashion designer Liz Claiborne:

> As the customers form a circle around her, she seems relaxed, although some of the customers are staring at her as if they were watching a TV screen rather than a real person. They stare with absolutely no expression on their faces. A few women look Liz up and down in the competitive way that some women size each other up. And then, of course, there are the ones that go up to talk to Liz.[46]

How would you like to be gazed at by a couch potato? As Marilyn Monroe said, "When you're famous you kind of run into human nature in a raw kind of way. It stirs up envy, fame does. People feel fame gives them some sort of privilege to walk up to you and say anything, and it won't hurt your feelings—like it's happening to your clothing."[47]

A fashion photo or advertisement is a frozen image, antithetical to the livingness, the movement which must, by definition, be part of the beauty you see in people in your daily life. When what you think of as beautiful corresponds to a model's still picture or film, it's actually a series of stills or dots which, when run through a machine, create the illusion of movement, a *stillness* that imitates movement. Days of work go into those mass-media moments of carefully orchestrated beauty. It is an act, and this act is the model's job. Singer Helen Reddy articulates the distinction between glamor and beauty: "Beauty is something that touches your soul. It could be a sunset or a melodic phrase or a human face. But I think it's totally separate and distinct from glamor. Glamor is good packaging."[48]

When we see the price paid for glamor, it starts to lose its magic power over us. We take back our own power, and with our power we gain mystique which can be an essential part of our own beauty. Writer E.L. Doctorow reminds us glamor and fame are just not that central to a good life:

> Mythic auras are now pretty much manufactured. You can buy yourself one. But more to the point, the issue of renown is not something that figures usefully in your private life. You can't subsist on it; it's not that nourishing. Every day you do your work. Every day you work you begin as if you've never written a word before. And you live with people, family and friends and colleagues who've known you for a long time and for whom your renown isn't a hot issue either.[49]

It's our job to overcome the intimidation of the glamorous other. Look at how deep in the body self-esteem goes, and follow it deeper. Look at intimidation as more energy: "OK, I'm intimidated, I'll take it on as power wanting expression. What do I want to do with it?"

Remember that this glamor-love is dangerous. What martial artist Terry Dobson wrote about the dangers of beauty in combat applies equally well here:

My teacher used to teach us to look between the eyes instead of into the eyes because you can become enthralled with the beauty of the other person and be unable to deal with his attack. This other person might not be as refined as you are. All he will see is a sucker who has fallen into his eyes and he will take your head off. So, if you have the ability to see another person's beauty, you have to avoid becoming a prisoner to it.[50]

Look at your own past in relationship to this issue. Write about it.

• What does glamor mean to you?
• Under what circumstances would you like glamor in your life?
• What makes you feel glamorous?
• If you want glamor in your life, are you prepared for it?

Most of us do not know how to deal with people's reactions.[51] In real life, it takes a lot of fortitude to be radiant, say, at a friend's wedding, and respond graciously when you realize most women are giving you the evil eye. Escaping to the powder room, you stand before the mirror and notice that conversation has stopped. You can feel them thinking, and may even hear them saying, "She's got a lot of nerve. Who does she think she is?" Is it a worthwhile price to pay for loveliness? Wouldn't you rather continue being a shlump?

Feeling enviousness and being the target of it are both corrosive. When we define ourselves as worthless nobodies, our envy and malice toward the glamorized other whom we perceive as "It" feels justified: because we are nothing, our feelings don't matter. We are just weightless yearning. They matter, they are Somebody. We imagine being envied as the pinnacle of success, not realizing the others' yearning for our state would not give us peace, reliability, or happiness. Whom do you envy? When will you stop feeding that envy?

Consider your vulnerability when you look at a clothing ad or story. Finding and understanding the substance beneath your surface provides an antidote to an addiction to their idea of what will make you beautiful. Once you taste your own power, the pretty promises of advertising, like evanescent illusions, lose their power to sway.

5. *The importance of being dreamy*

Glamor can serve a positive function, according to Roland Barthes: "[T]he image makes the purchase unnecessary, it replaces it; we can intoxicate ourselves on images, identify ourselves oneirically with the model, and, in reality, follow Fashion merely by purchasing a few boutique accessories. . . ."[52] Sometimes magazines are merely comforting. The publisher of *W* and *Women's Wear Daily* sees that as his magazine's purpose: "The readers want to visualize in full color a world they don't necessarily know, want to dream and fantasize."[53] A friend recovering from alcoholism says the keys to her recovery were sappy movies, AA meetings, and fashion magazines. She needed something non-damaging that she could use to "zone herself out." Fashion magazines can be wonderful for a little vacation, or a way to float through an afternoon if you have the sniffles. Unlike escapes such as drunkenness and moviegoing, with magazines you can stop and start again, reading as needed, controlling the pace with which you ingest the information. This wonderful dream, Barthes noted, "combines unlimited buying power, the promise of beauty, the thrill of the city, and the delight of a perfect idle super-activity."[54]

A great deal of speculation has gone on about the "enduring fascination commercial fashion photography holds for its female viewers."[55] Some muse about the charge between the gazer and the image. This looking does not become absorbed into the system as self-love, even though supposedly we are looking to make ourselves more lovely. Is it lesbian? Is it vampiric? Does it matter?

We can't wear that much sex out the door. The camera allows with impunity the changes and revealings we don't allow ourselves or we are not allowed to make in our own lives. Perhaps the mass acceptance of these sexy beautiful images reflects the innocent desire that someday we too will be able to wear our sexuality and beauty, like the model in the photograph, without fear of reprisal.

Do you distinguish between real clothes that make you happy and the dreaminess of perusing fashion magazines? The magazines, as dreamsites, generate far more revenue than many fashion designers. *Vogue* has millions of readers. Only thousands buy couture. Some would argue the dreaming prevents us from acting in our lives, while others argue that dreaming is a necessary break. A real livable garment has a quality of homeyness—we are at home in it, and it suits us. The fashion magazine clothes are images of fantasy the way *Architectural Digest* shows fantasies of furnishing: the plump-pillowed homes with the fresh flowers, unstained rugs, no toys on the floor, no dust, no "evidence of human occupation."[56] Conversely, what makes a garment moving and comprehensible to the self and to others, like a wonderful room, is "the imprint of [its] inhabitants."[57] Not that you look as if you slept in your clothes; rather, you look like you. Hence the alien-ness of fashion, as writer Iris Marion Young notes: "All the projections of the fashion-beauty complex have this in common: they are images of what I am not."[58] Fashion, like a dream, is a huge unregulated mass of images. Our job/responsibility is to make sense of it for ourselves, to our own satisfaction, so we can thoughtfully accommodate clothes into our wardrobes.

This leads to the need to answer clearly the following questions:

- What do I get from fashion, its magazines and reportage, that supports me?
- What messages have I absorbed that do not support me?
- How do I disengage from the negatives?
- How can I get more of the good?

6. A love/hate relationship with fashion

Not surprisingly, given the grossness, crudity, and lack of genuine concern for the customer of most fashion industry pronouncements, fashion comes up against our resistance, resulting in the love/hate relationship. This has been with us as long as human civilization. Tertullian, a writer in ancient Rome, adhered rigorously to the fashions of the day while complaining of his toga: "It is not a garment, but a burden." He further whined that it was complicated to get it to drape properly, and it nearly always inhibited movement.[59] Jewelry designer Lisa Graves comments:

When I was a teenager, living a "hippie" life, I had braces (my one connection with the modern world). Every time I went to the orthodontist, issues of *Vogue* would be sitting in the waiting room. I would go through, "Should I look at it or shouldn't I?" It promoted these things that I didn't agree with: money and ideas of beauty. I felt bad looking at it. But on the other hand, I was so interested in the clothes, so attracted to it. I finally decided that clothing could be like art. That made it okay.

To my surprise, many of the clothes lovers I interviewed weren't interested in media fashion. Serious shopper Libby Granett has no use for or interest in the magazines: "I know nothing about the world of fashion." Tom Hassett, thrift store aficionado, says that what's fashionable "is instinctively what's to be avoided." His usually pleasing features organize into a look of plaintive disgust: "Fashion seems ironic. It's the opposite of how Jean-Louis Trintignant or Marcello Mastroianni would go about choosing anything for themselves, which is going into it with a certain gravity and with the personal intuition intact."

Despite the horrible things the fashion industry can do, at the bottom of it, for many involved, is love of clothes. The joy of fashion lies in its irrepressible enthusiasm and its use of the most wonderful materials on earth to express "the purely decorative, evocative, and utterly irrational."[60] This is not tracked and rarely discussed, although it's often mocked. *Vogue* writer Charles Gandee noted:

> Here at *Vogue*, there is a sacred ritual of sorts, which is performed at irregular intervals by the various editors and their assistants who toil away in the taffeta-lined trenches of the fashion department. It's called a fashion moment, and what it entails is this: Someone will hold up a John Galliano bias-cut silk dress fresh off the plane from Paris, a Gianni Versace silver lamé micromini just in from Milan, or a Liza Bruce vinyl bikini recently landed from London, and ten thin young women in black clothes will instantly stop what they're doing, fling themselves on the garment, and shriek and gasp and clutch their breasts as if their hearts were about to explode. And then, just as surely as night follows day, they'll all scream, "Fabulous!". . . It's at moments such as these that the fashion industry effectively lifts up its skirt and reveals itself . . .[61]

Emily Cho summarizes the good in fashion:

> [F]ashion is stimulating and useful . . . the changes that are fundamental to fashion are also essential and integral to society. Once you understand the phenomenon of fashion, you should no longer feel intimidated or insecure. Inspired by fashion, you will be able to blend your own taste and style with the knowledge of what can and should, according to the temper of the times, be worn in a given setting.[62]

Is she just justifying her own professional existence? Well, yes and no. She's also saying, "Take the reins, baby." Some people like fashion because of the metaphor. They have an urge to stand on the razor's edge of the present and express that moment, as Blumer said, "to be abreast of what has good standing, to express new tastes which are emerging in a changing world."[63]

There are good ways to use fashion . . . and good reasons to ignore it; for instance, when fashion discriminates in the nastiest way against things that cannot be "fixed" (for example, our physical structure or racial heritage); when it is ageist and undemocratic; or when to look great on fashion's terms is impossible or requires a kind of ferocious tenacity most of us are not willing to dedicate to this art. Personal style consultant Sharon Frederick advocates discerning the difference:

> There's a point where you have to take responsibility and say, "It's in fashion, but it's not for me." There are a whole lot of things in fashion. So if I'm giving that up, don't feel sorry for me. There's plenty more.

Knowing what you love that *isn't* in fashion is useful, too. Because fashion cycles, if you care about dressing in relationship to that, the look will have its moment again. Even if it isn't "in," if it makes you look and feel terrific, what difference does it make? That's not a rhetorical question.

7. *The numbers involved and a glimpse at the costs of production*

I have shut my little sister in from life and light
(For a rose, for a ribbon, for a wreath across my hair).
—Margaret Widdemer[64]

We who care passionately about clothes owe it to ourselves to be educated about the numbers involved, to know who gets exploited and why. The fashion industry's primary purpose is making money. We often forget this.

Annual industry cash flow today is $1.3 trillion,[65] and the sixty main producers in the garment industry employ eleven million people in the developed world. Some major fashion houses are wealthier than whole countries.[66] How to attempt to comprehend this? Consider that Liz Claiborne's sales volume is over $1 billion a year. What does this mean in terms of quantity of goods? In any one season Claiborne has over 5,500,000 pieces of apparel in stores throughout the U.S.; they ship 35 million garments and accessories a year,[67] and manufacture from 1,000 to 150,000 pieces per style in twenty-six different countries.[68]

If we know garments are made overseas, the word "imported" on a clothing label may falsely convey elite mystique. Many women[69] and children working outside the U.S. produce garments for less than $1.00 a day in conditions tantamount to slave laborers'.

If you think designers pay better, think again: a haute couture evening gown still costs the equivalent of about a year's salary of the seamstress who made it. The same was true in 1900.[70] On the advertising/promotion side, people are as grossly overpaid as the manufacturer's labor is underpaid. Top models earn $20,000 for a day's work, and the photographer shooting the pictures is often paid double that.[71] Why this kind of money? Because many of us have enough stuff, it takes a lot of talent and beauty to persuade us to buy more stuff we don't need. The industry rewards those persuaders accordingly. In addition, the hype about what models and photographers are paid stimulates consumer excitement about products. This means more profit.[72]

I don't dispute the multinationals' right to profit; however, I question the obscene size of that profit as long as the laborers who create the profit are denied basic human rights. When Congress pressed other countries to include those rights—the rights of workers to freely organize, the right to enforce health and safety regulations, and the outlawing of the use of child labor[73]—in NAFTA, the free trade agreement, the most flagrant violators refused to sign. The agreement passed through Congress without those rights. As the *New York Times* comments:

> Few countries . . . are prepared to allow international trade inspectors to come into their factories and press questions like this: "Excuse me, how old is that little girl who is gluing the leather soles of those shoes?" or "Could you show us how you treat the chemicals coming out of this factory before you dump them in the river?" Or even: "Why do you imprison workers who demand to make more than fifty cents an hour?"[74]

Much of the clothing actually made in the United States is subcontracted to sweatshop laborers earning less than sixty-five cents an hour and working nonstop from nine in the morning to midnight.[75] Fashion designer Camille DePedrini comments on problems that designers who are concerned with ethical production face when trying to pay fair wages:

> This whole idea of paying people nothing to make a garment is kind of wacky. Hank Ford, a designer, said to me yesterday, "People want everything under a hundred dollars, but they want it to be beautiful." So what do you give them? What can you make them that they're going to love? Maybe you make underwear. And you make it really perfect and beautiful because it's small and you can sell it for a little.
>
> To take the time now to do all those little touches that they used to do, you have to charge people a lot. I took a dress to the sewer's today, and it's not back yet because she had to hem it, but I wanted her to finish it—totally line it inside so none of the seams were showing and make it all perfect inside. Well, it's going to be really expensive. It took her all day.

The rag trade also uses fiber and fabric produced at the cost of unacceptable damage to the environment. For example, in most areas, production of cotton, the "natural" fiber, consumes more pesticides than that of any other agricultural crop.[76] The answer is not to turn to our furry friends, the sheep. Even though they look cute, they "turn out to be some of the most destructive grazers in the animal kingdom."[77] Similarly, fur and leather use raise obvious ethical dilemmas.[78]

What can be done in the face of this overwhelming unpleasantness? A lot. Several small companies in the United States are manufacturing beautiful fabrics without pesticides or toxic dyes. Among them is Fox Fibre cottons, which grows cotton in different colors. Color-grown-in fabric has interesting properties, notes grower Sally Fox: "The big advantage is that the color doesn't fade. In fact, the color intensifies with every washing. . . . It's great to pull your clothes out of the dryer and they're actually better-looking. It's so uplifting."[79]

While we don't do so well with garments after we're finished with them (only about twenty-five percent of garments are reused or recycled as wiping cloths, car seat stuffing, and carpet padding),[80] Patagonia, the sportswear company, has made a start of it by manufacturing polarplus clothes out of what they call Synchilla, a fabric made from recycled plastic soda bottles.

Not a single fashion magazine uses paper made from recycled fiber, and because of the processes used in making the magazines glossy, they aren't recyclable. Many local libraries provide bins where magazines can be left for other community members to take and read. As the saying goes, "reduce, reuse, recycle," in that order.

If this is important to you, find out where the clothes you love are manufactured and under what conditions. If you don't like it, contact the manufacturers and complain. Contact your congressional representatives, and your local stores, and complain. Or boycott. Have someone make your clothes for you, or make them yourself. When buying sneakers, for example, I try to get New Balance brand, because seventy percent of the shoes they produce are made in the United States. Write to the magazines and ask them to use recycled and recyclable paper.

The post–World War II American idea of an endless fashionable present where one can—as if in a dream—continually buy more and more, ties into a false 1950s notion that the world is endlessly exploitable, that our resources are infinite. As we are beginning to notice, our resources are finite.

Even before we peek in the closet or set foot in a store, we have some depressing facts to deal with. Like all aspects of fashion, these issues are political. Consider where you stand, and if taking action is important to you, act on it.

8. *Consider the potential for bias*

Given the reprehensible conditions under which most of our clothing is manufactured, we've still got to figure out what to wear. How good is the information in the fashion magazines? Consider the potential for bias by looking at the revenue of a typical fashion magazine. *Vogue* brings in $87 million a year. Roughly two-thirds of that revenue is generated by advertisements.[81] The issue is not so much that the magazines accept financial incentives, but rather that, as a result, their staffs write things that aren't true. Nicholas Coleridge, managing director of the British arm of the Condé Nast empire, points out a "disturbing new refinement of insider-dealing": The advertiser who shows "eighty particular garments in his paid-for advertisement pages" wants "forty particular ones used in the editorial."

> This effectively leaves the fashion editor impotent, since the pages no longer reflect her own taste and choice, only the merchandising strategy of the advertiser. It also legislates against the mixing of clothes by different designers. . . . It was regarded as the primary part of the editor's job to synthesize different collections into a coherent modernism. This is now discouraged by the designers, particularly the Milanese who insist that their message is delivered pure.[82]

Thousands of people design exquisite, wonderful, innovative clothes. Their work, however, goes unreported and unrecognized. The possibilities for looking great, as dictated by the fashion magazines, are limited to the work of about twenty designers, most of whom have paid for the privilege of being mentioned.

When some fashion writers get sick of the charade, they give away vital clues to the game of looking fabulous. *Miami Herald* fashion writer Peggy Landers reports:

Once you've been around the cycle once, you become aware that these designers need the hot, extreme statement to generate news value and excitement, that while the clothes may be tighter or looser or a different color or a new fabric, it's all pretty much the same.[83]

How do you figure out what to wear? In part, with a clear-eyed understanding that the relationship between the fashion advertising industry and your wardrobe happiness may be small, or even nonexistent. Since what people who work in fashion at the highest level wear varies little—they look for clothes that flatter them—consider, if you wish to emulate them, what styles and types of clothes flatter you best. The discovery of this is mapped throughout the rest of the book.

9. *The overreported, underacknowledged fashion shift*

The nineteenth-century transition to a mass-production-based economy caused popularization of mass adherence to one fashion. Anthropologist Edmund Carpenter observes:

"Mass production of identical goods required mass consumption of identical goods. Current fashion was like currency: private dress was counterfeit." Nobody walked around in anything but what everybody else was walking around in. Circle skirts and circle pins. "Private dress was as unacceptable as a three-dollar bill. Fashion was obedience to public form. A woman wore one kind of dress or another kind of dress simply because it was done. By everybody."[84]

With so many years of mass-produced clothing behind us, and so much of it in circulation, many fashions have become familiar and acceptable. Paradoxically, the fashion industry loses its power over us as it follows the fashion. Except for the teenagers who are busy "finding themselves" through following trends, nothing has gone out. Nothing has left. Fashion scholar Gilles Lipovetsky notes:

When all lengths and widths are possible, when multitudes of styles go side by side, when vintage clothing is in style, when looking old-fashioned might be the height of fashion, it becomes difficult indeed to be categorically unfashionable. . . . [F]ashion's "dictatorship" is over along with the social rejection of unfashionableness.[85]

The freedom to select from many fashions and wear exactly what we want is a dual-edged liberty. "On one hand nobody need be forced into an outfit that is patently unflattering, but on the other hand, without a steely sense of your own taste and direction, the countless options can be merely bewildering."[86]

The designers are also noticing that we are beginning to pull our own strings. Superstar designer Donna Karan comments:

"Sometimes I wonder about what we do here. . . . We sit here in our wonderful atmosphere creating our own stimulations, but who gets it? Like the whole short thing. If women didn't go out and buy short last year, the whole thing passed them by, and now long is back again. They have to realize that they no longer have to buy what we tell them to. It all happens so fast. All they have to do is sit tight and their old clothes will be back in style."

"Don't let them hear you say that," says one of the editors.[87]

People are turning away from the dictates of fashion in droves, and this has sent retailers and manufacturers scrambling.[88]

In 1995, Azzedine Alaïa was the first of the couture designers to acknowledge that fashion is not "synonymous with change" by publicly reissuing favorite clothes from previous collections. "I've reintroduced clothes I designed in the past because there are people who want them." He maintains that "clothes don't die. You merely forget them, then bring them back."[89]

In case you're worried, Laurel Fenenga reassures us that this transition doesn't mean we'll lose fashion:

We'll always buy fashion because it feeds boredom. Right now, fashion is terrific. You can wear whatever you want. Very few jobs tell you you have to dress like an idiot. More and more people are saying, 'I want to be comfortable.' Clothes really are fantastic in terms of wearability. And yet we still are always looking for the exciting, the visually stimulating.

In garments for the masses, the overwhelming clothing choice, regardless of fashion, is the "relaxed American sportswear that you can wear without having to suck in your stomach."[90] This mode of dress began to be popular on a large scale during World War II when America was cut off from Paris as a fashion source—Americans went to Europe to fight, not to observe and copy the designers' lines. American designers had to create their own style, which has only increased in popularity over the last five decades.

Among people I interviewed there seems to be a consensus "canon" of clothes and suitable silhouettes that, once fashionable, are so good they stick around and attain the status of belonging to the twentieth-century greats. Among the garments are blue jeans (especially Levi's 501s), loafers, leather jackets, button-down shirts, T-shirts, boxer shorts, twin sets, crewneck sweaters, silk scarves, basic dresses and skirts, trench coats, cardigans, Hawaiian shirts . . . things people actually buy and wear over and over again because they work well and look good. There is a certain relief that these styles created through mass production—and hence easily available—have proven valuable. These classics might provide part of a solution to the fashion-disgusted person who nonetheless wishes to appear current, to be visually aligned with present time.[91] The fashionability of these classics would imply a different definition of good fashion than Paris' or Seventh Avenue's each spring and fall.

So here is what is new, current, and staying: knowing your own taste. The rest of this book addresses ways to acquire this knowledge of self. You can look for this outside yourself in shops, in magazines, and on television, but until you look inside and evaluate what works for you—what you feel comfortable in—with your individual body, unique features, and specific preferences as a reference point, you'll foolishly spend energy, attention, and money.

Just because magazines present an unattainable beauty ideal doesn't mean you have to buy into it. Just because their bone-thin, listless vision is limited doesn't mean yours has to be. Much information in the modern world is transmitted through visual cues—an endless spew of information. Nothing in that realm will encourage you to use alternative sensing to enrich your life. The wake-up call, the way out of a fashion-induced self-hatred trap involves giving the overstimulated vision a break by tuning in to other ways of perceiving. Your underused senses such as hearing, smell, and touch; balance, gravity, muscular tension, and flex; feeling your body moving through space; your memory; your history—all can nurture a healthy, gorgeous alternative.

Sight is useful to locate something once the inner vision has fully formed the object. However, a good relationship with your wardrobe, like anything else, must arise from the natural, comfortable, easy movements of your own system, must be deeply felt in meditative mode, and must be fully formed long before the shopping expedition occurs.

In order to begin to establish these inner criteria, you start by examining your relationship with the personal politics of frivolity.

Notes:

1. Nash, Eric P., Ed. "Does fashion matter?" *New York Times Magazine.* October 24, 1993. Page 52.

2. Phizacklea. Page 57.

3. Betts, Katherine. "Working It Out." *Vogue.* August 1993. Page 222.

4. "The eye of the needle." *New York Times Magazine.* February 20, 1994. Page 48-52.

5. Betts, Katherine. "Very Fitting." *Vogue.* July 1994. Page 50.

6. Morris. Page 84.

7. Davis. Page 150.

8. Davis. Page 142.

9. Daria. Page 161.

10. Deeny, Godfrey. "Fashville." *W.* April 1994. Page 84.

11. Flügel. Page 133.

12. Benstock. Page 268-9.

13. In a world where the potential weekly audience for American television and advertising is over a billion people, the idea of Western affluence in the form of unattainable fashionable clothes, body, and hair styles becomes a subversive kind of export. The media function as the magic mirror through which we think we see the real things of the world. With few exceptions, the media are not teaching us to see ourselves and our own beauty. We see a world of white and well-lit people, which the majority of us aren't. They take us to a narrow arena of fantasy, where product endorsements decide what goods appear on the shows, and very strange people act and dress in ways entirely unlifelike. No real issues are raised beyond personal ones (not surprising when two of the four major television networks are owned by companies which also produce nuclear weapons; *The Simpsons,* of course, airs on Fox). In the media we see the unattainable loveliness of the "beautiful," convincing us that through mimicry we can be transformed, live their lives. As sociologist Stewart Ewen has noted: "Style taught people that they could gain comfort from self-estrangement" [Ewen, Page 76]. We leave our skins. Popular culture has helped perpetuate our obsessions with clothes and beauty, even in stories as innocuous as those seen in children's movies. The Walt Disney version of the fairy tale *Snow White* depicts a woman who will kill to be the most beautiful; Disney's *101 Dalmatians'* plot is driven by a woman who wants a dogskin coat, for which she is willing to kill; Clark Kent becomes Superman in a quick change of outfit (neatly avoiding indecent exposure) in a public phone booth; Cinderella can go to the ball because of her magical new dress; Dorothy gets her ruby slippers on the road to Oz. We learn that clothes have magical powers.

14. Goodwin, Jan. "From the Valley of the Chador." *Mirabella.* April 1994. Page 106.

15. Davis. Page 199.

16. Davis. Page 198.

17. Davis. Page 183.

18. Davis. Page 182.

19. Lurie. Page 93.

20. Was the ancient philosopher Heraclitus talking about fashion? Fragment 50: "As they step into the same river, other and still other waters flow upon them." Fragment 51: "One cannot step twice into the same river, nor can one grasp any mortal substance in a stable condition, but it scatters and again gathers: it forms and dissolves, and approaches and departs."

Milliner and store owner Chandra Cho has a more psychological take on it: "There's one way of interpreting dreams so that everybody in the dream is an extension of you and they're holding up signs trying to tell you something. That's how the fashion world is. Everybody is an extension of you, and they're just trying to tell you." She laughs and continues, "Yeah, it's all a dream."

This life we lead is transient and hard to grasp, but worth moving in and with. Clothes can be a part of that movement. In the most earthbound sense, they move with us as we move, and can facilitate or hinder our expression of movement. Fashion is another expression of that change. Perhaps a resistance to and hostility toward fashion reflects uneasiness with the knowledge that our lives are nearly as transient as the fashions—one moment we are here, the next moment gone. And fashion with its "in"s and "out"s never makes any pretense to the contrary. Is fashion another way of marking or mourning the swift passage of time?

21. Merriam. Page 41.

22. Madsen. Page 124.

23. Langer. Page 208-9.

24. Sproles. Page 130.

25. Sproles. Page 134.

26. Sproles. Page 135.

27. Bell. Page 12.

28. Finklestein. Page 130.

29. Wallach. Page 17. This sentence is unfairly drawn out of context from a terrific book.

30. Ewen. Page 244.

31. Lipovetsky. Page 155.

32. "Huge Recall of Rayon Skirts Made in India. Filmy Garments Burn Fast." *San Francisco Chronicle*. August 13, 1994. See also Hinds, Julie, "Q & A about skirt fire safety." *Detroit News and Free Press*. August 13, 1994, C-1.

33. The emphasis on youthfulness has also had a positive result. The optimist Lipovetsky notes, "The idealized meaning of 'youthfulness' led to a detachment from luxury clothing, which was identified with the old world. . . . Clothes could be casual, crude, torn, worn, unstitched, sloppy, ripped, or frayed: all these features, which had been strictly taboo, began to be incorporated into the field of fashion. By recycling signs of 'inferiority,' fashion pursued its democratic dynamics" [Lipovetsky. Page 100].

34. Gross, Amy. "The View from the 44th Floor." *Elle*. January 1996. Page 26.

35. Williams, Christopher. "Getting Down and Dirty." *Terrain*. August 1995. Page 1.

36. Ephron. Page 78.

37. See former top model Susan Moncur's *They Still Shoot Models My Age* for more information.

38. Gross. Page 241.

39. Gross. Page 486.

40. Even store mannequins carry on the charade of a false feminine ideal: a recent *British Medical Journal* report stated women whose measurements match those of the average store mannequin don't weigh enough to menstruate normally [Wall, Cara. "Fashion Fax." *Glamour.* September 1993. Page 216].

41. Ewen. Page 90.

42. Gross. Page 219.

43. Cho, Emily and Linda Grover. *Looking Terrific.* Page 54.

44. Riding the wave of the sewing machine's and fashion magazines' increasing popularity, "designer clothing" gained credence in the public imagination. This was most apparent in the nineteenth-century rise of the fortune and attitude of the first major couturier, Charles Frederick Worth, who custom-made individually fitted gowns for the courts of Europe. Why do we value photography, aside from the child's love of glossy pretty pictures? In the film *Designing Women*, the Gregory Peck character describes fashion shows as religious shrines, rites which put clothes and fashion in the place of God, and demand a great sacrifice, the huge cost. All veneration has a price. The status of God began to fade with the breakup of the divine rule of kings and the rise of merchants in the Renaissance, but this didn't take away the human need to love and worship. Without having the old structures, perhaps some choose to idolize fashion to fulfill that yearning. In some ways we are still the naive peasants awed by the paintings on the walls of the church, seeing God in the stained-glass windows. We look at a fashion picture, at the thin, painted model, and pre-verbally, instinctively worship and love beauty. The innocent aspirant thinks, "This is what we should be, this is what women are like, this is what I can be, what I must make myself."

45. Garber. Page 353. At its core, fashionable glamor may be Zen-like in its celebration of nothing but change.

46. Daria. Page 156.

47. Mailer, Norman. *Of Women and Their Elegance.* Page 24.

48. Scavullo. Page 128.

49. *At Random.* Number 6. Fall 1993. Page 62.

50. Dobson, Terry. *It's a Lot Like Dancing.* Page 120.

51. Orbach, Susie. *Fat Is a Feminist Issue.* Page 92.

52. Barthes. Page 17.

53. Fairchild. Page 75.

54. Barthes. Page 253.

55. Benstock. Page 213.

56. Rybczynski. Page 17.

57. Rybczynski. Page 17.

58. Benstock. Page 201.

59. Batterberry. Page 197.

60. Fraser. Page 231.

61. Gandee, Charles. "Fashion Victim." *Vogue.* January 1995. Page 72.

62. Cho/Grover. Page 43.

63. Davis. Page 116.

64. Goldsmith, Olivia. *Fashionably Late.* Page 247.

65. "Style Flash." *Self.* October 1993. Page 105.

66. Coleridge, Nicholas. *The Fashion Conspiracy.* Page 271.

67. Daria, Irene. *The Fashion Cycle.* Page 9.

68. Daria. Page 14.

69. The clothing work force is 80% female [Phizacklea. Page 3].

70. Fraser, Kennedy. *The Fashionable Mind.* Page 138.

71. McDowell, Colin. *The Designer Scam.* Page 4.

72. So much has been said about the evils of advertising that we tune it out as background noise. The subtle and elusive issue of responsibility could bear a little attention. Former fashion designer Colin McDowell observes that advertising conveniently forgets that "fashion's force is based on emulation, and what a designer or photographer proposes is tantamount to an edict for millions of young women who see their appearance as their major currency" [McDowell. Page 206]. Advertising is not solely responsible, but the industry has an unclaimed responsibility. Advertising executive Tony Bodinetz explains:

> I don't think you can just point the finger and blame advertising, because advertising never leads. But admittedly it is very quick to sense what is happening on the streets or around the world and to jump on a bandwagon . . . it cannot escape its share of the responsibility for confirming the view that to "join the club" you've got to look like this, smell like this, speak like this and dress like this. [Chapkis. Page 40]

While ultimately personal style should be the individual's responsibility, something in me gets annoyed when superstar designer Sonia Rykiel says, "It's you who dictate fashion" [Benstock. Page 106]. This buys into the idea that the media can't be that important, can't be that subversively influential. We forget that some of the best salespeople in history have devoted themselves to this field. As Ruth Preston, *New York Post* fashion editor, said of Bill Blass, "He could sell the eyelashes off a hog" [Kelly. Page 111]. The advertisers use every tool they can to get you yearning for something—they keep repeating—only buying can fulfill. The reason it works? As someone once said: "You can't get enough of what you don't really want." By promising the "good life," they get you yearning for something goods can't satisfy. If you've got an endless shopping hunger, what other hungers do you have as well? Do you get enough solitude? Do you feel beloved? Do you get enough rest? What makes you feel truly satisfied?

73. Phizacklea. Page 106.

74. Sanger, David E. "Trade agreement ends long debate but not conflicts." *New York Times.* December 14, 1994. Page A-23.

75. Lii, Janey H. "Week in sweatshop reveals grim conspiracy of poor." *New York Times.* March 12, 1995. Page 1.

76. 1993 Press Release on Natural Cotton Colours, Inc. Background, P.O. Box 791, Wasco, CA 93280.

77. Feldon, Leah. *Dress Like a Million*. Page 58.

78. Ethics come up a lot more with leather and fur than with silk production, which relies upon the death of many worms.

79. Infusino, Divina. *VISaVIS*. August 1992. Page 56.

80. "Esprit bets on recycled fabric." *San Francisco Examiner*. September 1, 1993. Page B-3.

81. Coleridge. Page 249.

82. Coleridge. Page 211. Most of the fashion magazine is already advertising; even most of the editorial section is advertising, too. So the "point of view" you see is really what the manufacturers want you to purchase. However little editorial content is left, it's important to look at it differently from how you look at the ads. This brief moment in the magazine is the one creative expression the editor, writers, and photographers get. There may be something there.

83. Satran. Page 249.

84. Kelly. Page 168.

85. Lipovetsky. Page 119.

86. Procter. Page 6.

87. Daria. Page 205.

88. "Across the women's apparel industry, a stunning reality—that millions of women have lost interest in buying clothes—is starting to sink in. The industry is entering the third year of a slump that is baffling most retailers and fashion marketers. The usual magnets, fads and bargains are failing to pull women back into stores." *Wall Street Journal*. February 28, 1995. Page 1.

89. La Ferla, Ruth. "Back to the Future." *Elle*. July 1995. Page 106.

90. McDowell. Page 101.

91. See the *Chic Simple* series of publications for more information.

Open and Clothed

Questionnaire

1. When someone labels your love for clothes as frivolous, do you respond,
   a) "Is *not*," and stick out your tongue?
   b) With a whimper?
   c) "A little frivolity is good for the soul," and smile mysteriously?

2. What frivolities do you allow yourself?

3. What do you consider too frivolous to indulge in? Why?

4. What, if any, frivolities do you long for but deny yourself? Who suffers for it?

5. What allows you an experience of grace? If you moved through life like a swan moves along the surface of the water, what would you wear?

The Personal Politics of Frivolity

Dress is a very foolish thing. Yet it is a very foolish thing for a man not to be well dressed.
—Lord Chesterfield, 1745[1]

Personal style consultant Barbara Jay comments, "Clothes have not always been considered so frivolous. As Alison Lurie, who wrote *The Language of Clothes*, says, clothes have been a function of cultural status. The slaves in Egypt weren't allowed to wear any clothes at all, and we can see how, at various points in the history of clothing, people have been more or less elaborately dressed to indicate their status." We can see this in the sumptuary laws issued throughout history by royalty to prevent people of certain social classes from wearing, for example, ermine, purple, or specific kinds of fabric. Jay continues, "It's still with us to a certain degree because the work of the very best designers and the very best and most opulent fabrics can only be afforded by those who have means."

The kind of status employed today by the lucky few who can afford couture has a profoundly different impact than the sumptuary laws of yesterday did. When the finest clothes were associated with royalty, mocking the love of luxury could result in death. Napoleon was known to criticize women of his court if he saw them more than once in the same dress on the same day, asking, "Madame, is that the only dress you possess?"[2] and thus controlling them by sending them scurrying for new clothes. He wanted to make France the center of the fashion industry and, more importantly, knew that if he could make the court obsessed with clothing, it would distract them from politics and allow him to rule unimpeded.

Today there is no court, no emperor, and he has no new clothes; anyone with money can buy fancy clothes. And everyone is free to criticize. It's useful to note that the expression "fashion victims" was coined by the very industry rag that created them, *Women's Wear Daily*. Their in-and-out lists are the closest we come to any sort of fashionable court today, outside of the mini-courts formed by our private circles. And their lists only attend to the very rich, connected, or famous. Maybe our discomfort with the fall of the hierarchy, with the difficulty in discerning who is to be respected by the way they dress, is reflected in our dismissal of clothing as frivolous. Democracy, by definition, would seem to eliminate or disdain such categories. With all people created equal, how do we determine what is acceptable, who is superior? How do we establish criteria?

While status ambivalence may contribute to accusations of frivolity, Judeo-Christian teaching may also add fuel to the fire. Some fundamentalists bawl that by loving clothes, ornament, and show, we align ourselves with the biblical harlots. For example, Isaiah 3:16-24:

> Then the Lord said: Because the women of Zion hold themselves high and walk with necks outstretched and wanton glances moving with mincing gait and jingling feet, the Lord will give the women of Zion bald heads, the Lord will strip the hair from their foreheads. In that day the Lord will take away all finery.[3]

What the women are doing seems innocuous. Yet to the author it seemed deserving of contempt and punishment. This leads the reflecting mind to note with amusement the value the male writer(s?)

of this text placed on a full head of hair. Perhaps the male author(s) of this text could think of no greater suffering than the baldness nature had inflicted on him (them).

Centuries after the Bible was written, prohibitions emigrated to America for religious reasons with the Pilgrims. Barbara Jay sees a correlation between the accusation of frivolity and this aspect of our history when asking why an interest in dress is considered silly: "Why is it such a put-down? Traditionally, clothes have been considered very frivolous. We live in America. This is a Puritan culture." The Puritans had rules regarding modesty in dress. People were outcast, and later, at Salem, were burned at the stake for disobeying rules. Jay continues:

> So we are very moralistic. On one hand, one's image is not supposed to be very important because of this heritage. On the other hand, we're totally image-oriented in this culture. So much is surface. Women are really caught between a rock and a hard place, particularly women who are shopping compulsively, women whose self-esteem is not intact. For some reason, they're considered frivolous because they are interested in something so "stupid" as clothes.

Simplicity in dress (as opposed to love of adornment) was also celebrated by the early patriots for political reasons. They sought to encourage American independence, to influence people not to want Europe's goods. Fashion historian Caroline Rennolds Milbank notes that before American fashion there was an American style which had its roots in "the patriotic determination, after the Revolutionary War, to wear home grown, home spun, and home sewn clothes." George and Martha Washington, as well as religious groups such as the Amish and the Quakers, set the example. "Simplicity in dress celebrated both self-sufficiency and the freedoms inherent in a democracy."[4]

As America prospered, love of dress and finery grew more popular. Until the Industrial Revolution, among the wealthy, both men and women participated with equal enthusiasm in indulgence in fine clothing. Many men, now remembered for other things here and abroad, were known in their time as great dandies, among them naturalist John James Audubon, writer Charles Dickens, and statesman Benjamin Disraeli. Most wealthy men renounced fashion in favor of the uniform business suit at the dawn of the Industrial Age. These men seized the world as their oyster, and gave women the home and wardrobe—a bad trade. As the new possessors of fancy dress, women were only allowed expression in realms judged frivolous or secondary to the important men's activities; at that time these included secretarial work, and still include contact sports. Limited to such a small sphere of expression, women's clothes grew more and more intricate. Davis notes:

> Women, having to manipulate a more complex code, could more easily (through mismatches, exaggerations, neglect or obsessive preoccupation with detail, etc.) "make mistakes" and be thought gauche, fussy, dowdy, vulgar. . . .[5]

Laws made by men kept women in this narrow sphere of expression, and then ridiculed them for using that sphere. Writer Iris Young comments:

Misogynist mythology gloats in its portrayal of woman as frivolous body decorators. Well trained to meet the gaze that evaluates us for our finery, for how well we show him off, we then are condemned as sentimental, superficial, duplicitous, because we attend to and sometimes learn to love the glamorous arts. The male gazers paint us gazing at ourselves at our toilet, before the table they call a vanity.[6]

Even in the second half of the twentieth century, some take this viewpoint to its most illogical extreme. Former *Women's Wear Daily* publisher John Fairchild said that ". . . the whole Women's Lib thing is silly. A woman can get anything she wants by being charming."[7]

The fashion illustrator Vertes urges a more moderate overview of the issue:

Fashion must not be examined indifferently nor yet with an eye that is too critical. Now that men no longer wear frills or satin breeches, they are inclined to frown at the mere mention of Fashion. Come, gentlemen, show a little indulgence for masterpieces in silk and lace! Don't lose your temper over a few feathers and ribbons![8]

Every woman with whom I spoke about her love of clothes and/or shopping apologized because she's afraid that she sounds obsessive, saying to me, "You must think I'm . . . " or "I'm sorry that I'm talking so much. . . ." Not a single man did. The men talked about the topic with pleasure and confidence. One man, having just shown me his blue lace ball gown, commented, "Somehow I didn't think about it until just now how exposing and strange this is." He didn't apologize. I told him I wasn't shocked. (I wasn't.) And he responded, "I figured. I don't have lace panties or anything." And then he went on to discuss his athletic socks.

Men make fun of women, of what they don't understand. Do I understand? Recently, I saw a billboard on La Brea Avenue in Los Angeles: "The problems of the world do not include what to wear. Protest." Part of the perverse deliciousness of this message is that it's not clear if this is an ad or a hijacked billboard. It tells us that fashion is trivial relative to the *real* issues. True, clothing is not health care or homelessness, but it matters. You have to wear clothes every day. The ambiguity of the source of the message on La Brea reflects the current political slant on the judgments about people involved in fashion. Is this itch to dress beautifully merely one of society's ways of preventing us from examining what's important? Are we being controlled? Joanne Finkelstein, author of *The Fashioned Self*, believes interest in appearance and dress lecherously saps the energy available to make a difference in the world, and to make meaningful connections with others: "To focus so closely on one's style of appearance is to become distracted from concerns that are more morally transcendental, such as involvement with the politics or injustices of the day; such attention to self-adornment has the effect of curtailing or closing off social and political consciousness."[9] Later she continues, "Human sociality becomes a trade in fashionable items; it is emptied of its spontaneity and easy companionship to become dominated instead by the necessity to display material goods, control impressions and cultivate reputation."[10]

Does an excessive interest in clothes benumb? Sure, there are people overinvolved with the fashion/image industry, mindless simps wandering from one plastic surgeon to the next,[11] but there are, and have always been, vigorously engaged political people who love clothing. Queen Elizabeth I was extremely interested in clothes. Former head of Planned Parenthood Faye Wattleton is a fabulous dresser. And I could devote a whole chapter to Hillary Clinton's hair. Clothes lover Jeremy Stone comments:

> Men can spend a lot of money on cars and symbols of their masculinity and stereos and CD players and sports events. Men are allowed to spend all of this money on special equipment, special things, clothing associated with different sports, but when it comes to women and clothes that they actually wear to work and in their everyday life, clothes that have to do with them feeling positive and comfortable in their bodies, it's a subject of jokes, ridicule, and sarcasm by men.

(A really good baseball glove costs over $200. For that kind of money you don't even get a pair!) Many of the traditionally "female" areas of recreation still get trivialized overtly and covertly in our society, as if women don't need to relax or rest, as if doing two-thirds of the world's hourly labor is not enough.[12]

What is it about fashion that brings up strong feelings? What so frightens men that they have to marginalize love of clothing and shopping? Perhaps, in part, they fear the power of transformation. In sport, the uniform remains a constant. It's easy; you know who your friends and enemies are. You know whom to root for. There's our team and their team, and they're the bad guys. There are better players and worse players, and the great players. There are fixed rules to the game, and referees to tell you if you've gone out of line. Sport is easy; you always know where you stand. It ends when the game is over.

Clothes and fashion say that you can't tell your friends from your enemies by looking at them. You have to look deeper. Anyone can buy the look, the gang's uniform. Life is about looking deeper.

Fashion involves a shifting wind of opinion, and playing with it involves sensing that change before others do and risking demonstrating the excitement about how beauty expresses itself in the next week, month, or season. Fashion requires making personal choices that affect how you feel and are perceived all the working hours. It is a game with some consequences, a game which does not end when you put down the magazine. Fashion is harder than sport, because there are no written rules that everyone has agreed to follow. Rather, there is an agreement that the rules constantly change, and that is part of the fun. Winning the game of fashion is defined differently by different "authorities," but who is defined as an authority varies from culture to culture and person to person. Perhaps this frightens some people.

It's also peculiar how women turn against women on this issue. A great many of us forget our history, and don't know our possibilities. Today women call fashion frivolous, too, with the idea that just wearing old jeans and T-shirts is a way around it. *Beauty Secrets* author Wendy Chapkis asks the question, "How did women's *liberation* end up on the side of the sensible over the sexual, the 'efficient, upright and honest' over the colorful and fun?"[13] We broke fashion's unilateral power over us during the feminist revolution. No longer were dictates from on high obeyed with a "charming docility." Shari Benstock and Suzanne Ferriss comment:

> Feminists of a generation ago, echoing their suffragist precursors, taught women that interest in dress and beauty was the result of a socially produced false consciousness that placed women in league with patriarchal and capitalist power structures. High fashion signaled (hetero)sexual and social oppression, and even "real clothes"—what we wore every day— cinched waists, smoothed out curves and bumps, and constrained our movements. What a relief to unhook brassieres, unzip girdles, and step out of the cage of Jackie Kennedy box suits. Letting our hair down, we proclaimed Our Bodies Ourselves. If our shoes pinched, we went barefoot.[14]

The feminist insistence on clothes that actually were comfortable was part of what changed fashion forever, supporting a new multi-channeled course of fashion. Yet somehow sisterhood incorporated a stance of disapproval. Carol Ascher speaks to this disapproval, asking, What if self-decoration gives women a sense of potency to act in the world? Responding to a feminist moralism she hears in her head, Ascher says, "The idea that clothing ought to yield a magical shift in one's feelings about oneself stems from an austere, prudish rationalism in which one does not allow oneself any comfort or pampering that goes beyond the logical 'necessity' into that unreasoned wild place where we all ultimately live."[15]

All this brouhaha leads to the popular stance that a deep interest in clothes is unnatural. Fashion is scorned as superficial. We are not supposed to care about pleasing the eyes through bodily ornament the same way the way we can love beautiful music, wonderful food, the scent of roses and rain, the feel of worn-soft wood or a cat's back. Somehow the desire to show others' eyes beauty when those eyes are looking at you in clothes is a vain, dishonest waste.

Laurel Fenenga takes the criticism to its logical extreme: "Well, let's bomb the Louvre while we're at it." Closer to the essence of our subject, architecture expert Witold Rybczynski observes:

> The notion that what is artless must be better than what is not requires a precarious leap in reasoning, but for all that it carries great weight with the American public—at least judging from the dozens of advertisements that extol "being natural." It is a shallow conceit. A little reflection shows that all human culture is artificial, cooking no less than music, furniture no less than painting. Why prepare time-consuming sauces when a raw fruit would suffice? Why bother with musical instruments when the voice is pleasant enough? Why paint pictures when looking at nature is satisfying? Why sit up when you can squat?
> The answer is that it makes life richer, more interesting, and more pleasurable.[16]

While design can be awful, there's something deeper about the visual. As Laurel points out, you wouldn't accuse someone like Cézanne or Rembrandt of being superficial because they only work in a visual medium ("So two-dimensional of them!"). Why can't we see ourselves as wondrous, transient, three-dimensional works of art? What will let us allow ourselves to play in peace? What will give us some measure of acceptance of the things we truly love?

If we have a love of clothes, we're really stuck with it. Those of us who love clothes do so despite the haranguing of those less than sympathetic to our passion, the limits of our budgets, and our inner critic.

Maybe the anger and criticism our culture dumps on fashion and the love of display is a misplaced anger about other things. Laurel Fenenga comments:

> Our anger with fashion is a little bit like in a marriage: they say couples fight most about who left the cap off the toothpaste tube, the unwashed dishes, or who picks up the socks. Those are very small things. If you're fighting a lot, there's really something big that everybody's dancing around.
>
> The bitching about fashion is a little bit like dancing around the other things in your life that you don't really want to fix. You say, "Oh, these designers, they just design for young people."

It is true that the most visible fashion in magazines is shown on the young. However, because there are many clothes out there that suit people in all age groups, the anger behind this comment might also reflect a lack of peace with the changes wrought by time on a face and body. Laurel suggests the anger could also reflect "an overall frustration where you have an itch and you can't scratch it." She comments that in her generation, "growing up, everybody felt that they were going to be Grace Kelly or whoever. I wanted to be a princess like her." She laughs about the anger that may bubble up about such a frustrated expectation.

How do women get serious about clothes without self-recrimination? The climate is shifting; women are beginning to take a stand for their interest in clothes. Perhaps we claim our seriousness about clothes while differentiating ourselves from "most women." Daphne Stannard, for example, comments: "Clothing is serious for me in a way that isn't typically female. I don't spend all day thinking about my clothes." We acknowledge that an interest in fashion and clothes can be nourishing in other ways, as Iris Young observes: "I find three pleasures we take in clothes: touch, bonding, and fantasy."[17] We acknowledge that while it is not the Bomb, it's important. And we are selective about whom we share our love with. Clotheshorse Susan Zeidman comments, "When my boyfriend asks, 'Is that a new dress?' because I know he's critical about spending on clothing, I always answer, 'No.'"

Personal style consultant Joan Songer doesn't see an interest in wardrobe as frivolous at all:

> Like it or not, our culture pays back to women more dividends for looking good. When we talk about women going shopping, I think it's the opposite of frivolous. There's tremendous pressure for women to look good. And if you don't want to do it, then you pay a price. That's okay, too, particularly here in California, where women have a lot of choices. But the woman who does know how to dress herself beautifully whether she chooses to do it all the time or not has more confidence available to her.

A survey agrees with Joan, showing the shift in other ways. According to a national telephone poll, "American feminists see pride in their appearance as central to their self-respect. . . . Considering how busy women's lives are, taking time and money to care for yourself requires high self-esteem."[18]

How else do we counteract the outer and inner voices telling us our passions are ridiculous or trivial? Primo Levi wrote movingly of how, when people in the concentration camps were stripped of garments, their characters were fractured. They were deprived of something fundamentally human.[19] Clothing is integral to our sense of who we are. Who can look at the photos of the piles of glasses or shoes at Auschwitz and not be moved by the thought of the human beings who once wore those objects, who are no more?

Our clothes tell us and others that we are part of the mass of society, that we belong. When the yellow star accessories identified Jews as outcasts in World War II, King Christian of Denmark is believed to have said that if the gold star were introduced, he would be the first to wear one. This story illustrates the humanity of the people of Denmark, from the top down.[20]

With our clothing choices we can literally and symbolically do beautiful things. Style consultant Kathryn Hoover comments: "To express as much beauty as you can tap into within yourself is not an unholy thing to do." Besides, how can a little self-indulgence be that bad? We know it destroyed the Twelve Caesars, but then we don't have absolute power. We just have some loose change to pick up a lipstick every once in a while. *Women's Wear Daily* publisher John Fairchild redeems himself by concurring: "I know that self-indulgence is frowned upon these days, but I don't see how anything that gives life a romantic lift and a little joy can be put down as wrong."[21] While he has a financial interest in saying this, we still need to know who we are, and ornament is a way of exploring this. It's a time-honored reassurance as well as ridiculous good fun. Jeremy Stone comments:

> Vanity's a wonderful thing, especially as you get older and realize that there are a lot of things in life that you have to do for yourself, things that bring you pleasure, and you're lucky enough to be in touch with the fact that they bring you pleasure. There are very few things in life that bring pleasure these days that are not going to cause you to die of a disease.

Why else ignore the cry, "It's frivolous"? In her autobiography, *Me*, actress Katharine Hepburn shares her mother's advice for dealing with the tormentors who would have us forgo our passions for more "serious" pursuits: "Don't forsake those duties which keep you out of the nuthouse."

We can have it all. Artist Annabelle d'Huart insists that her preoccupation with her appearance isn't frivolous. "It's deliberate," she says gravely. "It's my way of resisting the ugliness, vulgarity, and aggressiveness of the world around me."[22]

This reminded me of an encounter I had a few years ago. The seed for this book was planted on a cold spring day in Boston in 1982, as the clear afternoon light slanted through the venetian blinds in my Italian professor's office. For a moment I looked up from my textbook and admired his attire. He, a kindly elegant gentleman of perhaps fifty, with a shock of white hair and a goatee, wore a simple wool sweater and a pair of wool pleated trousers and loafers. Color, weight of fabric, texture, and cut blended into a gift to the eye. His sweater fit him perfectly and was always in some subtly altered shade, perhaps still blue, but a grayer blue than expected, or a brown with some green in it. His trousers were also of extraordinary fabric, and his shoes were beautifully yet simply designed. I asked him the question that preyed on my mind: "You always dress beautifully, and what is that all about?" After thinking for a moment, he responded seriously:

> I am flattered and also embarrassed by your compliment. Thank you. I will tell you. I knew from an early age that the world can be a terrible place. In the war—World War II—I saw things so terrible I cannot mention them here. I realized then that if there are simple things I can do that can make life easier for other people, these things I will do. Among them, I dress so that people will look at me and see something pleasant to look upon, perhaps beautiful. So much of life is difficult. I want to do a small kindness. It is important to bring harmony and beauty back to this troubled world. I do not feel I am the most beautiful person on earth, but rather that it was important to me to give in this way, to know that I am making a contribution.

I think of him walking down the streets of Boston in his pleasant and simple clothes, and he seems to blend eloquently with the old stone buildings and the trees budding in spring. It seems to me that he was on to something.

The business of dressing is important, not just because the clothing industry is huge—what Barbara Jay calls "one of the great chug engines of this country"—and not just because the reason that people quested out from their tribes in the first place was in pursuit of food and cloth, but because dressing beautifully and harmoniously in a way that expresses your essence is a world-changing, world-defining act, a positive contribution, and—despite the negative hype criticizing fashion as frivolous, shallow, and vain—a public service. Beauty uplifts, inspires, and touches people who see us, people whom we will never know.

Notes:

1. Bell, Quentin. *On Human Finery*. Page 18.

2. Anspach, Karlyne. *The Why of Fashion*. Page 42.

3. Davis, Fred. *Fashion, Culture, and Identity*. Page 168.

4. Milbank, Caroline. *New York Fashions*. Page 8.

5. Davis, Fred. Page 41. Lawrence Langer adds the useful reminder, "Immodesty is seldom attributed to the male. He can display torso, arms, legs, and indeed practically every part of his body except one." [Langer. Page 74.]

6. Benstock, Shari and Suzanne Ferriss, Eds. *On Fashion*. Page 203. Should I remark about the chip firmly lodged on her shoulder, or just let her be?

7. Kelly, Katie. *The Wonderful World of Women's Wear Daily*. Page 57.

8. Vertes, Marcel. *Art and Fashion*. Page 7.

9. Finkelstein, Joanne. *The Fashioned Self*. Page 113.

10. Finkelstein, Joanne. Page 119.

11. See the searing British television comedy *Absolutely Fabulous*.

12. In this world, women perform two-thirds of the hourly labor, receive ten percent of the income, and hold one percent of the property according to Gayle Binion in "Human Rights: A Feminist Perspective," in *Human Rights Quarterly*, volume 17, number 3, August 1995, pages 509-526.

13. Chapkis, Wendy. *Beauty Secrets*. Page 131.

14. Benstock. Page 4.

15. Gaines. Page 6.

16. Rybczynski, Witold. *Home*. Page 80.

17. Benstock. Page 203.

18. Sandroff, Ronni. "Surprise! Feminists wear more makeup." *Glamour*. September 1993. Page 119.

19. Finkelstein. Page 111.

20. This is an urban legend. The Nazis never attempted to force badges on the people of Denmark because they knew how strongly the public sentiment was against such a measure. [*Encyclopaedia of the Holocaust*. Israel Gutman, Ed. Macmillan, New York: 1990. Volume 1. Page 142.]

21. Fairchild, John. *Chic Savages*. Page 35.

The Anguish of Sexiness

See that painted spectre,
The vampyre of the streets!
What foul demon wrecked her
Hoard of youthful sweets?
Made a crime of loveliness?
Oh! 'twas Dress—'twas Dress!
—*Harper's New Monthly Magazine,* 1858[1]

If a woman doesn't want to be looked at,
she should stay in bed with a cup of tea
and wait for the moment to pass.

—Designer Azzedine Alaïa[2]

Because we are all sensitive, the inadvertent or deliberate actions of other people can disturb us and make us feel horrible about our attractiveness or our sexuality. When I was in fourth grade, as I got on the bus one day, the bus driver put his hand on my shirt over my budding breast and said dismissively, "Huh. Not much there." When I was about eight, the housekeeper made me pose naked for pictures (because her boyfriend liked them, she said) and threatened to kill me if I told anyone. My guess is I was not alone in receiving their attentions and that there are a lot of people like this out there.

Those two experiences caused me to feel ambivalence about my changing body, a body I had previously accepted unquestioningly. They forced me into an awareness that my femaleness might have different meanings to different people, and that my body could be violated without my consent. People might forcibly impose meanings on my body that were not there, among them the idea of my acquiescence where I felt none and the suggestion of desire where none had had time to blossom. At the same time I felt a guilty intoxication from my body's fleeting ability to gather attention. I still ran with the boys, ran faster than the boys, wrestled with the boys, and usually beat the boys. Soon, my desire to do so ebbed.

Welcome to adolescence. Welcome to your adult female body. Emotions about one's sexuality begin to develop when one is young, and sorting them out must include examining formative experiences. What has this to do with clothing? Until sexuality is sorted out, clothing choices are made in part unconsciously, and confusions are acted out. For obvious reasons it's useful to be clear and aware about your own relationship to the issue.

In response to my experiences, I became defensive; I shied away from the driver as I got on the bus, or stayed after school. I told the housekeeper if she did it again I would tell my mother. I wore only long-sleeved, loose shirts and long baggy pants. Some children respond to inappropriate adult behavior by wearing provocative clothing—acting out the role others want them to play. It was years before I felt safe enough to define my body even by tucking in my shirt. This is often characteristic of abused children, and gives a worrisome edge to the recent teen fashion of contrasting baggy with excessively tight-fitting clothes.

If you were abused as a child, are the choices you made then still useful to you as an adult? What might be some alternatives? Identify the people who abused you and what they did. How does what happened color the way you approach living, sexuality, clothing? The intensity of the attractiveness problem is compounded by about a thousand issues. Eleven of these are listed below.

1. It's basic animal behavior.

Sexualized dress is the humanized form of mating plumage. However, we've reversed the sex roles and dress. In the animal kingdom males are the dandies, while females need camouflage so that they can protect and raise the young. Scent actually forms a large part of what attracts animals to each other; humans bathe too much to make that useful. Sheila Jackman, director of the Division of Human Sexuality at the Albert Einstein College of Medicine, comments, "We've kind of wiped out our pheromones so we attract with plumage we call clothing."[3]

Humans, unlike other animals, do not have a time of year when they're fertile. Because females are permanently available for mating, males are continually on the sexual hunt.[4] Melissa Batchelder comments:

A woman who dresses provocatively is going to have to expect that kind of attention. Anybody who's going to be really honest and fair to the whole philosophy of male/female or sexual relations is going to have to admit that there is an element there that is just animal nature. We fluff our feathers for one another.

2. Since we use clothes to define our erogenous zones, we don't really know where to put them.

[T]he female body consists of a series of sterilized zones, which are those exposed by the fashion which is just going out, and an erogenous zone, which will be the point of interest for the fashion which is just coming in. This erogenous zone is always shifting, and it is the business of fashion to pursue it without ever actually catching it up. It is obvious that if you really catch it up you are immediately arrested for indecent exposure. If you almost catch it up you are celebrated as a leader of fashion.

— James Laver, fashion historian[5]

What's sexy changes. In China the bound foot was considered erotic, in Japan the back of a woman's neck.[6] In the Victorian era, Alison Lurie noted, "leg" was so suggestive a concept that "the well-turned limbs of pianos might be modestly shrouded in fringed brocade."[7] Legs were so "sexual" that the royalty denied possessing them: "A would-be donor of silk stockings to a royal bride was rebuked for the indiscreet implications of his intended gift by the statement, 'The Queen of Spain has no legs.' "[8] This hysterical concern with modesty was paradoxical considering that the clothes women wore outlined and enhanced the curve of the breast, and the shaped skirts created an exaggerated curve of the bottom (but logical in light of the fact that, as Anne Hollander notes, "since women wore no underpants, the sight of the nude leg undoubtedly carried rather intense associations with undefended nudity higher up.")[9] Sociologist Fred Davis suggests that this dance between the hidden and revealed is what sexiness is all about. What do we do when we want to escape the sexiness of clothes? We try being modest. It's the opposite, right? Wrong. Flügel points to the clincher: "Modesty is essentially correlated with desire. Its purpose is to fight desire, but in so doing it rekindles it, so that a circular process is inevitably set in motion."[10]

- What do you like to hide?
- What do you like to reveal?
- How does this differ from what you like to see hidden and revealed in others?

Your expression of sexuality can be completely hidden. Melissa Batchelder adds, "I used to think that it was wasted if it wasn't illustrated. For me, now, there's nothing more sexually satisfying when you're not having sex than wearing a great lingerie set or something in an environment where no one in the world is going to know it. . . . It's the safest sex I'll ever have."

3. For many people, clothes are solely about sex.

The designer who plans them, the dressmaker who sells them, the divine or the moralist who denounces them, the historian of dress who reviews them as they successively occupy the stage for such brief years or months as may be allotted to them—all are alike agreed that their ultimate purpose, often indeed their overt and conscious purpose, is to add to the sexual attractiveness of their wearers, and to stimulate the sexual interest of admirers of the opposite sex and the envy of rivals of the same sex.

—J.C. Flügel, *The Psychology of Clothes*[11]

How we can have our beauty and not be treated as a commodity is an ancient riddle. The use of clothing for sexual attraction is the most ancient sartorial practice. According to archaeologist Elizabeth Wayland Barber, European scholars were horrified when a complete skirt made of string was dug up at Egtved because string skirts don't provide for either warmth or modesty. They are worn by women to "attract the eye precisely to the specifically female sexual areas by framing them, presenting them, or playing peekaboo with them."[12]

In addition to actual skirts which have been found at digs, archaeologists have also discovered statuettes of women wearing string skirts, apparently related to childbirth or fertility. Although we left the cave thousands of years ago, our training remains. In ordinary life today, it's hard for any woman to dress for comfort on a hot day and protect herself from being "read" as a bimbo. The two get snarled as we wear fewer clothes, as we get closer to that string skirt.

4. No matter how safe a garment seems, someone will think it is a juicy turn-on.

What is attractive to one person repulses another. You never know what will provoke the creep. He's nuts, and hence hard to predict. Among the nice guys, there's no telling what turns them on, either. Even when fashion designers classify garb as sexy, it's hopeless: Designer Hardy Amies once said that the most erotic sight of dress he had ever seen was "properly garbed nuns playing tennis, wimples and all."[13] Seeing the wimple very differently, my friend Sarah, a product of Catholic schooling, describes the arrival of a teacher: "The nun descended like a black cloud." According to Pamela Satran, women's ideas of sexiness vary according to their age, class, upbringing, and politics, and also may differ from men's ideas of sexiness: "For one thing, men tend to see all women's clothing—even items like nursing shoes that to women are decidedly nonsexy—as sexier than women do."[14]

How do you want to deal with the possibility of creeps? If you enjoy dressing up, employ selective sexiness. Be careful where you choose to wear your fabulousness. Go ahead and wear that sequined G-string bikini, but among people whom you trust; or keep bodyguards and carry a tiny working sequined pistol in each hand. If you're going to be leaving your home, arrange for rides or protection. Most movie stars do, so why shouldn't you? Friends enjoy playing posse. For the sake of the pleasures of dress, become proficient in a self-defense art—when you know you can protect yourself, you can more effectively focus your attention in dangerous situations. Exercise street smarts: regardless of your sex, wear flat shoes and clothing you can run in whenever possible. Tote the pumps. Advertising executive Stacey Lamiero suggests wearing stilettos only in bed. Maybe that's the only place for them—there they don't affect your spine and the way you move, and if your partner gets too frisky you have weapons to fend him off.

While in clothes, your body language can clearly announce your lack of interest in sex and your enjoyment of dressing, not everyone will be able to read that announcement. Be prepared to tell them if they get too forward. You have to know how to say "No" and how to get help fast. Quick tip: Yelling "Fire!" repeatedly at the top of your lungs will get help a hell of a lot faster than yelling "Help!"

5. The law punishes women for their dress.

One warm spring Sunday, I'm sitting at an outdoor cafe in Chicago with actress Andrea Gall and her girlfriends. One woman talks about how, when wearing something great, there's always an implied or lurking threat of male violence, "as if men are not responsible for their own lust, as if women were responsible for men's sexual feeling." The rest of the table nods knowingly. Someone else mentions the vulnerability of being a "babe," how looking great has a dark side that should not be. Even though clothes won't protect you, they can be used against you in a court of law.

One of Andrea's friends mentions the notorious "you-asked-for-it" court judgment. This case shows up repeatedly in discussions among women. It is shocking evidence of the imbalance between how men and women are treated. A Florida jury ruled recently in a rape case that the plaintiff had "asked for it" because of what she was wearing.[15] The jury was wrong, but they had the power to decide. Someone else mentions that women are disproportionately punished by the law: "The average prison sentence in the U.S. for a woman who kills her husband: fifteen to twenty years. For a man who kills his wife: two to six years."[16]

Where does the difference in men's and women's perceptions come from? According to Flügel:

> Men may, therefore (rightly from their own standpoint), accuse women of being immodest; and women (also rightly from theirs) may reply, either that sexuality was seen where none was present (i.e., consciously recognized), or that they—the women—have a more "natural" and "healthy" attitude to the body (i.e., that they can enjoy the pleasures of exposure without apprehending or intending any concomitant genital desire).[17]

Flügel wrote about woman as the traditional scapegoat, the "guilty temptress"[18] made responsible for man's sexual desires. Another of Andrea's friends comments, "The normal thought that pops into my head is, 'You got a problem with your dick, bub? It's your problem!'" While it is men's responsibility to keep it in their pants, they can enforce their viewpoint with threats and violence, rather than accept their moral responsibility as creatures with greater physical power, to protect and defend the weaker from danger rather than exploit them. How do they handle responsibility? Every nine seconds a woman is beaten by her husband or boyfriend. Domestic violence is the leading cause of serious injury to American women, more common than muggings and car crashes combined.[19]

When a man says to me, "You're so pretty when you smile," I want to hit him. For centuries, for women, smiling has been related to accommodating and "making nice." It is a gesture with which the powerless ingratiate themselves with the powerful. I fear that compliment rewards an almost instinctive and self-denigrating behavior. Although his comment never intends this, it causes me to fear my that face showing relaxation or intensity—my natural states—is unattractive. The societal code still yammers about women being nice and pretty. We are supposed to smile to demonstrate our availability, approachability, helpfulness. Alice Koller reminds us that when the wolf bares her teeth it's a snarl, but when humans bare their teeth we think it's about friendliness.

6. Dressing has changed so much in the past few decades that even if a person were trying to read the signals correctly she would be flummoxed by the fact that there are no rules.

Advertisers urge sexually provocative clothes upon youngsters as effectively as they urge new autos on their parents. Tawdry and sleazy are synonymous with desirable according to the magazines. The same outfit that communicates "hip" to a young girl on the college campus says "prostitute" for a woman turning tricks on San Pablo Avenue a few miles away. Nice girls don't, for example, show their underwear. Yet frilly, lacy, deliberately observable underwear is sold for little girls.

Perhaps the current pressure to embrace the bimbo look also has to do with its being at one ideologically with a consumer culture whose overarching messages are of the "use-me," "throwaway" kind.[20] We have disposable diapers, paper towels, refrigerators that are cheaper to throw away than to fix. Disposable, usable women fit in perfectly. Women are commodities to sell objects; "keeping" a woman is portrayed as the goal of many magazine and TV ads. The idea of women as objects that run down and must be replaced can fuel the frenzy behind women's make-up purchases.

What sexual signals confuse you? What signals do you want to communicate?

7. Clothing disapproval is one way parents unclearly communicate with children about appropriate use of sexuality.

One clothes collector in her mid-fifties describes how her mother's fears and concerns about her emerging sexuality manifested themselves:

Once when I was about five years old, I was trying to approximate my mother's breasts by stuffing toilet paper under my T-shirt. I was running around in the yard, and when my mother saw me she hauled me into the house. She said, "Go out and cut yourself a lilac switch, and don't you ever do that again." And I got switched for it.

Events like this may bubble on the back burner for decades. The dangers are all the more menacing because they are merely implied (and we are punished), never voiced, never explained. What unclear messages did you receive from your family about sexuality and clothing?

8. The anguish of sexiness is perhaps most fundamentally the anxiety of the perpetually hunted.

An emotional undertow denying the issue resides in comments such as: "You think everyone wants you? Who are you kidding?" The anguish of sexiness is perhaps most fundamentally the anxiety of the perpetually hunted, who is told it is all in her head: "You shouldn't worry." Meanwhile she can feel the draining pull of the gaze, even when it never reaches the point of physical contact.

The pervasiveness of this assault is revealed by Timothy Beneke, author of *Men on Rape,* who discusses some of the language of attraction, and offers a psychological perspective on dating from many men's points of view. "Clearly, to men, a woman's *appearance* is a weapon." He quotes phrases men use to describe women's looks, "She's a *knockout!*" "That woman is *ravishing!*" "What a *bombshell!*" "She's really *stunning!*" He states heterosexual men can feel attacked by a woman's beauty. This relates to how men understand sex: "If sex is an achievement, then the presence of an attractive woman may result in one's feeling like a failure. One's self-worth or 'manhood' may become subtly (or not so subtly) at issue in her presence."

He thinks he couldn't win the beautiful woman: she would choose someone richer, smarter, or better looking, and he resents that. And his feelings of inadequacy become her fault. If he's hostile enough, he may try to make the woman feel as degraded as he does, through any action from a demeaning sexual remark to rape.[21] Or he can ask her out on a date—in the common vernacular, he can "hit on her." Women also correlate certain looks, specifically high fashion, with violence—"dressed to kill." What effects of your presence are denied or unspoken by others?

9. Attractiveness can cause discomfort.

Often on a day when I look pulled together, coordinated, and chic, a phenomenon occurs which makes me uneasy: men glom onto me with their eyes. Not everybody, but enough people so that the duration and quality of the eye contact people make with me, or the glance I receive, changes. The eye contact lengthens. Sometimes I feel as if I were being sucked in, drunk, through their eyes. I think, "Oh, I've captured it. I've done something." Who knows what links into someone else's idea of attractive? The same outfit doesn't always create the same result. I go for test runs to the supermarket, to the bookstore, down the main street. I feel some uncomfortable I-am-one-up-on-you feeling. Men are exposed by their rapt dependent gaze (not unlike a baby at the breast). I resent it. I feel isolated from humanity, too cute to be a member of the crowd. The relationship, created by the gazer's gaze and myself as desired object, feels unbalanced at a deep level.

So there I am at the Motion Picture Studio Christmas Party at the fabulous ranch of the attractive studio founder. I'm single, he's single. So what if he's twenty years older than I am? I'm wearing a beautiful peach silk dress that I bought at a thrift store for seven dollars. I figure it was meant to be: He'll see me across a crowded dance floor. Our eyes will lock. He'll ask me to dance, marry, live with him forever. I thought the whole thing through. I'm already spending his money, riding his horses, redecorating, making him peanut butter sandwiches. . . .

What really happened: I'm standing on the edge of the dance floor with my friend Judith, the music is pounding, nobody asks me to dance. I figure "What the hell" and just close my eyes and start swaying to the music, enjoying sensing the rhythm in my body. I feel behind me that prickling oddness of someone staring at me and turn to open my eyes to see it is he! I scowl instinctively and turn away. By the time I realize what I've done and turn back to face him, he's vanished.

When you've got it all "together," how do you feel?

10. Unspoken rules for containing women's sexual expression (however ridiculous) are vigorously enforced.

Many people seem to enjoy the enforcer's role, snapping out the line, "You asked for it." Heaven forfend you should enjoy being on display. Clothing scholar Grace Margaret Morton chides us: "Do your clothes claim too much attention? The looks you get may imply contempt rather than admiration."[22] She is not alone. The dressing books counsel us to avoid drawing looks to ourselves. Leah Feldon suggests:

Keep it simple. If you do decide to go all out and call attention to yourself, make sure you can handle the reactions. If you wear a transparent blouse you are going to get stares and comments, plain and simple. So take responsibility for your choices. No whining allowed.[23]

"No whining allowed?" I think a little whining is in order here. "She has no one to blame but herself" for his lack of control over his own libido? Because he is stronger than she is, has the law behind him, because it's the law of the jungle here in civilization?

This trick of confinement by warning, by veiled threats, is not new. The Reverend Wettenhhal Wilkes wrote to a Young Lady in 1740: "The negligence of loose attire/May oft' invite to loose desire."[24] In 1925 the Roman Catholic Archbishop of Naples announced that God, in his anger about "a skirt which reached no further than the knee,"[25] had caused a recent earthquake.

Women also have voluntarily chided, cajoled, controlled, and threatened each other for centuries. Witness the preaching of the Victorian writer, Mrs. Sherwood:

> But if a woman laces herself into a sixteen inch belt, and then clothes herself in brocade, satin, and bright colors, and makes herself conspicuous, she should not object to the fact that men, seeing her throw aside her mantle, comment upon her charms in no measured terms. She has no one to blame but herself.[26]

Currently, at work, some "well-meaning soul" may take us aside and tell us what is "too much." One woman received advice on professional dressing when she started working at Marshall Field's: "I remember one of the store's top buyers saying, 'Never wear anything that jingles,' which was very good advice, because it's distracting. 'And nothing that wiggles, yourself or your clothes.'"[27]

I thought, "Why can't we wiggle? Why can't the people who are upset by the movements of our bodies, by our self-expression, just GET OVER IT?" To my surprise, I then found myself participating. My friend Karen was giving me a ride up Broadway. At a red light, a young woman, tall and slender, in a short, tight, fluffy, pale pink sweater-dress crossed the street in front of our car. I thought, "What a bimbo," just as Karen said, "She has courage." After a moment's shame I had to agree with her. Think of a woman looking as if she enjoyed the loveliness of her body, the bouncing breasts, the moving hips. How do you feel about such a person? Is she "asking for it"? Do you desire her, envy her, or even hate her? How often do you think, "Bless her and good luck to her in this crazy world"? Fabulous-scarf-wearer and legal assistant Melissa Batchelder, a woman much more level-headed than I, examines how these rules and warnings play out in a law firm and how they are changing:

> I think it's silly not to acknowledge that the way that you dress is going to have an effect on the people around you. That's the reason this place here, for example, has rules like "A woman cannot show too much of her chest," or whatever the rule is. [Employees are actually given a manual containing a page of such dictates.] And yet, what are they really saying? Are they willing to admit that they can be seduced? Or are they saying that it's inappropriate? Well, why is it inappropriate? What's it got to do with performance?

She also notes that office rules change as women become more powerful:

Things have certainly changed just in the time that I've been doing this work—in terms of what's acceptable and not acceptable in terms of clothing. When I first started in this business, a woman didn't wear culottes. It was completely unacceptable. Now, there's an enormous change in the amount of skin that a woman shows in the office. Some, not all. It's a very interesting concept, how things have evolved. And yet we seem to be trying to pretend that they haven't. Economically and philosophically, women are obviously more powerful, so they're going to dress more like they want to dress. And they're going to be less willing to accept what a man says is appropriate. This is why that little blue suit with the little tie has gone out the window.

Melissa had a calming effect on my nerves, which allowed me to ask the necessary questions. If explicit or implicit warnings gave you information about sexuality, about your looks and body, how did it make you feel? What decisions did you make about your appearance at that time? Are those decisions still appropriate to the person you are today?

11. Consider the flip side, the anxiety of not feeling attractive.

The extent to which you "buy in" to your value, relating to how men value you in the sexual market, will be reflected in the extent to which you prize conventional attractiveness, feel sold out by your aging, and feel panicked by the once-unwelcome attention no longer coming your way.

The insistent messages bleated by the media (about, for example, staying fashionable, staying slim, smelling good, and not having bags under your eyes) have a corrosive effect on normal women trying to lead good lives. Germaine Greer comments: "Women might well ask, When in this life will I be allowed to let myself go?"[28] This insistence on training to be a magnet for men overrides the messages which actually can contribute to a life that is of value: Find the things that interest you and do them. Develop your intelligence, feed your curiosity, care for your soul. What has this to do with clothes? These actions allow our lives a depth which informs surfaces with meaning. If you are relaxed in nature, taking a walk in the woods or on the beach, how could they sell that to you? If you love to read, how could that be marketed (beyond best-seller hype) when all the books eventually show up at the library where you can borrow for free? It costs nothing to use a library to educate yourself, to train yourself, to make yourself brilliant. Isak Dinesen wrote, "Women . . . when they are old enough to have done with the business of being women, and can let loose their strength, must be the most powerful creatures in the world."[29] There's no need to wait to be old. Give yourself pleasure and unleash your intelligence. If you like to putter around the house or walk around the neighborhood, if you like to figure out math problems or . . . you begin to get the picture. The life that is marketed to us, for the most part, is not a life that is fulfilling. It is the vision of the same life for everyone, owning a fancy stereo and computer, a big house, expensive running shoes, and two new cars. Attractiveness is part of that prefabricated picture.

Once we buy into the system, and into making ourselves conventionally attractive, we are then co-opted into this idea of remaining attractive. This raises Greer's ire:

The very notion of remaining attractive is replete with the contradictions that break women's hearts. A woman cannot make herself attractive; she can only be found attractive. She can only remain attractive if someone remains attracted to her. . . . Her desperate attempts to do the impossible, to guide the whim of another, are the basis of a billion-dollar beauty industry. All their lives women have never felt attractive enough. They have struggled through their thirties and forties to remain attractively slim, firm-bodied, glossy-haired and bright-eyed. Now, in the fifties, "remaining attractive" becomes more than a full-time job.[30]

The truth that we all age continually butts into the fantasy. Society dictates ways a woman should look as she ages to "remain in the running." It's all useless information. As actress Cybill Shepherd commented, facelifts don't make you look younger, they make you look tighter. Nothing will stop those superficial men who have bought into the "beauty myth" from turning away from a lovely woman as time changes her face. And nothing will convince a brainwashed woman who desperately desires to hold onto the dreaminess of being found attractive in that specific way that she can't control her fate or her face.

What do we do? How do we adjust to the change in our faces and our bodies? Although it is reassuring to know I (as a woman) have value because I am desired, this is not a good goal to dress for or rely upon for my sense of my worth, depending as it does on a "hit" from someone else's approval.

What will give you the excuse to be yourself? We must allow ourselves to play, in whatever form it takes. I think of my usually dowdy Aunt Florence, who at age 82 appeared at my cousin's wedding celebration at the Rainbow Room in a long shimmering white beaded dress, fur stole, and a bright blond wig. She looked at my puzzled expression and said with a mischievous smile, "I'm going through my Marilyn Monroe phase."

In order to consider all these issues and not get spun around by a million perspectives, define what sexiness means to you. Why bother? Well, for those who were jarred out of our own inner timing, it's a good idea to realign and heal, if only for the sake of skin tone, darling. Clarity about sexuality may lead to good sex, and good sex improves the complexion.

1. Consider the psychology of sexiness, how you feel about your own and what you want to communicate. What contradictions do you live with? Make a study of the primary causes of erotic response and choose carefully when and where you wear, paint, or exhibit them.

2. How do you experience your sexuality and what do you want to express about it? What do you think looks attractive, and what, if anything, marks the borders or the relations among attractive, sexy, and dangerous for you?

3. How do you want to feel when you dress, for example for work, for play, for formal events? When does it feel safe, desirable, or appropriate to be sexy?

4. How do your definitions of sexy differ from the conventions of your family, your peer group, your neighborhood, your job? To what extent are you willing to deal with the flak that comes with challenging conventions? Does desiring not to look oversexed or cheap limit the way you

dress in any way? Do any tarty looks please you? How is this different from your professional dress? Have you ever found yourself in public in too sexy an outfit, caught "with your pants down," so to speak? What was behind this clothing choice?

5. Take a moment to explore the facets of your own expression. If this part of your personality were laid out in a picture book or notebook, what would the pictures or notes reveal? How does this express itself in your life? What about what turns you on is absurd? If you can't find anything, look closer. As we all know, sexuality is funny.

6. Try purchasing and filling up your wardrobe with "bad clothes" that you feel attracted to and scared of. Thrift stores supply them on the cheap. Invite them in for a visit and play. No one has to see you in them. The forbidden-clothes category includes whatever works for you: the sexy, the tacky, the buttoned-up, the polyester, whatever!

Construct fantasies of glitter, lace, and glue; check out the nearest big city costume rental store. Playing dress-up—sexy or not—can be ridiculously satisfying. Halloween functions as an annual excuse, but in the privacy of your home you are free to do anything, and free to hold costume parties any time of year. I recently attended a costume wedding where the bride came as a chunk of pineapple and the groom as a cube of lime jello. After their vows, the pineapple entered the lime jello, and actual pineapple chunks lodged in small squares of jello were circulated among the guests for consumption. I dressed as a blooming rose and my date wore a giant bee suit.

7. Read poetry. Jane Kenyon wrote:

> *The shirt touches his neck*
> *and smooths over his back.*
> *It slides down his sides.*
> *It even goes down below his belt—*
> *down into his pants.*
> *Lucky shirt.*[31]

Robert Herrick wrote:

> *When as in silks my Julia goes,*
> *Then, then (me thinks) how sweetly flowes*
> *That liquefaction of her clothes.*
> *Next, when I cast mine eyes and see*
> *That brave Vibration each way free;*
> *O how that glittering taketh me!*[32]

Notes:

1. Batterberry, Michael and Ariane. *Mirror, Mirror*. Page 11.
2. "People Are Talking About." *Vogue*. November 1995. Page 132.
3. Satran, Pamela Redmond. *Dressing Smart*. Page 147.
4. Glynn, Prudence. *Skin to Skin*. Page 20.
5. Laver, James. *Modesty in Dress*. Page 97.
6. Batterberry, Michael and Ariane. *Mirror, Mirror*. Page 11.
7. Lurie, Alison. *The Language of Clothes*. Page 40.
8. Flügel, J. C. *The Psychology of Clothes*. Page 66.
9. Urquhart, Rachel. "Seeing Through Clothes." *Vogue*. January 1996. Page 137.
10. Flügel. Page 192.
11. Flügel. Page 26.
12. Barber, Elizabeth Wayland. *Women's Work The First 20,000 Years*. Page 59.
13. Glynn. Page 94.
14. Satran, Pamela Redmond. *Dressing Smart*. Page 149.
15. Benstock, Shari and Suzanne Ferriss. *On Fashion*. Page 62.
16. *Elle*. November 1993.
17. Flügel. Page 109.
18. Flügel. Page 110.
19. From the "First comprehensive national health survey of American women, July 1993," The Commonwealth Fund in New York City. Cited by the Family Violence Prevention Fund in San Francisco, (415) 252-8900.
20. Ribiero, Aileen. *Dress and Morality*. Page 168.
21. Baker, Nancy C. *The Beauty Trap*. Pages 44-45. The analysis of Beneke contains her ideas.
22. Morton. Page 278.
23. Feldon, Leah. *Dress Like a Million*. Page 170.
24. Bailey, Adrian. *The Passion for Fashion*. Page 28.
25. Laver, James. *Costume and Fashion*. Page 232.
26. Batterberry. Page 249.
27. Wallach, Janet. *Looks That Work*. Page 63.
28. Greer, Germaine. *The Change*. Page 113.
29. Heilbrun, Carolyn G. *Writing a Woman's Life*. Page 128.
30. Greer. Page 112.
31. From the poem "The Shirt" by Jane Kenyon, which appeared in *From Room to Room*. Alicejamesbooks, 1978.
32. From *Selections from the Poetry of Robert Herrick*. Harper & Brothers, 1882.

Questionnaire

(*Fill in the blanks.*)

1. In my family, I am the _____ one.

2. a) My mother wears/wore a lot of _____.
   b) (*check one*)
   _____ I wouldn't be caught dead in this.
   _____ I wear this a lot and it looks terrible on me.
   _____ I probably would look good in this but no way will I ever wear it.
   _____ I solemnly vowed never to wear this but somehow my wardrobe contains many examples of this awful phenomenon.

3. My mother is so good-looking and looks so perfect all the time, I _____ .

4. My mother's clothing style was a constant source of embarrassment to me as I was growing up, (*check one*)
   _____ and remains so to this day.
   _____ and now I realize I was wrong.
   _____ and now I find, to my mortification, that I dress a lot like her.
   _____ so I reacted by dressing like _____.

4. My father looks like _____.

5. My sister/brother is an embarrassment to me. I don't like to be seen with _____ because s/he looks so _____.

6. Regarding other relatives, _____ looks great because _____.
   _____ doesn't because _____. She really should wear _____.

7. I look like _____.
   (*family member/pet name*)

8. My body type is the same as _____.
   (*mother's/therapist's name*)

9. In elementary school, I wanted to look like _____. This was _____ unlikely.
   (*adverb*)
   She wore_____.

10. In high school, I dressed like a _____. If I had to do it again,
    _____ a) I would wear _____.
    _____ b) I would kill myself.

Childhood

This chapter is full of stories intended to reawaken your memories. The details, sequences, and flavors of your story are important.

What clothes do you remember from childhood, fondly or with loathing?

Art dealer Nick Debs thinks about how his clothing tastes evolved. "When I was a kid, I didn't think about it. I had a pair of purple corduroys that I just loved and wore all the time, wide-wale grape-colored corduroys with a little bell bottom on them. They were very funny, but they were great. I wore them out, until they had huge holes in them." Somehow I can't see him in them now. "No," he laughs. "This was what, 1969? and I was five. . . . Then when I was older, I basically wore my father's hand-me-downs."

Computer expert Bart Shulman remembers a shirt:

I was four and it was mustard colored with a tight collar, a T-shirt-type collar, but not elasticky at all, so it was always a struggle to get over my head. The collar had black stripes on it.

I remember wearing that shirt all the time. I didn't like putting it on because it was hard to get it over my head, but I liked wearing it. I was Bart the Mustard Bottle.

Following the deeper emotions, a series of questions emerges: Who in your family do you look like? How do they dress? Are there ways they dress that you do or don't want to incorporate? What role does your upbringing play in your clothing selection today?

I asked interviewees the following:

- When you first became aware of clothes, how did you become aware of them?
- Was it with pleasure or discomfort?
- If people disapproved, where did it hurt?
- What did people say or do, and what were your resulting feelings?
- Are clothing decisions you make today based on those early experiences? Do these decisions serve you?
- In adolescence, who did you want to look like and what did you want to wear? What did you end up wearing, and how did it feel?
- What were your limits? Do these limits influence your dress today?

Why can't we just pull something out of the closet, look in the mirror, decide it looks good, and wear it? If we emerged from childhood unaffected by the things which were done "for our own good," or done against us, then no exploration would be necessary. If you are completely clear about the formative influences of your family and your childhood, fine; you get a medal. Skip this part. (When Joan Songer tells her wardrobe class that we choose our parents and come into a family environment based on the greatest amount of delusion we can handle, she always gets an enormous laugh.)

The relative importance of appearance is first defined by the parents. After Laurel Fenenga's baby was born and she heard him cry for the first time, she thought, "Thank goodness, I've got the nice cry. A new mother doesn't care if the baby looks like a hippopotamus if the baby has a nice cry."

I spoke with an attractive woman in her early fifties who was viewed very differently as a baby (she works in the fashion industry now):

My birth mother, who was seventeen, was going to give me up for adoption, but she had a very long labor—more than thirty hours. People were ready to adopt me and take me into their lives, but she insisted on seeing me. The doctor said, "I don't think you should." She insisted. She said the minute she saw me, she fell in love. She thought I was the most beautiful baby. Her perception of me made her keep me at least for a while until she realized she wasn't able to take care of a baby.

The perception that she was beautiful continued to play a significant role in her upbringing, in the ways that beauty was and was not allowed to be enhanced:

My adoptive parents also thought that I was just a beautiful little baby. However, my mother did not believe that children had the right to have control over their own lives, their appearance and their behavior. She thought all girls should have permanents, and would inflict permanents on us at regular intervals. I hated them. She thought that my color was green. So I was always dressed in green. And my sister was dressed in yellow. Okay, fine. I didn't have any particular desire to wear yellow. But I had to wear what she made me wear. My mother felt we should wear Buster Brown brown lace-up oxfords with socks.

My mother had been subjected to the advances of a brother-in-law, and generally did not trust the inclinations of men. She wanted to protect the female children from them. Therefore, we were to be attired modestly. I entered puberty rather young. I started developing breasts when I was ten or eleven. My figure began to form. She was scared I might turn out to be like my birth mother, so I wasn't allowed to show my legs. I wasn't allowed to be a cheerleader because cheerleaders' skirts were too short.

I got control of my own destiny when I was twelve years old. I put my foot down. I was not going to let her do my hair ever again. I was not going to let her commit the degradations she committed upon my hair. And I put up enough of a fuss that she didn't.

Today this woman appears elegantly attired at any function she attends. People often compliment her on her attractiveness. And, not surprisingly, given the emphasis—unconscious or not—on costuming to prevent inappropriate sexual activity in her childhood, after much reflection and consideration about these matters she has an innocent penchant for garments that might be considered "naughty" in her private life.

Negative events in childhood can stimulate an interest in clothing and the costuming arts. Fong Wong—a fabulous dresser who grew up in China—was harassed one day by soldiers of the Cultural Revolution for wearing a pretty dress. She was in first grade. She called them bullies, and resolved to have beautiful clothes always.

From the age of four or so onward, my sister and I, garbed in fancy dress, were trotted out to meet guests at my parents' cocktail parties. Sometimes we would hold the hors d'oeuvre tray and be cooed over. My response to that was to dig in and resist finery. This attitude was cemented in adolescence after noticing my pleasure in wearing some particularly shocking garments I bought at the Salvation Army: "That's the way I am and if they don't like it, tough." This attitude has both served and not served me in my adult life. In the last few years I find myself taking pleasure in wearing elegant clothes, but I enjoy shopping for this garb only at thrift stores.

Daphne Stannard, despite her family's lack of attention to appearances when she was growing up, developed an interest in clothes:

I grew up in an academic family. Academics typically are allowed to run free with their clothing. They can wear their turtleneck backwards with the tag right there and go out in public, and that's kosher. You look more like an academic if you look like that because your head is in the clouds. I grew up with less fashion appropriateness than most kids for that reason.

Writer Rhonda Pretlow talks about her background:

In high school, I was never appropriate because I grew up really poor, and I never had the money for the Puma sneakers, the Gloria Vanderbilt jeans, or whatever. I just wore hand-me-down clothes. So I got into this mind-set that, "well, clothes aren't important. Clothes don't matter." It was sour grapes because I couldn't afford the clothes that everybody else was wearing.

But now I realize that they do matter, in terms of how much attention you call to yourself in a negative or positive way. I wear clothes just to be treated the way I want to be treated. If I want attention, I'll wear something that would reveal me in a more sexual way. If I want to be ignored, I'll wear something where I'm just going to blend into what the majority of the people are wearing.

For those who loved clothes and were financially enabled to play, costuming often assumed an important role. For Mary Armentrout, a choreographer who has been dancing and making up dances since she was three or four, costuming is part of her earliest memories:

I had fantastic costumes when I was little, like a duck bill made out of papier-mâché with a little yellow tutu. I'm not afraid to wear things that I feel good in, whereas other people might balk at wearing this hat, for example.

She points to her enormous black fake fur hat. "If I see something in the mirror that clicks for me, I don't have too much of a problem wearing it."

On a hot August day just before fourth grade started, I pulled my mom into a store because in the window was a blue tie-dye T-shirt with a sequined turtle on the front: my first true clothes love. Even though the total outfit, including the matching pants (I didn't like them separately, but they made the outfit) cost over twenty dollars, I wheedled her into buying it for me. Delighted, I wore it at once. In the first wash, the sequins discolored and dropped off. Only the pants were wearable. I began to stop having confidence about choices made based on love.

An awareness of what others around me wore gradually dawned. Before sixth grade, in the annual pre-school clothes shop, I came upon a sale table covered with "alligator shirts" in B. Altman's boy's department. All the kids were wearing alligator shirts then. And they were on sale! I made Mom buy me a whole bunch of different ones and proudly wore one to school, thrilled that I'd figured out how to fit in. I was swiftly informed that these were odd alligator shirts, different from the ones everyone else wore. The alligators were the wrong color and the shirts were the wrong weight of cotton jersey.

Shopping began to seem to me to be stupid and fruitless. I couldn't buy for love, I couldn't buy for conformity. Mom would not be persuaded to go out and buy me the "right" kind of alligator shirt after she had just bought me five perfectly good new shirts cheap.

Jeremy Stone has always been interested in clothes as well, especially the idea of wearing costume. She comments:

Halloween was a big deal. I gave a lot of thought to who I was going to be. I chose characters like Medusa or Circe. I had theme birthday parties where everyone had to come in costume. One was "Come as Your Favorite Goddess." I was interested in the historical implications of costume and characters from history that you could be. I loved Marie Antoinette. I read five different biographies about her in third grade. I was interested in the clothes, the costumes, the whole period.

Then I went on an executed-queens kick. I loved reading biographies about different women in history. Reading about other people and seeing the choices that they made and the things they did was like a road map. Costume was a way of trying on all these different fantasies and identities. I was very curious about who I was going to be when I grew up.

- What did your childhood clothes mean to you?
- How has this affected you?
- Can you recall specific outfits or costumes you loved or hated?
- Why did you wear them?
- Can you hear any echoes of your feelings about childhood clothes in your choice of presentation today?
- Are there styles you are locked into that you wish you weren't?
- Are there aspects of garments you wore in your childhood that you would like to incorporate into your presentation today? From our childhoods most of us remember at least the color of a beloved or significant garment. What do you recall?

Adolescence and the agony of junior high and high school

How we think about our looks and dress was formed in part in the crucible of high school. I noticed when researching this chapter that adolescents are so sensitive about their appearance, so sensitive to being looked at, that when I glanced at them they sometimes flinched.

Some use adolescence for exploring beauty and dating, others find identity in becoming an extreme—the class clown or the rebel. Some find themselves the Homecoming Queen, in the spotlight of positive attention, while for others their poverty—the financial status of their parents as demonstrated by the clothes they cannot afford to wear—becomes a cause of excruciating self-consciousness. Others find themselves, for various reasons, with a strong desire to follow the crowd.

Exploring beauty and dating

At adolescence, an involvement with fashion and clothing can empower young women to experiment with what adulthood means. We are looking for models, to know who we are and what we can become. During this time women are closest in age to the fashion models. Yet, unless we turn to high-level prostitution, have a sugar daddy, or become a top model, we can't afford the clothes the models wear. Many teens do not have parental permission or funding to choose their own clothes.

When Jeremy Stone changed from an all-girl to a co-ed school, she focused her interest on presentation, who she wanted "them" to think she was:

I wanted to wear the right thing and fit in. I used to carefully study what my next-door neighbor wore and looked at all the other girls at the bus stop.

Clothes were a way of trying to figure out my identity as a blossoming young woman, and also a way of testing out different theories about boys. I was alternately fascinated by and disgusted with how incredibly transparent . . . what suckers they were. I saw early on that they had this total obsession with the way girls looked, and it pissed me off. In eighth grade, I did a lot with clothes to test out my theories about boys. School was my laboratory. Experiments with boys on a daily basis were based on my "readings" in *Seventeen* magazine. I was going steady with four different guys at the same time. It was ridiculous. I realized, "These people don't even know me. They just want to go steady with me and call me every night because of the way I look." That irritated me, but it was also sort of exciting.

In high school, at first I pursued ultimate beauty. I went on incredible fitness campaigns, and got down to what I thought my perfection was. I was into looking like a model and got off on the reactions I got. I thought it was a real source of power. Clothes were a way of exploring sexual identity without being sexual. Clothes were also my way of thinking about and exploring my feelings about myself. I discovered that physical beauty can be so much an illusion. All you have to do is get one really bad haircut and wear a really unflattering outfit, and you see how people's reactions change based on how you look.

After a while, I got so disgusted by it that I gained weight and cut my hair short. When I saw the change in the way people responded to me, I loved it. I thought, "This way you can experience life without illusions. You can make yourself look neuter." I then went through a time of real conscious testing and physical change. It got to a point where my stepmother said to me, "You could not make yourself more unattractive if you tried." Part of me really liked it. I looked so unlike me.

She took from that time an understanding of how to play the clothes game. Only later, with maturity, would she return to the pleasure and enjoyment of clothing.

Homecoming Queen

I never could quite balance the idea that Debbie Epidendio was her high school's Homecoming Queen (in 1978) with the fact that she's one of the nicest people you'd want to meet. I asked her how she became Homecoming Queen. She responded:

I really don't know. I knew a lot of people in school just from saying hello and talking to them about different things. Not to mention that I had three brothers there, too.

When you're chosen as a finalist, it's in front of the whole school. All of a sudden, all of this attention is on you, and it's very different from when it's not. But after the night I was chosen Homecoming Queen was the strangest. You're chosen and you're standing up there, and they make all the other girls get off the stage. Then you get off the stage, and that's it. It's over. After the ceremony that night—I don't think I even changed clothes—we went out. I was carrying around all these flowers, and my mom said, "Do you want me to take the flowers for you?" I said, "No. No. I'll carry them around." I still wanted the recognition that I didn't have anymore.

I still have the outfit. I even still have the crown. It's either in a drawer or in the Halloween costume box, but I still have it. The next night at the crowning, I wore a long formal dress, one that I had from a prior prom.

She shows me pictures. I comment it's different from what I expected. (I mean, her story.) She thinks I'm talking about her dress and asks, "Did you expect it to look like a fairy princess dress?" When I was in high school, I took comfort in the idea that some people went through this hard time without effort, that for them it wasn't painful. Maybe I've just seen too many movies. Debbie says:

In high school, I was always wanting to go on diets because I didn't feel as good as the other girls who always got boyfriends and everything. It was really tough. I was in love with this guy and just couldn't get him. So, no, I don't see that from the outside. I was constantly wishing that I could redo something, wishing that I had different hair, different skin, a different body. I had a great time in high school, but it was the most stressed-out time—not the school part of it but the social part. I think going through high school is the hardest time in anybody's life.

Just as we all suspected, the Homecoming Queen suffered with the rest of us.

Class Clown

Where does the class clown come from? Lex Eurich talks about the transition from having Mom choose the clothes to having some autonomy in choice.

When I was a kid, my mom dressed me how she wanted to. I was a very good kid in general. I don't think I ever put up a fight about my clothes. In the transition period when I started to buy my own clothes, we fought a little bit about it. Because she was very traditional she wanted me to look "nice," to have nice pretty clothes without holes in them.

Lex became more confrontational in her clothes: "I'm sure part of it came from the fact that I didn't have a boyfriend, thought I was ugly. I wanted to be more outrageous than pretty. I wanted attention, but not for beauty." She went to a public school, but it had a country club atmosphere to it: "Everyone had the turtlenecks with the little hearts on them, and chinos or jeans. I don't think anyone ever had a tattoo in my whole high school history. If they did, it was on their butt." It was very clean-cut, white-bread, upper-middle-class:

I hated the whole popularity thing, and also I was always lusting after these boys who had no interest in me. I never got a boyfriend because I picked all the wrong guys, these horrible torture boys who would torture me forever, and never be interested in me.

She would buy the most outlandish, obnoxious, disgusting clothing to get attention. "I was trying to prove that I wasn't like them, that I didn't have to live by their standards. Yet I was such a good girl. I got such good grades. Maybe clothes were my only outlet." She was Class Clown senior year.

A lot of it had to do with my obnoxious mouth, but probably a lot had to do with my clothes. I had what my brother called "peed-on leopardskin pants." They're skin-tight, okay? They were white denim, with black leopard print all over, and they were splattered with neon yellow. And then I bought this awful acrylic bright neon yellow V-neck sweater. This was early eighties. Neon was very hip then, but not in my high school. And these black ankle boots with straps and buckles all over them—very early eighties. Duran Duran. I would wear that outfit, and I felt so cool, so different. Then I would jump up on desks and pontificate or whatever. I don't know what I was doing. It was a totally fabulous outfit.

Lex still has the outfit in a box marked "Clothes Lex Thinks Will Someday Amuse Her Children."

Me and my girlfriends were obnoxious together in a socially sanctioned way. We never drank much. No drugs. Rarely boys. It was always just in-school, fooling-around, loudmouth clowning kind of stuff.

Following the crowd

Wouldn't it be better then if she wore something just a little bit different, her mother ventured.
"You don't understand," the daughter wailed. "If you don't look like everybody else,
nobody will pay any attention to you!"

—Eve Merriam, *Figleaf*[1]

I grew up in the suburbs. Anytime I wore something out of the ordinary, I would "get it." In the eighth grade, a pack of girls came up and started kicking me because I wore the wrong shoes. School culture had rules about every garment, head to toe.[2] My friend who put her foot down about her mother's home permanents talks about her experience encountering class culture. In eighth grade, because she had grown, her aunt gave her some hand-me-downs. "I could actually fit into the clothing of my slender and very attractive aunt. I didn't realize what a figure I had, but she had bought some very nice clothes for work." She specifically remembers a wonderful winter white skirt and pullover raglan-sleeve top: "I wore that the first day of eighth grade and mouths dropped. People wondered, 'Who is this?'"

The people who raised her were poor. Her father, who grew up on a farm, was a real do-it-yourself guy. He worked for the telephone company, and had built a barn and a pigpen out of old discarded telephone poles. He kept chickens and cows and a pig, and they had a garden. Nearly everything they ate came from their one-acre spread.

When I started going to school and making friends with kids around the neighborhood, I discovered the middle class, which we weren't. And I observed how they set their table, how they kept house, and how they dressed and that they went to church and we didn't.

By then they'd moved to a trailer court. She started working when she was about nine. She mowed lawns, did some baby-sitting, and helped an old woman tie strings on aprons that she made. She start making her own money. And with that money she would go to JC Penney's and buy little bits of fabric for her doll clothes.

By the time I declared my sartorial independence, I was twelve. I started trying to craft my own wardrobe, design my own clothes, and create my own patterns. They really didn't fit that well, but I wanted them to be small in the waist and show my figure.

Becoming overweight and having acne sent her into a nosedive. Her mother wouldn't let her pluck her eyebrows, shave under her arms, or shave her legs. She wouldn't let her use eye shadow, mascara, or lipstick. (She sneaked an eyebrow pencil to school.)

When I entered high school, I started taking more and more stands for myself about my appearance. I started making up my eyes, using eyebrow pencil to put shadow on the lids so that they didn't bug out, because boys called me "Bug Eye."

But I used to weep on Saturday morning with my mother and my aunt. I wept about my weight and my acne and the fact that people called me "trailer trash." They had sympathy for me and would comfort me. They said with pride, "You are not trailer trash, and those uppity people don't know."

Yet all of my desires to make myself more attractive they put down. They said: "You're putting on airs. You're riding a high horse." One thing I was permitted was my intelligence. They honored the fact that I did well in school and said, "Someday you'll grow up and get a scholarship and go to college," and I did.

I was an object of contempt to a lot of the kids partly because I was trailer trash, partly because I was smart. I was popular, too. I never could figure out why. Maybe the boys teased me that way because that's the way boys are. I wanted to be like the girls who were pretty and didn't have acne. They had real long eyelashes, and their hair was like the Breck girl's.

I made myself and bought for myself some pretty good-looking clothes. Mostly when I sewed for myself, I used black, and that is the base color for my wardrobe.

She also took from that time an understanding of how to dress her figure and an appreciation of the transformative power of makeup.

Rebel

The difference between the rebel and the clown is the rebel's underlying rage and willingness to battle. Once, in high school, I walked home from school. When I was about a half-mile from home, a police car pulled to a stop on the path in front of me. The officer got out and asked me what I was doing in the neighborhood. My Indian print skirt and other wild garb convinced him I didn't belong. Berkeley shook me even more when I moved out a few years later for college. There was nothing I could wear that would shock anyone. Everyone had seen it all and continued to see it on a daily basis. The inability to get a rise out of people, which had been a staple of my self-expression— annoyance as a form of attention-getting—led me to question what I really wanted to express and how I wanted to look.

Daphne Stannard expressed her rebelliousness through dress:

In college I was really out to shock people, and I was angry. I didn't fit in, but I didn't want to fit in. It only made me angrier that people didn't accept me. Once I was walking through the cafeteria and I passed the SAE sorority table. (They repulsed me, but I was also feeling sad that I didn't have a group to hang out with.) And someone threw a bunch of Tater Tots at me. It only made me angrier and more determined to stand out. Some people would cave in and say, "Fine. I'll go buy some Add-a-Beads." But frankly, it incensed me that they would do that to me. I went home and put outfits together that were visually obnoxious, bright red, orange, and green. I was out to shock. I'm not doing that anymore. Now I'm just at peace with myself. I'm at peace with my wardrobe.

I speak with her partner, Beau, who currently presents a much more conservative appearance. Beau says:

> My spouse and I met in college. She was a frequenter of thrift shops and wore these absolutely heinous-looking patterns, bag lady dresses, outrageous-looking things. I was one of the foremost representatives of the hippie generation. My hair was very long. We were not diametrically opposed, but we were representative of different stereotypes. Our points of view on fashion are probably somewhat closer today than they were then. She basically wears natural-fiber clothing now. I'm a great natural-fiber person. We both have interested eyes and influenced one another in certain ways. We both, from time to time, say to each other, "Gosh, I really like that," and buy an article of clothing for the other person.

From childhood onward, most of us can remember specific incidences of clothing-related mortification, the general role we played, and how that role was emphasized through clothing. What was your role?

During the first twenty years or more of life, school, family, friends, and the agonies of almost constant physical change have a major influence on what is worn. For many people, internalized voices representing these influences begin debating every time they need, say, a new pair of underwear. It becomes up to you to unravel the mixed messages.

Grandma and other family influences

To what extent is this interest in clothing "in the family"? You had to scratch, claw, and hunt for everything at my great-grandfather S. Klein's store. I was raised on Solomonesque shopping parables—stories of women who both fell upon the same dress and, screaming, pulled on their bit of the dress, hoping they could claim it, until they pulled it apart. Despite the wealth that accrued as a result of this store, the legacy of getting a deal, of not being cheated, meant that we religiously shopped discount. We often confused getting a deal with getting what we truly wanted. The battle between the two modes continues within me.

Do you throw out or do you save? Grandma, to the best of my knowledge, has never thrown out a dress. While I was visiting with her last year, she handed me a small wrinkled brown bag before dinner and said, "Look at it after dinner. You don't want to get food on it." For a couple of hours I sat in a restaurant with the paper bag under my chair, wondering what was in it.

Later that night, I opened the bag and discovered her sister's slip. This beautiful apricot silk confection had been in her sister's trousseau when she was married in the thirties. It's cut on the bias, with handmade lace. And of course, because it's Aunt Bea's, there's a cigarette hole in it, but that's OK; it's an exquisite thing.

When designer Camille Depedrini talks about her family and their clothing past, I sense her love for them and the richness these memories hold for her. Camille comments:

There was a place called Urado's Bridal Shop down the street from my grandmother's. My mother and her sister always got all their special-occasion dresses made at Urado's. My grandmother, too. My mother would tell me stories about how they'd hand-sew stuffed flowers on a dress. I am fascinated with the romance of that time and the family history.

There can be a dark side to a grandmother's influence, when her excessive preoccupation with self-decoration develops, leaving no room for other aspects of character. Another interviewee commented about a beloved grandmother's love of clothes:

She recently said to me, "Oh yes, I was wearing my Norell when Kennedy was shot." She is an incredibly intelligent woman who has used her mind to keep track of every detail about everything she has worn to any event. She's the only woman I know who can tell you what she was wearing on every day that had historical importance during her life.

Another friend commented about a beloved, if fashion-mad, grandma, "She chooses her moods by her dress labels."

If there are styles, fabrics, preferences, pieces of jewelry, memories, or even sentimental garments you bring with you as part of your heritage, what are they? What do they mean to you? How do they fit in with how you see yourself? Stacey Lamiero comments:

My dad's mother was very theatrical. She was quite a wild one. She wore platform shoes, scarves, and turbans until she died. I think she was buried in them. In the fifties, she rode a Harley. Harley is the Cadillac of motorcycles, you know. She was flamboyant in her own way, and perhaps I pick up a bit of my aplomb from that side of the family.

Stacey can see sources of it in her family, but to a great extent she is self-made. This led me to understand a principle of dressing:

IF YOU DON'T HAVE IT IN YOUR FAMILY, MAKE IT UP!

What kind of ancestors would you have preferred? Talk to them (in private, or the men in white coats will take you away). Dress for them. Amuse yourself.

Mother

What do our mothers have to do with how we choose clothes, how we see ourselves, how we dress?[3] Whether one imitates or rebels against a mother's sometimes contradictory and complex sartorial instructions, our adolescent hopes for loving and gentle mothering can be ravaged in the battlefield of the dressing room. A sly comment about an admired new garment can ruin it for us forever. Sometimes with clothing, traditionally a woman's "realm," we see our mother's and our own true colors reflected with a peculiar and unsettling brilliance. One woman recalls standing in a dressing room with her mother while both tried on the same outfit.

"Look, Ma," the young woman said. "We're identical!"

"No," her mother replied.

"No?"

"I look better," her mom said. The young woman later took her revenge when she and her mother went to an Armani boutique. The mother tried on some jackets which didn't fit and then the daughter tried on a navy dress that looked terrific on her.

Genuine love for us is expressed along with the oblique messages mothers think they must tell us. The result is not nearly as damaging when conveyed with obvious if misguided love, as when the message is conveyed with viciousness by a mother too damaged to love. These formative discussions often take place during adolescence, when we are hormonally tormented, hence vulnerable, and not at our best. I comment to style consultant Kathryn Hoover, "Some people will only shop alone because their experiences with their mothers so demented them." She responds, "It can be a vicious thing that happens between mother and daughter."

I spoke with a friend at lunch overlooking a blooming rose garden. An attractive woman in her late twenties, she is wearing a dark blue silk outfit with matching hose and black ankle-high cowboy boots. She says, "I don't want to look like a Barbie doll." She has blond hair, blue eyes, and a little turned-up nose. I tell her I see some innate Barbie possibilities here.

My mother would love you for that. Thank you very much. Recently, my mother called me on the telephone a few times, wanting to talk to me about something. I thought it was regarding Father's Day. When I finally got her on the phone, she got very quiet and apologetic and then said, "I think we need to talk about something that I've dropped hints to you about before and given you money just to take care of by yourself. I tell you to spend the money on whatever you want to spend it on. And you never seem to spend it on what I think you should be spending it on, which is getting your face waxed." I nearly dropped the phone. I'm doing acupuncture. I'm letting my hair grow out. I'm losing weight. I'm getting in shape. I'm doing all kinds of things, but that doesn't matter because I have facial hair. So I'm walking around feeling like Santa Claus today.

What are our mothers thinking? I guess it could be construed as pure viciousness, but there is a different subtext—Sandy's mom just wants what's best for her daughter.

Often parental good sense doesn't make sense until much later. In cold weather, Mom frequently told me to wear a scarf, a garment I was unable to comprehend until adulthood. As a child, I thought a scarf was an itchy suffocation and strangulation device; now I enjoy scarves for their color, warmth, and comfort.

Stacey Lamiero mentions the power struggles with her mother over appearance that occurred as she grew into adulthood:

My mom used to get on my case, saying, "You're not wearing enough makeup." Because I didn't. As I've gotten older, I've pulled myself together more. I care about it more. When I was younger, I didn't care, and my mom and I used to do battle royale. I'd show up to go to lunch in white jeans and a blue T-shirt, and she'd say, "Is that what you're wearing?" She'd pull out her beautiful, expensive cashmere jacket, and I'd think, "This is it. I've got a blazer in the car." But we get along better now. We always got along, but that truly was a point of friction. I pulled it together for myself later, not for her. I did it for me.

Memories related to mothers and clothes differ widely. Some of us remember the dazzling mother preparing to go out for the evening. One recalled the changed aura of Mom as she was preparing for a ball, her hair perfect, the makeup mirror, the magical boxes and strange drawers opened, pearls unhidden, her perfume trailing her through the house, the intense closeness of the floral scent as Mother kissed the children goodnight and rubbed the lipstick off the child's cheek with her thumb, her fancy jewelry and pretty dress, the strange lights on at night. Jeremy Stone remarks:

After she and Dad divorced, Mom would go on dates to the symphony wearing this dress we called "the Blue Danube"—a deep cobalt blue, satin, strapless number with a full skirt. When I was a little girl, I thought my mother was just like a movie star. I thought she was the most beautiful person in the world. She had a little makeup table that had a gold mirror with light bulbs all around it, just like Hollywood. I used to love to sit and look in that mirror and turn on the lights and put on lipstick. At the same time, I felt that my mother, who was a really beautiful woman, never really enjoyed her looks. It seemed she always wanted to look more serious or more intelligent, and she didn't think, "I'm a beautiful woman, and isn't it great? Isn't it fun?"

Designer Camille DePedrini talks about the influence her mother and family had on her sense of style:

My mother was very modern. In the sixties, she worked for Bloomingdale's, in the couture department. She wore all kinds of wild couture things. My mother wore white leather outfits, Courrèges-type stuff with little gold hooks on the coats, but really tasteful. When I was really, really young, she would take me shopping, and I had real expensive clothes.

And I had an aunt who didn't have any children who used to buy me incredible dresses at this place called Shirlby's that specialized in dresses for girls. My aunt and my mother would say, "Shirlby's dresses are so wonderful because they're really good quality and the hems are really big." I'd wear the same dress for years and they'd just let the hem down.

I learned a lot about quality and things being made nicely. When I was nine my mom let me buy my first pair of shoes by myself. They were shocking pink and turquoise suede. My mom thought they were funny, but she said, "Well, you have to wear them, so that's your taste."

She always dressed kind of shockingly, but tastefully. I was taught to mix quality and taste but also have independence . . . and it was okay to be kooky. Kooky is tasteful, too.

Camille was the first of many to say: "My mother would say to me, 'It's always better to have a few nice pieces of clothing than a bunch of things.'" She continues:

I have some very good suits made by contemporary designers. I believe you should have a really good coat and a nice suit or two and really good shoes and a good purse. But it's fine to have quite a few of these funny little dresses, too. My closet is all mixed—my real life and my fantasy life. I think of myself as a theatrical person who doesn't actually perform. The performance is wherever it happens, the spontaneous performance of the day. I take advantage of whatever events I get to go to to dress up.

Laurel Fenenga finds her taste today to be similar to her mom's. She wears classic plain clothes, slightly oversized. She comments this was not always the case. As a child, her taste was different: "My mother was even more practical than I am. I wanted to wear froufy little princess dresses." She gestures as if she's rearranging her imaginary fluffy skirt so it stands out; hopefully, there's lots of crinoline underneath.

But my mother dressed me in jeans. I was wearing my brother's hand-me-downs. I have three sisters, but my brother and I were close in age. The only sweet thing about my wardrobe, when I was very small, was that I wore wonderful little Swiss embroidered suspenders because otherwise my pants would fall down. But I liked really froufrou things.

 I guess once I reached adulthood, I turned into my mother. I like clothes to be really practical, but I like them to be quirky. I'll wear big bows in my hair, and I will, more often than not, wear clothes that look like they belong on a child. Right now, I'm wearing shorts, but they're too long and they're also too big.

Sometimes as you sort out who's who, you find a bunch of clothes in your closet in your mother's taste. I did, and I boxed them up and sent them to her. My shopping mistakes are usually clothes that suit my mother. After I sent Mom the Anne Klein gray pants and Ellen Tracy blue jacket, she called me to tell me these clothes impressed her dry cleaner: "He said he was thrilled that I was finally getting quality clothes." Influence goes both ways: perhaps by remembering with sympathy that we influenced our mothers (from the very beginning: we changed their silhouette from regular to huge), we can begin to understand and come to peace with their part in our clothing identity.

 Sometimes our mothers only know how to care for us in the language of beauty. It is their way of expressing love, their adult version of "Wear your muffler." And if these are their limits, we must accept them. After surgery, Margo Kaufman wrote about seeing her mother:

When I was finally ambulatory, she schlepped me out of hospital garb into a dainty gown. Instantly, I felt better. Then she pulled out a bottle of Chanel polish. "Lie down," she ordered. "Let me do your toes."[4]

Maybe we can't change our mothers. (If you've had any luck changing yours, write a book. It's a guaranteed best-seller.) We can, however, change ourselves, and not pass the nonsense on. It's the Great Work, deciding whatever evil was done to us stops with us.

 Libby Granett has faced this issue head-on with her daughter, Annie. I mention my mother's rationalizing not buying a gorgeous shirt: "One go-round with chocolate ice cream, and it's all over for the suit." Libby responds:

I think I've made Annie crazy with that kind of stuff. At three years old, she was holding things up and saying, "Will this stain?"

When I heard her say that I thought, "Oh, God, I've got to stop this." Now she knows that spilling things makes me crazy, which is nonsense. She's a kid. And then I say, "But she needs to learn how to take care of the things that she owns. So where's the line?"

Part of Libby's pleasure in shopping comes from the memories of shopping with her mother. Even though shopping was fraught with tension, they did it as a team. They also used to walk to the library together in the early evenings in the springtime. Her mother enjoyed shopping and loved clothes, colors, and textures. She was very into thrift stores. Libby both loved and hated it. "I loved the fact that we got to rummage around and explore, and she would come up with the most amazing kinds of things, but if necessary I would make up stories, saying that they came from cousins, but certainly not that we bought them from thrift stores."

As she got older, and thrift stores became an "in" thing to do, she realized once again how far ahead of the game her mother always was. "I probably made her suffer to some extent for something that ultimately I came to really enjoy, and she died too soon for me to let her know that." Her mother died when Libby was twenty-one.

I've had some very good cathartic dreams about it where she forgives me. The most wonderful dream is that she's wearing these gorgeous capes and robes which she got at a thrift store and I'm terribly apologetic and I really feel awkward, but I ask if I can borrow them. She says, "See, it's okay."

I say, "Yeah, yeah. I'm so sorry."

She says, "Hey, it's okay. You just had to grow into it." And so we make up for it in this dream. I wasn't an adult for very long while she was still alive so we never got to talk about any of these things. I never really saw her as a woman separate from being my mother. From what I remember, from what I see in pictures, we had a similar body type. She was shorter than I am and couldn't wear anything but flats. In the fifties, that was pretty unfashionable. She was always ahead of her time in terms of style and clothing.

Libby talks about the intergenerational echoes of her mother and her daughter:

I remember as a small child wearing knee socks, and one of the elastics on one of the socks was stretched out so it kept falling down. It drove me crazy, and it drove my mother crazy that I kept pulling it up. She said, "What do you think? Everybody's going to be staring at your socks?" But in a lot of ways, she taught me that people were going to be looking at me so I should be conscious of those things. It felt very contradictory, and made me feel a little nuts.

Recently Annie graduated from third grade. She would have felt perfectly fine not having a new dress. In any case, we went shopping for a dress. We got this wonderful dress that comes sort of to mid-calf on her. I thought that she should either wear no socks at all, or tights, or long knee socks, because if she wore regular socks there would be about a two-inch gap between her dress and her socks, and that would look funny. It was getting late, and we were both getting hot and tired. I wanted to make one more stop to see if we could find the socks. She had had enough. She said, "Mommy, do you think everybody's going to be looking at my socks? They're more interested in other people." I thought, "Who is she to say this to me? I'm the mom." But she was absolutely right. If she can start out like this . . .

She used to wear the most bizarre patterns of clothes together, and it would make me crazy. My husband would say, "She's thrilled with these combinations she's put together. Who cares whether they go together or not?" Even as she got older and started talking, she would say, "What do you mean they don't go together? Who says they don't go together?"

"Well, they just don't," I'd say.

"Well, I think they do." That was perfectly fine with her. And I dropped it. It was the voice of my mother and the voice of Them, They, which made absolutely no sense to a three-year-old or a five-year-old, and if I'm lucky they won't make sense to a twelve- or fifteen-year-old. It's been a huge growing experience for me to let go of those rules.

Dads

Fathers' clothes influence was not characterized by their engagement with us, but rather by the example they set. Sons tend to talk more about their father's influence than their mother's.

A beautifully dressed father can lead one to be educated in the ways of style and also to understand that what works for Dad doesn't always work for the son. Still, it doesn't have that tense, insistent air that the mother/daughter clothing bond can have. One friend comments, "My father has supported the Ralph Lauren store in Dallas almost singlehandedly for many years." My friend is confident in his own more casual eclectic style.

A father's terrible clothes sense can influence one as much as good sense. When I asked attorney David Simons if there was anything about his sense of style he can trace to family influence, he looked at me and said, "Yeah. More their lack of style." I suggested he take the cloak of anonymity, and he responded:

No. He knows who he is. He's my father. My dad prides himself on it so I know it won't offend him. He's actually gotten better over the years, primarily because I started to buy him clothes. I think back at some of the horrid things he's worn. . . . The favorites are the overalls. He used to wear these big blue overalls and he would do everything in them, cut wood in the yard, pick up dog doo. They were worn and thrashed. Then he would go watch my baseball game in them or go to dinner with friends. My stepmom would be mortified.

David saw something that he didn't want to provide the universe with another copy of. He always looks great. The day after his baby was born, he dropped by the office in a beautiful Polo T-shirt, crisp khakis, and moccasins. "You're exactly the opposite," I comment. He responds:

I have lame clothes, too. I have T-shirts and shorts. My wife likes me to look nice. So I do. That's part of it, too. So there is a family influence in my style: I just don't want to dress like that. Sorry, Dad. But he already knows it.

Where does David get his sense of style?

In college I really didn't have any money, so I wore 501s and T-shirts and shorts. It wasn't until I met my girlfriend—and now, wife—that I started dressing nicer. She started buying me clothes because she had money and I didn't. That's really when my sense of taste developed. I think it's always been there, but I just didn't have the money to see it out.

There can be tension over clothing between father and son, but it never seems to be an earthquake as it can be between father and daughter (over clothes that are too sexy) or mother and daughter (over who controls the daughter's looks). We are discussing what's wonderful about men's wardrobes, and Nick Debs comments:

My father had a silk bathrobe that somebody had given him. I stole it from my father. He was really pissed and he stole it back. But it was really nice. I used to wear it. It was my bathrobe for a long time. He doesn't wear it.

Nick's unhappiness seems justified to me. Considering his father doesn't wear the robe, I think he should give it back to Nick.

Fathers, when they are not uptight about realizing their daughters are growing up and hitting puberty with a thud (and coming to grips with their adult and sexual selves), are often quite dear and clueless. Melissa Batchelder says:

My father is color-blind. He always wanted to be in the Air Force. But if you're color-blind it's kind of hard to see planes in the sky. We always thought, Dad saved the country because he didn't get up in the air.

In his work, he had occasion to go back and forth from here to Europe. He would arrive in the European airports with all this foreign currency and knew he was supposed to get rid of it, but he didn't have any clue about how to do that. So he would go into the duty-free shops. He usually had been given strict instructions by my mother ahead of time to get perfume and scarves. He'd just say, "These colors . . ." and he'd hand over this money and the clerk in the duty-free shop would help pick out various scarves. Then he would come home with maybe six of them. My mother would open the suitcases and everybody would pick. My older sister's not interested in scarves. So generally my mother and I divvied up the proceeds. But it always struck me as funny because the attractiveness of it probably is completely lost on him.

Some dads are fashion victims in another sense. When I asked one dad about his wardrobe, he said resignedly, "I often would go looking for my favorite clothes in the closet and not find them. My daughter, who has similar coloring to me, would have taken it. I gave up on my relationship with my wardrobe when I saw my favorite shirt walking down the street on the back of my daughter's best friend. She'd traded it for one she liked better."

Some questions to consider:

1. Would I deprive my mother of anything if I changed the way I look to something more flattering, more effectively expressing myself? How am I protecting my mother by how I present myself today? To what extent does the way I dress validate my mother's idea of me? We have many reasons for dressing the way we do, or staying in a certain clothing mode long after we are (if we ever were) comfortable or happy with it.

2. When you were a child, were you embarrassed about clothes your mother wore? What would the other kids think of your mom when she wore those clothes? How did you respond? Whom did you want your mom to look like? Why? Are any of the things that used to embarrass you similar to what's in your wardrobe now? If so, why?

3. Is there a tug-of-war between you and your mom regarding who has the looks? Has she already won? How old is she? How old are you? How much longer do you want to play this out?

4. If your mother is or was a beauty (or was obsessed with her looks), how did this affect you? Was there anyone home beneath the surface?

5. What role did you play in your childhood home? Who was the star? Was your mother in the background in relation to your father or to her family? Were you in the background in relation to your mother? Today do you prefer to "stand out" or be in the background? Do you feel you have a choice? Where do you allow yourself to be in the spotlight in your life? Turn your attention to the role you play in the office. Are there parallels to the role you play in your home of origin?[5] What was dressing up like for you in childhood? What was Halloween like? What was your prom like? If you've married, what was your wedding like? Who taught you the most about dressing?

6. In your family, what lies were told about the value of appearances?

7. This dress-as-your-mother exercise comes from Susie Orbach's *Fat Is a Feminist Issue II.*

   [Kathy] thought that if she could try acting as her mother, she might be able to get the physical presence of her out of her system and in that way come to grips with her own physicalness. She suggested coming to the group dressed as her mother and seeing where that took her.

   The other women were so taken by her idea that each decided to dress up as her own mother. . . . Nearly everyone was shocked to realize how much like her mother she felt herself to be. . . . For nearly all the group members, it was a revelation to discover that they looked at themselves with what felt like their mother's eyes.[6]

8. How do your parents save and spend money? What did you learn from their habits? Do any of the messages you received about buying yourself things contradict each other? Write down the contradictions. Look at them.

9. Flügel comments, "Since clothes obviously protect us from cold, it is not surprising that they frequently become symbols of this aspect of the protective function of the mother. . . ."[7] Garments that don't work, clothes which leave us shivering with cold in winter or perspiring effusively in summer, are clothes that have failed us. Perhaps, if clothing failures are present chronically, they provide us paradoxically with the comfort of a familiar sense that the dysfunctional mother has failed us. In what ways do your clothes fail you?

10. How does your mother keep her closet? Susan Zeidman says, "I think of my mother's drawers with that fruity sour smell of sweat and old perfume. The ancient drawers packed in. Things on the bottom from her trousseau, things she hasn't worn since 1950." How does your father keep his clothes? Does he take care of them himself? Does he have anything you long to wear? How do you take care of your clothes?

11. Were your parents everything you wanted them to be? What did your mother say—purposefully or not—that stuck? What can you forgive them for? How can you come to peace with the things that make you crazy and get on with your life? What psychological clothing baggage did you bring with you into adulthood? Anything in your psyche that you need to give away to the Goodwill?

Notes:

1. Merriam, Eve. *Figleaf.* Page 45.

2. For more information, see Birnbaum's *Preppy Handbook.*

3. Except for the rare paternal freak-out when Dad roars, "Go upstairs right now and take that off, young lady"—the moment he realizes his baby girl has grown up—the dads of the women I spoke with remained remarkably aloof from sartorial proceedings.

4. Kaufman, Margo. "Sitting Pretty." Hers Column. *New York Times Magazine.* April 18, 1993. Page 16.

5. Paraphrased from Thompson, Jacqueline, ed. *Image Impact.* Page 11.

6. Orbach, Susie. *Fat Is a Feminist Issue II.* Page 99-100.

7. Flügel, J. C. *The Psychology of Clothes.* Page 82.

You Look Like Death

Death is the life-defining moment. Clothes issues revolving around death include dressing for your own burial, dressing the dead, dressing for funerals, and dealing with the clothes of the dead.

Dressing for dying

In order to be prepared, it's useful to know that at the very end of life, most people pee involuntarily, among other things. Death, like many important life activities (eating and sex among them), is a messy business.

What you are wearing will probably be less important at that point than finishing any life business you need to complete. What you wear to enter eternity is another matter entirely, a problem not solely of interest to our generation. Look to the mummies from the pyramids for early inspiration. You can't take "it" with you, but you can leave a lot of "you" behind.

Dressing for decomposition is the final sartorial act. Being "buried with one's boots on" has different connotations for everyone. Although you can give instructions all you want, in your will, to your friends, to your family, it will usually be someone else's choice whether you get your final dress-up wish fulfilled—unless, of course, you choose to jump off a cliff or are alerted to your pending burial as was Benjamin Guggenheim:

> Because it was Sunday evening on the *Titanic* when not all passengers were dressed for dinner, a number of fastidious persons, who would have had it otherwise, faced eternity in business dress. Unwilling to make an exit on this note of informality, the aged Benjamin Guggenheim summoned his valet and retired to his stateroom, presently to reappear in full evening dress with tails and his best studs. "Now we are dressed like gentlemen," he said, "and ready to go."[1]

Without a warning such as Guggenheim received—that your ocean liner has been irreversibly damaged and there aren't enough life rafts—there's no total control over the time and manner of death. I don't advocate suicide, at least not just to have control of what you're wearing while you die.

At my father's funeral they told me it was customary to bury the dead in a fine white linen shroud. This seemed inadequate to me (I was twelve), considering how thin he was and that winter was coming. When I thought of my father buried in the plain garment dictated by Orthodox Judaism, I felt sad. I pictured my father's body going into the cold ground in some pale white muumuu, his ribs and knee bones pointing sharply through the shift. I probably would have been better off not knowing the custom, picturing him in a warm cashmere sweater, his bomber jacket, a sturdy warm cap, woolen trousers, socks, and loafers.

Since this final outfit is your last chance to make a statement, consider what you'd like to wear (if the place your remains will rest permits it). You might make it easier on your survivors by organizing your favorite outfit and leaving clear instructions about the outfit's location. The mortuary is usually prepared to accommodate last-minute requests regarding dressing the dead, or this can be negotiated beforehand. If you have strong desires, do tell someone you can trust to be bossy enough to carry out your requests. I can't honestly say you'll regret it if you don't, but why miss an opportunity for a grand finale?

My friend Sarah's sister, who died in her forties, was buried, by request, in her Mickey Mouse ears. On the day of the funeral, when the balloon seller asked Sarah why she was buying balloons, Sarah told him it was for a funeral. He offered to get her black balloons. Sarah thought, "That's not the point." Her sister would've wanted the colored ones so she could see them float off into the sunshine.

What would I like to be buried in? What means so much to me that I'd like to take it to eternity? Nothing, really. But I don't want to go naked, and I don't want to wear the same thing everyone else in my tribe has worn for the past few thousand years. It's not my style. I certainly don't want to be made up for my burial. When I worked at the cemetery (you've got to start somewhere with a B.A. in English), the mortician used to come in after a funeral to boast that he'd made someone look far better in death than they ever looked in life. There was a camp element to his fascination with painting the faces of the dead. He'd talk about how amazed the mourners were at what he had created. But then he drove a glowing, bright blue 1960s hearse. I am not a face paint person. I don't want an open coffin. It's not in the tradition anyway.

I think I'd like to be buried in natural-fiber garments, something that will decompose at the same rate I will, but I want them to be in color. Maybe a nice old pair of jeans, a brightly colored T-shirt, and a big handmade wool sweater in another color and heavy socks in a third color. And my pearls. There's some fear . . . or rather a sense that I should dress to meet my maker in a way that makes me feel the most comfortable. Even if my maker is, quite simply, the Earth herself.

I'd like to be wearing nice underwear when I'm buried—nice by my standards, that is. I think of some cotton panties in a bright color, not pink. Maybe no bra, because in an ideal (zero-gravity?) world, I wouldn't need a bra. (The underwear issue arises again.) Why is the underwear I picture myself wearing in death nicer than what I wear now? Wouldn't it be better to enjoy now—while I still have the senses to appreciate them—the things I picture myself satisfied with into darkest eternity?

Isn't it time to go out and get a whole lot of nice new underwear?

Outspoken heretics can have different views of what they want to wear, but because of their views they might not have a choice. Look at Joan of Arc or my former secretary, Greg. When I asked him what he wanted to be buried in he said, "I'm not going to be buried, Andrea; I'm going to be burned at the stake."

Funeral home rip-offs

If this is something you want to take seriously, before you're gulping your last breaths, find out what the mortuary will charge to dress you. This added expense can run over $500. If you're to be cremated, often the mortuary will offer to just lay the clothes next to your body, to save your loved ones the expense of embalming you. Up to you. Figuring this out ahead of time spares the people grieving more surprise expenses.

Funeral homes will do anything to get more money out of you. In death, as in life, the opportunists prey on the vulnerable—see Jessica Mitford's *The American Way of Death*. I first discovered this in my job as cemetery secretary. With the mourners sitting across the desk from me, I'd call the mortuary to find there'd be an additional $75 charge to dress the body of a person whose funeral I'm arranging, and could I hold the line a minute? The director comes on to say the corpse also has to be embalmed (an additional $400) for it to be dressed. No cost to place the clothes with the body, however. I privately consult with the spouse. We decide to just put the clothes with the body and not tell the other mourners. The ashes will all be together. Sort of.

Finding the right clothes for someone to be buried in

My friend Tony, as he is dying, tells us that he wants to wear his snake bolero and the outfit he wore as a guest at Susie's wedding. He reminds us to check the pictures, and somehow, as he says it, it's still difficult to believe we will have to follow his request, that he will die.

I study him as he lies dying, watching the movement of his hand as it stirs the sheet, drinking in each infinite moment of his presence. So much life. This cannot die.

He can be dying. I'll grant that. I see an ebbing, a turning of the energy inward, a lessening of attention to surfaces—but only to brighten the embers that fire his soul.

He can be dying as long as his dying is forever and he does not go, does not vanish, as long as his presence doesn't disappear. "Like pulling your hand out of a bucket of water," Ethel Roberts used to say. "You leave and there are a few ripples and then nothing, as if you'd never been there at all."

Tony is cremated in clothes he looked so handsome in at Susie's wedding, the black shirt and trousers, grey double-breasted jacket, that bolero, black shoes, blue underwear, black socks, black shoes. The day after he died, his partner Alan found a picture of him from the party, so he could pick out the clothes. I sat with Alan as he hunted up his lover's chosen outfit, and it was hard to see the little blue undershorts, to choose which pair of black shoes, the shoes so empty. And it was lovely, finally, to see the whole thing laid out, to think of Tony going out with style.

Retail store manager Ed Perry has given his own passing serious thought:

You know, for a long time, I said I wanted to be cremated, and I didn't want anybody to see me after I was dead. I was really insistent on that. The more I thought about it, I thought, "That's really selfish of me. At that point, that's not even me. That's the body that I once was in."

So, lately, when everyone's asked me, I have said, "You know what? Whatever makes my survivors—my friends and my family that are left and have to bury me—happiest, let them do it." If they want to fly me up a flagpole naked, they can do it, because I'm dead!

I'm more concerned that I wear the appropriate outfit to someone else's funeral. My own funeral, I could care less. That is something that has a real strong symbolism for people.

When my grandmother passed away, my mother, who was real close to her, said, "Oh, you know, I just wish I could find a white dress with red polka dots for your grandmother to be buried in because she always wanted one." And my mom told me a story of how, when she was younger, she had a white dress with red polka dots and my grandmother always said she loved that dress and wished she had one like it.

For two days after her death, I ran around the mall I work in looking for one. Finally, I found the dress we buried my grandmother in. For my mom and me, it was something kind of special. This was something she never had, and of course, we should have got it for her when she was younger, but it was important for my mother. I was glad that I was able to get that together for her.

I say to Ed, "We are a funny species." "I know," he replies.

What to wear to someone else's funeral?

Many people died in my family when I was young. I realized early on that I needed a funeral suit. It's the only suit that I make sure I have in my closet because I'm usually too undone by funerals to be able to think, "What to wear?" So I have this incredibly fabulous black Donna Karan thing that I slither into and I look to-die-for and respectful at the same time. That solved the funeral problem. Funerals and court are two places in life where showing respect through sober dressing still actually matters.

The black clothes we associate with mourning are neither universal nor constant through time. In Egypt, people wore yellow, which represented withered leaves, while in Ethiopia, people wore grey symbolizing ashes. In Ancient Rome, men wore white and women violet.[2] My friend Dorothy wore a pink suit to her father's funeral. Why? "I wanted to capture his spirit." Black just wouldn't do.

The clothes of the dead after the funeral; clothing and the survivors

She wrapped me round like a cloak to keep all the hard and cold world off me.
—Thomas Carlyle, speaking of his dead wife[3]

I remember Dad's side of the huge cedar closet, the left-hand wall rack bristling with soft silk neckties, the long row of shaped suits, his shoes on the ground in ordered pairs, firmly treed. The upper part of his dresser had its locked doors and mysterious objects, a pocket watch, old photos, his bronzed baby slippers.

I remember his dresser drawers smelling so crisply of clean ironed shirts, the soft cashmere sweaters, forbidden fruit after his death, until I began to pillage. Once he was gone, the pain of the void that remained was softened by periodic raids into his shirts and sweaters, where the scent of him lingered. Even his old khaki military shorts folded neatly in a closet in the attic were put to use. I found comfort in being surrounded by his huge clothes. They're all gone now, twenty years later, worn out or donated to charity. My sister and I took the dress shirts and the crew-necked undershirts; my brother took the sweaters.

After my father died, I used to wear his clothes to feel more at home. They seemed a welcoming change, loose, cottony, well made. As my weight went up and down, I began donning his clothes for school, wearing the big shirts and sweaters over blue jeans. I liked the way they looked, even all rumpled up. If I wanted a fresh one, I would tear the blue paper strip which bound one from the cleaners, a trip made years before, loosen the shirt from its cardboard, and slide it on. I liked how Dad's favorite shirt—a deep dark cornflower blue—looked on me. It made me feel a little less alone. So what if it was false comfort? I felt needy and afraid—the bereaved take what they can get. I wore that beautiful blue shirt until the elbows were shredding and you could see through to my skin. And when it died, I mourned it.

The degree of comfort I felt in these clothes, surrounded by what had surrounded my father's body, could not even be touched by the teasing of my peers (at that time the style wasn't fashionable), and by the deans and administrators who periodically took me into their offices and lectured me about making clothes look more flattering, and how it would improve my life in ways I could only begin to imagine. As if I cared. "If you just wore things that fit you better you would be so much more attractive." "Don't you think that pearls and a men's shirt is presenting a sartorial incongruity, Miss Siegel?" "If you wear that to school one more time, I'm afraid I'm going to have to ask you to go home and change." Then they went on to explain to me how I was probably afraid of my femininity. This made me wince. So my first choices of clothing outside the sphere of shopping with my mother were into my father's memory.

Jeremy Stone talks about clothes and her late friend, artist Sylvia Lark:

I think it was Christmas day when Steve, the man that she had been involved with, called me to tell me that she had died. I took the phone and instinctively walked into the closet. I have a little stool in my closet because I'm not tall enough to reach some of my clothes, and I literally squatted in the closet on this stool. For some reason I felt very safe there.

I used to shop with Sylvia. When she passed away, her twin sister asked me to organize the clothes into boxes. I had so many positive associations with Sylvia's clothes. When I opened up the closet and looked at them, every outfit was a story to me. It was a party that we went to together, the day we went shopping and we bought that dress at Loehmann's or the Neiman Marcus Good Bye shop. I took an outfit I had bought with her and given her—not because I thought it looked good on me again, but because of our friendship. (We both tried on that outfit and I bought it thinking, "If it looks half as good on me as it does on Sylvia. . . . " It never quite did.) Opening my closet and seeing that outfit made me smile.

A lot of times when I go to my closet, I feel like there are all these people sort of in there. I look at different outfits, and I feel like, in some ways, people stay with you, different stories and things stay with you, and there are times when I go into my closet and I hear Sylvia saying to me, "No pleats! Ever. Never!" There are times when I feel a little presence in my closet. Because of all the different associations, it's very comforting to me.

Some things to consider

1. Do you have clothes you keep for sentimental reasons? What are the clothes and the reasons?

2. Do you have an emergency outfit to wear to funerals? If so, what is it? Does it need any modifications or repairs? (Better to do it now, between funerals, when you aren't so upset. We aren't so far from inadvertently enacting the ancient custom of rending our clothes in mourning, and it happens on the morning before a funeral when you think you're about to make a small repair.) If you don't have a funeral outfit, why not? Some avoid having one for superstitious reasons—maybe it will keep death away. What about you?

3. If you had your way, what would you wear for your date with eternity? Anything you love that you'll allow yourself to wear in death but not in life? Why? (One woman said this way she could be sure she wouldn't stain it.)[4]

4. Death as a metaphor: One of my teachers once talked about cannibalizing the dead, a gruesome image. She was referring to something similar to sucking at the bones of barbecue so you get all the goodness out of them. When someone dies, allow nothing that was good about them to become buried or lost. Remember all that you loved and admired about them, and live it, make it part of you, make it your own. If they dressed in a way that you love, study your memories and pictures of them, visualize yourself in those clothes, try making some part of that look or their spirit your own and see if it looks good on you. See how it makes you feel.

Notes:

1. Batterberry, Michael and Ariane. *Mirror, Mirror.* New York: Holt, Rinehart & Winston, 1977. Page 14.

2. Rosencranz, Mary Lou. *Clothing Concepts.* New York: Macmillan, 1972. Page 296.

3. Flügel, J.C. *The Psychology of Clothes.* Great Britain: The Hogarth Press, 1950. Page 81.

Speaking with Clothing

Should we be silent and not speak, our raiment
And state of bodies would bewray what life
We have led . . .

—William Shakespeare, *Coriolanus*[1]

The famous message of dress, the well-known language of clothes,
is often not doing any communicating at all;
a good deal of it is a form of private muttering.

—Anne Hollander, *Sex and Suits*[2]

The problem of language

If you aren't happy with what your clothes say, odds are you haven't woken up from the fashion-industry-created language nightmare. Fashion essayist Kennedy Fraser points out that for the industry, concepts like "understanding" and "usefulness" are only used to sell a product (not to educate the consumer). "Its tendency is to view perception and reflection as commodities, ideas as merchandise, and words as promotional tools."[3] Fashion's nonverbal messages don't get to the complex heart of the matter. From fashion, we learn neither how to speak about clothing nor how to speak with the clothing we wear. It shows us one type of body (the amenorrheic tall model) wearing one type of clothing (the dramatic and extreme). And somehow, from that example, the rest of us are supposed to figure out what to wear.

Alison Lurie points out, "Fashion is free speech, and one of the privileges, if not always one of the pleasures, of a free world."[4] The burden of interpreting this speech is the individual's responsibility and comes with the territory. People bristle at the idea that their clothing is communicating to others without their permission. Some become outraged, confusing dressing to send a message to people with a perceived compromise: dressing for people. Others display willful ignorance of our unasked-for responsibility in this ridiculous overly visually oriented culture. You can deny you're speaking this language, or not want to look at what you're saying, but communication happens anyway.

Emily Cho comments:

Trying to avoid the whole issue, people often think they can stay out of trouble by dressing in a nice neutral sort of way. Unfortunately, it is not possible to dress in a neutral way; whatever you wear makes a statement of some kind. Every time you dress, you're making choices and even an "I-don't-care" message is a clear statement.[5]

How are you supposed to master this language? Let's look at some more general ins and outs before we investigate the common language of clothes. (See the "Appropriateness" chapter for the latter.) The most interesting aspect of the problem with clothing's "utterances" is that miscommunication occurs in many forms. Not all language is as direct as the footwear of the ancient Greek courtesans whose sandals had soles studded with nails arranged to leave a footprint spelling out "Follow me."[6]

According to Lurie, "You can lie in the language of dress . . . [also there is] ambiguity, error, self-deception, misinterpretation, irony and framing."[7] Because clothing "speaks" metaphorically, it is subject to variations in individual interpretation, and flexible realistic expectations need to be in place regarding the results of using this tool. Another problem with the use of the language of clothing is the philosophical underpinnings upon which a belief in communication may be based.

What might language do?

Part of how others approach and deal with you is based upon their perception of how you have drawn this boundary called clothing. From seeing you, they think they know things about you. They may evaluate your "look" and make assumptions about your feelings about yourself and who you want to be, and about how you fit in. In dressing, humans behave like the animals we are. We seek to avoid being henpecked.

When discussing the ramifications of this issue, consultants sometimes go overboard, claiming that clothing communicates everything about you and, mastering the language of clothing can result in miracles. They are both right and wrong. Dressing appropriately helps, but you communicate your ability by doing a great job. We live in the era of the glass ceiling, not the glass slipper. The wardrobe symbolizing ability is not enough. Clothing can have a negative influence or a positive influence, but it doesn't provide the magic key to your heart's desire, unless your desire is the garment.

Wardrobe analysts, personal style counselors, and the fashion press intimidate us with the idea of the powerful messages we might inadvertently be sending with our clothes. The repetition of this theme becomes unnerving in the face of the fact that many of their offered communication solutions are untenable and dated. (The "individuality" and "statement" clothing, advertised by the industry, has a mass-produced extreme look. Not only does it lack uniqueness—thousands of pieces are made in each size—it also often looks remarkably unflattering. The clothes are meant to attract negative attention rather than enhancing the attractiveness of the wearer.) No one dares say that clothes always speak a regional dialect relative to the mores of the area. This requires close individual study for fluency. The dialect is subtle, nuanced, and ever-changing, hence difficult to teach. Clothing scholar Fred Davis comments, "The very same apparel ensemble that 'said' one thing last year will 'say' something quite different today and yet another thing next year."[8] When you hear someone say, in response to a third party's outfit, "Who does she think she is?" you might well consider the question nonrhetorical.

Many consultants discuss dressing as if it were a thing for others' security and pleasure, not your own personal and private delight. But in "real life," appearance significantly matters to others in only a few respects: if you are making a first impression (this becomes more important in big cities where nearly everyone is a stranger), if you are a public figure or a celebrity whose livelihood depends on appearance, if your work involves making a frequent positive visual impression on customers or clients, if your peers value highly visual communication, or if you go to court. Beyond that, clothing is really a private matter. If you love it, you play in this arena; if you don't, you do the minimum necessary to get dressed and invest your energy elsewhere. Clothing, to a large degree, can be enjoyed as a private language.

The clothing experts' emphasis on "clothes talk" also reflects a deeper problem: society's overemphasis on visual orientation. I think we look and eat too much and act, listen, touch, taste, smell, and feel too little. We lack balance, almost as if the eyeballs get heavier and heavier, eventually causing the body to topple over. The belief in the communicative powers of body and clothes reflects the desire that life, expressed through the body and adornment, means something. But by insisting on a conformist "look" to communicate meaning, according to Finkelstein, we are unwittingly embracing the pseudo-science of physiognomy.[9]

What's wrong with reading someone's character from their face or presentation? It doesn't account for individual variation. It doesn't include common differences such as the tics related to Tourette's Syndrome. The result of such a fixation on purely visual indices can result in a society whose primary interests are superficial. Presenting evidence of character from the natural endowments of face and body is a classic ploy of fiction and works well there. But we don't live fiction, we live life. The looks we may aspire to mean nothing about the content of our character. In endorsing physiognomy we ally ourselves philosophically alongside the Nazis who murdered millions because of the belief that a person's looks (derived from bloodlines) are all-important.

A bouquet of misinterpretations

Over and over again we see that clothes can be grossly misinterpreted: "One of the world's most famous criminologists once stated that the person who had made the best impression on him had been a woman who had poisoned her children for the insurance money, and the one who had made the worst impression on him had been a famous philanthropist and reformer."[10]

We frequently see this confusion in the outfit that spells "belonging" to a teenager. In these garments the youth feels together, with-it, part of the group. At the same time this garment may spell "jail bait" or "juvenile delinquent" to an outside observer.[11] A cut, a look, a color, a pattern may mean something different to the wearer than it does to the uninformed observer. For example, no one told me that when, as a teenager visiting an Italian city, I wore yellow, the Italians would naturally assume I was a prostitute and behave accordingly. I had a pair of beautiful new corduroy trousers the color of butter. Each time I wore them in Rome, Florence, or Sicily, men would call after me and grab me in a way that made me feel ashamed, while ignoring my other companions. Mayhem ensued. Finally a kind person let me know the cause. I ceased wearing the trousers for the duration of the trip and the unwelcome attentions diminished markedly. I did not know the centuries-old history of that color there, that around the fourteenth century, Venice first drew a connection between prostitutes and Jews, making them both wear yellow in the form of badges or scarves.[12]

Regardless of how complex our analysis of threads' talk, we may also fail for other reasons, perhaps because, as Kidwell observes, "many clothing messages are more like music: they are expressive in an indirect and allusive way."[13] In addition to the misreading, the destruction and deconstruction of the common Western visual language of clothing has been going on since the 1960s. Writer Karen De Witt notes:

> Fashion messages used to come in nice complementary packages. The shoes rhymed with the belt, the blouse with the scarf, the skirt with the jacket. But the tidy couplets have been scattered to every wind, and deciphering the message in the current combination is no easier than deciphering a hidden message in the Beatles song "Revolution No. 9" when it is played backward.[14]

Since the decline (marked by the proletarian-originated, hugely popular miniskirt) of the "couture-based" fashion declaiming from on high the look of the moment, the language began to babble in many tongues. Each group, each profession, each neighborhood has its own regional dialect, its own twists which are unreadable in any other milieu.[15] When my cousin Claudia moved from New York to Wisconsin to attend college, she was immediately struck by the big hair and make-up choices of the "preppies" on the Madison campus. She comments, "I wanted to take them aside and say, 'No. No. No. You're doing it all wrong.' Instead, I just laughed." She observes the feeling was probably mutual.

Discerning the language is further complicated by distrust of clothing itself. Clothing has been used as a metaphor for the language of deceit. Reb Nachman of Bratzlav, a late eighteenth- century Jewish mystic, asked that his followers not write down his teachings, but rather pass them on orally because, he said, "my words have no clothes. When one speaks to one's fellows, there arises a simple light and a returning light."[16] We think our ideas about nakedness are everyone's. The ancient Greeks thought nakedness was a good sign: "[A]mong the ancient Greeks a nakedly exposed body marked the presence of a strong rather than a vulnerable person—and more, someone who was civilized."[17] Nakedness is often perceived as innocence, purity, light. Nakedness is also correlated with lust, sin, and temptation. Life is confusing.

Miscommunication

We have moral ambivalence about deliberate miscommunication (like "dressing for success" at a horrible corporate job). We somehow feel it is wrong to camouflage. For some, this ambivalence is a hangover from the "let it all hang out" era. We can also see signs of Puritanism butting in again. Learning the arts of dress becomes a moral issue, and the ability to create illusion, immoral. We stridently tell ourselves we must speak the truth (which of course means drawing the most attention to the things about ourselves we don't feel at peace with: Look at my ample behind. Isn't my nose prominent?). We forget, as Emily Cho reminds us, that we can choose the qualities to feature, "and it is not a lie to stress the best."[18] You can emphasize your strong points and armor your weak points. You can feel safe and comfortable in the world.

Sometimes the miscommunication occurs because of gaps of understanding. For example, the physical discomfort the clothes cause are considered "worth it" because of the feeling of belonging that is created by wearing them. Finkelstein asserts that the belief that appearance expresses one's identity explains why women put themselves in painful shoes, corsets, surgery: their sense of self is at stake.[19] A woman who dresses that way doesn't realize that others apprehend her discomfort viscerally. They may see she is wearing something fabulous, but on another level they sense the dissonance, the physical discomfort. This is also tricky because often what is hidden by garments, if it is hidden with self-consciousness, draws attention to itself, as in the mystery behind the curtain.

Discordance can occur between what your clothes express and what your voice, body, or spirit is saying. A woman with a powerful muscular body in an extremely fitted ladylike suit might seem uncomfortable. Discordance can also be seen in the difference between the age of the wearer and the style of the clothes. We observe this when we see the child playing in her mother's fancy shoes. Also, as Lurie notes: "When the age gap between costume and wearer is greater, the offender is considered not only silly or pathetic, but a walking social embarrassment—the sartorial equivalent of someone who lies blatantly about his or her age."[20] Where in your life have your clothes been misinterpreted? Where do you see discord and miscommunication in your dress?

Clothing as a deliberate mask: Using clothing as a decoy for the private self

As a first step in looking at how you wish to speak, define to what extent you want your language of clothing to be a private one, and to what extent you want to communicate about yourself.

The experts also encourage us to use clothing to express ourselves: "If what you say with your clothing enhances your personality to the maximum, you have mastered the language of clothing."[21] But part of mastery of the language of clothing is knowing how to be silent, if you want or need to be private.

Strangers have no basis for interpreting you other than your looks, your clothes, the context in which they encounter you, and your manner. It is important to know what you want to communicate, and what you wish to keep private. What do you want to convey about yourself with your clothes? What aspects are nobody's business? What "looks" are safe only in private, among trusted friends or alone? (Perhaps a preference for S&M, a deep ambition to be a nudist, etc.) Is there anything which needs to be kept private in all cases? Designer Miuccia Prada suggests that because of the pressing, serious global problems which inform our lives, the expression of whatever happiness we are fortunate enough to feel may have become almost "forbidden." Consequently, she says, "the way to express this joy or sense of beauty has to be subtle. You have to keep it personal—you have to wear this richness in a manner that is private."[22]

Let us consider the private self—what you want no one to know. If you study and love what you choose to hide, the perceptible emotional charge will diminish or vanish, and the edge of attraction, the cat-and-mouse allure of it, will disappear. But in order to begin it is important to ask:

- What do I really love about myself and my life?
- Do I want to show any part of this to people through what I wear?
- How is this display manifested?

At the most basic level cat lovers might wear cat pins. A lover who is also a grandmother wears a closed locket with pictures of the beloved and the grandchildren. This is more private, more mysterious, and totally socially acceptable. In the Victorian era women would wear bracelets made from a lock of their beloved's hair. A woman who loves her legs might wear fitted leggings with her casual wear. A woman who thinks her small breasts are nobody's business might get a push-up bra to create the illusion of something exuberant, bouncy, in-your-face, and large, or wear bright shoes to direct attention elsewhere. Jeremy Stone comments:

> My theory is: With shoulder pads and control-top pantyhose, nobody needs to know. My thighs are my own personal business. Unless we're in love, you're not seeing my thighs anyway. I feel that it is really important no matter what your weight is to dress yourself in a way that really brings you pleasure. That's fun, but comfortable.

A woman who enjoys the sensuality of silk might do so in the privacy of her undergarments. Greta Garbo is said to have insisted, under the plainest clothes, that her lingerie be made of pure silk:

> "Why?" protested the studio. "No one's going to see it. It's terribly expensive and no one's going to know it's silk." "I shall know," retorted the star, "and I shall walk differently."[23]

Illusion becomes less effective as it becomes more allied with self-consciousness and planned with less awareness. A person generally ashamed of her body might wear huge garments that don't bear any correspondence to her body's shape. This becomes a magnet for people's eyes, because the person is wearing their discomfort writ large; in the same way that a young woman might eat huge amounts of food to "disappear" evidence of the sexual maturity of her body only to find that the resulting largeness attracts far more attention. It is important to know, and perhaps be doing, what you love, so that you can express that if you choose. It's the Great Work, what makes the whole thing spiritual.

Sometimes we wish our clothes to be very quiet. This subtle direct communication has everything to do with the message of uniforms. The purpose of a uniform (non-military for our purposes) is to fit in smoothly. Rough edges disappear beneath the everyman costume. The fundamental message of uniforms is privacy. By wearing the uniform of a group or class, you're expressing alliance to that group while camouflaging your own uniqueness, insuring privacy.

The school uniform conveys the message that the child goes to school and maybe the name of the school, whether they're male or female, and maybe their age, but often not. The uses of school uniforms become more apparent today, as they lead children away from the dangerous crimes involving yearning for someone else's garments. School uniforms have found new use as a safety feature. I think school uniforms are a good idea. Nick adds, "Exactly!" and laughs, "You know, so much for Tori Spelling!"

My friend Andrew objects: "Where I went to school there were no class differences. Having to wear uniforms would have just been one more way for the bossy idiots to boss us around. Make 'em optional. No public funds spent on uniforms." I wonder what we should do about the kids who kill for a pair of sneakers. Andrew observes the problem is not the clothes, but that no one wants to supervise the kids.

Boundaries in the clothing context refer to appropriate and natural limits of the self as they extend emotionally, psychically, and physically through clothes. When regarding boundaries and considering what you want to say with clothing, ask, What makes me feel safe? The boundaries marked by clothing you wear should reflect someone who is not an easy mark. If you want this, choose clothes that say "neutral" and "hands off" to the people around you. (There is, however, no substitute for common sense as a basic modus operandi. Stay out of dangerous places. Be prepared. Protect yourself.)

In the case of military uniforms, the message is obvious. You're a soldier, a weapon for the state, a member of the gang. Military uniforms reflect a willingness to be anonymous fodder, to sacrifice humanity in the interests of politics. The sacrifice of the individual for the (often questionable) benefit of the whole evokes a thrill in many, whether that of erotic pleasure or of horror is never quite clear. All that order, all those shiny things, all those rosy, fit young men. You figure it out.

Speaking

If there is a language, and you are interested in studying it, what aspect will you focus on, attend to? Where do you listen? What will the language's purpose be for you? Once aware of the potential power of our yapping clothes, we are still tongue-tied. We gather that "the right thing" to wear is a slippery and elusive issue; we despair with the awareness that "the right thing" changes. There is no uniform! There are no rules! It's easy to feel defeated by failed experiments, like the child who thought she was going to grammar school in the "in" shoes, only to find out hers were an "off" brand and the wrong color. (She said to me at the end of that day, "It's simple, I'll never show my face at school again. I'm running away to Paris.") She survived and returned to school. As she discovered, this doesn't mean you should give up on self-expression through clothing, but rather recognize with forgiveness and humor the imprecise nature of this communication.

The language of clothing needs to be reclaimed. Recognizing the complex and different ways the same garment can "speak" to the self and to others is an intimate part of this process. In addition, what clothes do, as we wear them, could use close study and accurate articulation, so that we can freshly describe what we seek from our wardrobes. Having words to describe clearly what we desire will give us power to move in the direction of that desire. The ultimate goal is knowledge of the language of the body, or of being. The words that come out of our mouths are only a fraction of what is possible in communication. We have music, scent, touch, the visual, etc. Why not stretch to study further fluency?

If our clothes must speak, and it seems that they do, how do we make them say what we want them to? We've tried lying or denying it exists. We just end up harassed and pissed. It's appalling, and galling. What to do? Ask the question: What do you want your clothes to say about you? For example, Libby Granett answers the question as follows:

> I hope to be saying that I have a sense of myself. On some level, they're saying that I'm comfortable with myself, that I have a style that represents me. One of the things that I've always strived for in my professional life is to be seen as both a competent professional and a reasonable, down-to-earth person with a sense of humor. That combination I look for and value in other people. Maybe to some extent that's what I look for in my clothing, too. I have a lot of things that I consider professionally correct but also a lot of frivolous, whimsical things. I like that combination.

She coaches people in an area where dressing usually does matter. "As an employment counselor, I take clothing pretty seriously in terms of what people say about themselves—in myself and others. I see that what people wear has a lot to say about who they are." If we are going to view dress as a form of communication, it is certainly complex. Our freedom to choose is part of the heady and powerful freedom that has come with the gains won by the civil rights and feminist movements.

It's a paradox that the traditional realms of women are also being rethought, that feminism would send you back to your closet for re-examination, that there's power to be found in your dresses, bras, and underwear, that all of you is learning to speak up. It can be useful in clarifying the issue to ask yourself:

- What do I want my clothes to say?
- If my clothes were given voice, what would they tell me about who I am and who I want to be?

And demand very specific answers to the questions.

Notes:

1. Flügel, J. C. *The Psychology of Clothes*. Page 15.

2. Updike, John. "The Seriousness Gap." *The New Yorker*. November 7, 1994. Page 245.

3. Fraser, Kennedy. *The Fashionable Mind*. Page 150.

4. Lurie, Alison. *The Language of Clothes*. Page 36.

5. Cho, Emily and Linda Grover. *Looking Terrific*. Page 22.

6. Laver, James. *Clothing and Fashion*. Page 33.

7. Lurie. Page 24.

8. Davis. Page 6.

9. Finkelstein, Joanne. *The Fashioned Self*. Page 29.

10. Ryan, Mary Shaw. *Clothing*. Page 31.

11. Lurie. Page 210.

12. Senett, Richard. *Flesh and Stone*. Page 240.

13. Kidwell, Claudia Brush and Valerie Steele, Eds. *Men and Women*. Page 6.

14. De Witt, Karen. "So, What Is That Leather Bustier Saying?" *New York Times*. The Week in Review. January 1, 1995. Page 2.

15. Lurie. Page 4.

16. Myerhoff, Barbara. *Number Our Days*. Page 272.

17. Senett. Page 33.

18. Cho. *Looking Terrific*. Page 23.

19. Finkelstein. Page 132.

20. Lurie. Page 56.

21. Cho. *Looking Terrific*. Page 25.

22. Sischy, Ingrid. "Some Clothes of One's Own." *The New Yorker*. February 7, 1994. Page 44.

23. Glynn, Prudence. *Skin to Skin*. Page 123.

Part 2
Expressive Fundamentals

Looking Inward to See Outward

If we have not quiet in our minds, outward comfort will do no more for us
than a golden slipper on a gouty foot.

—John Bunyan

Given the forces at work in the fashion world and personal history, you might think it would take a major miracle to understand how to find wardrobe bliss. Well, actually, no.

It's time to think, brood, meditate, and daydream, discovering what you think and getting specific. A robust sense of clothing includes desires, fantasies, and real life.

Does it seem mysterious how to figure out who "you" are and how "you" are expressed in clothes? The trick is getting to know what you know. Clothing consultant Leah Feldon observes:

> During my many years in the fashion business, clients and friends have come to me for advice and help in putting together their wardrobes. The conversations usually begin with comments like, "I have absolutely no fashion sense . . . . I have no idea what looks good on me. I'm not even sure what I like anymore. Help!" When we do meet, it always turns out that they are much better informed than they think they are . . . . They recognize easily enough when someone else is well dressed and can almost always point out the quality specifics. They can look through fashion magazines and quickly distinguish the tasteful from the tacky. But when it comes to themselves they seem to lose all objectivity . . . .[1]

Some want to have the answers without doing the work. It's soooooo UNFAIR that we aren't so dewy fresh and beautiful that everyone swoons when we enter a room. Please. It's work for everyone. There is some value to be gained from laboring for your rewards, from studying yourself like a work of art and figuring out what harmonizes with and enhances your uniqueness. From this work may emerge your grace, beauty, dignity, integrity, and distinction.

Why is there confusion?

We are taught to look outward rather than inward for cues. (The only introspection coaching tip we got was "Be yourself." Big help that is.) We are not even taught to look as far inward as our own surface. Because we constantly stride through two completely different universes, that of the world around us and that of the infinity inside us, it is useful to think of this boundary of clothes between the inner and outer person as an area where the inner and outer person meet, get to know one another, and come to a harmonious agreement. The agreement is important because, as Emily Cho writes, "If your new outer image does not merge with your self-image it remains a shell, something which you don and doff, and it will be apparent to others that it's just a surface thing— an exterior decoration."[2]

Part of the confusion stems from this knotty idea of self-expression. There are so many things you could be, and so many options to consider (because the range of acceptable modes of dressing for women has widened). This may initially make you want to crawl under a rock. Clothing image embraces your comfort, lifestyle, interests, activities, body shape and proportion, the degree of your relation to fashion, your personality, your coloring, your style, fabric, and color preferences, and your grooming. Yow! That's a tall order. You may wonder, Can I get room service from underneath the rock?

Personal style, as I understand it, means "coming to grips with who you really are,"[3] not creating a convincing veneer. Years of psychotherapy may help—but since this book is cheaper, there's no harm in plowing through the rest of it first.

Comfort

Can you be comfortable and fabulous? What causes the tension between the notion of dressing for one's peace of body and "looking terrific"? The factors which add up to individual comfort are unique to each person, and knowing the range and depth of your preferences becomes essential to understanding how clothes work well.

Everyone mentions comfort, which is a strangely elusive construct. Maybe it's just a buzzword. It deserves another look. According to Rybczynski:

> The word "comfortable" did not originally refer to enjoyment or contentment. Its Latin root was *confortare*—to strengthen or console—and this remained its meaning for centuries. We use it this way when we say "He was a comfort to his mother in her old age."[4]

Sometimes clothes give us what we perceive to be support and strength without actually feeling good on our bodies. For example, a friend who cycled from Vancouver to San Francisco disdained padded bike shorts for machismo reasons, but halfway through the trip needed to stuff socks into his gym shorts for padding.

Fashion uses the word "comfortable" to sell clothes despite its blatant absurdity in the context. For example, Carrie Donovan, fashion consultant to the *New York Times,* said of platform shoes: "Once you get the hang of walking in these 'elevators,' they are really very comfortable."[5] This sort of nonsense is always used to pump up the "new" look. The new comfortable corset, or stiletto, or head vise. Comfortable? There's media-comfortable and there's real comfortable. Real comfortable makes your breathing easier, makes your body feel good, allows you to move freely, stay warm, dry, or cool as needed, and do all the tasks you need to do without fear of damaging a garment or being inhibited by it.

Dale Goday and Molly Cochran, the authors of *Dressing Thin*, point out, "Most women don't realize that they don't *have* to be uncomfortable in their clothes. They were brought up to believe that 'you have to suffer to be beautiful.'"[6] It's amazing what women will say is comfortable, despite scarring, blisters, displaced organs, and bleeding. When I inquired about comfortable stilettos, a veteran shoe salesman told me gently that people seem to have broadly different tolerances for discomfort.[7] Goday cautions regarding clothes, "Be sure you can tell the difference between what you really *like* and what you've just gotten used to."[8] We grow to be at home with the things that irritate us, attached to things that make us unhappy. With a society thriving on its "dysfunction," discomfort is recognizable and familiar. In addition, there's a fine line between the comfort that leaves us poised and supported to lead vital lives and that which puts us to sleep.

Sometimes people wear uncomfortable clothes for no clear reason. When I worked downtown in a fancy law office with marble floors and guys with cufflinks, I hated what I had to wear. I blamed the clothes for the fact that I didn't feel comfortable there. I decided that it was because I was lazy and accustomed to casual clothes, and I panicked if I felt required to dress more formally. Closer to the truth was the fact that I didn't want to be there, and how I felt about how I looked reflected that. When I left, I dyed the twelve pairs of hose I had for work purple, blue and green, stuffed the legs with fill, and made three octopi. Swords into plowshares and all that.

How can you release yourself from custom in order to choose happiness? You start by just looking and feeling. In doing so, you begin to dance the awkward line of "Am I uncomfortable because I am out of my routine, or is this genuinely wrong for me?" The two feel distinctly different. Ask yourself the basics: What am I allergic to? What itches? As Leah Feldon notes:

> The trick is to really know the boundaries of your own comfort zone and put those boundaries right up there with your top fashion priorities. Make them nonnegotiable. My personal comfort zone includes being able to get my hands into a pair of pockets, sit yoga style, and move around.[9]

What makes me feel comfortable? Deep pockets in my skirts or trousers. Nothing slimy or slippery in the fabrics (mostly cotton, sometimes a little wool), bright colors, a little sparkle here and there. Shoes that fit and support my feet, shoes I can walk long distances in. Being covered up, pants rather than shorts, long-sleeved shirts rather than short-sleeve. What's on your list? What makes you feel comfortable?

Melissa Batchelder comments on wearing comfortable underwear under work clothes to her high-stress job: "It's the satisfaction of knowing that I really feel comfortable underneath what everybody else sees. There's something very satisfactory in knowing that you are comfortable when everything else going on around you is chaotic."

If you know your limits and respect them, you will avoid a lot of confusion in the clothing arena, and your beauty will be free to emerge. If you don't respect your limits, you'll wear things that are "sort of," that make you grimace or constrict your body so that others will viscerally perceive your discomfort even if it remains below your level of awareness.

What kinds of clothes feel comfortable to you? In private? In public? How do you like clothes to fit and to feel? If you could wear anything at all, what would you wear?

Be cautious. "Comfort" can blind when it comes to clothing. Things worn at home do not have to meet the eyes of critical strangers. These cocooning clothes can be all joy, nesting, color, and love. You can be in a soft fuzzy wonderland at home, but the outside world has stricter criteria. Because clothing has an aesthetic component, something can be both comfortable and make you look like a large, wet, blue rabbit. Something soft, broken in, wearable, worn in to your contours, can look worn out and woefully tired to others on Main Street. And often this becomes hard to see because the mirror doesn't reflect accurately. We screen how we look at ourselves.

Inner prohibitions

How do you get through the inner prohibitions regarding sexuality and frivolity, and the inhibiting internalized voices of family and society? It's useful to remember, as Cho says, that dressing well is "not a natural talent. It's a learnable skill. Just like your job. You can learn the basics . . . practice the principles . . . make a mistake now and then. And one day, sooner than you think, you've got the hang of it."[10]

Part of the inner prohibition has to do with the habit of self-deprecation. You can assign other tasks to the critical voice in your head. She is, after all, so discerning and incisive in her ability to judge, you can give her something useful to do while the rest of you works on something fun.

An impatient part of the self shouts, "I don't care about all this inner stuff; just make me look good!" In the same way that voice says, "I don't care about eating sensibly, I'll do that later; just help me lose ten pounds by Saturday." And then the quickly starved-off weight is just as quickly binged back on. How to deal with her? Tell her that in examining your motivations for dressing the way you do, you must, as Geneen Roth puts it, trust "that you developed these behaviors for good reasons and that before you can take them away, you must first discover their purpose. . . . If you're doing something that does not make sense, look deeper. It makes sense."[11]

It could be that dressing functions in your life as a way to express distress. If this is true, you must explore and reflect upon this before you will be able to let it go, if you want to let it go. Yesterday I saw a woman I wanted to ask about this. She walked into the grocery store in rags, with black lines painted on her cheeks and forehead. A fang-like bone pierced the bottom of her nose. Other bones pierced other parts of her face. Her clothes were brown rags; a bottle of fluid hung from her waist. She looked like a cavewoman camper. She was a walking protest of the strange war paint we wear today called makeup, a reminder of our roots in more tribal customs. Of course, because this occurred in Berkeley, nobody except me paid any attention to her. When I looked at her she asked me whether I thought Rome or Granny Smith apples were better for baking. Startled, I voted for Granny Smith. She thanked me, chose her apples, and walked away.

You may have a stake in dressing awkwardly, in not looking good. Some part of you is being satisfied, otherwise you wouldn't do it. In a similar way that Geneen Roth asks questions about food, I would ask about clothes: What needs does being dressed inharmoniously fulfill? What needs does being dressed poorly meet? What is the payoff from your sartorial mode? What would you lose by changing?

Often invisibility is the payoff. And it may be worth considering if it is worthwhile *not* to change, *not* to be seen and noticed. It may also be worthwhile to consider that *not* being seen is only vitally important for people whose lives depend on it. For example, Salman Rushdie should keep a low profile as long as there remains a price on his head.

Sometimes in our minds we have a scripted role for each type of person. Being well-dressed can be associated with a slew of changes in the way you lead your life. In dressing the way you do, you may be unconsciously seeking unvoiced advantages. What you want may become embodied in the idea of being beautifully dressed, how you want your life to be. The truth is, being well-dressed is just being well-dressed; and if there are things you want in your life, it is important to start moving toward them, in a gradual, sensible way. Some questions to ask:

1. How does the way you currently dress support, protect, and help you? What are the purposes and advantages of the way you currently dress?

2. What is the function of the way you dress? How do people interpret it in ways you like and don't like?

3. What are the societal expectations for the way you should dress? To what extent do you fulfill them? How do you feel about those expectations? Under what circumstances do expectations change?

4. What do you fantasize would occur if you dressed more beautifully and more true to yourself?

5. Complete the following sentence: "Sure, I'll dress up for special events, but there's no reason to look wonderful every day because _____."

6. Do you think people who wear nice clothes have a specific lifestyle? Would this mean having to give up the things you really enjoy? How would you finish this sentence: "Being well-dressed means I can't _____."

7. Finish the sentence: "I am waiting to be well dressed so I can _____."

8. Finish this sentence: "If I really began enjoying my wardrobe, _____."

9. "I wear what I wear because _____."

10. Do you see yourself having some sort of power in wonderful clothes that you don't have now? It might be useful to ask how and why you have withheld this power from yourself and attributed it to clothes, and how you can reappropriate this power so it becomes part of your essential self. This way, when you change your manner of dressing, you do not give up a method with which you have dealt with the world.[12]

Feeling your power doesn't mean you go out and buy ten pairs of new shoes, but rather that you avoid limiting self-image to something so restrictive you must burst out of it, or something so colorless it gives you no joy. Develop and expand your self-image to include the possibility of your comfort, beauty, confidence, and success, all emerging in a way that supports your life. No one says this is easy. Psychiatrist Ellen Berman observes that when women agonize over considering changing clothing style, the indecision often isn't about wearing "quieter clothes. The discomfort comes with a change in style which makes you more visible." (Changes may include more dramatic styles, colors, and accessories.) She adds that for women in particular, clothes are about "taking up space in the world, because you know people look at you, and you know they're making a judgment about you." The question to consider: "How much space do you want to take up?" She notes that women may have difficulty with this question because "most women have been trying not to take up too much space."[13]

What problem do you want to solve?

What are the causes of anguish or problems in your relationship with your wardrobe, the things that can't get clear or straight? Are they emotional? Technical? Both? There are as many issues as there are people. I always think of myself in clothes that I could never afford, that I have no excuse to wear anywhere. Sometimes I even go into the stores and try them on. It feels ridiculous. For me, the technical problem is getting quality at a price I'm willing to pay, and the emotional issue is forgiving myself for my fancy tastes. Choreographer Mary Armentrout, on the other hand, cites a purely technical problem: "If you dance a lot, you're always in leotard and tights. If I'm wearing tights, some of my pants can be too tight. . . . That was a big problem for me, finding clothes that went with leotards and tights." Understand what problems you are willing to solve. What will you absolutely not do under any circumstances, even if it's good for you? It's useful to know your limits. Experts say drinking six to eight glasses of water a day will make the skin glow. Well, fine, but I have no interest in spending as much time on the potty as such a regime requires. So forget it.

Using and abusing magical thinking

Human civilization first developed in warm climates, where clothing was unnecessary if not downright hampering. So why bother with clothes? According to Alison Lurie:

> The original purpose of clothing was magical. . . . A necklace of shark's teeth or a girdle of cowrie shells or feathers serves the same purpose as a prayer or spell. . . . The shark's teeth are believed to endow their wearer with the qualities of a fierce and successful fisherman. The cowrie shells, on the other hand . . . since they resemble the female sexual parts, . . . are thought to increase or preserve fertility.[14]

We might look at our garments today, and consider what we'd want from them if they did have magical powers. We can tailor our wardrobe to reflect our yearning for a better life, and in so doing encourage ourselves, much the same way a child plays superhero by having a piece of cloth wrapped around her shoulders. My electrician showed up the other day to discuss some work she would be doing on the house. She had a terrific chin-length haircut that precisely complemented her fine auburn hair, a lovely black long coat, black trousers, and boots. The accent of an abstract silver pin at her lapel made the outfit elegant. The pin was a copy of the Starship Enterprise insignia. Dave Grossman mentioned a hat:

> I have a top hat. I feel like a magician when I put it on. Sometimes I can reach into the hat and pull something out, not a rabbit, but a feeling or an idea. I actually carry things around in the hat sometimes. You take off the hat. You pull something out. People weren't expecting that, right? Anything people weren't expecting? Well, that's magic.

Discern the subtle difference between these sorts of clothes and the ones we lean upon to do far more than clothing is capable of. The "it will change my life" garment is a familiar refrain. Libby Granett comments:

> It's a constant joke between me and my friend Susannah. We always go shopping saying, "I'm going to find a pair of shoes (or the perfect somethings) that are going to change my life." I found myself saying that to her the other day, and her response was, "Oh, dear." It's come to that point where it's not good to be looking for a pair of shoes that are going to change your life.

However, Libby puts in a good word for garment's actual powers: "I also think that there's something about a certain style or color or fabric that does make you feel different. Those washed silks feel wonderful against your skin, and this more sensual feel to it could change how you're feeling about yourself." A math professor I know wears Hawaiian shirts to class to make his students comfortable, "and also because I like to. Math is stressful enough without the students being intimidated by the professor."

How do you feel about the clothes that would change your life? What is magical about clothing for you? Have you ever bought " the perfect thing"? Did the magic last as long as the garment did? How do you express spirituality, love of life, or beliefs through dressing? Do you believe this is impossible or not worthwhile? Why?

Clothes: Practical needs

At the most practical level, people need clothes in order to be comfortable with the weather and participate in society. Clothes are a home away from home, the shelter your body takes from the elements. They are your snail shell and first must protect you physically in order for you to feel beautiful and convey the assurance of your own beauty to others.

A turtleneck sweater will keep you warmer on a cold day than a V-necked one. Covering your ears with a hat or ear muffs on a windy day helps, too. A visor keeps the sun out of your eyes, and sunburn from your face. A hat keeps rain off your glasses. Wool socks keep your feet warm in boots, in rain and slush. Consider your basic physical needs for clothing and have this form the framework upon which all aesthetic and emotional needs are based. Often people ignore their basic needs in pursuit of a fashionable ideal, then look and feel uncomfortable and can't figure out why the look doesn't work. Today I saw a man dressed both creatively and protectively. While riding his unicycle down the sidewalk, he wore lycra bike clothes, which facilitate easy riding. His suit was hot pink (àla the Pink Panther). He had a hot pink lycra tail, pinned up for safety. He looked happy.

Consider the physical requirements you have for each season. This can be different from the fashion market's seasonal demands. (That you buy something rust-colored in September, for example, or starve yourself for a summer swimsuit. If you don't swim or sunbathe, you can forget the swimsuit.) How warm do you like to be in your clothes? Or how cool? It took me years to realize that when I feel cold, I notice it first as a feeling of hopelessness or despair. I could literally spend a whole weekend depressed and not realize that I could alter my mood by putting on a sweater or turning up the heat. In a hot climate, what a difference a lightweight garment makes on a sticky day! Considering the weather (including indoor climates) where you spend your time. List the different kinds of clothes you need for where you are.

Do you have wonderful things to wear for all climates you regularly experience? What would fill the gaps in your wardrobe?

Some basics about garments: How sturdy do you need your clothes to be just to deal with your limited budget and the way you wear clothes? What materials will be most durable for your needs? How do clothes that endure make you feel?

Inner work: Developing your senses

Know, first, who you are; and then adorn yourself accordingly.

—Epictetus, *Discourses*, 3.1[15]

For an impenetrable shield, stand inside yourself.

—Henry David Thoreau[16]

Without a sense of self, dealing with fashion and clothes becomes a fun-house hell hall of mirrors—everything gets distorted to varying degrees, depending on where the image is projected from: out-of-date childhood dictates, a fashion manufacturer, a spouse, a magazine, a movie star, a clothing store, etc. This visually overwhelming world is tricky enough *with* a sense of self. At least self-knowledge gives a trustworthy reference point. The broader and deeper the self-image, the better choices you make because you know who you are in your entirety.

How to begin to observe? Moshe Feldenkrais, a specialist in integrating body and self, observed, "Our self-image consists of four components involved in every action: movement, sensation, feeling, and thought."[17] This statement could use some unpacking. In order to know ourselves, we need to be aware of our body in motion and the range of possible movements, what suits us in moving, and what does not. With regard to sensation, we might begin to explore what we enjoy feeling and what we do not (touch, smell, sight, sound, gravity, and muscular resistance); we might begin to experiment with sensations we haven't felt before. Feel your body move through space as you walk and rest, touch different fabrics, smell flowers, see art, seek out any pleasure you normally avoid. Enjoyment is perhaps the most important sensation to explore; because our peculiarly Puritan-rooted society places such suspicion on freedom of joy, we often have less of a range there than we do with, say, anger. It is useful to ask, again and again, "What does pleasure mean to me?"[18] and listen for the answer, looking to develop a kind of virtuoso flexibility with sensation.

"Feeling" might be meant here as emotion, the range of emotional possibilities. It is especially useful to explore happiness, contentment, equanimity, balance, calm: How do you feel these things? How do you sustain these feelings? How can you reconnect to these states once the connection has been broken? How fast can you reconnect? "Thought" is also a world unto itself. As you move through space, tracking movement, sensation, and feeling, how do you use your mind? How do you direct your thoughts? When do your thoughts ramble off on their own? What do you enjoy thinking about?

How does all this relate to clothing? The above-mentioned facets comprise an important part of your self-image. If you don't know who you are, how will you know whom to dress? But, as Moshe Feldenkrais points out, this is complicated by the fact that "our self-image is never static."[19] As we strive to fix a self-image so we can hang clothing on it, we don't necessarily do so focusing on maximum flexibility and creativity. Often our self-image restricts us by falsely limiting our sense of what is possible. It "is smaller than our potential capacity."[20] We must observe ourselves, see how we limit ourselves, see where we are stingy—physically, mentally, and emotionally—with ourselves. Why? Freedom. As Feldenkrais put it, "If you know what you do, you can do what you want."

Once you have a "sense of self," it becomes possible to understand what you want, what all of you wants. If, while contemplating a course of action, you both spontaneously smile (a positive response) and ache in the belly (a negative response), you know how to choose what to do. You will know how to find satisfaction, instead of spinning around pursuing satisfaction.

How to start doing this? By gently taking your attention off self-criticism and placing it on self-observance. Over and over again. That's how you form a new habit. Why is it important to consider changing? Our habits of dress were acquired from childhood on, without our conscious consent and without our being educated about all the possibilities that dressing could hold.

Forming a self-image

The media conditions us to look for "A Whole New You!" in each outfit we purchase. Whichever "New You" you create each morning as you dress includes all of the old you. For instance, my background and education lead me to resonate with the old preppy look, even though part of the pleasure in that lies with the fantasy of my assimilation as a Jew into a high Episcopal milieu. Since it's only one facet of my past, I had to integrate this look without being subsumed by it. And since it has been so widely adopted by the mass culture in recent years, how do I wear it without it looking ironic or clone-like? Well, in my favor I have the contrast between my Semitic features and the clear crispness of oxford and khaki. I don't like the candy-colored coordinates of prep. And I love the boho style as well. With complexity of pattern and old style, thrift-shop clothes function as a way to offset and subvert a clear preppy message.

I was thinking about this as I was finishing a meal in a Chinese restaurant this evening. My fortune cookie read: "Simplicity and clarity should be your theme in dress." I had no idea what this meant. I immediately abandoned my musings on what I like, the preppy-sloppy look, and wondered, "Armani? Zoran?" (Not that I can afford that stuff.) The inner debate team entered the fray: "Think of the dry cleaning bills! I'm a machine-wash-and-dry sort of person. So back to the whimsical Woody Allen look, but is this who I want to be? Or is that a persona from another time who expressed herself in another time?"

What are your debates? It's worth getting clear about who and what were your clothing influences. What don't you want to look like? What real or imaginary people resonate with your sense of self? What is possible for you, tired-looking to you, fun for you? How do you unnecessarily limit yourself? If you could be anyone at all, who would you be? There are also various "looks" that are derived from cultural identities—Scottish tweeds, tartans and kilts, Japanese kimono and obi, German leiderhosen, etc. Do any of your cultural identities resonate with you? It is useful to begin to narrow down options from infinity to an abundant sense of wonderful workable choice. The marketplace offers everything. If you go to buy without knowing what you want, you'll get exhausted, endlessly distracted by the wonders of this merchandise-oriented society.

When you take this a step further, you look for thematic expressions in dress that answer the questions "What is your look?" or "What are your looks?" It may be more useful to look at looks as a sliding scale of possible moods, and see if any of them resonate with you. This exercise is as impossible as it is important. Figuring out the words to describe your look, as well as your spirit, is one way to get closer to solving this problem. Ask a dear friend to describe what's beautiful about you. Get it in writing. Tell her you can't stand any mean words, only kind ones. Deal with the embarrassment of asking for your love straight. Or if you can't, another way to think about this is to ask other people to describe their looks. Jeremy Stone says about her look:

I want to look professional, but interesting. Young, but also fairly sophisticated, and pretty jazzy. I like the word "slinky," and I like the expression "lean and mean," of which I'm neither. It's important to me to reflect a positive, upbeat image that inspires confidence.

Retail store manager Ed Perry says of his look:

I would say overall fairly conservative casual. I tend to buy a lot of clothes at Banana Republic because I like their stuff. I like the colors they do most times, and the fabrics. I buy some things at Eddie Bauer. Probably I spend 75% of my clothing budget in Banana Republic.

Ed's is a very classic look, but it's updated and modern. It has a certain *Casablanca* feel to it. When Stacey Lamiero walks in the room, what does she want people to see?

If people are going to look at me and form an opinion, I want them to think, "That person is attractive and looks like they have their shit together." I don't care if somebody says, "Wow." I think somebody who has their shit together is very attractive.

What looks do you want to avoid? What are the fashion identities or styles you've embraced and discarded? Nick Debs comments:

In high school, late adolescence, I went down the primrose path of the Astor Place, St. Mark's Place thrift-shop look—sort of dumb suburban kid discovering punk rock, the downtown scene. I'd get something to wear, but also I'd get it because it complemented, in a totally-unrelated-to-me way, something else in my wardrobe. They would look nice together...not necessarily on me. They'd kind of talk to each other in the closet.

They'd say, "I'm beautiful. Are you?" This was a very unfortunate waste of time, pathetic and ugly. But who knew?

How did he change? "It just sort of happened. You know, getting old, you lose a lot of desires." We both laugh. "Do you know what I mean?" he asks. "Yes," I reply, "and they come back."

Are any of the looks you love at odds with your own facial features or body type? How do you bring the looks into harmony with what's there? For example, I love the fragile ballerina look, complete with pale pink shoes and a pale leotard with a tiny bow at the neck. My features are full, and my complexion sallow. I honor my love of that delicacy by wearing a token of it, a string of pearls or a pretty ring, more in scale with my medium-large features, but honor my looks by wearing more sturdy, relaxed clothes. If I wear pale pink, it's in my socks, so my face doesn't look like a golden zucchini. I incorporate the baby ballerina inside without letting her take over.

In *Color to Color*, Patton and Brett suggest making a list with two columns as follows. Under the headings, fill in what you love and what simply isn't you. This exercise can be applied to specific areas (texture, color, style, shapes) as well as the big picture:

<u>Love It</u>   <u>Not Me</u>

Once you begin to get a sense of your basic body and facial-features "look," factor in your lifestyle and your inner sense of self. This answers part of the question "What is my style?"—or at least you have a bunch of indicative adjectives. Then you can begin to focus your clothing search to provide solid results. If the clothes you seem headed toward feel weird, daydream about wearing them. What about them makes you uncomfortable? What would need to change for them to be comfortable? Then hone your search accordingly.

In *Clothe Your Spirit*, Jennifer Robin offers an exercise for the clothes lover to find appropriate words to describe both inner and outer self, her spirit, and what she seeks through her wardrobe. Her list of descriptive possibilities follows. Circle the ones that apply to you. Add whatever suitable words come up.

ADJECTIVES DESCRIBING PHYSICAL ATTRIBUTES

Overall Body Design: curvy, angular, voluptuous, sumptuous, sensuous, straight, streamlined, lanky, long, sinewy, compact, sturdy, delicate, dainty, petite, soft, ripe, luscious

Shoulders: broad, straight, rounded, delicate, narrow, strong, squared

Legs: long, strong, slender, curvy, straight, powerful

Walk: quick, languorous, bouncy, boyish, athletic, leisurely, brisk, direct, sexy, swinging

Face Shape: soft, rounded, angular, curved, open, broad, heart-shaped, delicate, slender, long

Mouth/Smile: sexy, pert, bright, charming, slow, funny, winning, brilliant, sparkling, dazzling, pouty, determined, mobile, animated, spirited, fresh

Nose: strong, elegant, pert, perky, dramatic, distinctive, classic, aquiline

Eyes: twinkling, sparkling, intense, soft, gentle, kind, deep, sultry, sharp, bright, mysterious, expressive, wishful, eager, open, humorous, animated, clear, soulful, muted, molten

Hands/Feet: long, elegant, graceful, delicate, strong, sturdy

Coloring: dark, strong, delicate, fresh, healthy, intense, gentle, muted, soft, quiet, dramatic, warm, cool, subtle, deep, peachy, rosy, vibrant, striking, glowing, burnished, bright

ADJECTIVES DESCRIBING YOUR SPIRIT

feminine, womanly, gracious, serene, gentle, delicate, classic, romantic, fun, funny, childlike, little-kid, youthful, fresh, friendly, lively, bubbly, pixie, sprite, light, bright, lighthearted, clear, simple, cheerful, open, innocent, wholesome, eager, animated, mischievous, exuberant, charming, daring, wild, adventurous, rich, subtle, natural, relaxed, casual, warm, solid, earthy, true, honest, complex, thoughtful, wise, sincere, gypsy, athletic, movable, moving, energetic, strong, vibrant, free-flowing, free spirit, crackling, snappy, sparkling, artistic, creative, dynamic, buoyant, whimsical, traditional, conservative, straight, precise, rooted, grounded, formal, informal, elegant, refined, dramatic, sophisticated, intense, straightforward, streamlined, glittering, queenly, regal, princess-like, sensuous, ripe, luscious, fluid, spirited, playful, impish, zany, frolicsome, vivacious

FASHION TERMS

sophisticated, straightforward, free-flowing, earthy, classic, traditional, sturdy, rugged, athletic, simple, fresh, charming, clean, streamlined, delicate, romantic, crisp, casual, relaxed, informal, feminine, sexy, sensuous, graceful, dramatic, daring, striking, formal, wild, crazy, fun, tailored, conservative, ethnic, proper, prim, elegant, interesting, rich, soft[21]

Write down the words you circled on a separate page and play with them. Can you come up with a phrase that would "clothe your spirit," a group of words that describe how you want to look?

Robin suggests:

> Think of your terms in combination with each other. No single term used alone is going to feel just right. The individual combination is what describes your uniqueness. "Romantic" takes on a different meaning when combined with "sensuous gypsy" or "classic innocence." "Calm-sporty-traditional" or "calm-serene-gentle" conjure up different images.[22]

Resolving perceived conflicts among various self-images

When your clothes send messages that are inconsistent with your stated intentions—
when you want to be seen as sophisticated and sexy, for instance, but wear puffed-sleeve pink dresses,
or when you wear sloppy clothes to an interview for a job you say you want—
it can be evidence of a deep ambivalence. Interpreting and coming to terms with such a misalignment
may lead you to change your style . . . or your life.
—Pamela Redmond Satran, *Dressing Smart*[23]

Where are the gaps in your expression? What do you wear that makes you itch—emotionally? When I met with personal style consultant Barbara Jay on a hot summer day, I wore a denim shirt, a floral split skirt, pearls, and a white canvas hat. She analyzed my outfit briefly as we discussed clothing issues, talking about dealing with perceived conflicts between the self-image and the body image:

> For instance, if you had a ladylike body with a wild writer's spirit trapped inside, you could be unhappy unless you understood that you had to do your sportswear in a ladylike way. That's why the pearls work. That's why when you're wearing a denim shirt, it has basically a softness to it. It's not a real rough stone-washed hard-finish denim. It wouldn't work with you.

This whole dress issue may make you want to set fire to your wardrobe and start again, but I hope you haven't. Even if you did, without the tools to choose clothes differently and more effectively, you would re-create the same feelings in your closet that are there now. Instead, start to use daydreaming as a planning strategy. Fantasizing about change is a nonthreatening way of beginning to achieve the desired result. Daydreaming will also provide the satisfaction of winnowing down the fear. . . . The more emotionally prepared you are for a change in the way you dress, the better chance that the change will be effective for and supportive of you.

While it's fun to consider new roles you might play that require new clothes, most of your dreaming should be put toward what you need now, what your life is like now, and making that as good as it can be. Planning to buy, and spending money on a life you could have someday, will drain resources from your being present now.

Visualizing also allows you to test out possibilities to their limits without spending a cent. It's worth deciding whether the changes you are considering making are truly worth the costs.

Psychotherapists Muriel Goldfarb and Mara Gleckel observe:

[E]very change requires a trade-off. You will have to ask yourself if you are willing to make the sacrifices that accompany change in order to garner a totally new set of rewards. So be honest with yourself: Do you prefer the rewards that accompany the old [way of dressing]? Is the reason you're not attaining the new [style] because you're unwilling to give up the things—emotional, physical, financial, or other—that go with the old [style]?[24]

How do you do it? Find a comfortable, quiet spot where you will not be disturbed, close your eyes, and try out one of the following exercises. The first was inspired by Susie Orbach:

Visualize being well and poorly dressed in a social situation. How do you sit, move, talk, eat? Are your stances different when you are well dressed and when you are poorly dressed? Who responds to you? How do they respond? How do you feel in this social situation? Is there anything frightening about being well dressed? Does being well dressed bring up any negative feelings?[25]

One of the goals of visualizing is clearly uncovering what you want and think you can't have. A good general visualization to start with is Geneen Roth's exercise from *Why Weight?*: "If you were to decide that you were already fine the way you are, if you were to begin living as if you deserved love, satisfaction, success, and respect, what would you do? How would you live?"[26]

If all this seems too foreign to you, try something simple: Every day while doing mundane tasks, spend a few minutes imagining yourself well dressed while doing them. Watch for anything difficult about being well dressed in your daily routines.[27]

What are your assets?

Joan Songer suggests the following exercise: Get a piece of 8 1/2" X 11" paper. Draw a line down the middle. On the left side list your good points. You have ten minutes. What to do on the right side? She smiles, "We'll come back to that later." How kind are you when you perceive yourself?

From life sty to lifestyle

The very word "lifestyle" may make you shrink away in an agony of buzzword revulsion. But like so many clichés, there's something useful in it. Lifestyle is part of how the self-image expresses itself. Also, your lifestyle is part of what dictates what you want and need your clothes to do.

Lifestyle reflects that we live in many worlds. Often our challenge is how to span the worlds gracefully so we don't have to play superwoman. There are no pre-formatted charts I can show you to tell you what to wear. There are no lists of this many trousers and that many shirts. Just as "diets don't work," there is no wardrobe list which will tell you what to buy. At the most basic level, Moshe Feldenkrais reminds us to ask ourselves how we "speak-walk-fight-dance-rest."[28] From a study of our actions, we might better understand how we need to be clothed to perform them. More specific questions help paint a clearer picture:

1. What do you do? List your activities. All of them. List the places you go. What kinds of clothes are needed for each activity or place? "Underline the ones that need a definite change of clothing from what you would ordinarily wear."[29] Consider how the clothes will be used. How durable, pretty, sensible, flashy, etc. do they need to be? "Then make a list of the recurring events in your life, in their order of importance for your being well dressed."[30]

    Sometimes it's more important for your well-being to be well dressed at a once-a-year family gathering than at work. What are your priorities?

    How does your everyday look differ from your dress-up look? We often think that our casual clothes, the clothes we wear most of our leisure time, don't matter. As one woman said, "If I look like a large spotted fuzzy pillball, what difference does it make? The only people who are going to see me are my cat and my plants. . . . " It's worth considering style consultant Doris Pooser's idea that "every woman needs a casual look. Whether it's her everyday look or weekend look, it should be current and fun."[31]

    What are your jobs? What roles do you play? Work includes being a student, a volunteer, or a homemaker. We have left behind the idea that all the homemaker needs is a muumuu. Style consultant Jane Procter notes, "It's more than possible that you play chauffeur on the school run, office manager, grocery shopper, and company hostess, all without a chance to change. . . . "[32]

    What do you do in your private or non-work time: shop? weld? couch potato? work on projects at home? play or watch sports? go to the movies? What are your clothing needs for your social life? How do these leisure needs differ from your "work" needs? The private-life image of many people differs from their job-life image. They don't want to show up at work looking sloppy, sexy, or young, but that's fine at home. What's merely acceptable for you, and what would be optimal? Don't shy away from dressing well to honor your solitude rather than just slithering through.

    Several people suggested examining datebooks from previous years to remind yourself about the occasions that made you wail, "What do I wear?" What sorts of events do you never have the right clothes for?[33] Take a deep breath and take a look. Visualize the perfect outfit. Do you want to look even more closely at this issue? Some people like to keep a diary of how they dressed over a period of time, a week or a month or longer, recording at the end of each day how they felt during different times of the day, how they felt before dressing, how the clothes felt when they put them on, and at the end. Ilene Beckerman wrote *Love, Loss, & What I Wore* for her grandchildren. It has drawings of garments that had meaning for her and some notes explaining why. You can do the same.

2. Figure out the percentage of your time you spend on each activity. The places you spend the most time should perhaps be the places you spend the most money or effort on your wardrobe. Better to be happy most of the time, no? For example, if you work outside your home and your commute is a significant amount of time, include that on your list.

What are the gaps in your wardrobe, considering how much time you spend on each activity? Are you overloaded with clothes for a very small part of your life? What do you have too much of?

3. Your homework is to study looks. It's called "developing an eye." Rhonda Pretlow talks about where she got her sense of style: "When I got out of the Navy, I hadn't been wearing civilian clothes. So, I just looked at what everybody else was wearing, and I looked at what looked nice to me, and what image the people were putting out." There are also the traditional places to "look" at clothes—the magazines, movies, and media—but there are different ways of focusing your attention, so you see more, so you see newly.

The easiest way to do it is the aforementioned exercise—parking yourself with a nice hot drink in a good seat at a cafe in an interesting busy neighborhood in the biggest city near you—and look. Look out on the street, and watch the people go by. See what you like and don't like. Think about why. Bring a newspaper or a book so you'll have something to do when you don't want to watch for a while. Bring a notebook to jot down your observations.

As you watch, you can study the garments and how they are arranged, the accessories, the colors and textures, and how they are juxtaposed, as well as the more subtle relationships. Cho observes:

> Important clues can be gained not just from the clothing itself but from the context in which it is worn. Is a person in harmony or at odds with his or her "silent partner"? Is he or she too conscious of clothing? Does she preen? Does she sit or stand to show the clothing to advantage, or does she attempt to conceal it? Is that stranger you're watching having a quarrel with ill-fitting, uncomfortable shoes? Did he choose to make himself uncomfortable, and why? . . . Has a person chosen a garment that will allow her to be relaxed about what she is doing?[34]

Think of people you've noticed recently. Use your imagination to re-create what you saw. What caught your eye? A friend reports that she doesn't keep a written diary, she keeps a drawing diary. Each night before she goes to sleep she draws one thing she's seen that day from memory.

Movies can be fun, especially older ones. When I watched *Bell, Book and Candle*, a film about a witch, I loved her—wearing the all-black outfits that fit close to the body, and her going barefoot. Check out art books from the library that contain portraits. They are the best source of Western fashion history. You can stare all you want and people will just think you're terribly cultured.

You also can look at your own history. Emily Cho suggests a method: "Allow yourself, as I did recently, the luxury of spending an afternoon looking back over your life. In old pictures, you can generally see that coalescent quality that runs through your life. . . . "[35]

Are there things about the way you look which you want to emphasize? Are there clothes or styles you loved that you inexplicably abandoned? A little warning: Stay away from having someone take photographs so you can see what you look like. This is another version of buying into someone else's vision. Society trains us to look at photographs as real images. Photos are two-dimensional and we are three-dimensional. Unless the photographer both deeply loves us and is an expert at the use of the camera, the picture either may not portray us lovingly or may show us distorted by the lack of the photographer's art. And we may blame ourselves.

Make a collage. Collect images that please you from old newspapers, magazines, and catalogs. They don't necessarily have to be fashion pictures. Get a big sheet of paper (newsprint will do), some tape or glue, and scissors.

Would the clothes the models are wearing look good on you? You can quickly see if what you love in a picture is the clothes (not the fantasy) by putting your thumb over the model's face. Now what does the garment look like? Do you still like it? Can you see your head on the top of that outfit? Resist the urge to rip off the model's head. (It's not nice.)

Another way to study looks is to write about them. If, pen in hand, you take a few slow deep breaths, you can write down questions you have for yourself (such as "What do I want to wear?") and listen for the answers. It's useful not to edit as you write, but rather just let the words roll out and look them over later. You can ask the part of you that just knows, and she may well answer.[36]

Another entertaining written exercise involves writing a dialogue between you and your wardrobe. For example:

Me: Hello, old closet case, you sad state of affairs.

Clothes: I'm just clothes. You make of me what you will.

M: You don't support me. You don't love me. You don't make me beautiful.

C: My job is to cover, warm, and protect against the elements. I do my job. If you want more from me, then that's your business.

M: Huh? What do you mean? You've betrayed me and somehow I'm supposed to fix it?

C: I do my job. If you want to be a radiant flower, you have to choose clothing and buy clothing or trade for clothing that does that. You have to study beauty in painting, in art, in nature, on people. You have to not get jerked around by fashion or others' instructions. Go to the library, take out some portrait books. Start!

M: No instant solutions?

C: Correct. No instant solutions. Develop an eye.

M: Then what?

C: First things first.

M: But what do I wear?

C: You've been fine for thirty years. Another year of study won't kill you.

M: Oh.

C: *Try it. What have you got to lose?*

4. Things to try once: Play. Wear a big hat. As Joan Songer points out, "How are you going to find out how it feels to wear a hat that's big unless you wear it?" The same is true of any outrageous garment or style you admire or secretly pine for.

5. Let's look at some more anxiety-provoking activities, shall we? For example, meditation. We are taught to think of meditators as monks in robes "om"ing and eating brown rice. There are no rules about what we can use to calm, please, and orient ourselves. You can use meditation to improve your wardrobe. Meditation doesn't have to mean sitting on a cushion on a mountain in Tibet breathing in through your nose (one nostril only!) and out through your mouth. I prefer what I call "puttering meditation," which means being home alone with lovely music on, wandering around the house picking up things and putting them in their proper places. By the end I have a good sense of self—a confidence. To attain a meditative state, I sometimes read trashy magazines or take a hot bath. A few uninterrupted hours with either of those, and I'm relaxed, calm, and ready for anything. Meditation can be tricky because there's a subtle difference between being still and noticing the marvelousness, and being still and numbing the mind, spacing out. Shoot for the former.

6. Other people have found classes in figure drawing to be helpful for obtaining a realistic self-image. There are also classes in gentle movement (where you explore the possibilities of your structure, not where you try to painfully pummel yourself into some weird ideal).

7. Affirmations? Affirmations can be used as a sort of inner cheerleading squad to shout over the inner Iago. For instance, if you find you say to yourself over and over, "I am so fat. I hate my body," you could chant inwardly, "I love my body just as it is," to combat the "hellish villain." There are some problems with affirmations. Like paint over rust, if you don't do some deeper psychological work, the ugliness will come through again. You write the affirmation and then rite your mind's responses. It can be edifying. Just write the phrase and the response that comes to mind ten times, or twenty times, or until you run out of steam. And try it several days in a row. For example:

I dress beautifully.
You usually wear sweat clothes.

I dress beautifully.
There's a hole in your sock.

I dress beautifully.
Beautiful went out with the fifties.

I dress beautifully.
I'm ugly as a moose. This will never work.

I dress beautifully.
What is beautiful?

I dress beautifully.
In denim?

I dress beautifully.
Shut up, you fascist.

I dress beautifully.
I hope. In my dreams.

I dress beautifully.
Beauty is for Grace Kelly, not for me.

I dress beautifully.
OK, I give up.

I dress beautifully.
Enough already.

I dress beautifully.
Mommmmmmy!

I dress beautifully.
What is beautiful to me? Full skirts, fitted bodice. With my bazooms I could never pull it off.

It's not the goal to have a happy ending. Affirmations with responses are a kind of list. As such, they reveal your motivations.[37]

8. One of the places many people get lost in the "look" search is when they neglect to "finish" a look. In women's clothing a "look" is a total look. You may have figured out the perfect jacket, but no one looks at you and just sees a jacket. They take in the whole picture head to toe. The key question is: "Are all the components of my image in harmony with each other?"[38] The idea of a total finished look was a complete surprise to me. A look includes shoes, your underwear—what's underneath affects what's seen—your accessories, the relationship of what you're wearing on top to what you're wearing on the bottom, your hair, etc. It's a whole picture. Certain things, once you find suitable versions, will suit you on almost all occasions.

How do you think about putting a "look" together? What are the components of a "look" for you? Where are the gaps in the "look" of the outfits you assemble?

Where does all that welter of information—the inner world relating to dress, the ideas about clothing you bring from your history, and the feelings, lists, and ideas that go with a wardrobe—

leave you? We're looking for the experience of emotional completeness, manifest in an aesthetically integrated way. If you find your desire boils down to wanting what you don't have but being unsatisfied when you do have it, go deeper. Ask yourself what that's about. I craved silks, fabulous pouffy ball gowns, and satin ballroom slippers. My life requires nothing fancier than jeans. What was missing from my life that called out for such finery? I thought deeply and came up with activities: writing this book and making beautiful dolls out of silk. I came up satisfied.

Investigation to the depths of the self is required to emerge with "your heartfelt point of view."[39] Only from this can you find, in clothing, a kind of harmonious animism—that the clothes live as you live, and express what you want, so that you find a way of "breathing your own life into them."[40] From the emotional balance that comes with self-awareness, you prepare to receive the happiness of knowing what is yours.

Start taking steps toward that goal. Not going too fast is essential to success. Emily Cho writes:

Sometimes a client will try to move too quickly toward her desired image of herself. She'll dress beyond her role, become lost and slip back several steps. Dress just one step above where you are now, but let it be comfortable. Give yourself time to integrate each level of sophistication.[41]

We're looking to return to the house of the inner self, even if we notice it has a lot of outdated or broken furniture. We need to know this floor plan intimately before we turn our attention outward. This knowledge is your filter for the huge amount of information out there, so that what comes through the filter works beautifully for you.

You are going toward the place where "you're going to make every single garment you own a comfortable and good-looking one," but first we have to look at the body fundamentals, more fundamentals of the arts of dress, and shopping. Why? There you find what you want and how to get it, where interior meeting exterior creates harmonious blend.

Notes:

1. Feldon, Leah. *Dressing Rich*. Page 9.
2. Cho, Emily and Linda Grover. *Looking Terrific*. Page 197.
3. Cho and Grover. *Looking Terrific*. Page 77.
4. Rybczynski, Witold. *Home*. Page 20.
5. Donovan, Carrie. "On Higher Ground." *New York Times Magazine*. Page 34.
6. Goday, Dale and Molly Cochran. *Dressing Thin*. Page 16.
7. I didn't, for example, want to interview clothing fetishists. Latex and leatherwear have to do with the whole world of sadomasochistic bondage, which is intimately connected with the eroticization of discomfort. My gut response is, "Oh, please, life is uncomfortable enough."
8. Goday. Page 23.
9. Feldon, Leah. *Dress Like a Million*. Page 91.
10. Cho, Emily with Hermine Lueders. *Looking, Working, Living Terrific*. Page 38.
11. Roth, Geneen. *Breaking Free from Compulsive Eating*. Page 52.
12. Adapted from a passage from Orbach's *Fat Is a Feminist Issue*, page 63.
13. Satran, Pamela. *Dressing Smart*. Page 262.
14. Lurie, Alison. *The Language of Clothing*. Page 28-29. (Vintage)
15. Lurie. Page 60.
16. *Elle*. October 1993. Page 254.
17. Feldenkrais, Moshe. *Awareness Through Movement*. Page 10.
18. Susie Orbach, on page 150 of *Fat Is a Feminist Issue,* asks the question, "What does pleasure mean to her?" in the context of food, specifically eating cream donuts. Regardless of impetus for reflection on this issue, it is a worthwhile question.
19. Feldenkrais. Page 11.
20. Feldenkrais. Page 15.
21. Robin, Jennifer. *Clothe Your Spirit*. Page 53.
22. Robin. Page 53.
23. Satran. Page 254.
24. Thompson. Page 12.
25. Based on an exercise about seeing how feeling fat or feeling thin might serve the individual. From *Fat Is a Feminist Issue*, page 71.
26. Roth. Geneen. *Why Weight?* Page 38.
27. This was suggested by an exercise from Orbach's *Fat Is a Feminist Issue*, page 158.
28. Feldenkrais. Page 25.
29. Kentner, Bernice. *Tie Me Up with Rainbows*. Page 40.
30. Cho. *Looking Terrific*. Page 77.
31. Pooser, Doris. *Secrets of Style*. Page 8.
32. Procter, Jane. *Clothes Sense*. Page 6.
33. Procter. Page 20.

34. Cho. *Looking Terrific*. Page 37.
35. Cho. *Looking Terrific*. Page 73.
36. In *Writing Down the Bones*, Natalie Goldberg describes this process in depth.
37. Roth, Geneen. *Breaking Free from Compulsive Eating*. Pages 50-51.
38. Thompson. Page 20.
39. Feldon, Leah. *Dress Like a Million*. Page 4.
40. Feldon. *Dress Like A Million*. Page 5.
41. Cho. *Looking Terrific*. Page 88.

Help! My Body Keeps Changing!

Honor your body, which is your representative in this universe. Its magnificence is no accident.
It is the framework through which your works must come. . . .
Those who do not love the body or trust it do not love or trust the soul. . . .
Who muzzles the body or leashes it muzzles and leashes the soul.
The private body is the dwelling place of the private guise of God. . . .
The body is the soul in Earth-garments. It is the face of the soul turned toward the seasons.

—Jane Roberts[1]

If thoughts, feelings, self-image, and personal history reside within, then the body would seem to be external. After all, that's where the clothes lie. However, how you feel about your body and what you do to it influences how you wear your clothes. So, after you've looked at your interior, before you look at the clothes, you have to look at the body. The body bridges interior and exterior, and eloquently expresses the contradictions, paradoxes, and ambivalences we feel about this integration.

Much of importance about the body has to do with how you feel about the inevitable changes wrought by time upon flesh, about your body's fat and the food you eat, about how soul relates to body, and what actions you take as a result of these feelings. It's important to discover the changes you wish to impose upon your body as well as explore your direct experience within it. The next two chapters discuss this in depth. Were the body just a clothes hanger, dressing would be a whole lot easier.

Body changes

In reality, though, the female body is a constantly changing landscape. From the budding breasts of adolescence, through the rounded belly of pregnancy and generous curves of maturity, to . . . the deep creases of old age, our bodies weather and reshape. To call beauty only the still life of unchanging "perfection" is no praise for creatures so lively and diverse as womankind.

—Wendy Chapkis, *Beauty Secrets*[2]

We dress a different body at 85 than we do at 50, 30, 19, and 4. Many challenges face us as we weather these natural changes. To give up the pleasures of body or dress at 40, 50, 60, etc. in response to societal blather that "It's all downhill after_____" (fill in the year) is ludicrous considering you may have great years to the end of your life. Bodies do age, but that does not have to obliterate clothes love. Consider that late adolescence and early adulthood, the so-called "peak" of our bodily perfection, may also coincide with our time of greatest unease with ourselves. Though we can't hold onto the age of that young body, many hold on to the related anxiety throughout our lives. In eighth grade, one poor, hormone-crazed young man sought out my body in this way: Whenever I was within hearing distance he would remark, to my mortification (and probably his), upon my "watermelons." I still wrestle with the self-consciousness prompted by his comments.

If a picture is worth a thousand words, the media chime in with a few million of their own. Despite the hoopla surrounding the "new" over-40 models, most models are either teenagers or have barely graced their twenties, because the aforementioned youth, the dramatically unlived quality of the models' faces and bodies (mere bony curves), provides a counterpoint to the extreme garments they pose in. As writer Jennifer Egan notes: "In the fashion world of the '90s, teen-age models simulate an adulthood they've yet to experience for women who crave a youthful beauty they'll never achieve. Sweet 16 it's not."[3]

The movies are notorious for this youth emphasis. Superstar actress Meg Ryan has spoken of the difficulty of finding acting roles where a woman has experienced some life and love. When we do see aging celebrities, because they are the group most likely to embrace cosmetic surgery to deflect aging's signs, as columnist Ellen Goodman noted, these women

> raise the threshold of self-hate faster than the age span. . . . Those of us who failed to look like Brooke Shields at seventeen can now fail to look like Victoria Principal at thirty-three and like Linda Evans at forty-one and like Sophia Loren at fifty. When Gloria Steinem turned fifty . . . she updated her famous line from forty. She said, "This is what fifty looks like." With due apologies to the cult of mid-life beauty, allow me two words: "Not necessarily."[4]

The minute you start to "age," which of course we are all doing all the time, the Greek chorus of advertising starts to chime in at inconvenient moments, predicting tragedy. Women continually hear versions of what *Vogue* calls "the poisonous compliment 'she looks good for 40.'"[5] Women aren't allowed to age well, unlike men, rare books, fine cheese, T-bone steaks, or wine. We must mourn time instead of growing into it, agreeing with actress Tallulah Bankhead that "they aren't making mirrors the way they used to."[6]

There are contexts in which you can frame your body's changes and your beauty, other than those marked out by the media or pervasive stereotypes. Instead of wasting your yearning on fantasy, you can take back the power to define how you look by privately changing how you perceive yourself to a more accurate and supportive vision. Jennifer Robin suggests a preliminary exercise: "Instead of fearing your assets will disappear, imagine them growing clearer, sharper, more well defined every year."[7] Perhaps you will age fiercely and proudly, as did artists Georgia O'Keeffe and Louise Nevelson, dancer Martha Graham, and fashion editor Diana Vreeland. Writer Naomi Wolf offers another possibility for a woman's aging:

> [She] grows into her face. Lines trace her thought and radiate from the corners of her eyes after decades of laughter, closing together like fans as she smiles. . . . [I]n a precise calligraphy, thought has etched marks of concentration between her brows, and drawn across her forehead the horizontal creases of surprise, delight, compassion, and good talk. A lifetime of kissing, of speaking and weeping, shows expressively around a mouth scored like a leaf in motion. This skin loosens on her face and throat, giving her features a setting of sensual dignity. . . . When gray and white reflect in her hair, you could call it . . . silver or moonlight. Her body fills into itself, taking on gravity like a bather breasting water, growing generous with the rest of her. The darkening under her eyes, the weight of her lids, their minute cross-hatching, reveal that what she has been part of has left in her its complexity and richness. She is darker, stronger, looser, tougher, sexier.[8]

You can learn to honor the passage of time as it is mirrored in your features.

Many invest energy in products or services that claim to change the body or alter the changes wrought by time. Some seek temporary changes such as makeup, hair style, and scent, while others make more permanent changes such as plastic surgery and tattooing. These body changes are a way of saying, "This is the face I want to present to the world. This is the mask I want them to see." What face do you want the world to see?

Plastic surgery: The desire to be a cut above

Seeking surgery for psychological uplift? It doesn't address the problem. Find some good things to say about your nose. Can't find any? I'll help. The most important thing about your nose . . . Does it work? Can you breathe through it? Wonderful. Can you smell things? Fine. Be grateful; stay away from the knife. Celebrate your face. Find gorgeous accessories that echo the shapes of the features nature gave you. Play it up. If you want surgery to change your face or body, spend a year or two acting as if you already had it. Lead the life you would lead. See if you can have what you want without risking your life. That's an order.

An aside on tattooing

Tattooing, a surgical option often performed by people with no medical training, is momentarily in fashion, as if it were bad, rad, new, and different. We have the memory of the bacteria that lives only five days. Tattooing's been bad before. In 1584, Reginald Scot thought tattoos the devil's mark: "The Diuell giveth to euerie nouice a marke, either with his teeth or with his clawes."[9] Tattooing's been cool on and off for centuries. Even royalty have had tattoos. In 1910, for example, many—including Lady Randolph Churchill—got "Coronation tattoos" of the royal arms or a patriotic motto.[10] Part of tattooing's allure is that of writing in permanent ink. Yet, due to lasers, "permanence" is now a joke. Actor Johnny Depp's WINONA FOREVER tattoo has been altered to remove NA. Ah, another miracle of plastic surgery, which has all of the pain and none of the permanence of ritual scarification. If ever you admire my tattoos, trust that I got the rub-on stickers from a gumball machine.

Makeup: Playing in the paint pots

The problem with makeup in this culture reflects a larger problem, according to Susan Bixler: "People don't buy products or ideas on the basis of logic. They buy emotionally."[11] We will hang onto them even if we know we are being fooled. We prefer the scented beliefs to what we know to be true. Even the models fall for the beauty fantasy.

The cosmetics companies don't exist for the well-being of the women modeling. Cosmetics companies earn big bucks off our fondness for paint. Cosmetics are the first thing you usually see in department stores because stores know about and profit from everyone's rationalization, "Oh, I can afford a little makeup." Makeup sales, with their huge profit margins, keep stores afloat. Cosmetics account for about one percent of consumer spending on goods and services.[12] What does that mean in terms of profit? L'Oréal's sales reach over $7 billion annually[13] with 32,000 separate products on the market.[14] Factor in that only seven cents of each dollar you spend on lipstick actually pays for the cost to produce the product.[15] We're paying for packaging.[16] Since they're just giving us a dream, it sure as hell has to look good. Why do we put up with the cost? Chapkis responds: "An item that promises a fantasy by definition must be priced fantastically."[17] In the glut-of-goods society, we're willing to pay through the nose for the perception of quality, falling for that "technical" mumbo jumbo as men fall for high-"horsepower" cars.

Despite the snake-oil fantasy suggestions of makeup advertising, modern makeup, because of legal boundaries, cannot change you. If it did, it would be considered a drug, the FDA would need to test it and approve it, and you wouldn't be able to buy it over the counter.[18] We're kidding ourselves when we think we're "nourishing" our skin with products. Yes, cream on the skin does feel good, but it doesn't do anything. What "nourishes" skin is what nourishes the body: food. You have to eat well for your skin to look good, unless you're preadolescent. We kid ourselves when we starve on diet soda and other petrochemicals and think slathering goo will help the skin. Sleep well, eat well, stay out of the sun, exercise—boring advice, but true—and you'll have your miracle.

The antidote to the deceptive aspect of this, according to makeup artist and cosmetics manufacturer Bobbi Brown, is to realize, for example, "this line isn't going to make you younger, or taller, or make your wrinkles go away. It's simply going to make your skin look smoother so the makeup looks better."[19] Anna Levine adds that makeup limits the wearer to the type of artificial light used for the still camera: "God did not design light so it would fall correctly on your makeup."[20] Because of this, department stores most often display makeup under artificial light. When did you last sit in real daylight at a makeup counter?

If you're like most people, facts are not going to sway you. Maybe we can change that, but first let's look at what the emotional cycle is doing. Eve Merriam tracks how makeup products move through our lives:

> [F]rom Idealization to Frustration to Demoralization. The ideal imposed upon American women is the maintenance of youth. Since it is an idealization and not an attainable reality, the pursuit of such a false goal leads to frustration. One promised product does not achieve the effect. Another is tried. Another, and yet another. After a while, demoralization takes place. . . . She is properly demoralized, so that she does not query, what's wrong with this product? Instead she turns her frustration inward: What's wrong with me?[21]

We're so polite. We're trained to take it out on ourselves instead of demanding a world where this ridiculousness is diminished and realistic alternatives are offered.

A failure of the imagination results when we are asked to consider living outside this psychological loop in a non-traditional narrative fairy tale. We imagine we wouldn't want it, that there would be no beauty, we'd be forced to eat brown rice and wear overalls. I am mystified why we allow ourselves to be brainwashed into ferociously hanging onto the hope of a conventional life narrative. In the story, lovely woman meets handsome man, they marry, have careers, live happily ever after, have two children, a house, and a mini-van, send kids to college, have grandchildren. Why does this single story, always jump-started by Her beauty attracting Him, get embraced by hundreds of millions of people?

I am happier without makeup. I am such an expressive person that I might rub an eye if it itches, I might put my finger on my mouth if I'm thinking intently. My hands are constantly in my face, I rub my nose, or I eat something, and I hate coming away with paint on my hands and the fear I've smudged. When I wear makeup, I worry it doesn't look right. I don't want to spend energy on this, especially since I think I look fine without it. For me, that's comfortable. For other people it isn't. I think makeup is great in specific situations such as acting in plays, dressing for Halloween, or appearing at the Academy Awards.[22]

On the plus side, unguents, pastes, and powders used well can enhance the wearer's looks and psychologically support her. There are logical reasons to be pro-makeup. It's war paint. In the battleground known as work, painted ladies make more money. Studies done by a major beauty product manufacturer found women in the corporate world earned 20 percent more money when they wore makeup.[23] One might suspect the survey's sponsor but still wonder about the conclusion.

Today, makeup is available to everyone. Who wears makeup? The first wave of feminism was known for its desire to abolish the Feminine Mystique. Among the touted instruments of torture were bras (to be burned) and makeup. Today, feminists can enjoy their freedom and their paint pots. According to a recent survey, 63% of women who consider themselves feminists wear makeup every day, as opposed to 57% of non-feminists. "Among women who hold management positions . . . 83% of the feminists vs. 63% of non-feminists wear makeup every day."[24] The reality of who plays in the paint pots is quicker to change than the perception. Writer/activist Naomi Wolf comments, "We have no archetype for a serious female thinker who also gets manicures and is trying to work out a wedding menu."[25]

Jeremy Stone really enjoys makeup and has delighted in it for a long time.

I started really getting interested in it in fifth grade. I used to sit in front of my mother's mirror and put on lipstick. We had choir practice on Thursday nights, and I would put on really inappropriate makeup just to see what kind of reaction I could get. My mother, of course, pretended to not notice. I used to think, "I must have done a really good job. My mom doesn't even notice it."

Stacey Lamiero's mom is very into cosmetics. She also blows apart the youth mystique—she's a gorgeous, silver-maned woman, dramatic, classic, and fabulous. Stacey agrees:

My mom is lucky. And she spends about $100 a month at the Estée Lauder counter. She buys everything. I keep saying, "Mom, those makeups are nothing. You're paying for the pump and the package." But my mom is such a kick. She went in to the Estée Lauder counter just recently, and she said, "I need this foundation," and they said, "Oh, have you tried our new sheer foundation?" "No, I need the heavier one to cover these little lines I have on my nose." They said, "Well, you must not have heard of our face primer." She said, "No, I haven't. Tell me about it." And they bring out this thing—it's green. You put this green stuff on to cover your flaws and then you can use the sheer foundation. I said, "Mom. It's good marketing— instead of walking away with your one foundation, they sold you a foundation which was just as expensive but sheerer, and the green stuff." So she spent an extra thirty bucks. And I think that's hysterical. But she feels beautiful. She is beautiful.[26]

A brief interlude regarding nails

My grandmother has gorgeous hands. In her youth she was asked to be a hand model. She declined, as modeling was not something a lady did. Recently, when we were out to lunch, Grandma took a phone call at the table. Afterward, the woman at the next table came up to Grandma and said, "You're so fabulous. I love the gorgeous red nails against the black phone." Grandma said, "Thank you." Grandma inspires admiration wherever she goes.

Where Grandma goes, Mom follows. From early childhood on I could find my mother by following the scent trail of acetone. The beauty salon held the fascination of bottles arrayed on the polish tray. I tend to remember people's nails—once, on line at the DMV, I saw the talons of an old woman with her hand-carved cane and fingernails curled over and over in glossy enameled loops.

The arbiters of taste would demand we have a very specific kind of nail, the "classic" nail. Personal style consultant Doris Pooser dictates:

> And finally, my pet peeve—overly long fingernails. While lengths vary from season to season, really long nails never say style and class. And fortunately, in fashion, we are seeing a movement toward shorter nails; less color for day and work is always correct.[27]

But I'm not sure nails aren't more about fantasy than "communicating" something. Sure, if you work at a keyboard, your fingers have to be able to type accurately and well. Your nails must support that. If you garden, clam, dig in the sand or the dirt, if you work with your hands, long nails can get in the way. Still, I can't help having my sense of whimsy tickled by the colors and silly glossiness of long nails. I'm not alone. I try to call my friend Judith to ask her about this. Her friend Kirk answers, saying she can't come to the phone right now. He explains, "She's doing the flapping-her-hands-vigorously-to-dry-her-nails dance. It's very alluring." How do you trim your claws? What do you like them to look like? What feels best to you? Are there any absurdly decadent things you'd like to do with your nails you haven't tried yet?

Back to your shanim punim

Some questions to consider:

1. Where are the places in your makeup you feel unsure?

2. What do you love about makeup? What do you love about your un-made-up face?

3. The word "makeup" suggests you're making it up, creating an illusion. What illusion do you want to create? Is it realistic? What can be pretended and what looks false TO YOU? The rest of the world be damned, what do you like? What do you believe makeup can do for you? Does it? How long do you use a product before its magical powers wear off?

4. How many products that you buy do you use up? How much of your makeup expenditure is on mistakes?

5. If you spend a lot of money on makeup, even if it just sits, do you get sufficient pleasure from it that it's worth it to you? How can you make better choices?

6. You can play at department store makeup counters if you can survive the invasive salesladies. What strategies work for you?

7. Know yourself in relationship to your makeup. What face do you want to meet the world with?

8. What don't you know about makeup that you want to learn, and who can teach it to you? Where can you find the courage to find out? Consultant Karen Kaufman suggests that if someone is teaching you, have her do one side of your face the way you want it to be, and then train yourself by doing the other. She emphasizes that makeup is fun, not essential:

   You can look beautiful throwing clothing on in a flattering color and walking out the door. Makeup is just an enhancement. People often use makeup because they don't think that they're okay without it. They cannot possibly walk out that front door without full makeup on. We are fed that in this society. I'm passionate about trying to break that pattern. Makeup is a fun thing, but not when it becomes like being thin—that you can't even be considered a woman if you don't have makeup on.

9. Incorporate your personal history. Think about the first time you used lipstick. Clara Pierre remembers "furtive applications of Tangee 'Natural' in the girls' locker room immediately upon arrival at my secondary school each morning."

   It had the consistency of orange-flavored gelatin and was apt to break off at the base. . . . Meanwhile, Revlon waited in the wings until we became seniors and could drive to school and were permitted coffee at recess instead of chocolate milk. Acne receded and our lips blossomed with "Persian Melon" and "Powder Pink." The more adventurous among us wore "Orchids to You" or "Fire and Ice" to dances.[28]

10. Consider your politics when shopping for makeup, for example, regarding animal testing on makeup products and the philanthropic activities of the company. For further reference, *Personal Care with Principle* lists over 400 companies opposed to animal testing.[29]

We change physically throughout our lives, wondrous transformations fraught with new dangers and new pains. Some feel it as a burden, a drag. Others go through laughing. How will you ride your changes?

Changes to the body: Hair

Hair is the most exciting and terrifying part of the body. . . . It sits up there on top of practically every person's head, unavoidable, infinitely malleable. You can make it yucky, you can make it fluffy, you can stick stuff in it, and so on. And it isn't for anything but pleasure. It does, more or less, keep the scalp warm, but you can't rely on hair—it doesn't grow more thickly in cold climates. So it's out there, and since it has no function, it has nothing but meaning.
—Anne Hollander, an historian of art and dress[30]

When she realized what her situation in the world was and would probably always be she threw away every assumption she had learned and began at zero. First off, she cut her hair. That was the one thing she didn't want to think about anymore. Then she tackled the problem of trying to decide how she wanted to live and what was valuable to her. When am I happy and when am I sad and what is the difference? What do I need to know to stay alive? What is true in the world?
—Toni Morrison in *The Song of Solomon*[31]

One of the things I love about my friend Dave is that he has the longest, most beautiful curling brown hair of anyone I know. While hanging out with him, I take a deep breath and notice that Dave uses the shampoo that my old boyfriend used, and I feel pangs of melancholy. I tell Dave he has beautiful hair and ask him why he decided to let it grow.

Because it feels right. It fits that way. Your clothes have to fit you properly, your hair has to fit you properly, too. You have to allow it to flow out at the proper length and then you stop it right there.

I got a haircut recently because the ends of my hair weren't doing what I wanted them to do. They were tying themselves in knots, and I didn't like that. I became uncomfortable. So to punish them, I had them cut off. It's a good summer 'do, too. It's nice and short now. It stays out of the way. I could maybe even ride in a convertible with the top down.

His idea of a "summer 'do" is longer than my hair, which goes down below my shoulders. Dave comments on what might be traditionally considered a women's issue, "There's an in-between stage when you're growing your hair out when it sticks out and makes little wings at the side of your head." He puts the backs of his hands up against the sides of his head, and wriggles his fingers to demonstrate.

Your hair is totally out of control, and you have to have faith that it will get to the longer stage, and you'll be able to do what you want with it. But you have to find a temporary means of restraint. People try hats, bandannas, all kinds of different things before it actually fits back into the ponytail. Some people use grease.

Although many women experience significant hair loss, we suspect punk politics or chemotherapy, depending on the wardrobe. When a friend had chemotherapy, she did the punker black leather fashion thing and looked fabulous, if a little drawn about the eyes.

But let us move down the head a little to the beard. Women's facial hair is categorically not allowed in our culture, regardless of the fact that many women sprout hair naturally. Emotional wreckage can result, as we saw in the chapter where the mother harasses her adult daughter with the idea that the daughter's unnoticeable facial hair represents her true obstacle to the good life.

What are the hair rules where you live? How does your hair reflect your response to them? What would your hair do if given its head? And what about accessories?

Grooming accessories can change your life. When I was a child, each year as I blew out the burning candles on the birthday cake I wished for hair that was trouble-free, while knowing I should use this wish to end world hunger or lower the infant mortality rate. My fancy "quality" hairbrush did not go through my hair easily. I hated my hair and I hated brushing it. Because I avoided brushing, my hair would develop huge knots which my mother combed out periodically as I protested screaming and holding still. Then I lost the expensive British hairbrush and got a cheap plastic one to replace it. The cheap one, with its wide-set bristles, moved through my hair as if it were silk. I've had that brush for over fifteen years now. I've been friends with my hair all that time. It makes my hair look beautiful. For years, I didn't know the "problem" with my hair was my hairbrush. Do you have a hairbrush, accessories, and hair products you love? If not, why not? One person commented that she'd wanted to change her shampoo, but each time she went to the grocery for a new bottle, she told herself she was under too much stress to change now. Recently she realized she'd been saying that for three years, made herself stop a few moments to smell the different shampoos, and chose a new one.

Changes in haircut can be a way to assert or mark changes in one's life. Hair can also function as a literal curtain to the expression of your face. If you want to hide, this can work quite well.

Hair can communicate information to strangers that may or may not be accurate. Daphne Stannard, an intensive care nurse, has wild spikes of dark hair. She doesn't change her hairdo when she nurses. What kind of impact does this have? Why does she do it? Daphne comments, "Well, I can't change my 'do. I used to have it permed. I looked like a poodle. I had this big mop on my head." She didn't like the perm solution smell, the cost, or the painful procedure, and decided to grow it out and see what would happen.

I quickly found out it just feathers naturally. Really scary. I just can't deal with that. I can't look like Shaun Cassidy. I'd have to kill myself. So it just gets spiked up. Right now, I have to put junk in it to make it stand up. It's pretty happy.

With a fresh open-heart patient, I let the family come in for a few minutes after the patient had come back from the O. R. It's very intense, very critical for the first two hours because they're always unstable in transit, and we have to make sure all the drugs get transferred over from the anesthesia machines to our machines. For the first two hours, this patient was on a thread. I worked a twelve-hour shift so I was with them for the rest of the night, and after many hours, the family confided in me that they were really worried at first when they saw me because they thought that I would be a very severe nurse. It's tragic because it's just based upon my hair. I said, "What do you think of me now?" They said, "Oh, you're so caring. We just misjudged you. But we were worried at first."

When I was a child, my best friend Vicky got a bob, and I followed suit. Except for the first day, when it looked perfect because my mother's hairdresser cajoled and terrorized every strand into place with spray and able manipulation of a blow dryer, my hair never behaved again. I didn't understand that his cut went against the nature of what was coming out of my head.

In frustration, when I got to college, I got it cut really short. I kept it short for years. Gradually, I let it grow out, just to see what it did by itself. It seemed to fall in gentle wide curls. I've never seen anything like it on TV, and I'm not sure it's ever been in fashion, but it's lovely. Now it's long enough that I can twist it into a bun that holds without any pins. In winter, worn down, it keeps me warm. In summer, up, it keeps me cool. While I feel periodic urges for a buzz cut dyed white-blond, for the most part, allowing myself to discover its nature has given me joy and made me feel beautiful.

When to make a change? Louisa Rudeen reported one clear message in the *New York Times*:

Brimming with holiday spirit, I gave a handful of coins to an elderly woman who is a permanent fixture at the entrance to the subway at Eighth Avenue and 57th Street. She accepted them and began to speak. I leaned closer, awaiting a prophecy or blessing. "You've got to do something with that hairdo," she said.[32]

You change when you feel the need. But how to try new things? Jeremy Stone has experimented extensively with different hairstyles:

My first year in art school, I really got into changing the way I looked. I started doing all different things. I was dying my hair red. I permed it. I cut my hair really short. I bought wigs. And I would go every week to the photo booth at Woolworth's to document all these changes. I have a whole book of photos of different hair styles called *Transformations*.

What was she looking for?

I knew who I was, but I was looking for a reflection in the mirror that I could live with, that I was comfortable with, that embraced all the different facets of my personality and my interests, that I didn't feel was a compromise or focused towards anybody else's approval but my own.

Dave and I discuss uncomfortable looks, the haircuts that are held in place with spray and resemble helmets. Liz, who cut my hair, says that the "helmet" look is a statement. It takes a lot of labor to make it and a lot of leisure to maintain it. For the most part, we accept this socially sanctioned body distortion without comment, as we do with the makeup which paints strange expressions on our faces. Flügel comments:

> When hair is "dressed" . . . in various styles, either with the help of external instruments (combs, hair pins, etc.) or by imparting some unnatural shape to the hair itself, there has taken place what is, strictly speaking, a deformation of this part of the body. The reasons why we tend to look upon these artificial manipulations as fundamentally different from the mutilations or deformations referred to above, would seem to be . . . the procedures adopted have nonpermanent or irrevocable effects. Even the most lasting of "permanent waves" vanishes. . . . [33]

Is it going too far to call it a deformation? Perhaps. But hair inspires strong language and feeling. Many who shrink from the idea of a personal style consultant form a quasi-religious attachment to their hair "dresser," who is part shrink, part artist, all comforter. New York assertiveness trainer Perla Knie finds women in her workshops "view hairdressers as authority figures, like doctors and lawyers." She herself once put up with a haughty hairstylist because he kept saying to her, "If it wasn't for me, you'd still look like Brooklyn."[34]

Betsey, an artist who had long hair into her twenties, could never relate to people who were in tears after their haircut. "I looked at the cut and thought, 'Huh, it's OK.'" Now that she has shorter hair she understands. When she cut her hair she thought she'd found the right hairdresser. The first cut was great. The second cut was OK. The third cut was a disaster, and she vowed never to return. After this happened with several different stylists, she formulated a theory: They get used to you and stop paying attention. Each haircut is a risk, and you can't afford to get comfortable. Each time you must remind them: My hair does this up in front, remember if you cut it too short it. . . . You must be certain you are heard, that the cutter isn't saying, "Uh-huh, uh-huh, uh-huh," and slicing away without listening. This person wields sharpened objects upon your head. Make sure you trust him or her.

The fashion industry consultants, of which hairdressers are its least well-recompensed agents, perpetuate a myth about gray hair that it says "old,"[35] as if old = bad. Hair usually does gray because of age, but so what? That "so what?" sends as many as 65% of women to some type of hair color.[36] Not, thank god, jewelry rep Kathy Upton:

> I got my first grey hair when I was 17. And it didn't bother me at all. I said, "If I grow up to have a great grey mane, I'll be like Lauren Bacall." I think she tints her hair blonde now. But I will never tint my hair. I will never dye my hair. I glory in it, and I will never cut it short. I think it's a real statement, my grey hair.

Dave comments by briefly discussing the notion of dyeing his hair blue or working on dreadlocks. It's clear we're winding down. I ask him, "Any other hair thoughts, Dave?" He replies, "It's good to be hairy. It keeps you warm. What if I was stranded out in the wilderness in the middle of winter in the Yukon? I'd have a better chance of survival than the next guy. More hair covering my body."

Changes to the body: Scent

Check the ones that apply to you:

1. _____ Perfume makes me sneeze.

2. _____ I yearn to be told, "God, you smell wonderful!"

3. _____ When I notice someone's perfume, I wonder what they're trying to hide.

4. _____ I tuck perfume samples from magazines in my underwear drawer.

5. _____ Other (*please describe*)

Mom likes Chanel No. 5. The origin of the perfume's success has been attributed to the ability of American soldiers to pronounce it in post-World War II Paris. If you can ask for it, you can bring it home stateside to your girl. If not, it languishes on the shelves in a state of ennui.

Perfume is *the* moneymaker for many clothing designers. In magazines, we are presented with the alien other, a perfectly skinned, coiffed, dressed, sized woman. The only smells of her we get are carefully spaced designer fragrances made to deliberately leak into our reading. The many "realists" among us decide we can't look like her, but we can smell like she does. How much of what we pay for perfume is actually product? Eleven percent of the retail price goes for ingredients and packaging; thirty-two percent for the retailer; twelve percent for the manufacturer; seventeen percent for advertising and promotion; thirteen percent for overhead, and the rest for VAT (value-added tax in Europe)—fifteen percent on average.[37]

If this makes you want to seek alternatives, consider novelist Tom Robbins' suggestion in *Even Cowgirls Get the Blues* to use the perfumed clear liquid from your vagina behind the ears, and heaven knows what might result.[38] Robbins introduced me to the idea that scent is a kind of clothing or language, a put-on. Perspiration, the willingness to sweat and smell of it, communicates different things in different contexts. The idea of liking the smells that come from your own body runs contrary to the societally imposed idea that you should douche, deodorize, anoint with many mighty heavily scented cleansers this soiled sinful flesh. . . . Due to pernicious advertising we have become mortally afraid of our own sweat, our own stink, our own bodies, the different smells that come from different parts. We are saturated with perfume samples we really don't need, drowning out the pheromonal signals that humans seek in scent in the first place. Americans are probably the most obsessed with this. (For anyone raised off the farm in the U.S., the body odors of Europe are a complete surprise. One family member flew to India, didn't like the smell, and caught the next flight back.) Does perfume have to do with longing for sensuality in a sterile world?

We forget that not every culture has taken as great an interest in bathing as we have. People have used perfumes for most of recorded history in order to hide the smells of truly horrible things.

Cleopatra, for example, even soaked the sails of her ships and drenched the walls of her barges in scent.[39] Due to changes in cleaning habits, we've lost the smells that needed to be covered, but retain a holdover advertising-supported neurosis about smelly things. Our present-day culture has taken this concern with smells to new sanitized extremes.[40]

Scent is tricky, in that what you take home may not be what you end up with. Just like shoes that behave in the store but begin to pinch the moment they're unreturnable, scent has recalcitrant aspects. With scent, especially soap and shampoo, be careful. Body chemistry changes the scent after it makes contact with the skin. Sometimes the change is not pleasant.

Then we're told some men don't see clothes at all; they're led by their flaring nostrils into love. Glynn notes: "For a great many men it is the smell of materials which is exciting. Once again, the range of tastes is inexhaustible. . . . "[41] Scent is a much more forgiving medium; it's far less expensive than clothing as bait for the hook of "love." If your particular perfume, soap, deodorant, shampoo, baby powder, or garlicky meal causes you to attract something you'd rather not attract, you can always wash yourself or your clothes, or stop eating garlic, and start again.[42]

Samples are everywhere: in magazines, in stores. Usually, if you ask, a clerk in a department store will have the perfume sample of your choice squirreled away. If you're cagey, you can keep getting those tubes and never buy perfume at all. Unfortunately, I get carried away. I notice the department stores have trays with perfumes on them. I spray one hand, sniff it, think, "Don't mind it." I see something else I'm curious about, spritz the other hand, sniff, go "Yuck!" And then I spray over it something else, then spray a forearm with some other brand, and by the time I leave I'm drunk on the heady mixture of flowers and chemicals. People who walk near me look up, alarmed.

Scent is everywhere. How do I choose? Several times, over many years, when I hug my brother I notice I like the smell of his soap. I ask him for the brand and buy it. Due to the nasal numbness that occurs with long-term exposure, I can never smell the detergent on my clothes, so I just trust that if it smells good on Matt, it'll smell good on me. Until the-woman-who-almost-was-my-mother-in-law says, "You don't use Wisk?" OK, here's a testimonial, and they're not paying me. I try it, like it, and have stuck with it, regardless of the scent, which is not unpleasant.

But what about men?

When I was a kid, when the garbage man would drag his can up to the house to get our garbage, he always smelled so smoky that tobacco-scented air hung in the kitchen after he left. I asked Mom why he smoked and she said, "If he didn't smell like that, consider the alternative." He provided a courtesy "smoke screen" to us and perhaps to himself; odd that smoke would be a positive alternative. After Mom broke up with the man we called "Skunk Dew" (he worked for a couturier, and we hated his cologne), she dated a guy who smelled great, but we didn't think much of him either. When Mom stopped seeing him she cautioned me without explanation, "Never date a man who smells better than you do."

Why am I talking about how men smell? Shouldn't I be more worried about how I smell? (Sorry, I got distracted.) If you think you're wearing scent to attract men, you're kidding yourself. Here are the facts about what smells turn men on: pumpkin pie with either lavender or doughnut, and doughnut with black licorice.[43] Consider individual variation: when I eat peanut butter, the smell of it drives Andrew from the room.

How often I bathe, what I eat, whether or not I wear perfume, whether I work in the woods or in the city, affects how I smell and hence affects the perceptions of people I meet. But right now I just don't care that much (the luxury of the self-employed). I am not a traditional perfume person, much as I admire perfume people. I love that Grandma's sweaters all smell faintly of Bal à Versailles. Part of my love of this involves my craving for elegance and luxury, symbolized by the faintly perfumed.

What scents do you like and dislike? What perfumes are worn by members of your family, and what memories do they evoke? How do you choose perfume? Why do you discard it? When was the last time you allowed yourself to experiment with new perfumes in your soap, shampoo, laundry detergent, bathwater, etc.? What do you like about your body's smells? What do you want to smell like? To what extent do you want to change or blend with the smells of your body?

We've circled the body by looking at the changes imposed to its surface. Let us now examine more deeply our flesh.

Notes:

1. Roberts, Jane. *The Education of Oversoul* 7.

2. Chapkis, Wendy. *Beauty Secrets.* Page 17.

3. Egan, Jennifer. "James Is a Girl." *New York Times Magazine.* February 2, 1996. Page 26.

4. Chapkis. Page 10.

5. Gandee, Charles. "Dressing your age." *Vogue.* November 1993. Page 298.

6. Larkey. Page 113.

7. Robin, Jennifer. *Clothe Your Spirit.* Page 10.

8. Wolf, Naomi. Page 231.

9. Angeloglou, Maggie. *A History of Make-up.* Page 10.

10. Angeloglou. Page 117.

11. Bixler, Susan. *The Professional Image.* Page 229.

12. Finkelstein, Joanne. *The Fashioned Self.* Page 105.

13. McDowell, Colin. *The Designer Scam.* Page 109.

14. Lipovetsky, Gilles. *The Empire of Fashion.* Page 245.

15. Chapkis, Wendy. *Beauty Secrets.* Page 93.

16. Vienne, Veronique. "Designing Beauty: From the Outrageous to the Sublime." *Harper's Bazaar.* December 1994. Page 188. Packaging comprises a third of all municipal solid waste—over 200 million tons annually.

17. Chapkis, Wendy. Page 92.

18. Bixler. Page 191.

19. Wadkya, Sally. "Beauty's New Minimalist." *Vogue.* February 1995. Page 184.

20. Scavullo. Page 86.

21. Merriam. Page 166.

22. When looking at old photographs I always like the people who aren't made up . . . they look like real people, they're not the faces we laugh at. The older the picture, the more likely that the unmade-up women look better than the made-up ones.

23. Pooser. Page 91.

24. Sandroff, Ronni. "Surprise! Feminists wear more makeup." *Glamour.* September 1993. Page 119.

25. Karp, Jonathan. "Why feminists should stop blaming men." *At Random.* Number 6. Fall 1993. (*At Random* is an in-house book-advertising magazine published by Random House.)

26. Stacey wears makeup but not a whole lot of it:

Less is more. Somebody asked once, If you could only have one thing, one makeup on a desert island, what would it be? I would be torn between face powder and lipstick. I don't wear eye shadow, and I just started wearing eyeliner again. I don't know why. I look at it, and I think, "Why am I doing that?" Now, I have more makeup on, but I don't spend a lot of money. My lipstick is $3.99. The stick is green, and you put it on clear, and then it works with your different chemistries, supposedly.

It stains your lips. That's it. My mom puts on her beautiful Lancome and my attitude is, "Here's my green lipstick." My mom just shakes her head and says, "Can't you put that into a nice tube so that people don't know you're using $3.99 lipstick?" But, of course, my attitude is, "Look at this. Isn't this the greatest?"

27. Pooser. Page 94.

28. Pierre. Page 2.

29. Scruby, Jennifer. "Beauty with a Conscience." *Vogue*. February 1995. Page 160.

30. Friedman, Vanessa. "The Politics of Hair". *Vogue*. December 1994. Page 230.

31. Heilbrun. Page 127.

32. *New York Times*. January 22, 1995. Page A-17. West coast edition.

33. Flügel. Page 44.

34. Baker. Page 243.

35. Pooser. Page 93.

36. Bixler. Page 186.

37. McDowell. Page 105.

38. Robbins, Tom. *Even Cowgirls Get the Blues*. Houghton Mifflin Co.: Boston, 1976. Page 137.

39. Starzinger, Page Hill. "The story of eaux." *Harper's Bazaar*. March 1995. Page 92. Until the 18th century, when Dr. Ernst Platner came up with the idea that the skin needed to be clear of filth to breathe, people believed in the efficacy of staying dirty. His theory changed dress as well. Sennett notes for this reason, "Women lightened the weight of their clothes by using fabrics like muslin and cotton-silk; they cut gowns to drape more loosely on the human frame. . . . " Concurrent with that change, Western cities began to smell less fetid because sewer laws changed. In Paris the dumping of chamber pots on streets was prohibited. The sewers, instead of flowing openly by the roads, were moved underground. Even the shape of paving stones changed. (Because there was no need for room between the stones for feces, the stones were placed closer together.) [Sennett. Page 263]

40. The original American version of this fixation can be precisely dated from a 1919 advertisement for Odo-Ro-No, a deodorant cream which was the first to directly challenge readers to sniff their underarm area. [Stern, Jan and Michael. *Encyclopedia of Pop Culture*. Page 138.]

41. Glynn. Page 135.

42. Glynn. Page 135.

43. "Beauty flash." *Self*. July 1995. Page 47.

Body Acceptance

Now, I and most of the women I know have "problems" with our bodies. We discuss them as if we were talking about recalcitrant, maddening, sometimes defective children. We often behave like owners of bodies and not like the actual bodies ourselves. We are able, somehow, to undergo an out-of-body experience that leaves us hovering above. . . .

—Meg Wolitzer[1]

A recent magazine survey of 10,000 women concluded that 95% of us hate part or all of our bodies.[2] Before we get to clothes, we need to finish the discussion of the frame on which clothes move and rest. In order to have a fabulous relationship with your wardrobe, accepting your body is essential.

What you eat relates to your body and how you feel about it, but perhaps not in the way you think. At the risk of stating the elusive obvious, if you're crazy about food, it could be that the food is making you crazy. One of the symptoms of allergy can be craving. If you find yourself craving foods without cessation, get tested for food allergies. Allergy is technically defined as an immune system response. If you're not allergic, you could be sensitive. I am just sensitive, and my mouth bleeds like Dracula's after a good night when I eat products containing cane sugar. Dr. Theoron G. Randolph's work in clinical ecology, as outlined in the book *An Alternative Approach to Allergies* (Harper & Row, 1980), has made a start in examining food sensitivity. He tracks a correlation between sensitivity to certain foods and mood swings and depression.

The human diet over the past few hundred years has changed radically, while the human physique which digests the food is still equipped to handle roughly the same sort of whole-foods diet as that of the cave dweller. The foods associated with the modern Western lifestyle[3]— refined luxury items—have little to do with what's good for our bodies, what our ancestors used for nourishment for thousands of years before.[4] Joan Gussow, a professor of nutrition education, suggests that eating "highly processed, fatty, sugary, artificial snacks and convenience foods" seems to confuse the body's "programming" and may ultimately cause us to "stop trusting our bodies and start relying on other information, such as counting calories and fat grams, to determine what to eat, which throws everything out of whack. We end up eating mentally instead of relying on our body's regulating signals, which tell us when we're hungry or satisfied."[5]

In one case I know of, a friend's eating disorder, including the crazed cravings, vanished instantly—after years of her trying everything—when she eliminated refined foods from her diet. This does not deny an emotional component to eating disorders. But only after the strange food-sensitivity-induced cravings stopped was my friend ready to do the deep emotional work that can be accomplished with the support of a good therapist or a perspicacious group of friends.

If scientific reports of health risks associated with obesity were enough to change us, we'd all be bone-thin or at least aware of when we actually are thin. Instead, additional pernicious, culturally reinforced habits (aside from diet) keep our thoughts riveted with loathing upon all or parts of our bodies. This feeling manifests through the idea of "feeling fat" and the ideal of being thin, mercenary soldiers in the internal battles women wage over their bodies. The advantage of having this, or any, obsession is that you know how to focus. To find a way out of body hatred, you're going to need that. And it's worth doing because dressing a body you love is far more wonderful than dressing a body you hate.

Where does this come from?

I ask Libby Granett, "If your mom has the same body type as you and your daughter have, is it possible that this label 'overweight' actually isn't accurate, that your weight is actually appropriate?" Libby responds:

> That would be all well and good in a culture that didn't pay attention to those things, but if I need to shop in a department that's called "Macy Woman" or "Big and Beautiful," then what am I to believe? It's very tricky. Certainly it's become much less of an issue for me as I've gotten older and more comfortable with myself. But my mother didn't like her body, and she made it very clear to me that I have the body that she had. I grew up knowing that this was not an acceptable body.

Libby goes on to describe obsessive behavior with clothing that doesn't emerge from a vacuum. According to social worker Barbara Altman Bruno: "If you're a little girl watching your mother, one of the things you're bound to learn is to watch your weight all the time. We're raised to be at war with our outer selves. . . . "[6] We've heard too many times the now-familiar statistic about young girls dieting by age ten.[7] Women's food and body issues writer Susie Orbach comments:

> Rarely are our mothers and other female adults able to convey to a young woman that her body, whatever natural shape it has, is a source of pride and of beauty, since they themselves have not been able to feel that. We learn instead that our bodies are powerful in a negative sense, they can destabilize men and get us into trouble.[8]

Hating the body becomes a form of honoring our mothers by repeating their pattern. Without healthier models for female identity, we unconsciously assume body alienation to be part of that identity, rather than a product of the twisted ideals born of an illogical, gender-rigid past.

This learning is reinforced by the current media, in addition to their promulgating another false message: that our purpose is to mask (make up) who we are or alter our naturalness into a fantasy of who we want to be. The industries foster a viewpoint which misses the point by encouraging people to look outward, to value the appearance of warmth, safety, comfort, health, and well-being, while forgoing direct experience of them. We learn to prefer "looking" natural—an imitation—to "being natural." I don't know about you, but I recoil from the phrase "being natural," as it evokes unbathed bodies, braided armpit hair, blackheads, and a conspicuous lack of clean, tiled bathrooms.

We also absorb the idea we should "slim down" for men, when men love us with flesh on our bones. According to a recent study:

> Many American women still think they are too fat; they think that men would find them more attractive if they lost weight. But the men, clinging to an older ideal, think many women are too thin. . . . Meanwhile, the men are satisfied with the way they look, happily unaware that women tend to think that American men are also too fat.[9]

The fashion industry further contributes to the fat–thin headache by using extremely thin girls as our "models." Why? They "photograph well." Supermodel Linda Evangelista has commented that she's successful because today's clothes are made to look good on hangers and she's a clothes hanger. The fantasy presented to us looks very thin. The average model's actually twenty pounds thinner than she looks.[10] She's so thin that she carries padding with her to wear when designers fit clothes on her.[11] "Twenty years ago models weighed 8% less than average. Today models weigh 23% less than average."[12] At that weight the menstrual period usually stops or becomes irregular. According to a study by Eric Stice at Arizona State University, "Women with lots of TV and magazine exposure turned out to be the ones who idealized thinness, bought into prevailing gender stereotypes, disliked their own bodies—and showed symptoms of eating disorders. . . . " Stice reports, "We grabbed the most recent *Cosmopolitan* and took twelve images of idealized women, and twelve of normal-size humans. . . . Sure enough, we found that just looking at the *Cosmo* images provoked guilt, shame, depression, insecurity, stress, and body dissatisfaction."[13] Consultant Dale Goday asks the question we should ask ourselves more often when looking at these pictures: "Is being cadaverous really so terrific?"[14]

Some say we attempt to imitate the spirit of the times in striving for thinness. Stuart Ewen sees resonance of the flesh-stripped body in the contours of modernity, the lean lines of the office tower, of the credit card. However, he notes: "The haunted desire to conform to the modern contour is at war with the physical and emotional hungers of the individual."[15] Words like "spare," "clean," "pared down," and "stripped down" are used to define the "modern" sensibility. This sensibility impoverishes us.[16,17]

Our bodies need the flesh described by the Whitmanesque adjectives "turbulent, fleshy, sensual, eating, drinking and breeding." The modern sensibility doesn't include concepts such as warm, soft, sturdy, round, and solid.

Another school of thought says we want to look like men. Maybe we don't want their forms—come on, who would choose external genitalia?—but rather, we see in men's stylized flatness the embodiment, the access to autonomy, power, and freedom.[18]

Part of the work of ending the interior battle is lovingly tuning out the cacophony of "them" and tuning in to oneself by ceasing to turn the hate about this issue inward. A version of taking this step exists in Geneen Roth's statement, "I have experienced bouts of rage at a society that would drive woman to seek acceptance through fashionable emaciation, rage at what I was taught at home, and rage at myself for denying and distrusting who I am."[19] Rage functions as the energy source to move us forward to uncover the facts that underlie our personal battles. And the changing awareness about our bodies changes the way we wear our clothes.

We think we should weigh 100 pounds and be about 5'7". The average North American woman is 5'3.8" tall and weighs 144 pounds.[20] Clinically overweight at 5'4" doesn't even usually begin until 160 pounds.[21] We are conditioned, in part, by our myths and stories toward yearning for an impossible slenderness. Scarlett O'Hara had a 17" waist. I don't even have a 17" head. If the pencil-thin women were actually out there en masse, a vast number of books (not just the fantasy froth of fashion pap, feeding rapaciously on our discontent with ourselves) would be helping her to learn how to dress, like there are hundreds of books for everyone else. She ain't out there. We are big people. "One out of every three women in this country wears a Size 16 or larger; and 10 million of those women wear a Size 22 or larger."[22] We don't see our bodies clearly, regardless of their size: "47 percent of normal-weight women want to be thinner, and 16 percent of those who are already considered underweight want to be even thinner than they are."[23]

If you are caught up in believing you are too fat, in dieting and bingeing, in secret eating, in starving yourself, you can quickly get ensnared in the paradox formed by the juxtaposition of societal beliefs (dieting works) and direct experience (it doesn't).

How much does the diet industry earn by pouncing on people's insecurities? Billions of dollars a year.[24] Simultaneously, companies including Weight Watchers are being sued because diets don't work, because their programs are based on false promises. The National Institutes of Health reported that 90 to 95 percent of people who diet regain most or all of their weight within five years—many within one year.[25] We ignore that the body is our home and, in addition to having primitive dietary expectations, has its own encoded sense of the right size. As Gilday's documentary film *The Famine Within* reminds us, "The body seems to have its own preferred weight, which it protects with great vehemence."[26] Unconsciously echoing Gilday, Swift recounts that after dieting, "I, like 97 percent of the other weight-loss victims, gained back my weight. I went home to a size 18."[27] According to the *New York Times*:

> Anyone who has dieted knows how hard it is to keep the weight off. Now scientists at Rockefeller University know why. In a decade-long study of 41 volunteers, obese and lean, they discovered that the body changes its metabolism to foil attempts to lose—or gain—weight. . . . The findings were consistent: As soon as they gained an extra 10 percent, their metabolisms speeded up by 10 to 15 percent, pushing their weights down. The extra calories were burned by their muscles. As soon as they lost 10 percent, their metabolisms slowed down, again by 10 to 15 percent.[28]

(This plays right into the hopes and teachings of the gods of Frito-Lay by not noting that if you eat more like your primitive forebears, you also can shift your metabolism's set point.) It could be useful to ask yourself: What size does your body "go home" to? Look at the other people in your family—bodies tend to be similar. If you think you should weigh 20 pounds less than they do and you have the same frame, you may not be thinking clearly.

Since 90 to 95 percent of diets fail, and women persist in dieting anyway, this points to a pain so real and so deep that it blinds women to the fact that radical and extreme actions required of dieters result in failure. Why do we continue to bother? It's easy: we're exhausted and we don't know a better way. Each time we go to some other outside authority (be it a magazine, a TV quack, or even a "diet doctor") to tell us what to eat instead of listening to ourselves, we weaken the link between our own power and knowing and the ability to express it. Therein lies the route to couch potato-dom. We're trained to think of dieting as a responsible action. When we don't diet we're admonished for "letting ourselves go."

The temporary state of dieting sacrifices the needs of the whole person for a superficial result. We say we want slenderness, oh yes, we neeeeed it, but when push comes to shove, we protest with our whole selves, and lunge for the food.

Why do we get stuck in this arena? Why does something so "trivial" as dieting consume us? "After all, it's not the bomb, world hunger, or war," we say, ignoring the deep pain of our experience. It is no coincidence, Gilday points out, that these "disorders [are] centered on women's traditional spheres of expression, food and the body."[29] While a physiological component may also be operating, in addition we channel our obsessions, our inner battles about taking our personal power and place in the world, onto food. We interiorize our passions and not-so-safely express them through food. What happens when our values become channeled this way rather than toward engaging in the deeper issues of our lives? No one uses the word sinful anymore except in connection with dessert. According to a recent study, "Single women who have affairs with married men are generally untroubled by feelings of guilt; by contrast, many dieters feel powerful guilt and self-loathing after succumbing to a pint of Häagen-Dazs."[30]

Gilday reminds us that because food is now a metaphor for our values, fat has become a moral issue. An appetite for food reflects unladylike behavior; eating parallels sin in a world where men are allowed to bankrupt, with impunity, the nation's savings and loans.[31]

If you're wrapping your mind and life around a behavior pattern which doesn't work, this is more than just a diet issue. Gilday goes so far as to assert that there is no correlation between food and body size.[32] For years I joked that calories are an invention of the patriarchy to oppress women. I'm not sure how funny that is anymore. The idea of being thin was a fantasy I chose because I didn't know how to be present to and work with the reality of my life. Wanting and waiting to be thin controlled my buying clothes. I bought lovely things that were too small because "soon I'll be thin." I never bought for the body I am in "right now."

Feeling thin

The discussion regarding what to eat and when to starve subtly differs from the ongoing mental chatter that begins "I'm so fat. . . . If I were thin, I. . . . " A direct question to break through the "I'm so fat" litany is Susie Orbach's: "What kind of unreal expectations are attached to thinness?"[33] Everyone's answer is different. Consistently, the "look" of well-being is much more important to the dieter than actively fostering an interior state of well-being, because she doesn't know such direct experience is possible and sustainable. I've heard people looking at pictures of the starved and tortured in concentration camps and say only half-jokingly, "It would be OK if I were thin. It would be worth it."

Apprehension differs from reality. I ask Libby Granett, "Would you be different or would you present yourself differently if you weighed a different amount?" She responds:

> I think that I would end up spending a lot more money if I were thinner, if I had more choice about what I could wear. Because there are definitely more things to choose from in the smaller sizes. So my size keeps a curb on my spending. I would take more fashion risks if I were thinner, wear even more interesting things and a greater variety of things. It's not something that troubles me a lot, but it is true.

What does thin really feel like? For one thing, you bring your entire personality, rough edges and all, with you. It's a little colder because there's less padding. If you're eating sanely, your gastrointestinal tract calms down. If you're not eating foods that trigger binges or make you crazy, you've got a lot more time on your hands. If you don't work on your self-image, you still "feel fat." That's all. If you find yourself thinking, "Oh no, that wouldn't be me, I'd do it differently, I'd be _____" fill in the blank and get to work. Life begins now. It's time to start living.[34]

Please don't look at yourself and lie, "I will feel this way when I have lost five pounds." Who knows how you'll feel in five pounds? If you don't operate from the feelings you experience right now, the premise upon which any further knowledge is based will be corrupt. If you can't let go of the American woman's future-tripping mantra, "When I lose 5, 10, 25 (whatever) pounds, then . . .," say it in this way: "Despite the fact that I need to say, 'When I lose weight, then _____,' what is actually true right now is I'm beautiful."

"When I lose five pounds" is something people say to me when they want to say, "I don't want to deal with this right now," but they don't know how to say the words. A friend charges $500 an hour for his mathematical consulting business. He said he hoped it would make people stop calling, because he doesn't know how to say "No." People keep calling. He hasn't resolved his problem. "When I lose a few pounds" is a smoke screen, like charging $500 an hour, which doesn't resolve the problem. If the "real" you weighs ten pounds less and wears scarves, wear scarves and pretend. Who knows what might happen?

After I read Susie Orbach's *Fat Is a Feminist Issue*, I was idly thumbing through the classifieds one day and noticed an advertisement for custom-made pants for women. I weighed at least 170 at the time (I'm 5'1") and I expected to keep expanding forever. I called the seamstress, made an appointment, and was measured for the pants. We chose a beautiful, nearly wrinkle proof, beige, light weight wool. She made deep pockets in the front as I like them. When she finished, I put them on and twirled in front of the mirror. They were delightful. I had never felt so wonderful. By having these trousers made, I said to myself, "I value myself NOW. I am not waiting to be thin to appreciate and enhance myself." Soon afterward, for no apparent reason (I had recently stopped dieting, but didn't really believe in the process), I began to lose weight. The trousers have been way too big for many years. They're still beautiful. I keep them to remind me of when I started to love myself.

The ideal of "thin" represents a societally sanctioned body of lies we have swallowed whole-hog, including "Thin is good." Remember, "thin" does not equal "well." You wouldn't criticize a large flower.

Feeling fat

. . . Women are insane on the subject of their bodies. We all know that a paunchy guy with a bad haircut can be perfectly happy with himself, while a woman who's five pounds over her (self-decreed) ideal weight will attack herself in language she wouldn't use on a stray dog. Do you think we could possibly quit the self-haranguing? Is there any way we could just let ourselves live? Come to terms with the body we were dealt? Make peace . . . with the woman in the mirror?
—Amy Gross, *Elle* [35]

Part of the insanity Amy Gross refers to can be summed up in the ubiquitous phrase "I feel fat." Similar to the phrase "What an asshole" in that it describes a part of the body which everyone has as if it were the whole body, "I feel fat" is a phrase of deeply encoded language, allowing shared expression of despair without the possibility of redemption. Chapkis notes, "Among women, feeling fat, like feeling out of shape, has long been a metaphor for feeling powerless. Dieting and fitness training can be seen as attempts to regain control." She cites the 1984 body image survey of 33,000 women by *Glamour* magazine, where over three-quarters reported feeling too fat while "according to height/weight tables only one-quarter could be so described."[36]

Some live out their conflicts about fat through clothing, expressing to others what they cannot say to themselves, the anguish of what Dale Goday and Molly Cochran call the "closet fatty":

A "closet fatty" is anyone who thinks of herself as fat, but won't admit it. Witness the army of size 16 women out there squashed like sausages into size 12 clothes which "sort of" fit—meaning there's barely enough blood circulating in their crushed veins to sustain life. The message these women are trying to send is, "See, I wear a 12. I'm not fat!" But the one they're actually transmitting is, "I'm trying unsuccessfully to pass myself off as a 12 because I can't bear to admit that I'm a big woman. I hate who I am, and that's why I'm walking around in this uncomfortable disguise."[37]

Silencing the voice that says "I'm so fat" without delving into the fat's purpose doesn't serve us. We do things, even apparently destructive things like wallowing in the misery of "feeling fat," because at some level we are trying to help ourselves. Geneen Roth suggests some ways fat serves:

Fat becomes your protection from anything you need protection from: men, women, sexuality (blossoming or developed), frightening feelings of any sort; it becomes your rebellion, your way of telling your parents, your loves, the society around you, that you don't have to be who they want you to be. Fat becomes your way of talking. It says: I need help, go away, come closer, I can't, I won't, I'm angry, I'm sad. It becomes your vehicle for dealing with every problem you have.[38]

We start to shift out of the "I'm so fat" thinking when, for a moment, we stop the litany and notice something real. For example, the increasing size of a friend can reflect her happiness and contentment with herself. Lex says of a friend:

She looks really great these days. She's put on some weight, but she's also very healthy-looking, very tanned, and her hair is getting really long. It's kind of shaggy because she's trying to grow it out. She doesn't look as tense as she did. She's not so perfectly modulated or whatever in her hair and physique, but she looks really happy and healthy.

There are sartorial ways to neutralize that voice which says, nastily, "I'm so fat." Jeremy Stone says:

No matter how I feel, even if I feel fat, I'm going to dress as though I feel thin. If I look in the mirror and I'm wearing an outfit that I have thin associations with, I feel thinner when I wear it. I find when I'm wearing big, baggy, loose things for the most part, I feel fat again.

I also suggest setting up an effective internal United Nations. Assign part of your mind Buddha-duty—just monitoring the nasty voice that goes on about feeling fat and wanting to be thin. Simply practicing the art of watching the nasty thoughts seems to keep them from going ballistic.[39]

When I look at pictures or sculptures of Buddha, I notice he is always smiling and round-bellied. (No one ever said to Buddha, "Hey guy, what about that spare tire you're carrying around?" Of course, that was before tires were invented.) In martial arts training, I was told to stop holding in my stomach, that the body must know how to live with "Buddha belly." With practice, I found this position is more comfortable and easier to move with. Our societal ideal of a belly-pulled-in-tight is uncomfortable even for people whose professions require they maintain it. Actress Jamie Lee Curtis said once, before attending the Academy Awards, she was looking forward to the ceremony being over so she could stop holding in her stomach. I remember, at a workshop on food, the facilitator asking my friend Georgina, a slender woman in her late thirties, for a moment just to stop holding in her stomach. Letting go made her jaw relax. It made her weep. It made her look less hardened. Letting go of her mask of "control" allowed her the beginnings of understanding, a real self-control. When I relax my belly, people stop me to say, "Have you lost weight?" I feel happier.

Try ignoring all that chest-out/stomach-in crap and breathe fully in your belly and sense your feet on the ground . . . like a great martial artist. Try to hold your head up as if there's a ponytail on top, to which is attached several brightly colored helium balloons. Instead of sucking in your tummy in the dressing room, try letting it out in the new clothes. Then try buying clothes which fit a relaxed body.

This goes against the grain. And it works. We were raised to be the new women, strong and athletic, smart and successful. No one told us that one of the things our lovers would love about us, would comment about in wonder, was how soft we are. We get stuck in thinking our problems are about fat. Huge people can move gracefully and well, can look beautiful in their bodies. It's how they carry themselves, how they show they respect themselves that counts.

A word about support groups: To take a pro-women's-body stand in an anti-women's-body society is a radical act. You're going against the crowd, actually acting on the rugged-individualism shtick. You'll need support, perhaps. Seek it out, either by forming your own group[40] through an advertisement in the paper or on a computer bulletin board, or attending a bunch of Overeaters Anonymous meetings, trying out different ones to see if you can find one you like—the best ones are often weekend women's meetings. They're free.

Why bother doing all the work to resolve the food/fat/thin dilemma? Why not live with the yickety-yak that may have been your closest companion for years? For the purposes of this book, so that you can revel in undistracted glory in your clothes. The larger purpose is to enjoy your life. Dealing with feelings about fat and thin, dealing with a wacky mind, rather than allowing the feelings to rule you, is a way to start living more fully. Instead of waiting to be thin to live, you decide to start where you are, with what you've got. It's work. Here are signs that the mind is shifting:

My friend Sarah used to envy a mutual friend's skeletal skinniness, but now notices how our friend's body fills out clothes, that she doesn't like how bony butts look in trousers, that she feels trousers look better with a fleshy round behind in them.

Laurel, who was very thin before her pregnancy, talks about how her body changed after giving birth.

Now I'm on the other side of the coin. I think your weight is right when you feel healthy, when you feel like you can take a good walk. Your weight is wrong when you feel addled because you've eaten too little or you eat so much you're sluggish.

While mastectomy because of breast cancer isn't the answer for most people, Cathy found it liberating:

The mastectomy has actually helped free me from worrying about other people's ideas of how I should look. I used to worry that I was fat and ugly. I always thought I should lose weight. Now I really feel like I don't have to use those standards . . . I can't play the game anymore, and that's been very good.[41]

Mary, a dancer-choreographer, discusses how her viewpoint has evolved.

I was helped out by being in dance, specifically modern dance. Ballerinas definitely fall into this little anorexic syndrome, but modern dancers love to eat, and are generally heavier. You can get away with being fairly heavy and still do modern dance, which is good because I've always been heavy, and I probably will always be, for a dancer.

For some of us, this acceptance is much harder to come by. To find it, first look at your one perfect outfit. The colors all match. It's always beautiful, and, in certain situations, always appropriate. The outfit is, of course, your birthday suit, the body you were born in. It's perfect for bathing, skinny-dipping, hot-tubbing, for the sauna, for making love. It always fits. And despite what the media will have us believe, it is always lovely. One perfect outfit for so many occasions! It's easy care, ages beautifully, never needs ironing. It only needs love, attention, and respect. (And don't leave it in the sun too long.) These things cost nothing.[42]

Your job for the present moment is not to go shopping, not to buy anything new. Your job is to get to like yourself. When a therapist first suggested this idea, I was simply horrified. "Do you like yourself?" she asked. "Like myself?" I parroted, uncomfortably. I had a feeling there was a right answer to this question, but I didn't know what it was. Much later another asked, "Do you love yourself?" And I said, "Love myself? I don't even like myself." And my deficiency in this area seemed to me to be noteworthy.

The earth has often been seen as a living female body—Mother Earth. Countries and cities, too, have been seen as bodies. Perhaps peace with our bodies seems so difficult because of the difficulties of peace; strife and drama are glamorous. Peace is a tough body problem because it's also a world-view problem—as a militarily based country, we don't know how to live it. Perhaps through exploring some of the raveled edges of this body concept, we can begin to do the work of healing the tears in this country as well. Why? For the sake of world peace, and also for the sake of shopping: Shopping is so much easier when the body and soul are harmonious in clothes, when that "ahh" results. When the soul is present, the clothes look better.

Exercises

Wondering how to get the sense of the body and the soul in the clothes? Exercises! Before you start groaning, it's important to know that most of what I mean by exercise has nothing to do with muscle movement and heavy breathing. I abhor getting on hands and knees and repetitively pretending to pee on a fire hydrant. I think of exercises as a way to connect with a good sense of the body, an intimacy with it, a way of reconnecting with an abandoned inner road that had been sown with land mines of hatred.

The purpose of this portion of the book is to help you escape the obsessive rut of feeling fat or yearning to feel thin. Learn an alternative: feeling alive and good in your own skin. The exercises function like late spring in southern Alaska; they begin to break up the ice that covers the bays, and allow movement in. . . . It may be smelly, but it's kind of fun. Each exercise communicates to the body in a slightly different way. You don't have to do everything at once. Go slow. Do one exercise a year if need be. Go into each exercise and come out of it with the commitment to do what feels right for your body[43] glued firmly in the forefront of your brain. The "rigorous" exercise nonsense advocated by our society ignores that the body is capable of so much. The goal is not "burning away fat"; the goal is uncovering essence.

Writing exercises

Moving the pen across a page may be the deepest workout possible. Here are several variations.

1. If you treat the body as a stranger, perhaps you should begin an acquaintanceship by writing a letter to your body, and talking to your body as if she were someone you are interested in meeting.[44]

2. Overeaters Anonymous suggests writing your history of dieting. It might also be useful to write a history of movement, remembering ways of moving that you've loved and hated. If you're stuck, begin a page with the question, "How did I feel about high school gym class?"

3. When I tell my friend Patty, "I've spent my life camouflaging my shape," she suggests, "You're a writer, write a dialogue with your body." I refer to my body as "It" until Patty asks quietly, "It?" Patty suggests I find out what She wants to wear.

Questioner: What do you want to wear?

Answerer: Well there's this. I like protection from unkind eyes, I like to hide behind pillars of clothes. I am not safe in this world, I am hated and lusted for, I inspire extremes of emotion. I do not feel safe. And I do not know how to see and find safety.

So what I need is protection. Clothes that reveal nothing, clothes that obscure, clothes that dissemble my shape, my femaleness. I need to look like a modern eunuch. I need protection from hard eyes. This intense female needs a break from her intensity.

Q: How do I acknowledge you?

A: Listen, I was there for you through junior high, high school, college, and after. Through every triumph, every struggle, every defeat, every death, every sweet moment, I was there for you, working hard, pumping blood, feeding tissues, protecting you, giving shape. And I want an acknowledgment that I served you well and honorably. And I want it now.

Q: Anything else?

    A: Yes, please respect the overweight in others as a way of giving protection. They are protecting themselves. They are doing their best. Please do not subject them to the merciless scrutiny of the over-seeing eye. Please look at them with soft eyes.

4. Geneen Roth's book *Why Weight?* has many great writing exercises regarding food and body. If you want to do more writing exercises to explore your relationship with your wardrobe, you can substitute the word "clothes" or "shopping" when she asks you to make lists regarding "food" and "eating."

5. The words may not ever go away completely. Once a month the words "I'm so fat" run through my mind and I think, "Huh . . . period must be coming soon." And it is.

Food exercises

Swear off dieting. (Unless, of course, your doctor recommends you not eat or eat certain foods essential to your health.) Promise yourself you'll never diet again, and keep the promise. No more calorie counting, no more starvation, no more days with your mind numbed by the purity of a useless goal. How does the idea of not-dieting make you feel? What will happen?

What do you do instead? Eat what you want when you're hungry and stop when you're full. How? Practice. Wait to eat until you experience hunger and then ask yourself what and how much you want. Eat it. Pay attention to your body as you eat, stopping when your body signals "full." Sounds impossible? If the way you eat or don't eat makes you crazy, SEEK OUT EXPERT PROFESSIONAL HELP. Don't just settle for anyone. Read any of Geneen Roth's books, especially *Feeding the Hungry Heart* and *Breaking Free from Compulsive Eating*. She articulates the interior experience of a person seeking to stop dieting and coming to peace with food.

In order to be awake to your clothing, you need to awaken to your body and her needs, including the need for food. Part of doing this work is exploring the emotions that surface when you are not submerging them with food. The emotions are ancient; many dissatisfactions have been carried forward from childhood, and no amount of food will ever fill them.[45]

This is not something you do perfectly, like a diet, and then you binge because you've "fallen off." This is something to practice. So you ate past "full." Oh, well. Next time you'll try to be more attentive to "full." What do you want to do with the rest of your day? What else would you like to do aside from eating some more? Would taking a bath feel good? Reading a book? Writing?

When I started examining what I was hungry for, pausing briefly before I lunged for the refrigerator, often what I wanted wasn't food at all. It was joy, rest, or something else. For a while I liked to schlepp up to Stinson Beach, and wrapped in layers of clothes to protect me from the cold, I liked to take off my shoes and socks and walk along the shore. I always left there feeling opened up, awake, alive; these feelings informed everything I did for the rest of the day. I found new things I loved aside from food. My job became exploring and developing the dark continent which contains the maybe infinite number of something elses.

When I sought out food while listening to my hungers, the pleasure of eating regained its innocence. In looking to express the self truly through clothes, look for a body that truly expresses herself as well, feeds and satisfies herself. We live in a society where such luxuries are possible. Learn how to enjoy them. This is different from looking for approval in another's eyes, different from sneaking around looking to another for love or looking at chocolate or shopping to fill a furtive need for relaxation, different from desperately and vigilantly adopting some quack's opinion of what you should eat or what size your body should be.

Once you stop dieting, you notice that your body responds by finding a weight which feels great to move around in, and requires no effort or thought to maintain, only care. The point is not to be thin, it's to be healthy, to be able to approach food with sanity. Sanity creates an aura of almost mystical and unshakable beauty.

I lost forty pounds ten years ago by promising to stop dieting and to stop looking at the scale for validation. This promise, forged in my earlier, more physically expanded body, is the heart of the matter. It is more important than any size because it creates a freedom inside, and opens the self to a hard-earned acceptance of being large, beautiful, luscious. That was a glorious moment. I don't diet; I gave up on that. You can, too. A journalist friend wrote me about when she found her true calling: "I didn't really want to diet, I wanted to edit. I just had the letters scrambled."

Art exercises

For many people, there's a bridge to cross, from seeing beauty in other bodies to seeing the beauty in themselves. In the women's locker room at the swimming pool I saw many different naked bodies: stealing covert glances, I felt abashed and buoyant about how lovely they are. Yet, as I listened to how women talk about these bodies, I heard their sadness, distress, and self-alienation. Their friends' sympathetic murmurs, supportive of "the problem," make me want to spit. Their "figure problems" are problems of the psyche, not the body.

Studying art gave me nourishment I found nowhere else in my life. I also began drawing myself just to see what was there. I needed to see the body as a whole, not as individually wrapped parts. When we buy groceries, we see meat as legs, breasts, ribs. When we go to exercise class we work abs, thighs, butts. If we do see our body as parts, how can we suffuse our gaze with love?

Imagine a priceless work of sculpture, an exquisite work of art made from your figure. It exists. At some point in time people would've killed for your beauty. Remember, fashion changes, beauty remains.[46]

Imagination exercises

- What is the size of the protective bubble that surrounds you?
- How much "space" do you take up, or allow yourself to take up, in your life?
- Does it vary depending on whether you're on a city street or in your home? Does it vary depending on whether you're at work or with friends?

Melissa Batchelder mentions her small size. She doesn't dress like some petite people who dress cute. In fact, I don't think of her as small. Melissa replied:

Just recently when I went to the doctor's office, the nurse weighed me and she was astounded to realize that I was under a hundred pounds. She said, "I instinctively know what someone weighs when I'm getting ready to put them on the scale. I never would have guessed with you."

I perceive myself as very small in relation to other people. It doesn't particularly bother me because I've adjusted to it after forty years, but I'm very conscious of the fact that I may be shorter than someone.

They did a study a few years ago in San Quentin prison about the bubble that people have around them, the space in which you're allowed to stand if you're a stranger or an intimate friend. And in jails, the bubble they have across their shoulders and their front is very, very small. In back, it's considerably larger because they're much more aware of people behind them out to do them harm. Whereas most people have got it out in front, out in back, and less on the sides. For example, the Japanese people they studied seem to have a much smaller bubble because they're used to being in closer quarters and vice versa in less populated countries.

But for me, the bubble is a safety zone to keep people out. It's also a safety zone to keep myself in. It protects my emotional being as well as keeps people away.

I look at that almost as having as much of an effect on my way of existence as clothing. Because clothing to my mind is the visible part of that bubble. I think that the way that I dress and the way that people dress in general either enhances or defeats that bubble, or has a significant effect on the way that bubble fits.

What's your "safety bubble" like? Where does it need strengthening? Make the necessary repairs.

Mirror exercises

Do you hate looking at yourself in the mirror without any clothes on? I do.
—Alexandra Penney, Editor-in-Chief, *Self* magazine[47]

She was the editor-in-chief of one of the top women's magazines, the one that calls itself a "healthy" alternative to fashion magazines. For this position, they couldn't have hired someone who at least liked herself?[48]

Life is full of mirrors that spring upon us. If seeing yourself in this way depresses you, take comfort: at least you know you're not a vampire. Sometimes people use counseling to accept what the mirror reflects about their looks. Ann, a woman interviewed in Wendy Chapkis' *Beauty Secrets*, said, "About a year ago, I went into therapy, because who wants that shock every time you pass a department store window. I just needed to integrate what I really look like with who I am. You don't want to be confronted with your physical difference all the time. But the shock is enough to kill you if you keep hiding from it."[49] (Ann has diastrophic dwarfism.) And some people are happy about the reflection in the store window. Fashion scholar Iris Young comments, "I love to walk down a city street when I feel well dressed and to catch sight of my moving image in a store window, trying not to see myself seeing myself."[50]

In complete privacy, take off your clothes and look in a mirror. (By the way, if you are planning to spend some time looking at yourself naked, please make sure you're warm enough and stay warm.) Move your shoulders up, down, around. Notice how many ways there are to move your shoulders that look different from any picture of a woman you've ever seen. Notice what your range of movement is, what feels comfortable. Try that with other parts of your body as well, whatever you feel like moving. Put your clothes back on and look in the mirror. Do you see anything different?

Can you smile for yourself, at yourself, genuinely? How does it feel to be asked to smile?

Designer Sonia Rykiel, the inspiration behind Robert Altman's fashion film *Ready to Wear*, strongly advocates mirror gazing:

"Clothes are beautiful," she adds, "but they are only the wrapping, the decor. Attitude is a woman's manner of being. It is the way she sits, moves, walks and carries herself." This demeanor is achieved through self-knowledge and education, and once she has it, Rykiel states, a woman will look "fantastic in her eighties.". . . A woman must stand in front of the mirror for an hour, a day, a week or even a couple of months, the designer explains, to understand what she has to show and what she has to hide. "Once you know that," Rykiel says, "you can play with fashion. If you play, but don't know how, it's terrible."[51]

Rhonda Pretlow also suggests using the mirror as a self-teaching tool:

I would say spend a lot of time writing in your journal. Spend a lot of time alone, naked maybe, in a room looking at your body and getting in touch with who you are. Once you know who you are, then you'll automatically gravitate towards clothes that express that. You'll say, "This is incompatible with me. Ah, this is more me!" I think it will just happen. I'm not saying "Buy this" or "Buy that," because everyone's different. The garment has to be, it has to say, "you."

You're making a statement. You're saying who you are so you're not fooling people. You're not trying to fool them with your spandex girdle, your fake blonde bouffant hairstyle, your ten-inch nails, or whatever. Unless that's who you are.

Don't try to fool anyone. It should just be more of an expression of you. The only reason somebody wouldn't be able to do it is if they didn't know who the heck they are.

By the way, does anyone else find it odd that some ways we look at ourselves without benefit of a mirror are from a perspective no one else sees and no one comments on? We see a large shoulder, look down the arm to the hands. We look down the body, see the round breasts, perhaps the belly rising up like a mountain between? Perhaps we see the toes peeking out the top of the belly? Without using the mirror, how on earth could we be expected to have any perspective on our physiques?

Movement exercises

1. The Feldenkrais method, among others, offers exercises in movement where you don't have to move a muscle—someone else does it for you. The work is finding someone you feel good about working with.

2. Stance. It's worthwhile to try out the Susie Orbach experiment of "projecting different aspects of your personality through your stance."[52] You can pull down the curtains and play in front of the mirror. See how many different attitudes you can convey through your body. What does a strong, relaxed stance feel like? What does a happy body look like? Here's an abbreviated version of her exercise about inhabiting your body:

   > Sit down in the chair and close your eyes, follow your breathing for a moment and try to get a feel of your body from inside, and a mental picture of how you look sitting in the chair. . . .sit in a position that expresses how you feel about your body. . . . Now strike a confident pose . . . now an eager one . . . now an open attitude to the world . . . now a withdrawn stance. . . . Just feel the internal changes and the shifts you are required to make. . . . Now I'd like you to imagine that you are your ideal size. . . . What are you spontaneously expressing in this pose?. . . . Now try a series of poses just as you did before, only at your ideal size . . . open, withdrawn, eager, confident, reticent, and so on. . . . What are you afraid of, or what do you not want to express right now?. . . Now open your eyes, stand up and take a good look at your whole body in the mirror. . . . Stand comfortably and try to project a feeling of accepting and liking yourself . . . turn sideways so that you get another picture of yourself. . . . Just look, try not to judge. . . . Turn forwards again and, starting with your toes, look all the way up your body and, when you reach your head, look from your head all the way down. . . . Now turn frontwards and resume your usual stance. . . . What are the differences? . . . Now sit down on the chair as if you were your ideal size. . . . What do you see? . . . How would it be for you to hold this position regularly? . . . [53]

3. Diana Vreeland was emphatic on the contribution of good posture to a good life:

   > The back, you know, is the most important part of your body. I'm never tired at the end of a day—never. It's because of the way I sit. At the Metropolitan

Museum I have the same kitchen chair I used to have at *Vogue*. They sent it to me because nobody else would ever use such a hideous-looking thing in their swell offices—but it supports me at the base of my back, and that's what's important.[54]

The trick to good posture is having it so good you don't have to remember. I'm amazed at how wonderful it is to finally have a good chair to sit in as I write (I'm also amazed that I will deviously find ways to slump. Even in this chair, in which sitting up straight is comfortable, I have to constantly monitor myself.) I notice over and over how sitting up consciously after slumping affects my well-being.

4. The Naked Exercise: On a day you have all to yourself, risk going naked until you experience some desire to dress. When you feel the need for clothes, see how it feels for a minute or so.[55] What causes you to want to dress? What would you would wear if you could wear anything? The rules about dressing are not as solid as we think. My mother liked to houseclean in the nude while playing opera records really loud: "If you're alone, who cares?" Then she jumped in the shower and scrubbed off. None of her clothes got dirty.

When you dress, start with something you feel at home in. Put it on. Wear it around. Write a little about what it makes you feel like, what it gives you; think about how that could be translated to garments used for other purposes. Start to think about bringing that experience of comfort with you into every situation. In the privacy of your own room, with the shades drawn, do a dance that expresses what kind of comfort works for you in your life.

5. Movement as magic: Sports have a bad rep among women, because we're not taught to love movement for the joy of it. Sports are a way to punish our bodies into "shape." We're given strange uncomfortable "womanly" ways to walk, move, and hold ourselves. We forget what we knew as babies: how to move freely and joyfully. On a practical level, we are denied access to sports by a society that literally values men's movement more than women's: men's collegiate teams get 70 percent of all scholarships, 77 percent of all operating dollars, and 83 percent of all recruiting money.[56] How many professional women's sports teams can you name? How many have you seen on TV? We are systematically denied the benefit that love of sport and commitment to it can bring. The benefits are not just psychological. One study found, "High school girls who play sports are 80 percent less likely to get pregnant, 92 percent less likely to get involved in drugs and three times more likely to graduate."[57]

The martial art of Aikido astonished me when I first witnessed it, but it took me eleven years to actually try it.[58] And then I enjoyed the experience so much that the energy to hate my body diminished, then vanished. Swimming for twenty minutes does it too: "magic" occurs. Professional volleyball player Gabrielle Reece wrote in *Elle* magazine: "I am really focused on what happens to a woman's attitude when she feels healthy. Forget fancy clothes. Nothing feels more luxurious than feeling good in our own skin. Nothing."

About the French expression for this: bien dans ma peau—good in my own skin,[59] Pierre comments, "One can only deplore the gap in female psychology between the rarefied, mysteriously seductive world of high fashion—into which one can presumably enter only through the eye of a needle—and a reality that is far more exquisite with possibilities than women seem to want to recognize."[60]

Large body size is no excuse for non-participation. There are wonderful exercise classes available especially for large women. Nancy Roberts has talked extensively with large women about the positive side effects of these classes. Every woman emphasizes her feelings of achievement: "Just as dressing beautifully breaks down the 'fat and ugly' stereotype, so getting out there and doing something energetic starts to dispel the 'fat and lazy' image."[61]

Roberts discusses what happens during the complicated routines in dance classes for large women:

> The moving and the dancing become almost a sensual pleasure, and fat women aren't used to being sensual. Or if they are, they hide it very carefully. The only time they may get this same sort of pleasure is if they're very secure with the one man they've known for a long time and the lights are out. For big women to take joy in their bodies in the way that I think many slim women take for granted is a lovely thing to see.[62]

What's the key to making it in such a class? Have your primary commitment be to respect what your body is telling you, moment to moment. The minute the body sends the signal, "Gosh, this is killing me" and you ignore it, you've demonstrated a commitment to pain more important than commitment to success. Stop, give yourself a break, and try something that feels good. If you feel like trying again, don't work yourself to the point of brutality. Consider lap swimming: the water does the carrying, and because no one swims with glasses or contacts, your privacy is assured. The whole swimsuit purchase crisis is a moot point if the suit is actually just for swimming. Sensing movement for the joy of it (not to punish the transgressor who ate), as a regular practice, gradually supports the emergence of understanding and appreciation of your own unique beauty.

6. If you use the number from a scale as a weapon against yourself, perhaps don't use the scale. The number signifying your weight doesn't matter to dress. Instead, information about your true current proportions is essential to giving you the freedom to chose clothing that enhances what is beautiful. There is an excellent physical exercise you can do in your own home that always reaps enormous benefits. And you only have to do it once. Throw out your scale. I got a hammer and screwdriver, put on steel-toed boots, and after taking mine apart, smashed it to bits. It took longer than I thought it would, but it was an entirely worthwhile activity. If you don't have the energy for that, try putting your scale in a bag and donating it to charity.

By "acceptance," we do not mean "true love," or "deep spiritual communion"; no need to envision yourself accepting your figure with deep happiness and dancing down a garden path between rows of lavender and fuchsia flowering shrubs: these things are for the more advanced. Basic acceptance will suffice: looking at the facts and figures and saying, "Yes, this is so. From the trips to the doctor's office, I know my height to be. . . ." Facts are facts.

Touch your waist, rest your hands on your hips, feel your ribs by gently pressing the skin between your breasts and belly. Look at your feet. Touch your calves. Acceptance does not mean getting nasty about what you see. It means looking at the body and saying, "This is the way it is." Whenever possible, touch the skin and the muscle. Whenever possible, touch the skin to feel the bones . . . at your forehead, behind your neck, at your hands and feet (dozens of bones there), and knees and ankles. Press in to the hip, the pelvis; touch the elbow. It's all there, and the information is free. What color are your eyes? Your hair? What color is your skin? (Even albinos aren't truly white, and very few people are black like the sky which cushions the stars. Most people range from pale pinky mustard to cocoa-colored. Find some words to figure out what color you are.) What colors are your lips, your hands, your nipples? What colors are you?

So today, Sunday, I lie on the white-carpeted floor in the very sunny living room, and put my hands on my ribs. I feel them move as I breathe. I see blue sky, leaves beginning to notice fall, and the bright light of day. I finally have a body I enjoy. This is something worth dressing.

Notes:

1. Wolitzer, Meg. "Mirror Image." *Elle*. May 1994. Page 192.
2. Duffy, Mary. *The H-O-A-X Fashion Formula*. Page 12.
3. Temple, Norman and Denis Burkitt. *Western Diseases*. Page 154.
4. Ewen, Stuart. *All Consuming Images*. Page 32.
5. Fraser, Laura. "Fat-free but getting fatter." *Vogue*. January 1995. Page 93.
6. Berg, Rona. "85% of women don't like their bodies." *Self*. June 1994. Page 136.
7. Ibid.
8. Orbach, Susie. *Fat Is a Feminist Issue II*. Page 24.
9. Kidwell, Claudia and Valerie Steele, eds. *Men and Women*. Page 20.
10. Merriam, Eve. *Fig Leaf*. Page 76.
11. Daria, Irene. *The Fashion Cycle*. Page 122.
12. Gilday, Katherine. *The Famine Within*.
13. Stone, Elizabeth. "Can Vanna White Make You Sick?" *Elle*. June 1995. Page 38.
14. Goday, Dale and Molly Cochran. *Dressing Thin*. Page 10.
15. Ewen. Page 180.
16. Merriam. Page 209.
17. Kent Bloomer and Charles Moore observe something important and simple in too complex a way: "[O]ne of the most hazardous consequences of suppressing bodily experiences and themes in adult life may be a diminished ability to remember who and what we are. The expansion of our actual identity requires greater recognition of our sense of internal space as well as of the space around our bodies. Certainly if we continue to focus on external and novel experiences and on the sights and sounds delivered to us from the environment to the exclusion of renewing and expanding our primordial haptic experiences, we risk diminishing our access to a wealth of sensual detail developed within ourselves—our feelings of rhythm, of hard and soft edges, of huge and tiny elements, of openings and closures, and a myriad of landmarks and directions which, if taken together, form the core of our human identity." [Ewen. Page 184]
18. Kidwell. Page 9.
19. Roth, Geneen. *Feeding the Hungry Heart*. Page 191.
20. Gilday, Katherine. *The Famine Within*.
21. Tannen, Mary. "Playing the Numbers." *Vogue*. November 1994. Page 346.
22. Swift. Page 8.
23. Berg, Rona. "85% of women don't like their bodies." *Self*. June 1994. Page 136.
24. Benstock, Shari and Suzanne Ferris, eds. *On Fashion*. Page 38.
25. Stacey, Michelle. "How Weight Watchers Betrays You." *Elle*. April 1994. Page 175.
26. Gilday, Katherine. *The Famine Within*.
27. Swift, Pat and Maggie Mulhearn. *Great Looks*. Page 1.
28. Kolata, Gina. "The Catch-22 Rule of Losing Weight." *New York Times*. March 12, 1995. The Week in Review. Page 2.

29. Gilday, Katherine. *The Famine Within.*

30. Iggers, Jeremy. "Innocence lost." *Utne Reader.* November/December 1993. Page 56.

31. Gilday, Katherine. *The Famine Within.* By making even healthy pleasure a sin, does self-improvement become falsely equated with moral uplift? What happens, then, when self-improvement comes in conflict with other values, e.g., accepting a high-status but socially harmful job? Or what happens when self-improvement becomes a "liberating" experience for people overreacting to the problem? The personal is political, but how far can this be taken?

32. Gilday, Katherine. *The Famine Within.*

33. Orbach, Susie. *Fat Is a Feminist Issue.* Page 144.

34. Robin, Jennifer. *Clothe Your Spirit.* Page 20.

35. Gross, Amy. "Editor's Page." *Elle.* May 1994. Page 42.

36. Chapkis, Wendy. *Beauty Secrets.* Page 13.

37. Goday. Page 25.

38. Roth, Geneen. *Feeding the Hungry Heart.* Page 37.

39. In a spirit of gusto and hope, writer Ron Rosenbaum tells us of the good in fat, after taking the customary walk past the wonderfully fleshy, sensual paintings of Rubens. He extolls the joys of eating a Kobe beef steak from Japan: "After I took a couple of bites, tears literally welled up in my eyes—tears of joy, yes, tears of spiritual gratitude, tears that imitated the tears of fat welling up out of the tender matrix of red meat when my knife cut into it. But more than that, I think, they were tears of reunion, a spontaneous celebration of the primal reunion of body and soul, a juicy communion in the mingling of blood and fat with our own sweet, fatty, meaty, carnal innocence." [Rosenbaum, Ron. "An Ode to Fat." *Harper's Bazaar.* March 1994. Page 190.]

40. See Susie Orbach's guidelines in *Fat Is a Feminist Issue.*

41. Chapkis. Page 27.

42. Where did I get this idea? When we were twelve and studying for the Bas Mitzvah in Hebrew school, we read *Song of Solomon*:

> How beautiful are thy feet with shoes, O prince's daughter! The joints of thy thighs are like jewels, the work of the hands of a cunning workman. Thy navel is like a round goblet, which wanteth not liquor: the belly is like a heap of wheat set about with lilies. Thy two breasts are like two young roes that are twins. Thy neck is as a tower of ivory; thine eyes like the fish pools of Heshbon, by the gate of Bathrabbim: thy nose is as the tower of Lebanon which looketh toward Damascus. . . . How fair and how pleasant art thou, O love, for delights.

Jo in *Little Women* never thought she was fat. Neither did Laura in *Little House on the Prairie.* Lucy in *The Chronicles of Narnia* did not have a weight problem, nor did anyone suggest she lose a few pounds. Jane Eyre didn't sit at the top of a tower knowing that someday, if she lost weight, her prince would come. Cathy in *Wuthering Heights* did not hold her belly and think, "Fat fat fat. I'm so ugly." Cinderella just needed a new dress, Rapunzel just had to let her hair down, Dorothy just needed to click her shoes together and say, "There's no place like home." For my heroines, weight and fat were not the issue.

43. Roberts, Nancy. *Breaking All the Rules*. Page 180.

44. From a flyer by the Body Image Task Force, P.O. Box 934, Santa Cruz, CA 95061-0934.

45. Roth. *Feeding*. Page 178.

46. The idea of learning to see yourself through paintings and sculpture is played out clothes-wise in *The Triumph of Individual Style,* which suggests turning from looking at the beauty of art to seeing the beauty in oneself:

> By regarding yourself as a work of art at every stage or passage of your life, you will continue to revive your every feature with new character, so that it is never seen as an imperfection or flaw. Rather, each new line and shape, color or texture on your face and body is simply viewed as more new material for expressing yourself as a unique creation of time. [Mathis, Carla and Helen Connor. *The Triumph of Individual Style*. Page 7.]

47. Penney, Alexandra. "Letter from the editor." *Self.* June 1994. Page 133.

48. I'll stop ranting for a minute to discuss events in the history of mirrors that demonstrate other possibilities for what can be seen in them. The earliest known mirrors date from 4500 B.C. [Goldberg, Benjamin. *The Mirror and Man*. Page 27.] Until the modern age, people believed mirrors possessed magic powers. The ancient Chinese "believed that the mirror reveals to him who looks upon it the mask with which he faces the world. This self-study leads to self-knowledge, and self-knowledge to self-control, faithfulness, and steadfastness." [Goldberg. Page 48.] Mirrors became a powerful tool for deep "reflection." We will not be wasting our time today to gaze into a mirror and ask ourselves what our masks are, if we can learn to look with kindness and respect. The Greek mythic figure Narcissus caught sight of his reflection in the water and fell in love. We should be so lucky. Most of us gaze into mirrors with seemingly built-in self-loathing. Studies of people who describe themselves while looking in a mirror show that "most subjects experienced gross distortions of their perceived reflections in a multitude of strange ways. . . . The mirror often projects an image modified by the way we believe we appear." [Goldberg. Page 245.] Many women avoid the glance in the full-length mirror because they fear having to deal with the avalanche of criticism that comes with it. One person told me cheerfully that she liked her bathroom mirror a great deal. All she could see was her head, and that was all she liked about herself. I asked her how she saw herself and she ferreted through a drawer and pulled out a one-inch-square head shot on an old driver's license. "This is my image of myself," she said. I replied, "You have no body? You're only from the neck up?" "Yes," she said. We both laughed. She said, "Exactly! I actually am very dissociated with my body. I have my face and my mind, and then my body is just some weird free-floating thing which came with the package."

In Joan Songer's personal style class, when she suggested people look at themselves in the mirror—below the neck—there was a low uneasy murmur. What are your reasons for not looking? In 54 A.D. Paul talked of seeing "through a glass, darkly" [Goldberg. Page 117.] (more because mirrors weren't as well made then and the reflections they cast were shadowy—the modern glass mirror as we know it was invented in the Renaissance). Columnist William Safire comments, "The point is that wisdom will come when a person wrestles with his personal angel and comes face to face with God's grace: 'now I know in part: but then shall I know even as also I am known.'" [Safire, William. "The Goldilocks Recovery." *New York Times Magazine*. January 29, 1995. Page 18.]

Consider through what distorted mirrors you see yourself so cruelly. We look in the mirror and assume we are seeing reality; perhaps it is more accurate to say we are seeing the degree of self-hatred or self-love available to us. Wrestle with your personal angel. As mirrors became more available (not solely the property of royalty and priests) in the medieval period, artwork begins to warn of the problems of mirror-gazing: self-obsession. Tapestries show the dangers of too much mirror-gazing, the twin deadly sins of pride and lust. As the omnipresent practical mirror gradually replaced the rare holy or royal one, it became dissociated from theological warnings about metaphysics and associated with earthly distractions. People who were tired of being chastised for mirror-gazing would place a mirror inside a book so others would think they were reading.

Self-obsession, or obsession with one's looks, can be counterproductive, the mirror acting as a suck of time and thought. Graphic designer Jackie Thaw only allows herself a quick glance in the mirror before leaving the house, because she finds that once she starts looking she could spend hours fussing, time she'd rather spend elsewhere. Lex Eurich comments: "I will look in the mirror at the clothes and play with different shoe combinations or a different belt, but I'm never really looking at me. I'm looking at the clothes. . . ." Whom do you make your image for when you look in a mirror? What do you look at?

49. Chapkis. Page 20.
50. Benstock. Page 199.
51. Buckley, Richard. "Sonia Rykiel." *Mirabella*. December 1994. Page 150.
52. Orbach. Page 158.
53. Orbach, Susie. *Fat Is a Feminist Issue II*. Pages 149-151.
54. Vreeland, Diana. *DV*. Page 4.
55. Orbach. *Fat Is a Feminist Issue*. Page 118.
56. Nakao, Annie. "Playing a man's game for life." *San Francisco Examiner*. September 1, 1993. Page C-1.
57. Nakao. Page C-1.
58. See *Women in Aikido* by Andrea Siegel.
59. Pierre, Clara. *Looking Good*. Page 92.
60. Pierre. Page 92.
61. Roberts, Nancy. Page 180.
62. Roberts, Nancy. Page 176.

What Makes You Feel Beautiful?

Beauty is but the spirit breaking through the flesh.
—Rodin[1]

Everything has beauty, but not everyone sees it.
—Confucius[2]

Yesterday in the Rodin sculpture garden at Stanford, after looking around to be sure there were no guards, I touched them. I felt the muscle and bone beneath the surface. Up the backs I could feel the vertebrae, even though I couldn't see them. I felt calves, thighs, ankles, feet, backs, bellies, butts.

An Englishwoman with a plummy voice (she and a companion were the only other people there) walked up to me and asked abruptly, "What are you doing?" I explained, and then she started doing it, too. "Oh," she said. "Lovely." We who love beauty need to handle this vulnerable feeling carefully and with discretion.

Beauty is available to everyone, but the means to express our unique beauty may have been obscured. We compound our confusion by trying to paste the misinformation in circulation about beauty onto ourselves, before we have a direct experience of our own beauty.

If we get trapped into thinking we have to conform to the tall-blonde-skinny-young beauty cliché, no one wins except the people who profit from suckers (and, to a certain extent, the tall, blonde, etc. people). We become victims of the failure of the imaginations of those who run the American media. What can we say about a form where the hero can look like King Kong, but the heroine has to look like Jessica Lange? Does anyone detect a bias? The useless definition of beauty as the sole possession of celebrities with such appearances leaves most of us perpetually outside the warm room where beauty is appreciated. And coming close isn't close enough.

I remember a struggling anorectic friend, who is attractive that way, once saying to me that it was harder for her because she was so close to the ideal. She said she felt like a moth flying too close to the pure fire of a cultural shrine. Beauty scholar Nancy Baker comments that the advantages of being conventionally beautiful might turn into disadvantages as a woman ages, particularly if she has developed little other than her looks.

Psychologist Ellen Berscheid, who compared the happiness of middle-aged women, found that women who had been beautiful when young weren't as happy as women who had been more ordinary-looking. Also, the pretty women weren't as well-adjusted emotionally and were less satisfied with their lives than women who'd always been plain.[3]

We often confuse beauty with glamor. Glamor is available to anyone who wants to do the huge amount of work to create the frozen image for the photo or screen. No one jogs in sequins or swims in full maquillage. The only glamor-sanctioned movement is ballroom dance, and then you have to step backward in high heels all the time. If your beauty ideal is glamor, read Dianne Brill's *Boobs, Boys, and High Heels or How to Get Dressed in Just Under Six Hours*, a time-investment approach for va-va-va-voom glam. But don't expect to be able to breathe.

We may want glamor because we see it in fashion. Let's check out some more squirming insects under that rock. Olivia Goldsmith, author of the fashion-industry blockbuster *Fashionably Late* and co-author of the clothing self-help primer *Simple Isn't Easy,* wrote:

Fashion wasn't glamorous on the inside: it was all about production and a lot of hard work, kind of like a sausage factory. But it had to look glamorous, even if the designers didn't. If Gianfranco Ferré was overweight, if Mary MacFadden was bizarrely pale, if Donna Karan was chunky, and Karl Lagerfeld was balding, they juiced up their image by using models who weren't.[4]

Irene Daria, author of *The Fashion Cycle*, wrote about the external aspects of a model's work:

Modeling is supposed to be glamorous but almost every model I have ever come in contact with hates her job and does it only for the money. This poor beautiful girl, for instance, is spending her day standing around in high heels, bored in a windowless store, listening to music from the video and the hissing sound of the air-conditioning coming through vents. It's neither an easy job nor a stimulating one.[5]

Stuart Ewen points out the deeper downside to glamor: "The idealized human becomes the plastic human, able to maintain a perpetual smile, not one whose beauty requires a lingering familiarity, an intimacy."[6] Glamorous images are not touched, tasted, or smelled.

What is the media's responsibility? The apologists proclaim, "Mankind has always viewed beauty unrealistically,"[7] citing the example of the ancient Greeks who believed beauty was reason enough to forgive criminal activity. I believe we can't afford to wait for the media to change. There's no reason not to question this tyranny, poke holes in its cruel rule, and liberate ourselves from its confining vision.

Feminist foremother Betty Friedan comments that the influence of the women's movement has begun to change the way women perceive themselves: "There isn't a single image of physical beauty anymore. . . . There's a lot of individuality. . . . Somehow, women who before wouldn't have been considered pretty or beautiful, when they really feel good about themselves as people, look beautiful."[8]

Even if this new version of beauty is as "unrealistic" as the old ones, it's worth embracing. I asked many people, "What makes you feel beautiful?" Only a few had trouble with the question. One was a high school homecoming queen. Another, I fear, had lived too long in Los Angeles. Most people I spoke with don't possess the looks demanded by Hollywood, yet they had an experience of their own beauty. In retrospect, I theorized that perhaps everyone had a ready answer because I always asked "What makes you feel beautiful?" rather than, "What makes you look beautiful?" Looking beautiful is too charged an issue. "Looks" are a concept that has been commandeered by the media's airbrushed, computer-composite ideal. In addition, "looking beautiful" has the inherent problem of being attractive to *others*. As there are over 5.7 billion others on the planet, each with their own idea of beauty, this can be a problematic concept. What looks beautiful to me may not look beautiful to you. For example, on the train yesterday morning I saw a woman wearing a black kimono-style jacket over a black skirt, and black shoes. She had on a white shirt and a red Mickey Mouse tie, and little odd-shaped sunglasses. Her grey hair was in a bun. I said to her, "Excuse me, you look fabulous." She replied, "Thank you. My two grandchildren were at my house this weekend. I needed something to perk me up. Not bad for 62, huh?" I agreed.

Since we can't live with the certainty of enjoying others' appreciation, we who are interested might do well to learn to enjoy our own. "Feeling" beautiful implies an audience of one—you. Feeling beautiful starts inside, creating a joy and confidence which radiates to your surface and significantly influences those around you, so you "look" beautiful—bearing in mind that if you feel beautiful, it doesn't matter how many others "get it" because it's yours already.

The beauty truth? Francesco Scavullo, the *Cosmopolitan* cover photographer, states: "I think that there is beauty in everybody. You are born with it."[9] Don't start snorting yet. Appearances are the way we witness others' beauty through sight, a gift of light. The poets give us selective glimpses of this. Mostly we ignore them. Here writer Harold Brodkey talks about this quality:

> In sunlight, near the ocean, everyone is strangely wonderful-looking. I am not talking about beauty in terms of bones and muscle but about a quality that bodies have at the beach, and, in the city, in clothes: they give off a sense of the moment, a sense of pleasure—and a suggestion of some potential satisfaction to be had in moments ahead.[10]

Contrary to what the cosmetics and fashion industry would have us believe—that beauty must be bought—our experts disagree. Naomi Wolf, author of *The Beauty Myth,* observes:

> Light is in fact the issue, central to an innate way of seeing beauty that is shared by many, if not most women and me. . . . Some see that radiance as inseparable from love and intimacy. . . . Others might see it in a body's sexuality; still others, in vulnerability, or wit. It strikes one often from the face of someone telling a story or listening intently to someone else. Many have remarked on how the act of creation seems to illuminate people, and have noticed how it envelops most children—those who have not been told yet that they are not beautiful. . . . The [cosmetics industry] offer[s] to sell women back an imitation of the light that is ours already, the central grace we are forbidden to say that we see. . . . Women "know" that fashion photographs are professionally lit to imitate this radiant quality. But since we as women are trained to see ourselves as cheap imitations of fashion photographs, rather than seeing fashion photographs as cheap imitations of women, we are urged to study ways to light up our features as if they were photographs marred by motion, our faces handled like museum pieces, expertly lit with highlights, lowlights. . . .[11]

Wolf discusses encouraging and fostering one's own uniqueness. Resonating with Wolf, Eileen Sullivan talks about what makes her feel beautiful and how that relates to clothing:

> It's really an internal feeling. It's an energy. It's completely independent of clothes. A lot of times I'm naked. It's a feeling of peace, self-acceptance, and it can be with someone else or alone. . . . Clothes can be a way of expressing beauty, and it works when we know our own inner beauty. It's a cheap hit when we don't.

As I move through time and space, my face and body reflect the changes which occur. The fabrics, colors, and designs in which I feel most at ease, and that cause me to look my loveliest, may remain constant through time. This has nothing to do with fashion.

It would seem that beauty is our right as creatures with energy, the power of movement, and thought. We don't need to make ourselves distinctive through the most currently peddled "hot" styles. The closer we are to our own real work or path, to whatever calls us—without struggle—the closer we come to standing in the flow of that beauty and letting it flow through us. When talking with others about this, I notice that when someone can feel that they're beautiful in another's eyes, something softens in them, a barrier comes down. I was talking to a physicist about whether it's possible that people actually emanate light. He tried to disabuse me of this notion. Nonetheless, I have the sense that when people allow themselves to believe that they're beautiful, something changes about the way they present themselves. There's an ease about them that makes them more comfortable to be around.

What makes you feel beautiful? When I first sought help for my eating disorder, I was referred to a psychologist from Barbados. After I described my eating and body problem to him in humiliating detail, he beamed at me and said, "In my country, you would be considered a beautiful woman."

It was very sweet of him to try to be supportive, but no way did that comment address the fact that the food problem made me completely bonkers. I went through days obsessed with apple fritters, and where I was going to find my next chocolate bar? The sugar kept me racing. I couldn't connect thoughts. I did not feel beautiful. Much later I found what makes me feel beautiful: When I'm doing something I really love, I feel connected with it and I feel radiant. I look in the mirror, I like what I see. Yesterday, near sunset, I finished working for the day and went to the market to get milk for breakfast. I put my hair up, tucked my T-shirt into my jeans, donned a denim jacket, and left. In town, the flowers are just beginning to bloom, and the air was at that perfect pre-dusk coolness, damp and sweet with the scent of the flowers. As I walked along, enjoying walking, I caught sight of a huge rose, artichokes planted and blooming as flowers, a few poppies—and I felt beautiful. No one else was around. No ball gown or prince. I felt connected to the flowers and to the earth, comfortable and safe. I was part of my earth, a flower in another form. The judgments which so often slay me were absent.

Nothing in what I wore impeded me from feeling beautiful; the shirt was soft, everything fit, nothing was too tight, the colors suited me. I was conscious of a seamless connection to that moment in time. My relaxing after a long day, and the day relaxing into evening, seemed in harmony.

What made this trip to the market different from the others? I recently moved from a dangerous neighborhood to a safe one. When I walk now, I am actually safer, there are people with gardens here, I can see flowers. In the small gesture of tucking in my shirt, I admitted I have a shape. Underneath my jacket, I was defining my shape for me.

Only recently have I been realizing that my looks have a certain delicacy, my mouth is lovely, I have beautiful hands. Most of my life, I have felt awkward and clumsy, residue from adolescence, when, due to the general horrible awkwardness that goes with puberty, I felt crude, gross, graceless, hulking. My sense of self allied me with the Hunchback of Notre Dame.

That shadow haunts me to this day. When I turn to face it, to look at it and examine it more closely, little remains of an accurate self-perception. I sometimes have a tendency to walk into things, and I can be a little bit shy, but other than that, nothing rings true about this inner Nosferatu. The ghost in the attic turns out to be just some old shreds of dark chiffon, blowing in the breeze. When I was not ready to feel beautiful, nothing would convince me. Roth offers to those in that stage:

> You are gorgeous. You deserve satisfaction and laughter in your life. You deserve pleasure. You deserve love. I can tell you this a thousand times, but you won't believe me until you experience it yourself. You won't believe me until you begin acting as if you already believe it. . . . [12]

Jewelry rep Kathy Upton only recently made the transition to beginning to accept her own beauty: "Finally in my adulthood I've been able to reach a place where I was meant to be. And perhaps nature made it so I suffered a long time so that I could enter my beauty with grace. And I am very grateful. Yes, people tell me I'm beautiful. And I accept that."

Of the many people I interviewed, one who couldn't answer the question "What makes you feel beautiful?" kept comparing his looks to those of people he'd seen while living in Los Angeles. "You can take some solace if you think that L. A. is just full of mindless people, women in white go-go boots and vain, empty men. I think that L. A. is full of devastatingly creative, talented, and energetic people, and they're beautiful, too. Then there's not a lot of solace to take."

Many people have ambivalence about their beauty. Societal pressure to be beautiful for others can force us to rebellion or rage. This "beauty is duty" concept[13] is a relic from the era when women had no legal recourse to power. Any success they achieved in society often stemmed from their ability to catch a rich husband by manipulating their looks.

Debbie, the former Homecoming Queen, also couldn't see inner beauty emanating:

> On the outside, I don't perceive myself as beautiful at all, but I do know that I am a beautiful person inside because I'm a good person and because I'm a clean person. When I look in the mirror, I don't see it.

This was not what I expected. She's gorgeous. I asked if she could talk more about inner beauty.

> All my life, I've wanted to be more like my mom who never complains about anything. She's willing to bend over backwards for anybody. To me, she's a very good and beautiful person. Somebody could not be very beautiful to the eye, but if their inside is beautiful, then they are. If I see somebody on TV that looks like they have the perfect body, the perfect face, the perfect everything, they're pretty, but how can you really say that they're a beautiful person without knowing them? I know a lot of people put the outside beauty first, as opposed to the inside beauty, which is really sad.

Why doesn't she see herself as beautiful now? Debbie says, "I think it stems from insecurity inside." I joke, "So when you get really settled and you're fifty and you're really secure, you'll look in the mirror and think, 'I am really beautiful.' " Debbie laughs and says, "Hopefully."

Early in the interviews, soon after I talked with Debbie, I talked to my friend Lauren Meredith about this and got depressed. Both of them confirmed my darkest nightmares, that my theory about beauty would find no support. My friend said with a touch of sadness, "I don't know if I ever feel beautiful. When my husband tells me, that's something that makes me feel attractive."

I commented, "So it's more about love."

"Yes," she says. "It's always nice to get complimented. I think all of us enjoy a compliment be it because we're wearing something nice or because we look happy or whatever. But I don't look at myself in the mirror and think, 'Yeah, beautiful today.' " What does she see when she looks in the mirror? "Not enough sleep."

Lauren has truly wonderful clothes. I expected there would be some sort of natural correlation between having incredibly fabulous clothing and just thinking, "Oh, okay. I'm beautiful." Lauren comments:

> I think my clothes are pretty...I like them all. I don't wear things I don't like. I think the clothes I wear to work are work-appropriate. It's not like there would be room for variation in there. It's not like, "Oh, I'll wear something beautiful today, something trashy tomorrow." The variable is, "Oh, my hair's going—"

At this point Lauren extends her index fingers upward above her head and gestures with them as though there are spikes growing out of her head.

I'm interested in this socialization that allows these three people to think of themselves as not-beautiful. When I told them I see them as beautiful, the information was resisted or dismissed. I suspect the flickering thought, "Well, if you only knew . . . " —as if the evidence of my perception is not accurate. If I only knew what? That sometimes you don't wish people well? If I only knew how much you worry, what you fear, how hard life is for you? If I knew how "terrible" your skin was under that makeup? If only I could *really* see? At the time I didn't dare say, "Wake up."

Beauty is a birthright. The diversity of ethnicity is an enormous component in beauty, creating opportunities for expression and creativity unseen in the fashion magazines. My nose, which plumps toward the end, has its own natural grace, separate from the witchy-pointed alternatives available to the fashionable few.

When I talk with Laurel Fenenga about my wonderful grandma, I mention that Grandma and I were in a restaurant one day and she pulled up her skirt a few inches and said about the family legacy, "The legs. Our legs are always good."

Laurel comments, "I've heard older women say that the legs go last. I guess it's good that I attract leg men."

"Because you'll be beautiful forever," I say.

Laurel responds, "Well, you discover that the right men think you're beautiful no matter what.

It's really important that we choose a man who will be good to our soul, good to our children. And most of us overlook some of that, and that's not good. I looked a lot before I settled."

For Melissa Batchelder, feeling beautiful has to do with both a relationship with another and how she feels about herself. I had preconceived notions about how she would view the question, based on the fact that she has a variation on the all-American-girl look. She replied:

I probably feel most beautiful when everything is clicking for me. I can feel beautiful at work, which is a frightening concept. This is not where I put a lot of my energy emotionally. The other day, I did something that I've been avoiding doing. That was an emotional release and I felt great. That, to me, translates to beautiful.

I don't generally think of myself as beautiful in a physical sense. But emotionally, I put an enormous amount of energy toward a relationship, too much, in many respects, for some people. I'll go to the mat for anybody I really care for. I pay the price for it, but I feel that's part of what makes life worth living. If I demand a lot of somebody, it's not because I'm lazy and I don't want to do it myself. That to me is true beauty. I feel the most beautiful and I'm the most satisfied with myself when I accomplish what I set out to accomplish without hurting anybody.

Some people need a little push from their social circle to see the beauty in themselves. We sometimes can see beauty in friends that they can't see. We can help them along. This differs from relying on a person outside yourself to tell you you are valuable. It's more like the "spotter," the person who stands beside the gymnast to help her learn to do the back flip.

To my surprise and relief, every one of the rest of my interview subjects answered, without qualification, the question "What makes you feel beautiful?" Experts answered the question based on both their personal experience and their years of observing others grappling with this issue. Joan Songer said:

As we experience our own beauty, we are able then to express it, to share it with other people and allow them to participate in it and respond to it. It frees us to see beauty in another even though it may be very different.

Kathryn Hoover commented:

It isn't just the outfit, you know that. And it changes over time. Right now, I feel beautiful when I'm feeling very at ease and content. At that point, confidence is implied. There's a peaceable contentment that allows me to radiate beauty regardless of what I've got on my body.

What kinds of things support that?

I meditate and I pursue a spiritual practice. I spend quiet time with myself and my cat. In general what I do is I hold myself in a very loving way.

Designer Camille DePedrini said:

It's a combination of things: It's having gone to the gym enough that week, having a lot of love and encouragement in my life; and a great dress definitely can make me feel beautiful. A great dress, great fabric.

Barbara Jay said:

For me, it's the presence of the body in the clothes. The best thing I can do for myself is to really never lose sight of my body. I love my torso. When I can wear a T-shirt like this [she points to the black shirt she has on], then I don't get lost. It's Lycra. It's very fitted. The expression I use is very "to the body." It lets my body live. I'm always saying to people: "Let your body live."

Chandra Cho answered the question:

It has to do with the inner silence, the peacefulness, like you're on a tropical beach and the sun is beating down on you. You can hear the waves crashing in the distance, and then suddenly the sand and your body laying on the beach are floating off into the universe.

She laughed. I commented, "It's a tall order." Then I asked milliner Laurel Fenenga what makes her feel beautiful.

The first words that come to my mind are white linen or crisp, clean. . . . Having grown up on a farm, "clean" is the thing I have the least confidence about in terms of how I look. "Is my hair clean? I know I had a bath this morning, but am I clean?" That kind of thing. We were a pretty grubby bunch. That's probably why I like crisp little pleats. "Crisp" is the word, if I had to use one word. "She was wearing a nice, crisp shirt." Doesn't that just say it all right there? I said "confident," not "beautiful." Several times in this conversation I've linked those two. Beauty is, I would say, something really flowing and wispy, but when I have that on, I never feel as good as the feeling of being crisp. I almost always wear linen.

I had many expectations, but I never expected "crisp."
Part of real beauty for me is "bearing," moving my body as if I cared for it, moving with pride. Emily Cho observed:

Beauty is not as far out of reach as we think—if we'd just approach it from a different angle. People don't look at us with a disdainful eye fixed on that extra half-inch, those extra five pounds. They look at the whole person in front of them, and what they see is something we can do a lot more about, in a lot less time, than trimming half an inch, or losing five pounds.

What they see is how we carry ourselves, how straight we stand, how gracefully we move, how alive our faces are. How our clothes suit us, flatter us, attract people to us. In sum, people sense how happy we are just being who we are. And they respond accordingly. The secret is to make yourself aware of yourself as you enter a room or rise from a chair. Take a moment to collect yourself. Rise to your full height before you start walking forward. The minute you straighten up, hold yourself proudly, move gracefully; you'll be surprised at the improvement. The trick is to make yourself remember to do it.[14]

People not in the industry answered in a variety of ways. Tom Hassett said, "All I can think of to say is that I feel most beautiful when I feel most open." Daphne Stannard commented:

I think my beauty lies in my passion for life. "Beautiful," the word—I conjure up a woman in a long evening gown with pearls. I am never that. "Beautiful," maybe I don't identify with that word, but I definitely think I have a beauty to me. I think that people have always been drawn to me by my energy. I am a pretty energetic person. I think Beau's drawn to me for that reason.

I mentioned that her husband Beau lights up when he talks about her. Daphne said quietly, "Yeah. So that's a huge asset of mine. I don't know where it comes from. It's not something I manipulate. It's just there. It's just me."

Libby Granett related feeling beautiful to several factors:

A staff retreat I went on a couple of years ago comes to mind. I wore a flannel shirt with a lace undershirt that just poked out the top, and jeans. It felt like a nice combination. We were at this small beach house we'd rented for two days, developing a plan of action for the year. We had intense conversation with a lot of good ideas and brainstorming, and then we took breaks. We'd turn on the rock 'n' roll. Six out of ten of us were the same age. Fifties and sixties rock 'n' roll had a really deep core meaning to us. We would dance and then we'd go back to this intense conversation. Some people I knew and felt comfortable with others—the new staff—I didn't know. There was this sense of excitement and possibilities, a wonderful combination, and I felt beautiful that weekend.

Lex Eurich commented:

Sometimes I feel beautiful in a dress. Sometimes I feel beautiful in jeans. I feel more feminine sometimes in some things, but not necessarily more beautiful. No one our age or our generation thinks that women are more beautiful when they're in a special dress. I think we see beauty in women every day. You can get dressed up and you look special, but you don't necessarily look more beautiful. Gwen looks totally beautiful, partially because she's pregnant, and partially because she got her hair cut, and it's just a beautiful frame of her face. But she's just Gwen. She's just wearing what she always wears. So it's certainly not her clothes that are affecting my perception of her as more beautiful at this point in her life.

Nick Debs said of feeling beautiful:

> It's not a question of how I look because there's nothing I can do about the way I look. It's really a question of how my clothes are feeling on me. When I feel beautiful, I feel that my clothes are all of a piece and working together. I feel comfortable with my body.

What things support that feeling comfortable in his body?

> When I've been working hard physically or mentally. I'm not talking about staying up all night smoking cigarettes and drinking coffee to finish some dumb architecture project. That's when I feel hideous. That's when I *am* hideous, too; I mean really "Eeewww!" But rather when I've been able to solve a problem either in my head or by working on it physically.
>
> Or when I've been to a beautiful place. If I'm in a good frame of mind, I absorb it unless I'm completely out of sorts. I'm thinking about if we were to take a walk on Cape Cod, around the harbor there? I have this image in my head of a beautiful day and then jumping in the water and going for a swim. Or going rowing there in the water. That will do it. That will make me feel beautiful.

Stacey Lamiero talked about what makes her feel beautiful:

> One New Year's Eve, I had a minute total to pull myself together. I wore this dress that's quite fabuloso. It's black and it's kind of scalloped around the cleavage. Not a lot of cleavage, although if mine wasn't going so far south, there might have been. It's off-the-shoulder with those big tulle sleeves. It's a little too form-fitting, but it worked. My face was broken out, and I thought I looked like hell, but I swooped my hair up into a bun, put on the big earrings, glamor-pussed up the lipstick, and I walked out of there and thought, "I look hot." That's what does it.

Ed Perry observed that like a cat, he'd be most content if he could stop whatever he was doing every fifteen minutes and just groom. For Ed, beauty is "the whole package":

> I don't feel I look really great most times when I go to work because I'll be neat and tidy, but I'm cramped for time. I get up. I have an hour to get showered, dressed, and out of here. I just kind of throw it together in the morning. But if I really spend time getting something together for a special occasion, I can look really great. And then grooming comes into play, too. Not only how my clothes look and the fact that they are ironed, but also how I'm groomed has a huge influence.
>
> I wake up from a dream feeling beautiful to my core: I am on a trip with other martial artists in Eastern Europe. After training, a teacher I respect stops me to say, "I saw you. You are beautiful." I believe him. I know what he means. He's talking about my living from my central self, acting out of

some grace which is inherent in me. My face feels still and clear in that place. It doesn't mean I am one of the great fashion-plate "beauties" of the day. That's not what I want or who I am. He's talking about something real. I go to change out of my workout clothes and I think about trying to live my life from that place. If I can compose my face in that way, how to do IT really. I slip on a diamond ring with a good-sized round white diamond and prepare to go out. I wake up.

Some questions:

1. What do you hide that is beautiful? Do you have wonderful shoulders? Do you have strength? Do you have gorgeous teeth? Are your nails "to die for"? What about your mouth—is it full and soft and lovely? Is it small and well-shaped and adorable?

2. Who trained you to hide your beauty, to think of yourself as tainted? How can you untrain yourself?

3. What makes you feel beautiful?

Remember, flowers don't have to apologize, nor do budding trees in spring.

Notes:

1. Hauser, Gayelord. *Mirror, Mirror on the Wall*. Page 63.
2. Hauser, Gayelord. Page 168.
3. Baker, Nancy. *The Beauty Trap*. Page 151.
4. Goldsmith, Olivia. *Fashionably Late*. Page 207.
5. Daria, Irene. *The Fashion Cycle*. Page 152.
6. Ewen, Stuart. *All Consuming Images*. Page 85.
7. McDowell, Colin. *The Designer Scam*. Page 204.
8. Baker. Page 161.
9. Scavullo, Francesco. *Scavullo on Beauty*. Page 140.
10. Brodkey, Harold. "The Second Skin." *The New Yorker*. November 7, 1994. Page 115.
11. Wolf, Naomi. *The Beauty Myth*. Page 104-105.
12. Roth, Geneen. *Why Weight?* Page 31.
13. Kidwell, Claudia and Valerie Steele, eds. *Men and Women*. Page 37.
14. Cho, Emily and Hermine Lueders. *Looking, Working, Living Terrific*. Page 31.

Appropriateness for Work, Travel, and Being a Blob

It is only the shallow people who do not judge by appearances.
—Oscar Wilde, *The Picture of Dorian Gray* [1]

Why is appropriateness relevant and important if you're concerned with the inner realms and clothing? What difference do "They" (everyone else) make? As clothes lovers, we are no fools. Appropriateness marks the place where satisfying the inner and self-generated needs in dressing meets the mores and expectations of those around us.

Appropriateness also includes other issues. Daphne Stannard comments:

For fun, I have always used symbols in my presentation. I would wear religious symbols like the Jewish star and a cross on my earlobe. I thought, "Put Buddha in this ear, Jewish star over there. I'm multicultural. Isn't that good?" It wasn't until Beau said, "Some people take this really seriously, and you're just sort of making fun of it," that I thought, "Huh. That never dawned on me." So now I stay away from religious icons. Beau got me to see it in another way. I never set out to offend people.

In contrast, David Simons deliberately uses symbols in a political way. One Saturday when I was working at the law firm, David came in to work wearing a baseball hat with "X" embroidered on the front (short for "Malcolm X"). He said people had a different response to it in Walnut Creek, the conservative suburb where he lives, than they did in the city. I asked him to say more about that. David replied:

Why don't I start with why I wear it at all? I wear it primarily to create cognitive dissonance in white people. I wear it on my way to work or at the law firm on weekends. I have a briefcase when I'm on my way to work on weekends and I'm on the BART train. People look at my hat and they look at me and they think "gang man" or something like that. Then they see the briefcase and they're taken aback by it. I thrive on their discomfort. I want them to question why they categorize me because of the hat and because of my skin color and then maybe think, "Oh well . . . just because other black kids wear the hat doesn't necessarily mean that they're gang members or anything like that." In Walnut Creek, I may have the hat on, but I may not necessarily have my briefcase because I'm not going to work. So they don't have the dissonance factor. Walnut Creek is almost exclusively white. So the reaction is almost pure shock, like "What the fuck are you doing here?" In San Francisco, there's more diversity, and there's more enlightenment. People don't care as much. So I don't have that same reaction. And that's fine.

Back to earliest recorded times, clothing and ornament meant something to the larger society. According to clothing historian James Laver, in ancient Egypt simply "wearing clothes was a kind of class distinction."[2] Clothing-wise, we are social show-offs. Flügel sees, in clothing history, "when a new garment is adopted, there is a tendency for it to be put on over the old garment."[3]

For women, so much depended on appropriate dress. For many centuries, women couldn't work for money (except as prostitutes) or own property. Their sole commodity, their looks (enhanced by the appropriateness of their clothing), insured safe passage to a secure marriage and social position. Cinderella didn't get the prince's attention without the dress. Some resist this issue for fear of being distracted into being once again led around by the nose by an overdeveloped desire to please others. We know in a centuries-deep and intimate way that living for others' approval is a ruthless, fruitless game. Amy Hempel accurately describes the emotional consequences in summing up the interior state of lab rats: "Their affections are unpredictable, and here it's pertinent to remember that the most obsessive lab rats are the ones who are rewarded sometimes."[4]

Today, appropriateness is a matter of life or death in only a few cases. Emergency room nurse Daphne Stannard comments:

The only pair of glasses that I had that I enjoyed were some gunmetal wire-rims, and I had rose-colored lenses put in them. Cute. But, of course, I couldn't wear them to nurse in. I mean, you assess the color of a wound: "It's rose-colored. And his nail beds are rose-colored." It wasn't that practical.

Lawyers I spoke with said that regardless of how little this has to do with justice, if you go to court and you don't dress appropriately, showing respect for judge and jury, you can lose an edge you may never recover. Attorney David Simons comments:

Of course, when I go to court, I dress very conservatively. I go through this big debate—What's too far? What's too much? And I always opt for the conservative choice. Even though I could get away with a whole lot more, I end up wearing my blue suit, most likely a red tie, and a blue shirt. You don't want the judge to rule against you because you're offending him or her by the way you dress. You want everything going in your favor including respect for the court. Part of showing respect for the court is your decorum.

Conversely, clothing worn inappropriately, or the dread of that, can be harrowing. Several people I spoke with have enormous anxiety about work clothing. Some express their dissatisfaction through dress by wearing clothes that are slightly "off." One young male manager commented succinctly: "I haven't bought new clothes for work in years because I hate work, and I hate going to work, and I hate what I do." He then walked me over to his closet for the ratty-suit tour. Coworkers observing people who use clothes this way do not necessarily see what they are trying to say; they may not notice at all or assume the employee just lacks taste.

Anxiety about appropriateness can also be a peer pressure issue. One woman remembers buying the coveted "Levi's" brand pants on sale for five dollars when she was in seventh grade. When she wore the white canvas pants to school, everyone else was wearing corduroys in blue, emerald, brown, and tan. She defiantly wore the pants anyway: "I didn't have a choice . . . I got teased." Today, you're not seeking to join or maintain your status in the cool group in school; most adults are unable to sustain that level of in-group/out-group behavior once the responsibilities of career and raising a family are levied upon them. If one or more of the groups you participate in are that nasty, you might consider finding other places to socialize, work, or live.

Another form clothing anxiety takes is appropriateness denial exemplified by the phrase, "I just don't care." Awareness of a personal style or sense of image is not to be confused with the cry, "Don't bother . . . do your own thing." This stance has everything to do with reacting against good taste and seeking to offend it rather than finding what's true for oneself. My friend Sarah's son says, "You should wear what you want," and "It isn't important." Sarah senses an underlying edge of defiance against the idea that it is important. When thus accused, he retrenches and says it's morally wrong to be judged by appearance, so he'll act as if it isn't so.

True personal style frees itself from dress style that is merely reactive.[5] In mastering this, we acquaint ourselves with the societal, as well as with the inner constraints which prevent our style's full expression. Of course, the idea that one kind of garment is inherently more moral or in better taste than another is ludicrous. Flügel comments about this idea:

> It tends to distort the apprehension of reality by substituting a symbolic morality for an effective one, there being no essential connection between, say, a black coat and tight, stiff collar and the due sense of responsibility and duty for which these garments stand.[6]

It's important to dress in a way that respects our fundamental needs and desires, but denying our participation in a social context is dishonest. When we don't own up to this social influence, it will operate on us rather than our having control of it.

Those with rebellious streaks about clothing might feel a strong ambivalence about "appropriateness," likening it to conformity or finding it alarming or impossible. Nonetheless, it is important to have the skill of blending in. To achieve one's good ends—for example, if your intention is to create a sustainable non-exploitative economy—it might be useful, with a quick trip to the closet, to dress like the economists, bankers, or lawyers so you can mingle among them freely. Sartorial outrage doesn't always create a receptive environment for your eminently sensible ideas. If you need to persuade, familiarize yourself with the most effective tools. Realistically, in an arena where change is impossible, if They—the people with either real or imagined power over you— decide They don't want you, all the perfect suits and silk scarves in the world won't change Their minds. If They're sexist, racist, consumerist, horrible people, the right clothes will have little effect on Them if you're not born to their group.

Most people are not consciously aware of the persuasive power of clothing to communicate belonging, or member-of-tribe. Because of this, people can be manipulated for the good. It may relax others if you communicate through clothing: "People like us do this sort of thing." If one has a tendency toward tie-dye, multiple piercings, etc., one might take note of what Cho calls "Dressing True to Yourself—While Bowing to Circumstance":

There'll be times in business—and in your private life as well—when your position and surroundings will be quite different from the kind of person you are. How, then, should you dress? As the person you are—even if it makes you look quite out of place? Or as the occasion demands—even though you won't feel like you? This is one of the trickiest problems a woman faces in learning how to dress well. Not only because it comes up again and again, but because so much rides on how successfully she does it.

No matter what the situation, if you don't dress true to yourself, you're going to feel uncomfortable. You won't feel natural, honest, or relaxed. And when you're ill-at-ease, everyone else will be too.

On the other hand, if you don't take the circumstances into consideration, you're going to make the people you deal with uncomfortable. They'll feel you've distanced yourself—that you think you're better than they are . . . that you don't give much weight to their standards or customs or taste. In a word, that you either don't care, or you're not very bright. Probably both. And again, the unease will be catching.

It is not a cop-out to adjust your outfit to the situation. It's a kindness and a courtesy. The whole point of dressing well is that it makes everybody feel better. All it takes is a little thought and empathy.[7]

The first hurdle: Good taste and vulgarity

Some can't master appropriateness because they don't know about the good taste/bad taste canon, a hierarchy of clothing preferences never mentioned in fashion magazines. The negative poles of women's dressing identity—"bimbo" and "bag lady"—are similar to each other in that both show extremes of fit (too tight and bare, or too loose and covered), and both signify desperation for money. Fashion, with its chronic insensitivity, plays off our nervousness about poverty (not unrealistic considering the likelihood that, as women, we'll end up poor) by regularly creating "hot" bimbo looks (most of the internalized ramifications are discussed in the chapter on sexiness), as well as trendy bag lady looks. In contrast, for the rich and those who are interested in aspiring, what is known as "good taste" forms a prison all its own. Fashion writer Kennedy Fraser notes:

There is a cult of luxurious simplicity that is often mistaken for style, but this is only a sophisticated level of good taste. The woman who extols perfectly plain white silk shirts and perfectly plain black cashmere pants and who expresses utter loathing for frills and ruffles almost never really has style. Her kind of simplicity is costly, and it is usually timid. Although it seems arrogant, her dedication to monochrome unfussiness is inspired by fear.[8]

Good taste can be a terribly boring yoke to bear. After a while, comments Diana Vreeland, former editor of *Vogue*, one calls for the "spice," vulgarity:

Vulgarity is a very important ingredient in life. I'm a great believer in vulgarity—if it's got vitality. A little bad taste is like a nice splash of paprika. We all need a splash of bad taste—it's hearty, it's healthy, it's physical. . . . No taste is what I'm against.[9]

Good taste's war with flamboyance is a class issue. The upper classes can afford to take the time to learn to discern "good" taste. Flamboyance and vulgarity are the terrain of the streetwalker, the immigrant (and paradoxically, the rich women at their charity balls).

The current criteria for good taste in daily wear require a knowledge of tailoring and fashion history. Clothes rich in color, decorative frills, and exposure of the body's shape lost their appeal to the rich as they became available to the masses in the late 1800s. Quickly, "good" clothes slimmed down, losing their flounces, petticoats, and vibrancy. In contrast to previous centuries' ostentatious dress, where the wearer was encouraged, for example, to wear intricately hand-embroidered lace collars that eighteen virgins in a convent went blind to make, the classic "good taste" item—the little black dress—was initially derived by Chanel from the maid's uniform.[10] Barbara Jay comments:

The current stage is very minimalist. It hasn't always been that way, but it is a function of tailoring, and it's a function of fine fabric that falls beautifully. You have to have the eyes to see that. That's where clothing becomes such a badge of status that only the "right" people can see it. . . . Only your best competitors will know. It's a very insidious thing.

In order to understand this, we need more of a sense of the structures of good taste:

1. Good taste has to do with education. We need to know what a well-made quality garment is, how seams are sewn, what makes a good fabric, what is a good cut.

2. Good taste separates itself from the dictates of the couture. Since designers show extremes, we can assume good taste, for daily wear, does not. Instead, good taste favors neutral colors, natural fibers, low-key textures, unexaggerated silhouettes.

3. Good taste is "ladylike," not butch, for women: *Working Wardrobe* author Janet Wallach suggests women stay away from "the heavy, masculine look."[11] That's an interesting candy to suck on. Is masculinity heavy? Is that why women can't be?

4. Good taste is subtle: The famous dandy Beau Brummel put down a young man's compliment on his dress by saying, "I cannot be elegant, since you have noticed me."[12] Tom Hassett indicates the paradox in this: "The person who strives to avoid self-consciousness is the most self-conscious, in a way, of all." We laugh.

5. Good taste is understated; according to John Fairchild, "Good fashion is simple. Bad fashion is when a woman exaggerates."[13] If you don't have time to study every nuance of clothes (free time being the luxury of the idle rich), how can you know if you exaggerate? The idea of good taste then neglects the idea that an extreme garment or color may suit you beautifully. Nothing fancy, fussy, frilly, or fuchsia.

6. Good taste does not show a lot of skin in street clothes. The torso is nearly always covered. (Swimsuits aren't street clothes.) And good taste fits. The body is covered in such a way that it can move well beneath the clothes.

7. As Richard Gump of Gump's Department Store, the famous bastion of good taste, once wrote: "Any definition of good taste in absolute terms is, of course, an absurdity."[14] (If you encode it immovably, you can't control people with the concept. They can securely purchase it by pointing at a picture and saying, "I want that.")

An old, status-oriented rich woman recently moaned to Nicholas Coleridge: "Expensive clothes don't mean anything any longer. Anyone with money can afford to buy them."[15] She doesn't know that what she says has been true for centuries, and that, were the royalty around, they would say that about her.

It used to be you'd know a wannabe by the polyester in their oxford cloth shirt. Bless Lisa Birnbach's *Preppy Handbook*. With Birnbach's bible, the U.S. "old family" in-group cover was blown by the hugely successful J. Crew company and some others who have parodied the casual preppy wardrobe into clothes for the masses.[16]

The problem with good taste is not what it allows us to choose, but rather how it limits us. As Russell Lynes noted in *The Tastemakers*:

> Our great concern with taste for taste's sake has not increased our enjoyment in the arts; on the contrary it has put a damper on our pleasure. It has directed our attention away from the main issue and has focused it on the side issue of trying to discriminate between what is good taste and bad taste. Taste merely becomes a substitute for understanding and pleasure.[17]

Rigid adherence to good taste or appropriateness, to make a good impression, discounts the fact that most of our lives do not consist of first impressions; rather, our lives involve learning to live with ourselves.

- What do you consider good taste?
- What is the norm of good taste in your circle?
- Are there any ways in which good taste limits your pleasure?
- What sort of taste do you want to take with you into the world of your own expression?

The early psychologists of clothing and theorizers told us that dressing was all about upward mobility, Veblen's "conspicuous consumption," looking like the rich. If that's your goal, read Leah Feldon's *Dressing Rich*. For some, though, an elegant look doesn't suit them. Elegance might be a useful idea for you. Feel it out.

Anxiety's vultures

Without awareness of the importance of context, we can be manipulated by the fashion consultants who prey on our appropriateness anxiety. They crank up the tension with pronouncements like "Modern life is fast. Contacts are brief, and often we get just one chance to tell another human being who we are. We must make an instant statement."[18] Or "Considering that ninety percent of you is covered with clothing, at least in a business setting, ninety percent of that first impression is an impression of your clothing."[19] We've been told repeatedly that if we can clue into an appropriate way of dressing, we will reap benefits. In their insistence, they overlook, first, the vast area of misinterpretation and, second, that "wardrobe engineering won't do much for you if your work is lousy . . . or if you're one of an army of aspirants competing for the same spot."[20] I don't care how good your suit is, if you pick your nose in that job interview, you won't get the job. If the company has unspoken (and illegal) sex, race, age, weight, or appearance rules unrelated to job performance, you won't get the job.

Nonetheless, you are a part of many environments, and in these environments people choose specific dress. The aggregate dress of your contemporaries becomes the norm for appropriateness. You can dress within the range of that norm or not, but it's useful to have a clue about what those norms are. In terms of clothing rules made outside our own preference, appropriateness functions as the staid conservative brakes to fashion's wild, out-of-control ride. It's a natural progression: Know the psyche; then take the next step outward and know the body; then learn about the physical relationship with clothing; then the next layer expanding outward is knowing not just the peer group, but also the community. Today, your office, town, geographic area, school, exercise group, family, country, etc., all have distinct dress codes or leanings. In choosing what to wear, you are taking your place within the vast variety of codes, willingly asserting where you do or do not belong. Define the different areas of your life you dress for, the degree to which appropriateness really matters to you, and the level of appropriateness anxiety you can tolerate.

To dispel some anxiety, prepare yourself for situations where appropriate dress matters to you. If people are going to be catty, have realistic expectations so it doesn't surprise you. Give yourself more than enough time to choose an outfit that will suit both you and the situation.

Regardless of the event, remember: you don't have to go. You can, for example, marry another day. Make sure the sumptuous allure of the formal event doesn't distract you from meeting your real needs. And if you are designing the event yourself, be sure to design it to your specifications. Sarah Jurick remembers her niece's wedding where the bride's horses, Arabian mares, served as the bridesmaids, their manes decorated with garlands of flowers.

How, and to what extent, do you want to respond sartorially to others' expectations? Some dress for a man's approval or notice. Discern the difference between dressing for a man's approval (the victim's position) and dressing out of an overflowing generosity that shares your enjoyment of clothing with him while respecting yourself. Daphne comments that she and Beau sometimes dress for each other:

On the weekend when we're going to spend the whole day together, we choose each other's outfits for the day so that we like what we're going to see each other in. You don't see your own clothes. So it makes more sense that if I'm going to spend all day with you, I'd pick out what you're going to wear so I look at it and like it.

A lot of women's nagging dress anxiety has to do with worrying about what others think, regardless of whether they are living or dead. Among the men I interviewed, I heard significantly less clothing anxiety about "getting it right," perhaps because men's clothes are easier, and also perhaps because men aren't socialized to have clothing anxiety as an acceptable place to feel crazy. This anxiety about inappropriate (to the circumstances and one's mood) dressing, can lead one to attempt to try on everything in one's closet ten minutes before one is supposed to be at the event, and then dash out, leaving heaps of clothes around the room. In order to study appropriateness, you have to take a long, polite look around you at what people wear. Observe the different types of garments, and the age and sex of people who are wearing them.

- What colors, textures, styles, and proportions predominate?
- Do they vary from location to location?
- Do people with different roles tend toward different codes? What are they?
- Who looks attractive to you? Why?
- What would you feel comfortable in? Acceptable? Attractive?
- How do you want to look in this context; how do you want to be viewed?

If someone is wearing something you would love to try, ask them where they got it, and go try it on. If someone consistently dresses in a way you admire, ask them to lunch with the express purpose of talking about clothes. Ask them about their relationship with clothes and how they assemble outfits. Pay for lunch.

The job interview

Aside from major events where you need to dress up and day-to-day work—and dressing for dating, which has been written about ad nauseam—appropriate dressing is probably most important in a job interview. In addition to preparing intellectually for the interview (by researching the organization and finding out as much as you can about the work they do), you can use what Laurence Wrightsman calls "impression management."[21] Conveying respect and putting the interviewer at ease through dress are the primary goals.

Wallach sees it as a pleasurable act: "If you know what role you want to play, you can use clothing to get the part."[22] That's fine for someone who isn't prone to wardrobe freakout. How to rethink this in a calming way? Barbara Coffey comments:

A job interview is like a first date. It gives you a first impression of another person, tells you whether you want to continue the relationship, but it doesn't really tell you much about how the day-to-day living will be, and that, after all, is what a job is all about. . . . If you want to get ahead, dress as if you're already there. Put another way, pick the job you aspire to and dress as if you have that job.[23]

How to dress appropriately? Find out what they wear. If necessary, send in fashion-savvy friends as spies to case the joint. Test your outfit before the interview. When in doubt, err on the side of respectful formality.

Polish your shoes and get a great haircut. Clean your nails. Wash behind your ears. No, I am not your mother. For corporate jobs, David Simons advises:

> Never wear a brown suit on an interview. It's not alive enough. It's okay when you're a dead professional. I've seen brown in the office and it looks great. But for interviewing, you need a color that's more alive. You can't go nuts color-wise—wear blue or gray.

About women's accessories, Sharon Frederick comments, "You never go to a business interview with dangling earrings or big hoops moving or bracelets clanging. Nothing like that. They would want you out of that office as fast as they could get you out of there." Unless, of course, you're in a wiggling business. She comments about the other option:

> If you're not right for them, convey it immediately. Don't waste time. Don't send a double message. People will come to you who love the impression you're making. Those who need to will kind of step back.

Part of the self-consciousness of the interview is the sense that all eyes are upon you. Two aren't. Don't forget that you are interviewing *them,* too. Make time to turn the attention on them and get your questions answered. See Janet Wallach's books for more information.

Appropriateness for work

Unless you join a family business, any roles, restrictions, or rules dictated by your family exist only in your mind. It is useful to identify whose voices direct your choices, what they say, how much you really agree with, and what you really want . . . while attending to the new set of guidelines called "appropriateness."

Once you're gainfully employed, how do you figure out what's appropriate and accommodate to changes you have to make which may not suit your style? Daphne Stannard looks at appropriateness issues for the many different worlds she dresses for:

> I'm an Intensive Care Unit nurse, and I'm also a doctoral student. The ICU is such an intense place that family members don't need to deal with "groovy outfits." Nursing as a profession is very conservative in a socially imbedded way. I don't mean to imply that nurses themselves are conservative, but the "profession" is conservative.

I buy that, given the role we have when we take care of sick people. I take it very seriously. Families size you up the minute you enter the room. Usually the patients are very sick, so they're not sizing you up.

Daphne uses clothing to create a considerate, caring context for her nursing. In light of that, I ask her to describe what is piercing her right earlobe at this moment, as I wouldn't expect her to wear that to work. Daphne says:

This is my non-nursing identity, that's why. I'm wearing two plastic skeletons. One's matching my neon blue Doc Martens boots, and the other is red, matching my flannel miniskirt dress. I really like silly clothes. I like to look silly—not silly like I want to be laughed at, but silly like fashion is for fun. This is a really serious world, and one of the things that gives me a charge in the morning is to try to put together outfits that are funny, humorous, ha-ha.

Some work days she has to fit in more. She'll be helping to teach a class that day, or she's in a family faculty practice lab: "I have to wear things that I can tolerate, but that also are presentable." She wears a lot of skirts. And she'll wear leggings and flats without socks and a normal T-shirt.

She also has another set of clothes for consulting. She goes to hospitals and talks to nurses about their visitation policies for families. "And again, I can't wear anything too outrageous and be taken seriously." She wears a lot of rayon skirts and linen shirts: "It's tasteful, but I don't look like a power businesswoman or anything."

If you're a baker, a sanitation worker, or a doctor, it's obvious: you buy the uniform. The office worker also has a uniform, but the clues are more subtle. Every workplace has a uniform, even if it's "dress down."

Corporate culture has the clearest sartorial rules and by-laws about direct communication in the language of clothing, sometimes explicitly stated in employee manuals. Part of its unspoken law is that corporation work is a team sport. Wallach writes:

Wearing the uniform immediately says that you want to be on the team. . . . This may be a difficult concept for some women to accept. We were not generally brought up to be team players but rather to be the team's mascots or cheerleaders. . . . Men, in fact, are often quite proud of their particular uniform. For them, their school or club tie confirms that they are members of an elite group. Women traditionally have had a somewhat opposite view of dressing. A woman who walks into a room and sees someone else in her same outfit is sure to cringe.[24]

Men's uniform is suit, tie, shirt, shoes, and socks. It remains standard throughout. Women have more choices. For the world of work, jackets are the armor garment. Wallach comments: "I do think jackets are an important part of a wardrobe. Somehow, wearing a jacket equates to being one of the guys. . . ."[25]

In confronting the work uniform issue, we address a hidden truth: A great many women's suits are neither comfortable nor practical. Men's suits are often roomy, comfortable to sit down in, and made in durable quality fabrics that resist wrinkles and stains. Men's suits are usually neutral so that they can be worn many days without anyone noticing.

What makes a suit comfortable? It depends on what makes you comfortable. The five bottom-line questions to ask are:

- Can you sit down in it and work for a few hours without it turning into a mass of wrinkles when you rise?
- Does it fit your body well when you are sitting down, standing up, and walking?
- Does the fabric wear well, masking signs of wear and dirt?
- Is the style consistent with the style of the team?
- Do you like it?

Uniforms can be both practical and psychologically supportive. At the time of our interview, Lex Eurich volunteered at a children's arts center. When she went there to teach she'd wear old holey jeans with paint all over them and a T-shirt that she didn't care about getting paint on. When she attended arts center events, she'd wear "art lady clothes like funky, fun dresses. Looking like an art lady is important. It enhances my feeling that I belong there, because I'm in this position where I'm not a teacher but I want to be. It's important to me. It boosts me up." (She soon became the director of that arts center.)

Laurel Fenenga comments about corporate uniforms:

People say to me, I have to dress this way at work, I have to dress that way. What always comes out of my mouth is, "Are you sure you have to, are you sure this is something that's required in your job?" When I was working in retail, I would say to people, "Do you just feel that your boss or the corporation would not promote you?" If so, boy, we don't allow people to touch us physically, why do we let them touch our personalities?

In the late 1970s and early 1980s, many working women bit into the myth of the power suit and then found its promises false. When Melissa Batchelder started working as a legal assistant, she wore the blue suit, the white Oxford shirt, and the silk tie. At some point along the way, she realized, "I look like a little imitation man." People always suggested that "dress for success" would in some way make women advance, but she realized that short of becoming a lawyer, nothing would bring her more respect, status, or position. "All of a sudden, I said, 'This is crazy. And I'm not happy wearing this stuff.' So as it wore out, I stopped wearing it, and started wearing things that I really enjoyed more."

Expectations differ among jobs. For example, Alan Edelman of M.I.T. pointed out that, as a mathematician, he is expected to look "endearingly uncomfortable in a suit" at an interview. What are the expectations for your field? If you can't deal with appropriate dress for work, find a place with a ridiculously loose code. There are increasingly large numbers of great places to work where you can wear exactly what you want.

A brief digression concerning suitcases

One rainy day, I was exploring Grandma's attic and I came upon an old wardrobe trunk, its tan interior complete with drawers and extendable rack to hang clothes on. I wondered about the kind of life that would require the use of such a trunk—sturdy as a dresser and as heavy as one too. What did 19th-century travellers pack in their trunks? Mrs. Charles Moulton tells us that she took eleven trunks containing "eight day costumes (counting my travelling suit), the green cloth dress for the hunt, which I was told was absolutely necessary, seven ball dresses, five gowns for tea."[26] Travel needs and purposes were different in that era. I liked the distinction a designer made:

In Sarah Bernhardt's time, and for some considerable time after the war, travel meant leaving home for at least a month. . . . Unfortunately the most common form of travel is now the so-called "business trip," in which a physical transfer leaves the traveller, psychologically, in exactly the same place.[27]

As far as travel gear goes, the trunk bears no resemblance to today's lightweight plastic zippered satchel, small enough to fit under the airplane seat, containing a wardrobe that's light enough to easily tote about.

Travelling light vs. travelling heavy

Some travel light and others heavy. What emotional baggage do you travel with? If you travel heavy, does your need to feel at home, when you aren't literally at home, cause your luggage to weigh so much that you aren't mobile? Libby Granett's husband Dan likes to travel light. She comments:

When I first met Dan, he and his sister were driving to Alaska, and they were going to be there for at least two months. The morning they left, he got a brown paper bag and stashed some clothes in it. I was amazed. I would have spent weeks thinking about shopping, figuring out what combinations to wear. It didn't occur to him until then that he needed to do anything. He literally stuffed a bunch of clothes in a brown paper bag.

Ed Perry doesn't travel as light as Dan:

When we go on vacations, I pack coordinated outfits for every single day. I don't just throw stuff in a suitcase and "it's going to work out however." Everything is thought out beforehand and then my friends Alan and Tony laugh at me after the stuff comes out of the suitcase. I don't have the iron, but I have the steamer. I think, "Okay, even though I'm on vacation, I'm going to look the best I can before I go out the door."

The short list for travel

1. What do you need? What is appropriate where you are going? If you don't know, find out. Regarding weather, a good newspaper or the Internet lists the weather of every major city on the globe.

2. Buy lightweight, invincible luggage you are proud to be seen with. Why feel ashamed of your suitcases when you are meeting someone at an airport or checking into a hotel? Keep unique, distinctive luggage tags on your bags. You may be able to recognize your suitcase, but the person ahead of you at baggage claim may not.

3. Take along a good lightweight book.

4. If you travel often, always keep a plastic-lined, multi-compartment cosmetic bag packed for your needs. That way you won't forget necessities at the last minute. Refill everything when you get home. World traveller Sherlee Land says, "Always carry a separate little bag in case your luggage is lost, in your one hand carry-on. Have your medications in it, enough underwear, and a sweater, so that if the luggage is gone, your trip's not ruined for a couple of days." If you don't keep a bag packed, keep a list of what you need with your luggage.

5. What to wear while en route? I avoid the travelling-movie-star look (dark glasses, jeans, white T-shirt, and leather jacket) because if I'm going to sit for two or fourteen hours I want to be comfortable. For me, that means knit fabrics in a dark color (this diminishes my chance of arriving looking like a rumpled victim of a food fight). If I add pearls and pumps when the plane taxis to the gate, I feel ready to face the world. What suits you?

6. Re: packing for travel. It depends on your priorities. You can even write out your daily wardrobe on a list in advance. My primary criterion is weight—the lighter the bag, the happier I am.

7. When packing for work trips, consider if you can get by, like the guys do, with one good suit and several changes of shirt. That means one pair of shoes. This method affords enormous relief.

8. Maybe you're better off *not* taking the second lightweight bag in your luggage so that you won't buy more stuff.

9. Andrew suggests you pack at the very last minute so it will take as little time as possible. Having experienced him doing this, I strongly suggest you don't.

10. Alan Edelman points out that you don't need to be covered for all possibilities. If you're traveling to a city, you can buy anything you forgot.

Appropriate casual clothing

Appropriateness study is helpful to offset the "Ick Factor." Debbie Epidendio summarizes this: "If I'm real grubby one day and see somebody on the street that I haven't seen in years, I think, 'Oh, I look terrible!' That plays a part in how I feel." Take into account the "Ick Factor" when you are dressing for the part of your life that involves neither work nor travel. Have a standard level of dress so you feel both happy with what you wear and secure because you're prepared to run into So-and-So. One friend, a woman in her fifties, walks the dog every morning in the cashmere sweats required of her neighborhood, but comments, "No one has to know I'm not wearing any underwear and I feel FREE, FREE, FREE!"

Quick Questions:

• Where are you going?
• Who's going to see you?
• Do you care what they think?
• What's your worst nightmare of who you could run into?
• How much does it matter to you?

The bottom line: Stay comfortable. Make a distinction between considering others and considering the need to get job done. Make sure you have clothes appropriate for doing the job: aerobics shoes, gardening gloves, etc. Are there any essentials you cheat yourself out of? Some people use the appropriateness issue as an excuse to actually dress up as finely as they secretly want to.

The goal is dressing to avoid self-recrimination while supporting your well-being. You don't want to say afterward, "I'm so foolish." You want your basic level of dress to be high enough so that you can weather any encounter with "aplomb."

What's appropriate for being alone? Show self-respect.

The real work occurs in shifting, broadening and realigning your tolerance of others. Writer Maya Angelou comments, "Good manners and tolerance . . . are the highest manifestation of style."[28] At the same time you are studying your environments to determine the range of most appropriate garments for you to wear, you need to embark on an equally rigorous examination of your own biases about the way people look, in order to see if or how this affects the way you treat them. Then begin to correct your behavior.

The language of clothing gives everyone a different dialect. We have to remember humbly how often we misperceive. Dave Grossman gives an example:

My cousin was working as an aide with the Piedmont Police Department. She was in the dispatcher's office, handling calls. They got calls this one night about a strange black man in sweat clothes running through Piedmont. Everyone was really worried. The police stopped the guy to see what he was doing. He was the mayor of Oakland. He was out jogging.

Because of the prejudice running rampant in our society, appropriate dress, while not always signalling enough, can support one's ability to function in the world. Rhonda Pretlow comments on her need for appropriate dress:

As an Afro-American woman, there's such a pressure for me sometimes to be aware of my blackness in the world. Especially in the circles that I move in, which are primarily white. So I just don't like to think about other people looking at me. Maybe I want to look appropriate because I grew up with a lot of stereotypes—if I walk down the street looking baggy or something like that, people might mistake me for a homeless person.

I go into a lot of really nice stores, and I don't like people following me around like they think I'm going to steal something. I've been followed around a lot, and salespeople will say "Can I help you?" and give me a dirty look. Whether I like it or not, whether I admit it or not, people have a certain idea in their mind when they see you dressed in a certain way. I don't feel like I dress up when I go to the stores, but I guess I would. I normally just dress neat—even if I'm in a sweatshirt and sweatpants, I'm sure I look neat.

What's going to change people's attitudes so that if she walks into a store, they don't see her skin color first and make false assumptions about her? Rhonda replies, "What's going to change that is just more people living in the neighborhood, coming into the stores more often. I think it will change on its own." She says later, "All this fuss for a few yards of brown skin . . . would they prefer me in a plaid?"

I do a lot of instant clothing judging. I'm picky. I'll look someone over and think, "The color of her stockings doesn't go well with the color of her shoes." Then I think, "Andrea, you don't ever wear shoes. You wear sneakers. All the time." Debbie Epidendio reminds me, "And you can get sucked into it very easily if you don't keep reminding yourself. I think a lot of people do."

Balance this for yourself: While we can't control impressions, we may influence them. Given that, it seems that appropriateness matters because of what it can do for you, literally or psychologically, and what you can learn from it.

Notes:

1. Redman, Alvin, ed. *The Wit and Humor of Oscar Wilde*. Page 137.
2. Laver, James. *Costume and Fashion*. Page 16.
3. Flügel, J.C. *The Psychology of Clothes*. Page 175.
4. Hempel, Amy. "A Few Bad Men." *Elle*. February 1994. Page 114.
5. Lynes, Russell. *The Tastemakers*. Page 185.
6. Flügel. Page 197.
7. Cho, Emily and Hermine Lueders. *Looking, Working, Living Terrific*. Page 35.
8. Fraser, Kennedy. *The Fashionable Mind*. Page 79.
9. Vreeland, Diana. *DV.* Page 122.
10. Davis, Fred. *Fashion, Culture and Identity*. Page 57.
11. Wallach, Janet. *Looks That Work*. Page 152.
12. Fraser. Page 75.
13. Fairchild, John. *Chic Savages*. Page 19.
14. Lynes. Page 336.
15. Coleridge, Nicholas. *The Fashion Conspiracy*. Page 34.
16. It's hard to take preppy "good taste" seriously when you learn that the ultra-preppy Brooks Brothers started out as the first major mass producer of clothing in the mid-19th century. They made sailor suits.
17. Lynes. Page 339.
18. Cho, Emily and Linda Grover. *Looking Terrific*. Page 11.
19. Thompson, Jacqueline, ed. *Image Impact*. Page 24.
20. Lurie, Alison. *The Language of Clothes*. Page 118.
21. Thompson. Page 24.
22. Wallach, Janet. *Working Wardrobe*. Page 95.
23. Coffey, Barbara. *Glamour's Success Book*. Page 92.
24. Wallach. *Looks That Work*. Page 34-35.
25. Wallach. *Looks*. Page 48.
26. Bailey, Adrian. *The Passion for Fashion*. Page 84.
27. *Fashion: Poetry and Design*. Page 79.
28. Angelou, Maya. *Wouldn't Take Nothing for My Journey Now*. Page 28.

Part 3
Getting Into Clothes

The Components:
Color, Fabric, Proportions, Accessories, and the Dream of the Perfect Shoe

Before examining the surfaces that conspire to form your perfect look, it was important to look at the deeper fundamental issues, at what makes you feel close to yourself. Your different reasons for loving what you do add up to loving certain colors, fabrics, and styles. Consider, as well, clothing rules you don't feel like following. In respecting these aversions, aspects of your style also emerge. A third factor—harmony of color, fabric, and proportion relative to your own bodily colors, "fabrics," and proportions—is discussed here.

Color

Everyone sees color differently. This became apparent to me the day I ran into a friend who complimented me on my purple outfit. It was a blue outfit. How to choose? Rediscover how you see color. Kentner suggests you start by looking at your clothes and asking yourself which colors make you smile, which colors you like best, which make you feel restful, and which make your face more attractive.[1]

While certain colors look better on you than others, it is also true that when you're wearing something you love—whether it is in "your colors" or not—the joy you radiate may compensate for tonal imbalances between self and garment.

There are other ways to find the most flattering palette for you. Think of the basic bright rainbow. Add white and the rainbow lessens its intensity. Add even more white and it becomes pastel. Add grey or black to the basic rainbow and it gets all soft and muted, like colors seen through a foggy day. Add brown and the rainbow gets earthy. Your skin, hair, and eye colors are part of some variation on that rainbow. The rest of the spectrum of colors in the brightness, lightness, saturation, etc. that include your natural body colors, will make you look naturally lovely. An afternoon spent playing with a 10-pack of oil crayons and some paper in front of a mirror will teach you more than any text. Start by trying to replicate your skin, eye, and hair colors, then see what blues, purples, reds, greens, etc. look good with all those colors. Think about spending the $1.79 and a few hours.

No information about colors is useful, unless the colors are looked at in relation to the person who will be wearing them. Because people's skins usually range in color from yellow-beige or pink-beige to dark brown, the greatest contrast will show up in the green-blue-purple range, the other side of the color wheel from our own coloring. Sharon Frederick comments, "Your most dramatic colors are supposed to have the biggest impact on your coloring, your eyes, and your hair, equally in balance." Wearing a dramatic color can communicate respect for the formality or importance of an event. Sharon points out that the garment doesn't have to be "real froufrou, plunging, or cut down the back. The dress is rather simple, but the color gives the impact."

According to this theory, the exact opposite effect of the dramatic colors, that of subtlety and blending in—conveying trustworthiness and ease—can occur when you wear an extension of your natural eye color. A close match to the colors in the iris (not the black inner circle, but the ring of color around that pupil) has a flattering effect on the eyes.

Squint at yourself in the mirror, making the picture sort of fuzzy. Is there a dramatic difference between your skin and hair color? That degree of difference or contrast can be echoed in color contrasts in your clothing, not by wearing the colors of your skin and hair, but rather by wearing colors that are that degree of difference from each other. Larkey observes, "Regardless of your size, the stronger your body colors (skin and hair) are, the brighter your wardrobe colors should be."[2] Because strong contrast was in fashion for so long, we of more subtle contrasts tend to put ourselves down. Byers comments:

> What if you're nothing but the average American brown? . . . [S]tick to subtle effects. And remember this: vivid colors are for vivid types. Less definite types should wear softer shades or they will look washed out. If this disappoints you, stop and think—you can wear many more colors than a more striking type, so you will wear better, as it were. You need never become monotonous.[3]

If your skin, hair, and eye colors do not contrast much, try low-contrast clothing colors that echo the subtle differences in your body's colors. This will enhance your natural beauty.

Another way to look at color is to classify whether it is warmer (yellower), cooler (bluer), or neutral in relation to your natural skin, hair, and eye colors. Experts say choose colors that harmonize with your skin's (yellow or blue) undertone. If you can see this undertone, and it is, for instance, yellowish, consider trying the warmer coral reds rather than the cooler violet reds. Consider the peach pinks rather than the mauvey lavender pinks, the yellow-greens rather than the blue-greens, etc.

How would you define the range of colors you usually wear? Have you tried other ranges of color? How about soft pastels, jewel tones, medium-intensity colors, muddy grayed colors, or earth tones? It is very hard to stray from our habitual color paths, toward things we automatically dismiss, to retrain to look like a child would look, and move toward what moves us. Perhaps spend a day in a large store trying on clothes in strange colors and different ranges of color. Note your responses.

The most economical way to study this involves closely observing your body's response to color. Karen Kaufman designs clients' color palettes by draping many large squares of color around the neck and shoulders of clients and having them look in the mirror.

> It's interesting to watch the facial expressions. When it's the wrong color, their noses crunch up and their lips get a little pursed. Then I say, "Why does this strike you as not right?" They respond, "Oh, it makes me look pale." or "All I notice is the color," or "I look jaundiced."
>
> I notice a real change in breathing when a person sees the right color. The voice drops a little bit, the face relaxes. They'll say "Oooh, this looks good. My color looks even on my face. I look at me instead of the color."

Color consultant Naomi Tickle comments: "If you haven't seen the difference between when you put a color next to you and it works well for you and when it doesn't work well for you, that could be confusing. What you're looking for in all your colors is for your natural coloring to brighten, as if you turned a light on and said, 'Oh, yes.' It gets clearer." Colors that don't work make your skin look blotchy, your features look washed away. You look tired (while the colors may be very pretty, nobody notices you).

There are all sorts of ways to study color. You can also cut out pictures and keep color collage scrapbooks. You can use anything: feathers, ribbons, candy wrappers, magazine ads, sea glass, crayons, photos, fabric scraps, etc. You can go to the fabric store and ask for swatches of the colors you feel most drawn to. Tack them up on your bulletin board to contemplate. Laurel Fenenga comments:

The mother of my best friend in high school had a really big mirror that covered a wall. We'd go into her mother's sewing basket and look at yardage and we'd twist it around ourselves. It's an exercise about getting comfortable with your body, and about getting comfortable with wrapping things around you and seeing what colors you like, and rather than focussing on what you don't like, focus on "Do I like this color? How does this color make me feel?"

Wallach asks:

Do you feel strong in black, authoritative in grey, or do you feel more sincere in blue? Does your . . . skin light up against pale pastels or is the contrast more dramatic against black? Does red make you feel daring or do you feel dominant in purple? What color do you associate with each of the following adjectives: sophisticated? sincere? boring? conservative? aggressive? masculine? feminine? dowdy? sad? cheerful?

Add more adjectives to the list as you think of them, and as they apply to the life you lead or want to lead.[4]

Colors can also be used to create a better emotional state. Fashion writer Margaretta Byers suggests, "When you're at low ebb, give yourself a lift with a peach teagown."[5] Conversely, if you have something in a color which makes you look ghastly, wear it when you want sympathy. But make sure it's comfortable. When I wear black, my complexion gets strangely yellow, my eyes look ringed with red. I can "get better" fast by changing into a denim blue shirt, a color that makes me look rosy.

When shopping, don't pretend you can remember color in your head. Perfect color memory is rarer than perfect pitch. Bring the garment to match, snip out a scrap of fabric from the seam allowance (this has disaster potential), or use a color sample book. Pantone makes a good one.

Because colors look different in different lights, you have to check them under the light where you wear them. Department store buyers may never see the clothes in natural light. The Chicago Apparel Center—the central showplace for clothes distributed to stores covering the entire midwestern United States—has no windows because the department stores they sell to don't show clothes in natural light.

Fabric Fundamentals

Quiz [*Check the ones that apply to you.*]

_____I like wearing clothes made of natural fibers.

_____The only natural fiber I can stand is in my breakfast cereal.

_____I enjoy the sin in synthetics.

_____I like wearing clothes that shine or feel silky and smooth for specific events only (namely, _____).

_____I like wearing clothes that have rough textures, where the weave is visible.

_____I hunted and killed everything I'm wearing.

_____I like clothes that feel soft and cuddly.

_____I like fabrics that are crisp and have body of their own.

Where does a personal relationship with fiber and fabric begin? Camille DePedrini comments:

It goes back to my grandmother who was Italian. She had lots of linens. And in those days people ironed everything. She ironed all of the pillowcases and my grandfather's handkerchiefs. I used to stand next to her and iron. I'd have my little end of the ironing board, and she'd be on the big end . . . I loved that. I loved going through all of the linens. Things would be embroidered. They'd have fine little finishes on them and pretty colors. She'd crocheted the ends of tablecloths. It may have started there.

I love fabric. I think if it started as far back as my grandmother, it had to do with food, and eating on linen, and sleeping where I slept at her house, and what I slept on and the garden outside, the flowers and what sort of crocheted things the flowers were sitting on. It was very much a part of my life.

• Where does your fabric history begin?
• What memories do you have of garments or fabrics from your past?
• What do specific fabrics mean to you?

If you wish to explore the fabrics you enjoy wearing, you must investigate the evidence of your senses, especially touch, hearing, sight, and smell.

Touch

Our culture places a taboo on the gratification of touch. Touching in public is limited to hand-holding (one's opposite-sex lover only) plus an occasional hug or short kiss when saying good-bye. In accepting this, we voluntarily allow a curtain to fall between ourselves and our senses. Suspicion of touch extends to not enjoying or even being aware of what clothes feel like while we wear them, leading to the discomfort many tolerate in dress: shoes that cramp the feet, waistbands that rearrange one's internal organs, and shoulders shaped so that arms have no free range of movement. Paradoxically, women are supposed to be the beautiful ones while oblivious to the constraining aspects of our little gilded cages of clothing.

- What kind of fabrics do you like the feel of?
- What fabrics do you like to wear?
- Have you felt different wools from sheep, cashmere goats, camels, vicunas?
- Can you sense the difference between velvets made of cotton, rayon, and silk?
- Do you feel at ease in any of those?

Have you ever worn silk? Do you like it? Some say that it's the most elegant of fabrics. In silk's favor, it takes color beautifully and feels soft.[6] Experts write things like, "Silk screams money, elegance, fashion and sex. It drapes magnificently."[7] But do you want your clothes to scream? Ed Perry comments, "I know everyone just raves about silk, but it always feels clammy to me. I always feel wet and damp in silk."

Do you like cotton? It's a popular opinion. Test to be sure it's also yours. What do you like to feel? Can you feel a Sea Island cotton and know how it's different from a Greek or Indian cotton?[8]

What would you like to surround yourself with? If you had all the money in the world, what sorts of clothes would feel good from the inside out? A dear friend deeply loves the feel of pilly acrylic, but tells no one. It just isn't cool. However, in the privacy of his home and bed, he loves his blankets of that fabric. Sound strange? Glynn comments:

> The long-to-touch-you catalogue of fabrics is interesting, for it ranges from the apparently implacable gabardines and worsted twills—which say, particularly in sporting dress, "keep your hands off" but leave the impression of a lot of fun to be had under that dour and proper exterior—right through to the most innocent or calculated cheesecloth and chiffon.[9]

From childhood, I remember walking into a coat closet and surrounding myself with the tall draping fabrics, wool flannels and boucles, soft fluid beaver and rough dry leopard. Before I knew the politics, before I mourned the poor animals slaughtered, I savored the voluptuous beauty, felt the covering and protection, the musty smells mingled with good faint perfume, civilization, comfort, quality, and love. What do you remember touching?

Some ignore the easy clues of sensuality at their peril, spending money on garments that are "itchy and scratchy" only to have them languish unused in the closet. How to tell whether the touch of a fabric agrees with you? Fiber artist Kathryn Alexander suggests you put it around your neck: "You know how sensitive your neck is. If you can wear it around your neck for about five minutes without it bugging you, you can wear it next to your skin." In order to have a happy physical relationship with your wardrobe, it's important also to pursue more deeply your specific pleasures of touch. If you have issues about the forbiddenness of pleasure, explore them. Skip the shrink! Instead, do as fiber artist Cheryl Kolander suggests and learn more through fabric stores. Here she's talking about tactile comparisons of polyester and silk:

> Go to a local fabric shop and feel fabric of different fibers. . . . Look for the rack of "silky" synthetics, and feel each of them. Scrunch them up, smooth them on your cheek, then feel the silk. The most pronounced difference is the warmth of the silk. Silk is soft and warm, yet refreshing; synthetics are glassy, smooth and cold.[10]

Feldon adds:

> A label that reads "pure silk" means that no metallic salts have been added to increase the weight and give it a heavier "hand," but it doesn't indicate the actual weight of the cloth. The best way to train your eye and touch to discern between the "lightweights" and the "heavyweights" is by comparison. Take a look at some of the top designer silks, most of which are of excellent quality and the perfect weight. Then have a look at a few "special bargain" thirty-dollar blouses. You'll find yourself a very discerning customer in no time.[11]

You can also go to a thrift store (better than a department store because there's more fabric variety) and play "The Guessing Game." Touch a garment, guess its fabric content, and then check your hunch against the fabric information tag nestled in the collar or side seam. Expertise comes rapidly.

Obviously, respecting sensuality includes choosing clothing that's forgiving of perspiration. Almost everyone I interviewed mentioned some variation on "I sweat like a pig. Then, I sweat more." What are good fabrics for perspirers like us? Wool and cotton, according to *Stylewise* author McGill:

> In the right weight and weave, cotton is a good year-round fiber. It's good for cool weather because it's a hollow fiber that traps warm air. So it helps retain body heat. However, this hollowness allows cotton to absorb perspiration and permits that perspiration to evaporate, helping your body's natural air conditioning do a good job in summer.
>
> Wool is similar to cotton in its ability to be worn year round. (Again, if it's in the right weight and weave.) Why? Because wool fibers are twisted. . . . When these fibers are spun into yarn, natural air pockets trap warm air even better than cotton's hollow fibers. In summer, these allow perspiration to evaporate from the skin, albeit not as readily as does cotton, but readily enough if the wool fabric is light and thin. In a sense wool and cotton fluctuate in temperature with your skin.[12]

Natural fibers are said to "breathe," not as a kind of animism, but rather reflecting their flow-through qualities. Your skin breathes and needs to feel air through clothes.

Another tactile consideration in choosing clothes is weight. A down, fiberfill or Thinsulate coat will tend to feel light on the body, while a wool melton will be heavier. Wool sweaters can be downright airy, but wool with a lot of lanolin can make you feel as if you're wearing the living room rug. I don't like cotton sweaters because of their heavy weight relative to the warmth they offer. Others like the blanket-like security of the weight in clothes.

Close-fitting garments with a lot of stretch tend to be favored by those who like to feel resistance against their moving muscles. A completely constraining garment offers a different pleasure to others. Still others prefer clothes that offer no resistance to the body in motion. Many don't know that subtleties of this preference can be explored by observing the difference between wovens and knits. Barbara Jay comments, "A woven fabric is, just by virtue of the way it's designed, a more structured fabric." She makes a cross-hatching of her fingers to demonstrate.

People come to me who haven't been comfortable in their clothes, and can't figure out why. These women live in very moving, stretching, active, expressive bodies, and have to work in a bank, or in some profession that requires them to be dressed in a "corporate" way. They're wearing gabardine.

If knits aren't an appropriate alternative, she suggests her clients try crepe as opposed to gabardine.

Crepe is woven, but it often has greater drape unless you buy very expensive gabardine. Crepe isn't so heavy, it's softer, and it's often less tightly woven so there's literally more air that comes through the fabric. This can really affect how someone feels inside their clothes.

Shopping Touch Tests for Fabric

1. Grab the corner of the material and squeeze for twenty seconds with all your might. "If it wrinkles, you will have the same problem when you wear it."[13]

2. "Stretch the fabric between the thumbs and forefingers and hold for five seconds. If the yarns shift or slip apart easily, strain on the seams would be a problem at stress points."[14]

3. The Pill Test: "Fabrics made out of short fibers are more likely to pill. Take an inconspicuous corner and gently rub the right sides together; if this produces slight balls or pills, this will also happen in abrasion areas on your clothes such as the underarm and pant crotch."[15]

Hearing

Prudence Glynn observes, "And then there is the sound of materials. Swish. Rustle. Whisper. Starchy crackle. Rip."[16] Morton notes: "As some fabric surfaces touch one another, we are . . . conscious of sound, for example, in the characteristic scroop of silk."[17] Kathy, my former building manager, made a pair of pants for her son. When he picked the fabric—a heavy off-white cotton— she asked why he chose it. He said, "Listen," and then moved the fabric. "It makes the right sound."

Elegance can move soundlessly. Shoes don't squeak, belts and jewelry don't clank. No seams rip due to tightness and strain. There is no plastic "shush-shush" of thighs moving together as in a nylon track suit, or the vague sound of a thunderstorm made by an Ultrasuede garment entering a room. Once, on the job, when I walked into an executive conference room, a senior executive sitting with his back to me said, "Hello, Andrea," with the smug air of a ten-year-old nerd. I wondered how he knew who I was. As I walked over to take a chair, I noticed my shoes squeaking, and felt embarrassed.

What sounds do your clothes make? What cloth sounds do you like best?

Sight

Kathy Upton, commenting on fabric, recounts the discovery of her favorite garment:

When I was about thirty-five, I was getting business cards printed up. When I went into the print shop to place the order, the girl behind the counter was wearing the most wonderful dress I have ever seen. The perfect dress. I knew it had been made in the 1930s or 1940s. It was a wonderful deco print of deep forest green, chartreuse, taupe, ivory, and black. Very geometric.

She must have been about 5'8" or 5'9" and I'm not quite 5'3". Anyway, I looked at this girl in this dress, and I wanted that dress so much that I was ready to take off the clothes I had on, and I would have for that dress if I thought what I was wearing would fit her. That was my first impulse. The second was to find out if she would be willing to part with that dress. So I did what I do with anything that I'm enthusiastic about. I said, "I love that dress. I want that dress. I have to have that dress. How much would you want for that dress?" She recoiled a little. You can imagine why. She said, "Well. . . . "

I said, "Where did you get it?" Of course I knew that there's no way that that dress could be found anywhere because it came from a long time ago. She said, "Well, my boyfriend gave it to me."

I said, "Do you think he'd be mad at you if you sold it to me?" And she said, "Well, I guess not."

I said, "Would you take thirty dollars for it?" And she said, "Yes." I said, "Okay. Sold. You bring it here tomorrow and I'll be back tomorrow." Because they were closing.

I went back the next day with thirty bucks and I took that dress. That became my dress. I knew that it was acetate, but it was the most wonderful thing. And I wore it until now it's got holes in it. And I've got to figure out some way to take that fabric and do something else with it, the parts that aren't falling apart. And I love that dress. Oh, my God. When I wore that dress, I felt wonderful. I felt perfectly me.

How do you feel about patterns? Patterns, Wallach says, are usually "not as powerful" as solid colors: "The exception, of course, is pinstripes, which are as powerful as solid colors. Other menswear patterns, such as small checks, tweeds, tattersalls or glen plaids, all have authority. Slightly less intimidating but equally appropriate in the corporate arena are geometrics, paisleys and foulards."[18]

Patterns harmonious with the wearer, however, seem to correspond in some way with the scale and shape of her facial features and body. A person with large-scale features and a broad, expressive body might look more in tune with themselves in large-scale prints and/or jewelry, than in, for example, a tiny series-of-daisies print. A person with a teeny nose and a resemblance to the young Shirley Temple might look out of place in a dramatic, high-contrast black and white pattern of calla lilies. A person with curving, teardrop-shaped eyes might enjoy the resonance of her features with similar paisley prints.

Finding suitable textures is much simpler than finding patterns. Hair, skin, and clothing are all composed of different fibers or "fabrics." A texture that suits you will harmonize with your skin and hair texture. For example, if your skin has a naturally rough texture, or your hair is thick and full of wild body, you can play that off against highly textured fabric—such as wide-wale corduroy, tweeds, and deeply textured hand-knit sweaters—and make yourself luminous; or you can contrast it with fine-textured garments for drama.

Technical texture problems need to be addressed directly by the wearer, because the store won't clue you in. On a practical level, when considering silk remember the way a silk scarf will get snagged on a piece of unfinished wood when considering dressing for wood shop. Velcro closing on garments should be avoided with silk as well. Often fabrics that cling where they shouldn't can be freed by an intervening layer or slip of synthetic or silk.

McJimsey indicates some basic questions to ask when learning to look at fabric:

- How does the fabric handle?
- How does it drape?
- Is it opaque or sheer?
- Is there surface interest or is the surface plain?
- Is a specific occasion suggested by the luxury or durability of the fabric?
- Do color or the scale of the pattern of the fabric set limitations to its use?
- What type of silhouette—straight, bouffant, or draped—is best adapted to this fabric?
- What type of fullness: gathers, darts, or pleats?[19]

Ask yourself as you look at fabric why you like it or not. Study how the pattern and/or texture of the fabric effects the design of your features and the textures of your skin and hair.

Smell

Nick Debs comments, "My favorite is really freshly washed cotton sheets. The first day you put them on the bed, they feel really good and smell good, too." I like to touch cashmere but not wear it because it smells swampy if I perspire in it. Do clothes react to your body chemistry in a weird way? It could be the fabric. In wet wool, one smells like a miserable sheep caught in a rainstorm. Some like this smell very much, others don't.

Body proportions and clothing silhouettes

> *"There is no excellent beauty that hath not some strangeness in the proportion."*
> —Sir Francis Bacon (1561-1626) in his essay "Of Beauty"[20]

Today, looking great means choosing the outline that best suits your figure and self from among the many twentieth-century silhouettes. This can be overwhelming for someone who doesn't know her proportions and what silhouettes look terrific on her body. Proportion is key. When Joan

Songer first said this to me I nodded knowingly and cringed inwardly, wondering what she was talking about.

Proportion involves a far more individual and subtle way of seeing than the options presented in magazines. It doesn't fit into the in/out right/wrong black/white bad/good dichotomies that can be summed up in one page.

Proportion-sensitive dressing also refutes the idea of certain "classics" which look good on everyone. Amelia Fatt distinguishes between classics and "personal" classics: "To be a personal classic, a classic clothing shape must complement or flatter your own shape."[21] I read that and realized that's why squared blazers always look wrong on me. I'm rounded. The idea that added height compensates for accurate knowledge of proportion causes similar problems. We buy heels to be taller, throwing our spines out of whack and damaging our feet while getting no closer to resolving this issue.

Model Lauren Hutton points out, "People have to learn what their proportions are, not Christy Turlington's. Me, I have small bones and a big mouth."[22] She's 5'6 ½". They just dress her to appear tall. Proportion asks the question, "Who are you?" in terms of "What is your basic shape?" whether you lose that last five pounds or not. "Shape" means outline or silhouette, what we would see on a large sheet of paper if you lay down on it naked on your back and someone traced around your form with a crayon.

Step 1: Know the proportions of your body

Many people think they're familiar with their bodies, but they may only be familiar with hatred for their bodies. There's a wider range of information available than that one feeling. To find out more, answer the following questions:

1. Height (*circle one*) I am relatively short/medium/tall.

2. Figure (overall)
    ___ absolutely wonderfully abundant and full-bodied
    ___ in the wonderful medium range except for one (or more) area(s) which is/are
           fuller/narrower, namely: _____
    ___ wonderfully evenly proportioned
    ___ wonderfully slender except for one or more area(s) which is/are fuller/narrower,
           namely: _____
    ___ a skeleton (dead)

3. Figure (relation of parts to the whole)
    a) Which is wider, shoulders or hips? Neither?

    b) Am I relatively straight through the waist, or do I have a well-defined waist relative to my rib cage and hips?

    c) Am I relatively long-legged or short-legged or average compared with the rest of my body?

    d) Am I relatively short-torsoed or long-torsoed compared with the rest of my body?

If you can't see c) and d) in the mirror, do Connor's and Mathis's exercise: Using a piece of string, measure the length of your head from chin to top of forehead. Now measure from chin to waist. If it is two head lengths, you're in proportion; less than two, you're short-waisted; more than two, you're long-waisted. Now measure just from your crotch to the soles of your feet. If the distance is four head lengths, you're in proportion; less than four, your legs are relatively short; more than four, your legs are long.[23]

e) Are my arms shapely at the wrists? From wrist to forearm? All the way up the arm? (While we're out on limbs, how much of the shape of your arms do you like to cover loosely and how much do you like to show off? Showing off can occur through snugness of fit or exposure of skin.)

f) Are my legs shapely at the ankles, from ankle to knee, all the way up the leg? Fashion magazines give us some of the picture when they talk about hemlines, which are part of proportion. We then focus almost solely on them because hemlines are an easy thing to see. We miss two things: the rest of the silhouette and the fact that once you find the hemline(s) that make your legs and body look good, you can stick to that line. You don't have to follow the trendy skirt lengths which move up and down like a window shade communicating Morse code in a spy novel.

Regarding skirt length: Where do your legs look their best? If they're completely wonderful, how much sexual heat do you want to attract?

g) Am I relatively small-, medium-, or large-breasted compared to the size of my body?

h) Am I relatively curvy or straight? If my outlines are curvy in some places and straight in others, what are they?

i) Are my shoulders rounded, sloping, squared, or some other shape? If so, which?

j) From the side, where does my body go out and in? From the side, are the curves at bust, tummy, derriere, or elsewhere relatively large or small compared to the whole? (The French lovingly call that stomach curve "embonpoint." We could, too.)

k) On asymmetry, Connor and Mathis ask that you imagine a vertical line running down the center of your face dividing the face in half. "Do the halves mirror each other for the most part, or are they different?"

If your face is asymmetrically balanced, the asymmetrical styling details are in harmony with you, and in fact will make your asymmetrical face more active, emphatic, and exciting. . . . The question of symmetry versus asymmetry in the body is a consideration for the cut of your garments. Symmetrically cut clothing will not fit or fall properly on the asymmetrical body. Thus, if you have an asymmetrical body, then you will need to make necessary adjustments in your clothing or have your garments custom cut to conform to your body.[24]

Step 2: Choose emphasis or camouflage

Mary Armentrout indicates a useful distinction: We usually don't choose to wear a silhouette that makes us look naked, but rather we dress to play up or down different parts of our body through strategic cuts of fabric at different points of a garment. The silhouette you choose to wear also reflects where on the body you like clothes to fit snugly, casually, or loosely.

Flügel notes the deeper source of the tension between highlighting and masking. Decoration "beautif[ies] the bodily appearance, so as to attract the admiring glances of others and fortify one's self-esteem," while modesty is "utterly opposed to this. Modesty tends to make us hide such bodily excellencies as we may have and generally refrain from drawing the attention of others to ourselves."[25]

Procter writes: "Consider absolutely everything that you do or don't like about your body . . . it will become crystal clear what features need accentuating and which to play down—and this is where the right choice of clothes comes in."[26]

• Is there a silhouette you're accustomed to hiding behind, which leaves beautiful parts of your body unacknowledged? If so, why?
• What feelings do highlighting the hidden part bring up for you?

You're not expected to immediately let go of difficult body-related feelings. Rather, if camouflaging a body part, remember areas of pain deserve special attention, care, and quality cover. Some make tight clothes into a moral issue. They aren't. It's more useful to consider, if you wear your clothes "too tight," whether you are using your clothes to hold you when you want to be held by another person. Or is your small town too "uptight" and perhaps it's time for you to move someplace where you could dress the way you'd like?

In the need for clothes that fit or are loose around our bodies, some of us are like cats: our moods change. Sometimes the cat will curve her body close to the floor, avoiding your touch as you reach down to pet her. Sometimes she will rub her head against your leg or jump into your lap and sit on your newspaper, insisting that you make contact with her your first priority. What's true for you?

Sharon Frederick suggests that in studying fashion silhouettes, you look carefully at the overall shape indicated by the garment, not the clothes hanger (or clothes-hanger body) it's resting on.

As most of us do not possess the airbrushed looks of the fashion photo, what we can have (that they can't) is beauty with "distinction," distinction marking the qualities about us that are not conventionally "beautiful." This differs greatly from the condescension implicit in comments like "glasses give your face character."

You will find no agreement with me if you say that some part of you is bad or ugly. The choice you have is whether to enhance the feature or play it down. Connor and Mathis call our areas of distinction "body particulars." They distinguish between the goals of fashion and our goals as clothes lovers:

Since fashion trends are primarily about the "latest colors and fabrics" and about hemlines and silhouettes, most body particulars can't be viewed as either in or out of fashion. They just are. However, as you learn to accept and love each part of your body just as it is, you may well want to highlight that feature in an artistic way.[27]

Connor and Mathis further categorize some general ways to play up or play down a feature.

To highlight: (1) Use creative exposure to show off the feature. (2) Repeat and/or extend the line of the feature to emphasize it. (3) Add more dimension in the clothing to make the feature appear larger. (4) Surround a feature with more space to optically change its size. (5) Place an eye-catching element at or around the feature to draw attention to it.

To play down: (1) Cover up creatively to hide the feature. (2) Use line to direct eye away from the feature and/or break up space. (3) Create more dimension in the clothing to change the contour line. (4) Surround a feature with more space to optically change its size. (5) Use dominance elsewhere to divert the eye away from the feature. (6) Surround a feature with a large item to optically diminish its size.[28]

Step 3: Apply this to twentieth-century clothing silhouettes

What do we mean by finding the right silhouette or line for you? Connor and Mathis comment: "Basically, the principle is: Where your body is straight, have straight lines in your clothing; where your body is curved, have curved lines."[29] Then factor in what you want to camouflage and highlight. Finding clothes that express this has been simplified because, in the wide variety of twentieth-century silhouettes, all of which are current and fashionable, there are creative and expressive possibilities for every single body type.

Now that you know the game you are free to play it. Here's the starting place: Current fashion has a line corresponding to every known historical period. Do you have a favorite historical period? Is there a particular silhouette that works best for you? If so, what is it?

This does not mean going out and finding a genuine 1920s flapper dress if you have that sort of figure, although trying on vintage clothes in specific styles can be enlightening. The trick is to recognize the outline of the sort of garment that suits you in contemporary clothing. If it has an antecedent in fashion, it is a "classic" look. If it suits your shape, it is a "personal classic."

Silhouettes are often defined by how a garment looks when seen from the front. Clothing design modifications that flatter you when you're not seen from the front include pleats, bustles, and gathers. Many people look wonderful in more than one silhouette, depending on what they wish to play up or down.[30]

What silhouettes interest you? I love the drop-waist look—on other people. For dress-up, I prefer a modified ladylike 1950s silhouette with a fitted waist. For casual, I adopt slim jeans and an oversized sweater. Every person has their own individual take on the silhouette that works best for them. Mary Armentrout says of her style:

I have an image of a flapper as a twentieth-century, free, emancipated female. The silhouettes of the 1920s are very long and lean. They have no waist. They're totally flat-chested. The women don't have classically "female" or "feminine" haircuts. That fits my body shape, and it fits me. It's an empowering version of what females can be or what I want to be. It's a very beautiful image, not this kind of subservient-object image. It feels safe for me to play with versions of that updated in the clothes that are available.

Retired economist Jane Gelman says the basic silhouette she prefers is more sophisticated rather than childlike. She defines that silhouette as looser on top and more fitted on the bottom as opposed to more fitted through the bodice and looser from the waist down. Stacey Lamiero comments:

If anything, I downplayed my chest in my dressing. There was a time they used to sit up a little higher so any blouse you wore there was a hint, but then gravity set in. So now I wear the same blouse, and it doesn't have quite the same effect. And then about two years ago, all these women that I knew were getting breast enlargements, and they were wearing these low-cut things and showing them off, and suddenly I looked at myself and said, "Oh, I look so frumpy!" However, it did make me go out and buy things to make me show them off again.

I was always more apt to show my legs, and I like showing my legs as a better asset. I don't want to be thought of as, "Wow, look at her!" So I prefer to keep those downplayed.

I comment that it's hard being fabulous all over. Stacey agrees: "Oh, God, yes."

To test a silhouette on the body? Move in a garment that fits your lines and see how you feel. Look in the mirror as you move and see what parts look too loose and what parts look too tight. Try a different size if it isn't quite right. Consider trying another silhouette if you consistently have trouble getting clothes to fit you in the one you've chosen. If you can't see your outfit clearly, or you have difficulty getting the outfit to look balanced, the great Hollywood costume designer Edith Head would suggest another approach: "Put a paper bag over your head with two holes cut out for the eyes so you can see. Then look at yourself in a mirror."[31]

A good place to experiment with trying different silhouettes is a large thrift store. They have a wider silhouette selection than department stores because they sell a wider range of years of fashion.

Accessories

With accessories, you play the emphasis/camouflage/silhouette/color/texture game on a smaller scale. If you wish to play with ornamentation in a holistic way as it harmonizes with your face and body, acknowledge what you see of your body and the needs of your psyche in your choice of accessories. Although as women we're mostly raised to de-emphasize our distinctiveness and "play it small," the truth is that if you've got a big nose or a big mouth (or any dramatic, unusual, or unique feature), your accessories can play that up by retracing the shape of that feature. It's called style. As with all theories about harmony, you can try this one on, but if it doesn't fit, don't buy it. Once while shopping, Judy Newmark and a friend both admired a large necklace. Her friend said, "Oh, Judy, you buy it. You can wear it and I can't." Judy replied, "You know why I can wear it and you can't? Because I do and you don't."[32]

People also wear accessories for sentimental and practical reasons. The sentimental category includes family heirlooms, love tokens, and school insignia items. Practical uses include essential needs, for example, carrying stuff, seeing well, keeping warm, keeping time, and keeping the pants up. In fourth-century China, women used weapons as ornaments.[33] Given the confluence of three purposes—ornamental, sentimental, and practical—in the morning, as you don your accessories, note what your priorities are in each case. Are there any you'd like to change the emphasis of? In what direction?[34]

To explore this idea of playing up the harmony in our own features, Connor and Mathis suggest: "For your most harmonious neckline or necklace shape, all you need to do is repeat the shape that begins and ends at the widest part of your face and includes your jawline and chin."[35] This shape can be echoed through accessories, patterns, garment details, or all three. So, for example, if your chin comes to an angular point, you might find V-necked tops or V-shaped necklaces and earrings more becoming. If your chin is rounded, try crew- or round-necked garments and round jewelry. If your jaw is more oval, try reflecting the facial design accessories or garment details. The question becomes, "How do you want to enhance, honor, or note the line of your jaw?" The same principles can be applied to eye, nose, and mouth shapes. Connor and Mathis also suggest you factor in bone structure when choosing accessories and construction details of clothing:

[F]or the top of the body, look at the scale of your wrists; for the bottom of the body, look at the scale of your ankles. . . . It is possible for a small-sized woman to have medium or large scale bone structure. It is also possible for a large-sized woman to have medium or small scale bone structure, as seen in the bronze *Walking Woman* by Gaston Lachaise. This is why we look at the wrists and ankles, because bone structure is most evident there.[36]

Connor and Mathis note that if the scale of your body is large and grand, try medium to large and grand scale accessories. If you use small scale accessories, group them "in large clusters or amounts in order to be in scale." If your body is small in scale, use smaller scale accessories. If you prefer larger things, use fewer large things.[37]

Accessories case study: Coats

Capes, shawls, cloaks, jackets, and other coats are primary. To call them accessories is in no way meant to diminish the centrality of their psychological and practical functions. *Moda* cites two purposes of such cover-ups: "Extension: the desire to occupy more space. Concentration: the desire to enclose oneself in a circular gesture as if the body wished to isolate itself from the world and close in upon itself."[38] Flügel elaborates on coats' protective elements:

. . . against the general unfriendliness of the world as a whole; or, expressed more psychologically, a reassurance against the lack of love. If we are in unfriendly surroundings, whether human or natural, we tend, as it were, to button up, to draw our garments closely round us. . . . Under the friendly influence of the sun, on the other hand, we throw off our outer coverings, or carry them more loosely, so that they no longer envelop us and isolate us from the external world. These influences are, I think, not to be accounted for entirely by the temperature.[39]

- What experience do you seek from your coat?
- What is your coat history? One friend remembers how the warmth of a new down-filled coat shocked him into realizing how cold he'd been for years. Knowing what you need your coat to do, emotionally, practically, and aesthetically, can help you know where to look for such a coat, and, more importantly, how to know if you've found it.
- What temperatures do you need your coat for?
- Do you need a coat that is waterproof, water repellent, or neither?
- Do you like a heavy or a light coat? A waterproof synthetic can feel almost weightless on the body, but a wool coat breathes so you don't end up in a slimy pool of sweat.
- What is your budget? A good synthetic or fabric-blend coat purchased new can be far less expensive than a good natural-fiber coat, but the natural-fiber coat may last a lot longer.
- When considering a coat, know how many pockets you need. Plunge your hands in the pockets to feel if they're deep enough.
- Consider the fit of the coat. Does it close easily?
- Can you move in it?
- Lift your arms above your head. How does it feel?
- Is there anything else specific you need a coat to do?
- Must you have a hood, or an inside pocket?
- Something else? A friend who rides a motorcycle had a leather jacket made with extra-long sleeves, because he found, when reaching for the handlebars in a normal coat, the sleeves went halfway to his elbow.

If a coat does not meet all your practical needs, DO NOT BUY IT. A coat is a large enough investment—if bought at regular retail—that it is worth having it meet your baseline requirements, without compromises.

How to look at style specifics as you're trying the coat on? Fatt suggests you "consider what you will be wearing under your coat. Check carefully length, body width, sleeve width, armhole depth, and the neck."[40] Do all the coat's outlines—including waistline—work well with you and your clothes? In choosing a coat, consider what goes with the color of the clothes you own that you like. Darker colors won't show dirt as much, while lighter colors won't show dandruff or white cat hair. A dark-colored coat with a subtle pattern will tend to not look as stained as a solid dark color. Also, since a coat is worn from the shoulders down, the color at the collar should flatter your face. And you should really love it. Wallach suggests, "If you're going to use your coat for both daytime and evening, a dark color may be appropriate. Colors such as black and navy look smart during the day and dressy at night."[41]

How would you describe the perfect coat? What qualities of your current coat(s) work or don't work for you? One woman gave an elaborate explanation of the coat she desired and concluded, "And I can't afford anything more than $5.95." She found the coat. Anything is possible.

Accessories case study: The bag

Handbags took their current place in women's wardrobes in the late eighteenth century. Fashion suddenly shifted to a garment so lightweight and filmy that the pockets and pouches usually sewn into the huge skirts of women's dresses and petticoats could no longer be hidden there. Ribiero notes that the white muslin chemise dress was "the sartorial success story of the 1780s. . . . It was based on the chemise or shift which women wore as their main undergarment."[42] Laver comments that this eighteenth-century slip dress made a little handbag—known as the "reticule" or "ridicule"[43]—absolutely necessary. It was also called the "indispensable." Curious that it was considered both ridiculous and indispensable, oui? In the twentieth century, far from the fashions of the 1780s which made bags a necessity, Diana Vreeland made an attempt to liberate women from the handbag:

> One of those early days at *Harper's Bazaar* I had a brainwave! . . . I said to an editor ambling around the hall, "I've got the best idea!" I took him into my office. "We're going to eliminate all handbags."
>
> I told him how I would do the whole magazine just showing what you can do with pockets and how the silhouette is improved and so on, and also one's walk—there's nothing that limits a woman's walk like a pocketbook.
>
> Well, the man ran from my office the way you run for the police! He rushed into Carmel's office and said, "Diana's going crazy! Get hold of her."
>
> So Carmel came down and said, "Listen, Diana, I think you've lost your mind. Do you realize that our income from handbag advertising is God knows how many millions a year?!"
>
> Well, she was correct, of course. It's the same as if they cut out men's ties. The country'd be destitute.[44]

The fashion industry has a stake in your carrying a handbag. Do you? In 1930, from a man's perspective, Flügel advocated the practicality of the "hands free" sack over the use of pockets:

> The need for carrying about a number of small articles is one of the graver disadvantages of civilization, and it is time that the problem of how this need can best be met should be seriously tackled. . . .
>
> The advantages of having the loose articles contained in a bag, pouch, or wallet (or at least in a few of these receptacles), rather than in a great number of pockets, is pretty obvious; but so, also, is the benefit of having this receptacle securely attached to the body, thus leaving free the hands.[45]

Flügel's suggestions point to the "fanny pack" (zippered side turned to the front for security) and the backpack, which have conveniently entered fashion's stream. Of course Flügel didn't have to deal with a problem caused by the knapsack: straps crossing the shoulders in front of the body defines a feminine bust line in a way that draws a great deal of attention.

Neither of these two suggest the obvious solution to the heavy bag problem: Stop carrying around so much stuff!

- What do you need to carry in a bag?
- What is the best toting device for your needs: handbag, backpack, or forklift?
- How you maintain and organize your bag should be seriously considered when choosing one. What size does it need to be so there's really room for everything? Absolutely ruthless self-honesty is critical in choosing a suitable purse size. Like buying clothes for "when I lose five pounds," buying a purse for a person who carries less stuff (not you) is a complete waste of money. Really. I once spent over $600 on a purse for that "other" me.
- Are you choosing bags made up of materials strong enough to hold up under the kind of wear you inflict?
- Do you have shoulder, neck, or back pain as the result of carrying around too heavy a bag? If so, part of the weight problem may be the weight of the bag itself.
- If it's a shoulder bag, is the strap the right length so the bag falls in the most comfortable, practical place? (If not, a good shoe repair person can fix almost anything.)
- And finally the aesthetic decisions, which can be incorporated easily after practical choices are made: What color, shape, and style of bag will coordinate effectively with the kind of clothes you wear?

Bixler's advice about wallets is also true of purses and backpacks and suitcases: "Carry only what you need."[46] However, people show an enormous amount of resistance to removing never-used items from their bags and wallets. They also carry unused ten-year-old keys on their key chains.

Fiedorek thinks this kind of chaos is an appropriateness issue, odd considering the handbag is a private place. She says the stuff floating around in your bag is a mini-universe: "The less little bits of paper (receipts, gum wrappers, tissues, parking lot tickets) you have floating round in your bag, the better. People do see in, often when you least expect it."[47] Leopold agrees, regarding the hand-held purse: "A clutch bag should always look neat and flat—not like a stuffed flounder."[48]

Cleaning out your wallet and purse provides the same sort of pleasure as flossing. I'm grateful I do it. Today, when I leave the house I usually take four things: wallet, keys, pen, and notepad. If I'm going to need my checkbook and calendar (contained in one small folder/wallet), I add them.

Take a moment to list the information you carry in your wallet on a piece of paper. Note every card and its serial number, as well as contact numbers, so if your wallet is lost or stolen, you can quickly replace the lost items.

Accessories case study: Jewelry

Chanel said, "Jewelry isn't meant to make you look rich, it's meant to adorn you, and that's not the same thing at all."[49] Everyone has different jewelry preferences. Some people don certain pieces of jewelry as a constant in their life just as they brush their teeth. Bart Shulman comments about the jewelry he wears:

> The first things I put on every morning are my rings, and then my pouch. I have a little leather pouch, about two inches wide by three inches long, kidney-shaped, and in it are some rocks, a crystal, and a little tiny clay goddess and stuff like that. As small, significant things enter my life, I cram them in there.

Consider that the most sentimental piece of jewelry, the wedding ring, originated as a token of business exchange. The Romans exchanged rings at the conclusion of a contract. Eventually this custom also included betrothal agreements. After the father and husband-to-be agreed on the dowry, a ring was placed on the bride-to-be. The Romans also began the tradition of placing the ring on the third finger, believing "a nerve or vein ran from that finger to the heart."[50]

I'm a jewelry minimalist. On fancy occasions I put on a strand of pearls and sometimes a gold bangle. I don't like the weight. Stacey Lamiero is also a minimalist for different reasons: "I don't like to wear too much jewelry. I guess I'm holding out for that big, huge bauble." She'd look good in big rocks. Stacey says, "I think I would, too. There's nothing subtle about my jewelry. So I've got to keep that open."

What do you like to wear? What would you like to try? If you're interested in the look of fine jewelry, experiment with inexpensive good fakes to get the look right before you make a huge investment in something that might just sit in your underwear drawer calling out to burglars, "Steal me!" It is easy to purchase ridiculously expensive unsuitable fine jewelry whether we have money or not. One woman said, "That's the reason God invented credit cards." The distraction of a beautiful object can blind us to its irrelevance to our lives or its lack of enhancement to our person. Amelia Fatt comments that some women will look at a pair of emerald earrings against a black velvet backdrop and ooh and ahh over the workmanship, the setting, the perfect color and facets, etc. "All of this may be true; unfortunately, the woman is not made out of black velvet."[51]

To put the brakes on: Get educated about carats, stone treatments, flaws, GIA scales, and certifications. (Diamonds aren't costly because they're rare, they're costly because the DeBeers family has a stranglehold on the market.) "Don't buy gemstones when you are tired. Your color perceptions are not as clear."[52] If you find these instructions irritating, you're caught up in the romance. Wake up.

To discover what suits you in real or costume jewelry, figure out your boundaries. If you must wear something for sentimental reasons even if it makes you look like a rhino, fine, I'm not going to wrestle it off you. But consider also choosing jewelry that really complements your looks.

Gold has a yellow undertone, silver a blue one. If your skin color has a yellow undertone, gold might be more flattering; likewise silver for blue.

Barbara Jay also points out that many people don't look at the difference between how they look in "a metal that's burnished and a metal that's high-shine, and it makes a big difference." Do you prefer to sparkle, shimmer, or glow? Textural differences can also be seen, as Barbara notes, between a shimmery pearl-white and a flat ivory-white: "Different people wear pearls and bone." This again relates to the texture of your features, whether they are glossy, gleaming, or relatively matte. Even though they're the "same" color, the quality evoked by the different textures is very different. How do you see it? With difficulty. Barbara responds, "Sometimes I can really say exactly what it is. Other times the client and I are both looking in the mirror at her, and we just notice she's breathing easier."

Ornament is another way to provide the emphasis discussed in the silhouette section. Leopold notes, "Jewelry directs the eye where the woman wants it to go."[53]

Common sense: Use accessories to finish the outfits you own. Find and note combinations you love, so when you need to look terrific, you can do it easily.

Shoes

> *Life is so awful, so ugly and messy and rushed.*
> *But in a pair of beautiful shoes, you forget your problems.*
> —Manolo Blahnik, shoe maker[54]

In the realm of accessories, shoes are another duchy entirely. A subject of passionate fantasy, shoes seem to be the item most often purchased with blatant disregard for the essential needs of the wearer. Why?

Women especially develop emotional and aesthetic relationships with their shoes. As one shoe lover who buys at least one pair of shoes a month fancifully puts it, "Shoes follow me home. 'Can I keep 'em, Mom? They're so cute, Mom.'" Why such quantity? She describes shoes "as a way to exercise my multiple personalities. I don't ask, 'Is this shoe me?' I think 'I could be that shoe or I could be that shoe. . . .'" Later, she continues, "You don't think, 'Does it fit with my wardrobe?' You love the shoe for what it is, and it's you." This attitude does not come from a vacuum. Her mother used to sleep with her new shoes because she loved them so.

For the right shoe, does the cost issue slip away? Lex responds, "It becomes far less important, that's for sure." Stacey comments:

> If I do see something that I really like, I can justify that. I had my mom buy me a pair of little flat shoes for my birthday. They were kelly green Anne Klein's. My mom said, "What can you wear those shoes with?" and I said, "I just can. I know it." I had them resoled about three times until finally they started getting a hole through the top. I loved them. And my mom had to say later, "You're right. You got a lot of use out of those shoes."

When a woman who loves shoes finds a shoe that is beautiful to her as well as comfortable, something akin to rapture occurs. The Queen of Romania went to Ferragamo soon after she'd been banished from the throne. Ferragamo watched as she paced the floor of his salon in her first pair of Ferragamo shoes, and asked her, "Do your feet feel free?" "Free?" she replied. "In these shoes, my toes seem to be swimming. This is one freedom they will never take away from me."[55]

Before stilettos

In the fourteenth century, the pope condemned shoes that were so long they had to be reinforced with whalebone.[56] In seventeenth-century Venice, women wore platform shoes as high as twenty inches, initially to keep them above street filth, but later for social status.[57] Shoes have also offended with their width. Queen Mary eventually put a stop to shoes widening with a declaration that the toe's width must not exceed six inches.[58] It had gradually become more and more duck-billed in shape.

Common to all, as many point out, is the hampering of female mobility. Today's version is the high-heeled shoe. As Susan Bixler, author of *The Professional Image*, puts it: "You have a nice suit, you're all put together, and then you look down and all of a sudden the feet are just screaming sex!"[59] There is also much current public outcry similar to that of previous centuries. Even shoe lovers are not indiscriminate in their passions. Lex states:

> Heels are torture devices invented by men to keep women from doing what they need to do in life. Heels, like long nails, impair the physical ability of women to get things done. High heels will keep you on a pedestal. You can't run in them. You can barely walk in them. I know people who have completely ruined their feet, their Achilles tendons.

Walk behind someone in pumps as they walk down the street. Watch their ankles and think about the effect over time of that adjusting and shaking on the rest of their body. If we wear heels for "ourselves," because they're comfortable, maybe we should look around and see what else we call comfortable, take a deep breath and see if it really is.

Stacey puts in a word in favor of high heels: "If I have a skirt on, I love to wear high heels." I comment that a lot of women feel that heels are somehow debilitating. Does she feel differently? Stacey replies, "I think they probably aren't real good for you. But everything we do just about isn't good for us." Why does she wear them?

> It's not so much what other people see or who I'm going to impress. It's how I feel. I just have a few things that when I put them on, I feel like I can do anything. You know what it is? I think it's the confidence—if people are attracted to you—it's not what you're wearing. It's how you feel about yourself. When I put on these outfits, they make me feel good, and then I think I exude something.

Stacey is convinced, and I remain admiring but incredulous. Podiatrist Eliot Wenger substantiates Stacey's point of view: "Obviously there are people who can wear high heels with impunity and they have no problems." Others, he comments,

> have a high threshold of pain or choose to ignore the pain. . . . I get people coming in quite often who have painful feet and they're wearing high heels that don't fit. . . . If someone is in a job where they have to wear high heels or something equivalent to that, you try to compromise with them as much as you can with common sense. If they're walking around in

233

an office or they're seeing clients, then of course they wear their shoes. But if they're sitting behind a desk, they can certainly take them off.

As we've heard ad nauseam, heel wearing is correlated with serious medical problems. In one study, a doctor found in fifteen years of foot operations that women suffered ninety-four percent of bunions, eighty-one percent of hammertoes, eighty-nine percent of neuromas (thickening of a nerve in the foot usually associated with heels), and ninety percent of bunionettes (bumps on the outside of the foot). And seventy-five percent of these problems could be attributed to compression of the forefoot by narrow-toed, high-heeled shoes.[60]

But for someone to leave their beloved heels, they have to have direct repeated negative experiences. Melissa Batchelder comments:

I used to wear high heels. I walk a lot, and I walk fast naturally. As a result, a couple of times, I've broken the bones in my foot from the pounding. I thought, "I must be out of my mind to think that this is in some way attractive. Am I really fooling people into thinking that I'm taller? Not likely." So I stopped.

Women can be nutty about the heels issue, and they also can be nutty vis-à-vis shoes' size. In another study, ninety percent of the women surveyed said they wore shoes too small for their feet.[61] Ouch. What about resulting foot problems? According to a USC study, eighty-six percent of women can blame their foot problems on undersized shoes.[62] One study blames heels, another blames small shoes. Regardless, it's clear there's something wrong.

- Do you buy shoes because you want to be the person who would wear them or because they truly fit?
- What would life be like if you never felt pinching or pain in your feet, if your connection to the earth, through your soles, was always one of ease?
- If someone taught you to value image over direct sensation, how can you acknowledge them, and then move on to beautiful shoes which also support you and help you feel welcome here?
- How to find shoes that fit? Dr. Wenger says; "It's common sense. The first thing you want to do is look at your foot and see if it has any semblance or relationship to what the shoe looks like."

Exercises

1. The next page has been left blank deliberately. Get a pen or a pencil, take your shoe and sock off one foot and trace that foot. If your foot is too big for the page, tape another sheet to it so you can trace the entire foot. Do not alter the size of your foot to fit onto the page. Look at your tracing of your foot.

   Feet are shaped like feet for a reason. There are twenty-six bones in each foot, and many muscles, and all of them serve a purpose—to help you walk and move.

   Place the appropriate foot of each pair of shoes you own over the tracing of your foot. If the tracing is larger than the shoe, put the pair in one pile. If the shoe is larger than the tracing, put the pair in another pile.

   You don't have to do anything with the shoes that are too small. You may think you have to have this pair for that event and that pair because it goes with this outfit. Fine. Bear in mind two things: "that outfit" was created at the expense of your essential comfort, and without consideration for your moving with ease in the world. "That outfit" is part of the problem. But, if you give those shoes away, or sell them at a consignment shop, someone else who has embarked on a quest for the perfect shoe, whose foot is two sizes smaller than yours, might achieve nirvana thanks to your contribution.

2. Feel your feet move against the ground while you walk; try to feel the different bones and muscles moving. Wiggle your toes periodically. Try interlacing your toes. (Don't hold the position for more than a few seconds.)

3. The average person walks the equivalent of two trips around the world in her lifetime[63] and sweats a half a pint of moisture a day from the 250,000 sweat glands in her feet, facts that should be reason enough for buying decent-fitting shoes. The synthetic vs. natural-fiber issue really matters here. Synthetics don't breathe.

4. If you can't find shoes, there's always barefoot. Slippers are also important. I originally bought slippers because the downstairs neighbor complained I thumped early in the morning. I then realized I thumped because I was running because my feet were cold because I didn't have slippers. The slippers I bought are soft and warm, I can slip my feet in them from a standing position, they are wide enough so my feet feel relaxed and not squashed, and they have a hard sole so I can put out the trash without ruining them. Since none of my other shoes are quite as fulfilling, maybe I should never leave the house.

5. What are your criteria for shoes? How do you let go of shoes that don't work?

6. Shoe lovers' purchases are affected by mood more than need. Reebok estimates that its customers own six to seven pairs of athletic shoes. Eighty percent of those shoes aren't used for the activity they're designed for.[64] To break through the hypnotic hold of apair of shoes, look at what you need, match the type of shoe to the purpose of the outfit, and feel the fit.[65] Like all addicts, we need to learn to keep it simple. Do you need more than two pairs of shoes for work? How many pairs do you need for travel?

If these questions make you feel defensive, consider the following eight-step process for shoe purchases. (Most of this comes directly from Norman's *How to Buy Great Shoes that Fit*, except where noted.)

1. Bring inserts and get the hosiery right.[66]

2. Since the shoe industry has no standard measurements for size,[67] and the difference in length between a half size (say, 7 to 7½) is 1/6 of an inch,[68] always try the next two sizes larger to get the greatest comfort.

3. Don't just sashay up to the nearest mirror, look at the shoes for a few moments, and then sit back down.[69] Walk hard and fast on a hard surface.

4. Feel the fit. Can you wiggle your toes easily?[70]

5. Never ask anyone else how a shoe looks. They'll tell you, "It's the last shoe of its kind on earth"; "You can break them in"; "The shoes are returnable"; "A shoemaker can make alterations after you buy them." These are all red flags. Avoid the $300 shoe mistake I made.

6. After daydreaming about some yellow leather thongs with a bunch of brightly colored leather fruit on top (this might appeal only to me and to some Miami residents who are chauffeured around in pale yellow Rolls-Royces), when I tried them on, alas, I noticed my toes drooping over the front of the sandal. I let them stay in the store. Look at the shoes in a full-length mirror last. Why? Rapture has to be experienced physically, in your walk and movement, as well as visually. Otherwise it's easy to kid yourself about fulfilling the dream of the perfect shoe.

7. I have vivid memories from childhood of leaving the Stride-Rite store each fall carrying a brightly colored, helium-filled balloon and wearing my new shoes. I have grown up to learn: Shoes that feel comfortable in the store may never feel comfortable at home. In the store, feet are on their best behavior. They may not be entirely honest with you, even though they're attached to your body. An essential part of shoe shopping occurs after you take them home: trying them on with everything you own. If you must wear them outdoors during the test period, cover the soles with masking tape. Sharon Frederick suggests, "When they do not work, when they kill you, and you have to return them, you peel it off, and there're no marks on the sole. The store doesn't care that you tried the shoes. They look for the marks, that's all." If they get scuffed inadvertently, and they're not the shoes for you, have a shoemaker revarnish them before you return them. I'm not advocating questionable activity, such as returning shoes you've gotten good wear from; just don't keep shoes that cause you pain.

8. Maintenance and repair. Diana Vreeland, who had the soles of her shoes polished after she wore them,[71] said of a good shoe repair:

This is a serious subject with me. At *last* . . . we're on a serious subject. This isn't fashion stuff—this is the *real thing*. I always say, "I hope to God I die in a town with a good tailor, a good shoemaker, and perhaps someone who's interested in a little *quelque chose d'autre*," but all I *really* care about is that shoemaker. Everyone should have a shoemaker they go to as seriously as they go to their doctor.[72]

You now are equipped to fulfill your destiny of finding the perfect shoe.

How does this all fit together? Color, fabric, and proportion in harmonious blend provide you with wonderful outfits. Accessories are the finishing touch. The perfect shoe takes this ensemble over the top into rapture. Now, let us examine how it all gets put together and stored.

Notes:

1. Kentner, Bernice. *Tie Me Up with Rainbows*. Page 153.
2. Larkey, Jan. *Flatter Your Figure*. Page 92.
3. Byers, Margaretta with Consuelo Kamholz. *Designing Women*. Page 97.
4. Wallach, Janet. *Working Wardrobe*. Page 40.
5. Byers. Page 108.
6. What makes for good or bad silk? According to Bixler, "The variation in silk prices often depends on whether the silk came from cultured or uncultured silkworms, something that relates to the silkworms' diets, rather than to their exposure to good music and art. The cultured worm has the costlier and more controlled diet and provides the more expensive, finer-textured silk. The uncultured worm is left to scrounge for food, and produces uneven thread." Bixler, *The Professional Image*. Page 67.
7. Goday, Dale and Molly Cochran. *Dressing Thin*. Page 79.
8. "In England we first hear of cotton in the late twelfth century. . . . Cotton was supposed to be the wool of certain mysterious Scythian sheep. These lambs grew on shrubs, each cradled in its downy pod. Except for the fact that the stalk was attached to the soil, they were like little downy creatures who gamboled in the English fields. Fortunately this stem was flexible and permitted them to bend down and graze on the adjacent herbage. When, however, all grass within this narrow orbit had been eaten, the lambs naturally and wisely proceeded to expire. Both wool and flesh were then available. Short of a fire breathing dragon, no animal could have been more satisfactory to the Middle Ages. The actual cotton plant was tame beside it. To whom belongs the distinguished honor of this discovery, I can not determine." [M. D. C. Crawford, *The Heritage of Cotton*. Page 4.]
9. Glynn, Prudence. *Skin to Skin*. Page 133.
10. Kolander, Cheryl. *A Silk Worker's Notebook*. Page 10.
11. Feldon, Leah. *Dressing Rich*. Page 86.
12. McGill, Leonard. *Stylewise*. Page 132.
13. Kentner. Page 50.
14. Weiland, Barbara and Leslie Wood. *Clothes Sense*. Page 53.
15. Weiland. Page 53.
16. Glynn. Page 135.
17. Morton, Grace. *The Arts of Costume and Personal Appearance*. Page 118.
18. Wallach, Janet. *Looks That Work*. Page 98.
19. McJimsey, Harriet. *Art in Clothing Selection*. Pages 126-127.
20. Morton. Page 83.
21. Fatt, Amelia. *Conservative Chic*. Page 23.
22. Pener, Degen. "Lauren Hutton's shopping spree." *Elle*. February 1994. Page 172.
23. Mathis, Carla and Helen Connor. *The Triumph of Individual Style*. Page 42.
24. Mathis. Pages 89-90.
25. Flügel. Page 20.

26. Procter. Page 12.

27. Mathis. Page 59.

28. Mathis. Page 59. For more information on this topic, their book, *The Triumph of Individual Style*, has some wonderful sections on what to choose when you want to play up or play down a feature.

29. Mathis. Page 12.

30. Below are listed forty-four (yes, forty-four) of the classic silhouettes of the twentieth century. This list, though roughly chronological, is by no means comprehensive.

1. Turn-of-the-century dress included clothes that consistently hid the whole leg in skirts. These designs flatter a woman who wishes to play down an ample derriere and full legs. The fitted upper-torso variation favors a woman who wishes to emphasize a small waist, although the long full skirt can be topped with almost any sort of waist, bust, or shoulder camouflage or emphasis and still be considered "classic." A modern take on this would be not nearly as fitted (no need for girdles of whalebone). Of course, the exact patterns and colors of fabric available then are unavailable now, and the longish full skirts, for reasons of convenience, no longer sweep the floor except in some formal wear. This silhouette contains the delicious paradox of professed modesty, while exaggerating the curved outlines of the breasts and butt. A long skirt can be an excellent device to play up ankles, revealed by the bottom hem, or, if the ankles are shy, a long skirt with boots can relieve them of any nervousness.

2. The period from 1900 to 1910 saw the introduction of the shirtwaist dress. This garment favors many figures, hence its consistent popularity in fashion. Here the classic "white shirt" first made an appearance in contemporary fashion for women, though examples of it have been found in the tombs of the ancient Egyptians. The shirtwaist usually is cut for the evenly proportioned at the waist—neither the long- nor the short-waisted seek out that silhouette, though empire and hip-belted shirtwaists have shown up in the last few years.

3. Poiret's designs from 1909 to 1914 included "exotic" kimono looks, or enveloping capes that tapered toward the ankle. Trousers appeared as harem pants, full through the leg, tapering toward the ankle. If you like complete and voluminous coverage for your figure, adopt this oval or round silhouette. Through the artful use of pleats and tailoring, the updated version does not hobble the wearer as Poiret's did. One woman who favors this look commented, "I wear oversized garments, not to hide something ugly, but to hide something beautiful. In the privacy of my home, I traipse about however I please, but out in the world I need to feel dramatic but not provocative." For more information, see any book with drawings by Léon Bakst. Freeing the body from the corset, Poiret's fashions allowed for a relaxed torso while drawing attention to interesting hands and faces. Often, little else showed.

4. Clothes made for women during World War I were the first to allow full mobility (so that they could serve in the war effort). These clothes, using less fabric, both freed women from the corset and didn't hobble them. Out went boning, fullness, and

bustle, and in came careful crafty tailoring, using the limits imposed for fabric rationing to artfully conceal and reveal the figure. These designs favor someone who likes to wear an evenly proportioned or long-waisted silhouette that reveals nothing above the ankles, while hanging close to the body.

5. During and after World War I, clothing reflected the spirit of the times—it had the guts knocked out of it. The horror of the Great War rendered ludicrous the idea of a controlled, structured, orderly life. This was reflected in fashion. Bailey comments: "The current need for expression of brevity in style arose from the post-war feeling that the dearly held traditions and beliefs in our society had been blown away, along with the lives of millions of young men, so what was the point of maintaining old values and elegant manners of dress?" [Bailey, Adrian. *The Passion for Fashion*. Page 133.]

   Clothes without apparent structure date from this time. So, if you favor unstructured looks, start your research here.

6. and 7. War was followed by wardrobe revolution. The twenties marked the introduction of the masculine silhouette (the bloomers favored by Amelia Bloomer in the 1880s didn't really catch on fashion-wise until the culottes of the 1970s) by Chanel, who adapted casual menswear fabrics and silhouettes to womenswear. Also introduced was the straight silhouette, which favors the waistless and small-breasted.

8. and 9. The style of dress which is full on the top two-thirds, and narrow on the bottom third favors those wishing to dress a full torso and narrow legs. Women's business suits that are large on top and narrow through the skirt echo this silhouette in a fusion with menswear style. Also in the 1920s, for the first time fashion saw hems of dresses and skirts rise to the knee, revealing the shape of the lower leg.

10. The 1930s brought to prominence the great clothes of Madeleine Vionnet, whose bias cuts and to-the-body dressing enhanced a figure with some flesh on her who was also small-busted. The bias cut, which relies on fabric sewn so the warp and woof are laid X-wise on the body (instead of the usual +++ construction) favors a woman who enjoys revealing the curves of her body through fabric, because the way the fabric is sewn makes the body's shape show through.

11. "[In the] 1930s women signified their willingness and ability to help bear the burdens of the world by literally squaring their shoulders. . . . " Regardless of your actual shoulder definitions, these styles made you broad. Shoulder pads entered women's clothes.

12. In the 1930s fuller skirts brought back a waist to clothing. The garments camouflaged the thighs while showing off the calves and bust.

13. The 1930s were also the time of fitted Hollywood glamor and no fabric limits. The extremely sophisticated, complicated tailored clothes were ideal for people who loved dressing itself as an intricate time-consuming art. Vionnet also practiced this, but hers was an ethereal feminine look, not the tailored masculine-influenced style. A cleverly tailored garment can camouflage nearly any subtlety of the body seeking shelter from inquisitive eyes.

14. Also for the first time, formal menswear fabrics and jacket cuts were shown on women (both with trousers and skirts). Think of Marlene Dietrich and Greta Garbo in the menswear suits.

15. The 1940s silhouettes reflected fabric rationing of the Second World War. The garments fit close to the body, flattering those who were spare of form. Because the fashion capital Paris was shut down by war, Americans learned for the first time to appreciate our own sensibility. The sleek streamlined practical clothes demanded by the limitations of war later became our signature "sportswear."

16. Dior distracted us from all that with the postwar "New Look." His designs favored women with figures like upturned flowers, and "nipped in waists." [Milbank, Caroline. *New York Fashion*. Page 16.] This pleases women who want to play up large hips, delicate ankles, a tiny waist, and sloping shoulders. (His was not the first wasp waist; the ancient Minoans liked them too. [Flügel. Page 43.]) The postwar silhouette was exaggeratedly "female," a repopulating gesture. Modifications of this silhouette favor all figures with a defined waist.

17-21. The fifties brought about a series of fashionable silhouettes for a variety of figures. The A-line works on the small-busted woman with little waist definition and generous hips. The "trapeze" garment falls straight from broad shoulders, camouflaging all else. (However, wearing this dress in a strong wind can provide others with a complete view of your underwear.) The princess line, first presented by Worth, achieved eminence in the 1950s. This fit-and-flare style is narrow through the top and waist and wider below. This unbelted style can create the illusion of a waist where there is none. The H-line garment flatters a woman with evenly matched shoulders and hips and little waist definition, and the ill-named sack dress camouflages all but highlights lovely lower legs and, when worn sleeveless, well-shaped arms. All these structured garments were often lined and also made with great attention to cut despite their deceptively simple outlines. They favor dressing a woman with an "adult" figure, not a childlike one.

22. The 1950s teenagers brought interesting changes to fashion. The first baby diesel dykes wore their elder brother's denims and flannels, providing a tomboy clothes option for teens of all shapes. (And Katharine Hepburn showed her beautifully bony frame in her tailored menswear tweeds.)

23. Teenagers wore poodle skirts, saddle shoes, and cardigans. This silhouette resembles the turn-of-the-century look, only with lower legs revealed. It favors those wishing to camouflage ample derrieres and highlight the bosom, the defined waist, and shapely calves and ankles.

24. The jumper also was worn by teens.

25. The "bad" kids, thank God, brought into fashion the James Dean look, with their Levis and leather jackets—the first time in fashion women with slender hips and legs, and tiny behinds could play up their appeal.

26. Some of the Beat "chicks" wore all black with capri pants, showing the leg's shape all the way to the hip. The boxy tops in fashion masked any definition in the upper torso. A leisurely wealthy version of this silhouette was worn by Jackie Kennedy, shown at ease wearing white capri pants, boxy silk Pucci shirts, and sunglasses.

27. The garments of the 1960s, with their straight silhouettes, said with childlike simplicity "Enough already!" to the sometimes exaggerated femininity of 1950s clothes. Clothing became cartoonlike in its "purity," echoing the fantastic new world of space travel. Fashion saw the miniskirt with tights, dresses that were straight from shoulder to hem, no emphasis of hips, waist, or breast, even tent dresses. These sorts of cuts favor those with evenly proportioned shoulders and hips, seeking no waist emphasis through belt or cut, pretending to enhance only the small-chested while actually flattering almost any high bosom. Tent dresses cover everything except the calves.

28. In the late 1960s the hippies came forth, most in opposition to the Vietnam war (and some perhaps just in solidarity with the Beatles). They took fashion even further away from exaggerating a female body as designated for reproduction. One of their radical idealized looks was poor country Grandma, as Lurie notes.

29. The 1970s, with women's lib, marked the entry of the completely loose and forgiving silhouette, the fashion of the garment defined by the use of color, pattern, and fabric. Acres of colored crinkled gauze, gypsy "native" looks, and takes on nomadic traditional clothes filled the stores. This period also marked the re-entrance of the caftan for all figures.

30. We also saw clothes flared at wrist and ankle (seeking camouflage there anyone?) on narrow bodies. This worked on the bony, small-bosomed younger sophisticate, who preferred a "sharp" garment more aggressively revealing of her figure. Among the many services feminism provided, it created a multiplicity of fashion silhouettes that meant beauty was available to all. Some men, hopping on the bandwagon, even took the liberty of taking a moment to be dandies, reclaiming a sartorial splendor which had been their right prior to the industrial revolution. But they quickly, meekly scurried back into Levis and chinos once fashion told them to. The hardcore preppy look began to assert itself among the gay subculture and was quickly re-adopted by mainstream male fashion. They haven't budged an inch since. What about the Seattle Look? This was picked up by teenagers, and didn't go much further. See item 40.

31. Women took into account menswear, womenswear and feminism as they cruised through the 1970s. True "unisex" fashion came into play and women were encouraged to try actual men's clothes, not just clothes cut to look like men's. The archetypal loose menswear silhouette was defined by Diane Keaton in the film *Annie Hall*.

32. Some women and many teens, enjoying an exaggerated tartlike femininity, wore jeans so tight they had to lie down to zip them. This look favors the perilously slim or those who wish to show definition of the entire lower body.

33. Others surrendered to the ease of men's loose jeans and flannel shirts. (This forgiving look works for everyone who wants it.)

34. Women entering the workforce pounced on the power suit and quickly mutated the garment to make it their own. Suits—camouflage acquired to enter the business world of men—can mask the whole body except the lower leg and ankle.

35. In the 1980s menswear's previously unexplored realms, namely boxer shorts and athletic clothes, made their way into the territory of women's leisure wardrobes, with varieties for all figures.

36. We saw feminization of the power suit, integrating the female curves, done most beautifully by Armani and popularized for the masses with class by Liz Claiborne.

37. St. John knits began its climb to huge success with women's knit business clothes you could wear for travel without getting wrinkled.

38. L.A. style brought in the combination of blazers and blue jeans and the completely covered top over fairly well-defined legs.

39. In the 1990s anything goes. Hip-hop music gave us clothes worn oversized and backward. The voluminous garments worked on all figures, although few successfully resolved the problem of how to keep the pants up.

40. Rock music gave us grunge, wearing rags and calling it fashion. It only worked on those young enough to look like teenagers. Everyone else looked homeless.

41. Fashion borrows from the last unexplored closet, the kids'. I expect clothes for adults patterned after toddler clothes any minute now.

42. We also see variations on Charlie Chaplin's look, little over big, in baby-Ts worn with baggy pants.

43. More children's-wear influences can be seen in empire-waisted dresses and fragile garments worn with big clunky shoes (à la dress-up in Mommy's closet).

44. Women began to comment on the fact that you could watch a fashion trend go by and feel secure in paying no attention to it. The most popular of the oversized variations, the big overshirt worn with leggings, was adopted with pleasure and comfort by many who just wished to play up their legs and nothing else.

31. Morris, Bernadine. *The Fashion Makers*. Page 109.
32. Satran. Page 221.
33. Garber, Marjorie. *Vested Interests*. Page 21.
34. In addition to accessories, garment details, such as the width of seams and belts, as well as detail stitching, pockets, belt buckles, decorative buttons, bows, etc. [Mathis. Page 103] can also be chosen to relate to the scale of facial features and hands, the silhouette, color, etc.
35. Mathis. Page 51.
36. Mathis. Pages 97-99.
37. Mathis. Page 1-5.
38. *Fashion: Poetry and Design Approaches to Creativity*. Page 43.
39. Flügel. Page 77.

40. Fatt. Page 135.

41. Wallach. *Looks That Work*. Page 190.

42. Ribiero, Aileen. *Dress and Morality*. Page 115.

43. Laver, James. *Clothing and Fashion*. Page 153.

44. Vreeland. Page 89.

45. Flügel. Pages 186-187.

46. Bixler. Page 181.

47. Fiedorek, Mary. *Executive Style*. Page 75.

48. Leopold, Allison and Anne Marie Cloutier. *Short Chic*. Page 179.

49. Batterberry, Michael and Ariane Batterberry. *Mirror, Mirror*. Page 319.

50. Avery, James with Karen Jackson. *The Right Jewelry for You*. Page 61.

51. Fatt. Page 89.

52. Avery. Page 170.

53. Leopold. Page 173.

54. La Fela, Ruth. "What's sex got to do with it?" *Elle*. September 1993. Page 294.

55. Green, Lisa. "If the Shoe Fits." Review of *Shoemaker of Dreams* by Salvatore Ferragamo. *Elle*. June 1994. Page 50.

56. Rosencranz, Mary Lou. *Clothing Concepts*. Page 191.

57. Pierre. Page 183.

58. Brooke, Iris. *Footwear*. Page 41.

59. Bixler, Susan. *The Professional Image*. Page 59.

60. Berg, Rona. "High Heel Hell." *Vogue*. February 1995. Page 224.

61. "Health Department Footnotes." *Lears*. July 1992. Page 34.

62. Berg, Rona. "High Heel Hell". *Vogue*. February 1995. Page 224.

63. Wagenvoord, James and Fiona St. Aubyn. *ClothesCare*. Page 23.

64. Dominguez, Joe and Vicki Robin. *Your Money or Your Life*. Page 84.

65. Goday. Page 92.

66. Norman, Scott. *How to Buy Great Shoes That Fit*. Page 41.

67. Norman. Page 51.

68. Norman. Page 41.

69. Norman. Page 17.

70. Wagenvoord and St. Aubyn. Page 23.

71. Wallach. *Looks That Work*. Page 122.

72. Vreeland. Page 162.

Dressing:
Facing Your Closet's Contents, Maintenance, and the Dark Side

There are lots of good reasons why you should not clean out your closet. List yours:

1. I can't clean out my closet because:
   a) I don't have time.
   b) I'm afraid to open the door.
   c) As Marlow said of Kurtz, "The horror, the horror."

2. My closet looks like: _____.

3. If my closet only contained clothes I liked that fit, _____.

4. My clothes mean so much to me. (*Sigh.*) I can't let go of _____ because _____. Even though _____ (*item of clothing*) upsets me, I have to keep it because _____. (Who is going to catch you? Who will be hurt? Whose body would you need so it would fit?)

5. Closet history is a personal matter. Who or what is metaphorically in your closet?

6. List the top ten embarrassments of your closet. What do you wish you had never laid eyes on?

7. How much is enough?

8. How is your closet like your family?

9. How many complete outfits do you own? How many do you need?

Why clean out closets?

Every morning when we get dressed, we must face our closets, for better or worse. The degree to which our clothes and the organization of our closets please us not only affects how we dress, but also affects the humor with which we face the day.

The modern woman's closet takes its lead from Queen Elizabeth I, the first person to have "suites of 'clothes rooms' rather than the traditional chests."[1] There she stored over three thousand dresses, eighty wigs, and the crown jewels.[2] Prior to the industrial revolution, however, the "common" woman had, at most, two outfits—one everyday dress and one for "good"—which, when not in use, hung on a clothes hook. I suspect your clothes collection is slightly larger. Merriam characterizes an average one: "We may not actually wear it, but there the stuff is, piling up in our closets and bureau drawers, like some kind of horrible science-fiction blob that keeps on enlarging no matter what we try to do to stop it."[3] This too-full closet is an embarrassing, uncomfortable mirror of affluence. Some avoid facing their closets because they don't want to acknowledge the abundance of their lives, but our closet problem is real. I encourage you to face yours. Though resolution is difficult, the aftereffects—clear thinking and a relaxing generosity—make it worthwhile.

The goal of this book is neither that you have four perfect things hanging in an almost empty closet, nor that you have outfits in every color that can be transformed fifteen clever ways with the cunning use of accessories, but rather that you discover the sort of closet you want and figure out how to get yours that way. People have different ideal closets. Laurel Fenenga says of her own:

> I don't want to maximize the variety because then when I go on a trip, I'm schizophrenic. I don't know what to put in the suitcase—"Maybe I'll be having a green day. Maybe I'll be having a whatever." I'm best off having fewer choices, but more what I really like in those choices.

She points to her linen shirt and shorts: "I know that I'm going to feel fine in this. I don't have to put it on and then decide I feel fine in it, or see if it fits and then decide. I know I'm going to like it before I put it on, and I like that."

Libby Granett prefers a different kind of closet: "I'm a cheap shopper. I don't spend a lot of money on one item. Instead of having five tasteful, expensive outfits that I can always be proud of wearing, I have a closet full of chatchkas, of shmatas . . . not really. Most of them aren't things that I would feel embarrassed to wear, but I do have lots and lots of variety."

Jeremy Stone keeps clothes not just for daily wear, but also for sentimental reasons and creative costuming:

> My closet is a library of all the different personalities, periods and stories I can live. Some outfits are very reassuring, comfortable and comforting. I have outfits I look at and think, "Oh, this is so-and-so's favorite outfit." Or "So-and-so hated this outfit. Good. I'll wear it now."

Amy Fine Collins believes "opening a closet door should be like arriving at a really good party where everyone you see is someone you like."[4] The owners of the above-mentioned closets have resolved two central questions:

1. What do you want your closet to be like?
2. What do you love about the clothes you have?

At this point, you might be seized by the urge to go shopping. Forgo it. First, face your closet as it is. Why? If you don't know where you are on the clothes map, you won't be able to figure out how to get to your destination. Carol Jackson characterizes four different types of troubled closets:

> Most common is simple accumulation of clothes, one outfit at a time, by the woman who buys for events as they occur. Her closet contains a shirt here, a pair of shoes there. Each was purchased to go with something now discarded, and it currently matches nothing. . . .
> Then there is the closet containing too many clothes. This woman buys impulsively, never gets rid of anything, and has decision confusion when it is time to get dressed or go shopping.

A third problem is common to the woman whose weight fluctuates. She has three wardrobes, each in a different size, so she has both too many and too few clothes.

Last is the problem of too few clothes, either because the woman has financial limitations . . . because she is depriving herself (feeling guilty or waiting to lose weight) . . . because she feels insecure about what to buy, or because her lifestyle centers around blue jeans.[5]

I don't expect you to have a perfect closet; most women don't. Fiedorek found that nearly 80% of the executives she asked admitted to owning clothes they wished they didn't.[6]

If you look in your closet and want to weep, this may not be a symptom of your closet's needs, but rather may indicate dissatisfactions elsewhere in your life that need attention. The process of cleaning out your closet may honestly allow you to face other problems as well. On the deepest level, as Goldfein writes, you clean out your closet to "learn to discard things that no longer have a meaningful part in your life."[7]

Organizing your closet can include getting rid of clothes you'll never wear again, getting the proper hardware to store your clothes, finishing outfits that lack something essential, and assembling outfits that meet your needs. Without doing this, you end up with what Cam Smith Solari calls incomplete cycles:

Having things half-finished and lying around can make a person feel tired and unhappy. Attention gets stuck on those incomplete cycles of action. Finishing projects, answering mail, finishing the hem, picking up the papers, whatever . . . makes a person feel good and ready to do new things. So if I'm not being as productive as I want to be and things aren't going quite right, I make a list of all the incomplete cycles I have (even the very minor ones) and I finish them . . . and then I have a lot more energy and it is easier to work.[8]

With Goday's goal in mind, that your "entire wardrobe is totally functional and each item in it makes you look good,"[9] I used the information about color, fabric, and proportion and started looking around my closet, slowly throwing out or giving away stuff that didn't suit me. I was creating more emptiness so I could begin to see, in the space that was left, what I really wanted to look like, who I really wanted around me, what sort of life I wanted to have. The physical clutter was like the chatter in my mind—it distracted—and sometimes even convinced me that I was stuck: "This is how life is. You don't like it? Tough."

If you can't bear the thought of giving something away, you can put it in a box in a garage. I have a box of stuff under the bed which I look at every few years, and I can't bear to part with it. These clothes serve me far better out of sight.

You can do it slowly or you can do it in one fell swoop, once a year or every six months or so. The advantage to the marathon clean-out is you get the big picture. The advantage to the one-by-one approach is it's less shocking. It all boils down to how you remove band-aids—do you peel slowly or rip them off with a jerk? We'll address the big clean-out in depth. The same principles apply to the slow process. The first time is the hardest.

Case study: Heather's closet

Last spring, my cousin Heather asked me to help her clean out her closet. A law student with shoulder-length brown hair and sky blue eyes, she's also one of the toughest and most tenacious negotiators I know. She met me at her front door wearing a white T-shirt and gingham checked shorts. She lives in a charming apartment, with a private outdoor garden, in the heart of San Francisco. Her home is decorated simply in cream and pastel colors with some really fine pictures on the walls: a large work of a woman in a hat and some small, brightly colored abstracts. She has two large closets: one rarely used that contains mostly coats, and one for clothes. She also has two large antique dressers. My tone in supporting her closet-clearing was tough, a reflection of what I've come to know works with her. To her it shows seriousness and commitment. This was her first closet-cleaning.

After eating a small snack, we brought a few boxes of plastic bags into the bedroom and settled down in front of one of the closets. We came up with the following questions to support her in figuring out what she wants:

1. Do you really like the way you look in it?
2. What roles do you play?
3. Over the next year, any new roles?
4. How do you want to feel in your clothes?
5. How do you like your clothes to fit?
6. What do you want your closet to be like?
7. How do you want to look?
8. What impression do you want to make?
9. What looks do you want to avoid?
10. What makes you feel good in your body?
11. Does this reflect who you are right now?
12. The bottom-line question turned out to be: How much is enough? She said, "If in my wildest fantasy I can imagine wearing something, I hold onto it. I have so many outfits to wash the car in, you wouldn't believe. I never wash the car."

She added, "I'm afraid that this is going to be sort of an adversarial experience." So that my goals would be in line with hers, eliminating the possibility of an adversarial experience, I asked her again, "What's your goal for the afternoon?" She responded, "I would love to get rid of some of this stuff. In a way, I need to have it taken away from me because I don't part willingly."

I asked what words she needs to hear so we actually accomplish this. She replied, "Well, 'No' is a good word." We both laughed. She continued, "Or 'When was the last time you wore this?' Or 'Have you ever had a good experience in this outfit? Or getting out of this outfit?' "

She said, "Let's start with the dresser. That's one of my biggest excesses." As we worked, it became increasingly clear that Heather wasn't ready to have a closet full of clothes she loved and wore. This can't be forced, so I worked with her at the level she was willing to work at (getting rid of a great many worn, tired-out, or just plain bad clothes), and we did a huge amount of good work. In helping her clean out her closets, I was aware I was doing something that's literally stripping away. She felt vulnerable. My job was to be supportive. When she said things like, "This isn't so bad. I'm doing great!" I affirmed, "You are doing really well." As we worked, four categories emerged: 1) It's a keeper, 2) It needs maintenance, 3) Maybe, 4) Get rid of it. Only the keepers went back in the closet.

After her dresser, we went into her closets. Below are twenty-five excuses she came up with for keeping things she didn't really want. Perhaps you can come up with additions of your own.

1. They're hand-me-downs. "This sweater my brother-in-law Vinny got rid of. I thought it was a perfectly good ski sweater, and I didn't see any reason . . . " She never wears it.

2. They're clothes for a heavier or lighter body than hers. Clothes for a different body than the one you currently walk around in have no business in the closet you face every morning.

3. Emotional reasons: "I feel a sentimental attachment." "It's a gift." She holds up a sweater her mom knit. "I can give this to my kids." She does not have kids. I think about that, too: Carrying something around you don't like for twenty years so your children can tell you they don't like it.

4. Variations on "It's worn/stained/holey/faded or it ran but . . . " Regarding these, experts urge, "Toss out all those nobody-will-see-me-anyway uglies—all of them."[10]

5. We're slaves to quality. It's another form of self-torture. She says, "Oh, my God. A beautiful $50 shirt, it's Ralph Lauren!" She doesn't wear it. We toss it.

6. It belongs to someone else. "This was an old roommate's, and she left it with me for some strange reason." If something is genuinely someone else's property, return it.

7. It looks good on someone else. "At a party yesterday, one of my friends was wearing this exact shirt and it looked terrific on her. It looked better on her than it looks on me, but it's a nice color, and I like it. . . . Actually it's just too long and the neck's too high."[11]

8. Her voice says "Yes" while her body says "No." She pulls out a T-shirt, "This is cotton."
   Does she wear it? "Yes." I wait.
   "I'm trying to decide how much I really like this."
   I say, "You don't. You're not breathing." Like many people, she stops breathing when she doesn't like something. The shirt goes in the bag. Her body signals in other ways, like grimacing. She holds up another pair of pants, frowns, and says, "Brand-new." It goes in the toss-out bag.

9. It fits her self-image, but not herself. "I have an image of myself in this little white eyelet sundress, looking very pretty, young, and happy. Getting rid of the dress means divorcing myself from that image." She puts the dress in her lap and holds up a T-shirt that says, "Real skiers don't have real jobs." We list her self-images so that she doesn't lose the feelings she likes about clothes she doesn't wear, and then get rid of the clothes.

10. She loves one aspect of it: "I love this color. What do you think of this shirt?" Mary Fiedorek comments, "If you're questioning something, chances are others will, too. Eliminate it, and indecisiveness vanishes with it."[12] This category is much like clothes that start you thinking, "If only . . . "[13]

11. It's a special-occasion garment. People remember how much money they invested in the garment and completely overlook its hideousness.

12. She pulls out a pair of shorts and says, "Where did these come from?" As if that were reason enough to keep them. She moves to put them back in the drawer. I say, "Do you wear them?" She throws them into the toss-out bag.

13. It was a great deal! Heather pulls out a silk bathrobe. I say, "It's pretty. Do you wear it?" She replies, "I got a good deal on it." I tell her the word "bargain" is a shopper's warning flag. It drops in the give-away bag. (Free clothes, such as promotional T-shirts, are also a waste of energy unless you love them.)

14. She doesn't actually wear it, but. . . . She introduces an exotic outfit. "This is a great thing! I've never worn it . . . so I guess I don't think it's that great. Would you throw this out?"

15. She once loved it. She holds up a pair of multicolored, worn-out exercise leggings. "I've loved these for a long time. They're getting really old. But aren't they beautiful? They're Impressionistic."

    "Tell them how much you've loved them and appreciated them and let them go. You deserve better than that." She sighs and puts them in the bag.[14]

16. She's saving it for the shoulder pads. I pull out a dress. She says, "I haven't worn that in five years. You can take the clothes, but don't take the shoulder pads." After a few of these garments, I ask how many sets of shoulder pads she wears at once. How many does she need to save? "I only save the Velcro ones."

17. "It matches." "It's part of a set." "It's part of a pair." I hold up a single thick wool sock.
    "That's a ski sock," Heather explains helpfully.
    "You ski on one leg?"
    She says, "I probably have the other one somewhere." The degree to which socks are apart from their mates is directly related to how little they are worn.

18. It's a classic. A black dress emerges. Heather says, "It's timeless. Turn it around. That's the back."
    "No, that's the back. Can we put this upstairs?" We put it in the rarely-used closet.
    We have to ignore a much propagated falsehood of closet-cleaning: "If you don't wear it after one/two/three (pick one) years, throw it out." The relative truth of this varies from person to person. I haven't worn The Dress that makes me look like Audrey Hepburn's slightly more zaftig younger sister in five years. I haven't had an occasion. But no way am I throwing it out. You must decide for yourself. Grandma hasn't thrown out a dress in sixty-five years.

19. Get rid of all the dangerous or haunted clothes. Cho cites the example of the outfit that:

    > deliberately opens its seams (usually in a sneaky way under the arms), develops creases across the lap and even insists upon falling off its hanger. It clenches its zippered teeth in a rage so you can't even get out of the bloody thing, and it's the first to announce with glee that you've just gained two pounds.[15]

20. It belongs elsewhere. When we are going through the lingerie area I ask, "Have you considered using a desk to keep all your paperwork in instead of your underwear drawer?" She says she'll take it under consideration.

21. She thinks it could be wearable. I pull out a striped cloth belt from some long-gone garment. Heather looks at me. "Claire was throwing it out, and I said, 'I think I could use that for something.'" I say, "Someone's going to love it." Heather sighs as she drops it in the bag.

22. She invested in it. "That is a watch that I bought for Steve right before we broke up." I've known her thirty years. I ask, "Who's Steve?"

    "My ex-boyfriend. Can you give a watch you bought for one person to somebody else? The batteries are run down because it's five years old but it's brand-new. I'm not going to throw out a $150 watch." She doesn't throw it out. But she'll have it, unused, forever.

23. She can get away with it. "I loved this blouse, but it is totally rayon and polyester. Can I get away with this?"

    "Why keep clothes with an identity of 'Can I get away with it?' Why not just have clothes that are fabulous?" It goes.

24. She's just thinking. Heather pauses for a moment over a shirt.

    I say, "If you have to think—"

    "Okay." She heaves a big sigh and puts it in the "maybe" pile. I wasn't encouraging mindless obedience to me. I was just trying to teach her when her body's giving her information. In that case, what she called "thinking" caused her body to go still and her breath to stop.

25. This doesn't take up very much room. I look at a teensy piece of workout wear and say, "When was the last time you wore that?"

    "I don't know, but these all go together. They don't take up much room."

    "They don't need relatives."

    She resists at length. I give up: "Okay I'm not going to push this one." We laugh. They go back in the drawer.

Despite all the excuses, Heather was surprisingly willing to let go of things. By the end, she still had enough clothes to wear a different outfit every day for two months. When we finished, Heather said, "Let me sit with my clothing for a minute. . . . I think we better get it to the Salvation Army. Already in my mind there are a couple of things in the bags that I'm considering diving back in for."

We loaded the car, drove the stuff over to Goodwill, and donated it. After I left Heather's apartment, someone mistook Heather's "maybe" pile for trash and threw it out. Heather was initially upset about this, but seemed to forget about it rather quickly.

If you're still hesitating, here's an excellent way to decide whether to get rid of something: Try it on.

The above advice and examples show ways to understand it's time to throw things out. There are more ways; what are yours?

After closet-cleaning checklist

Unless you learn from your mistakes, closet-cleaning is worthless. Before loading the car, Heather and I looked at what was left and she answered the following questions.

1. Do you tend to buy the same item over and over? If so, what? For Heather, it was black leggings. At the end of our work, fifteen pairs of black leggings still hung in her closet.

2. Are there areas of your life you have far too few clothes for? Be specific. Heather had nothing for her impending job interviews.

3. Are there parts of your body you have enough for and other parts you don't? Olivia Goldsmith observed:

> When I went through the closet experience, I realized I was the victim of a strange phenomenon: I had twenty-five jackets and shirts that looked pretty good but virtually nothing to wear on the bottom! No wonder my closet was full but I didn't have a thing to wear! Once I noticed the pattern I knew the reason for it. I like the upper half of my body and I enjoy shopping for it. I can't say the same about my hips and thighs. But after my realization, I also knew why I had such a hard time putting myself together. I simply didn't have any whole outfits.[16]

At the next level beyond where Heather was ready to go, where one only keeps clothes one loves, Karen Kaufman described her process:

> I used to buy things because a salesperson said it looked good. I had a closet full of clothing that I did not wear. When I cleaned out my closet, I realized how much it had affected me to walk in every day and think, "Oh, I hate this closet. I really hate this dress." I had someone help me clean out my closet. When I was a kid, I never got to pick my own clothes, or I got to pick them from within a very limited range. We bought a lot on sale, and so we'd buy ten dresses for ten dollars. I ended up with a lot of clothes that I never liked, that I always felt uncomfortable in. I carried with me the idea that I didn't have the ability to choose my own clothes, choose the colors, the materials, all of that. It wasn't until I started "doing" my own colors and having someone work with me that I started to see what kind of taste I had. I ended up with a quarter of what I'd had in my closet. It was fearful for me to see this few clothes in my closet, but the truth was they were the only things I wore that I really liked.

After the throw-outs, maybes, and maintenance garments are separated from your working wardrobe, look for habits of buying that don't serve you. Also, reflect further on what's good in your wardrobe, what you love about what you wear. Fatt elaborates:

> Style . . . is an ongoing process of selection. And, in selecting, what one eliminates is often as or more important than what one includes. You can have the money to buy whatever . . . but you still need to pull everything together into some kind of synthesis for yourself in order to have a style—and coordination is the tool for doing that. . . . Personal style is based on selectivity: this color rather than that one, this print rather than that one, this cut rather than that one.[17]

What to do with discards? Put them aside, out of your daily traffic flow. You can keep them, but nobody says you have to look at them every day. If you can't bear to have them leave the closet, put a sheet over the rejects and hang them in the most remote corner, or put them in a bag, box, or suitcase and store them under the bed, in an attic, or in the garage. If you can't bear the idea that they go to strangers, Roth suggests:

> Plan a "clothes" day with your friends: ask everyone to bring clothes they no longer wear, and when they arrive with their bundles, put them in piles on the floor. Look through the piles, let everyone try clothes on. You can all go home with something new to wear.[18]

Give them away or sell them at a resale shop or a garage sale. "Whatever, just get them out of your life."[19]

Maintenance

In eastern Europe, Slavic women sought the help of a pagan goddess named Mokosh or Mokusha, who walked at night spinning wool and to whom they prayed for help both with spinning and with doing the laundry.[20] Not only a spiritual or personal matter, maintenance is also correlated with the public persona, the self in society. Lurie notes: "Cleanliness may not always be next to godliness, but it is usually regarded as a sign of respectability or at least of self-respect. It is also a sign of status, since to be clean and neat always involves the expense of time and money."[21]

What's left for us relatively normal people who just love clothes? Do the maintenance. There are wonderful books on clothing maintenance.[22] The section below includes some basic suggestions. The primary directive, as you know, is "OBEY THE CARE TAG SEWN INTO THE GARMENT." Also, save garment hang tags so you will know the fiber content, since some cleaning agents damage certain fibers.[23] Read the instructions on the soapbox as well and follow them, or else terrible things might ensue. There is the perhaps apocryphal story of one of the early synthetic dresses:

> Mrs. Diana Vreeland of *Harper's Bazaar* once sent a Schiaparelli dress to the cleaner's. The next day she received a telephone call informing her with regret that the dress had been put into the cleaning fluid and there was nothing left of it. Mrs. Vreeland, who unbelievingly

insisted on seeing the remains, was told that there was literally nothing at the bottom of the pan.[24]

In addition, if you have separate wardrobes for separate seasons, or need to put items in storage for any reason, care for them first. Otherwise, stains and body perspiration, though often invisible, may set. They then show up after the clothes are laundered.[25]

The basics? "Keep clothes brushed, sponged, spots removed and not jammed in the closet."[26] Also, as you dress, consider what you'll be doing in the clothes, and prepare. For example, "Newspaper thumbing and light-colored clothing don't mix—or do, but in a smudgy way. Since you're not going to skip the paper just because you've donned a cream-colored jacket, you might try buying a carton of moist towelettes to use after scanning the headlines."[27] Don't buy clothes you can't afford to maintain.

What are the maintenance basics? Inspect your clothes and fix them before it is too late. Resurrect the humble idea of mending. Watch out for drooping hems and pilling. Are you a high maintenance or a low-maintenance sort of person? If you like to keep things in good shape, this sort of attentiveness will appeal to you. If not, chose clothes that last forever so they don't discomfit you. There is no real stigma attached to being low-maintenance. History misleads us about the player's level of concern with clothes care when it tells us "some 1,200-year-old silk garments, like Charlemagne's silk coronation gown, circa AD 800 are still in mint condition."[28] What isn't mentioned is that Charlemagne mostly wore otter-skin pelts.[29]

Define how much of a slob you are by nature and choose clothes accordingly, rather than take absurd vows to change your ways. I approach life in a jump-in-the-puddle sort of way, and expect my clothes to support that. Does this mean lots of Gore-tex? Maybe someday, but for now, for example, it means silk only shows up in scarves with a wild pattern to hide the stains, and I always put the scarf away in a bag, a pocket, or a sleeve before I start eating.

Maintenance can be seen as a habit, or a ritual act that must be repeated for maximum efficacy. Cho suggests "developing a rhythm of care."[30] Many fixes you can do yourself. Cleaning is the obvious one. Some people love hand washing and find it meditative. I don't. Even my delicate lingerie gets tossed into a zippered mesh bag and into the machine. To my ongoing dismay, if I don't take care of my clothes, they don't get clean. One dirty sweater I looked at for a year, fully expecting someone else (who?) to pick it up and clean it. When I complain about doing laundry, Grandma reminds me that she remembers when people used to wash clothes in big pots that boiled on the stove and were stirred with big wooden sticks. I should be grateful.

Even with all the care instructions from garment and cleanser followed, the application of water can be a moment of dread. If the garment was glued together instead of sewn, if the fabric isn't colorfast, if it was made with pre-treated fabric designed to have "hanger appeal" in the store but not to continue to look that way after washing, you will find out now. My first grown-up swimsuit was an expensive navy lycra and gold lamé knockout for an evening high school pool party. I felt fabulous until I got in the pool and the suit began to dissolve. Cleaning is the moment of truth for some garments. Will it endure for years as a beloved object, or is it just a one-night stand?

Wagenvoord notes: "Woolens should be washed in cold water. Think of the lambs out in all weather—they are used to cold water."[31] While browsing through a tony San Francisco thrift shop, I overheard the lady who runs it saying to a customer:

> Well, I gave some of my sweaters to my girl to take to the cleaners one day, and when she gave them back to me they were so full and soft and lustrous I asked her, "Where did you take these?"
> She said, "I used shampoo and a little conditioner."
> I said, "Shampoo?"
> She said, "I washed them."
> I said, "You what?"
> She replied, "They're just hair, Mrs. Rose, wool is just hair. So I put them in the sink and washed them with shampoo, and then when I was rinsing them out, I put in a little conditioner."

Mrs. Rose turned to her friend and said, "Can you imagine?"

At the time, no, I couldn't imagine, but when my I-feel-like-Hepburn grey flannel trousers needed cleaning, I thought, "I hate the chemical smell and crunchy feel of garments after they've been dry cleaned." I ignored the primary directive and shampooed my trousers. I don't recommend this for everyone. The risk is there; the implied threat behind every tag which says "DRY CLEAN ONLY" is that your clothes will be ruined forever. (I later destroyed an Armani wool/silk blend shirt this way.)

When I approached this oracle for an interview, alas, she refused.

Pressing also provides reinvigoration of clothing in a different way. Some who love the steamy detergent smell of ironing feel a kind of peace upon hearing the steam sizzle, and know that one chooses an iron because it feels comfortable and balanced in one's hand.[32] A friend sometimes does a load of laundry just to iron a specific item.

And then there's linen. I admire people who have the energy to wear linen because wearing linen implies a relationship with an iron that I just don't have. Several people came to linen's defense. Laurel comments: "No, no, no. First of all, I love to iron. Secondly, my husband is the best ironer in the world." Stacey Lamiero, a non-ironer, comments about a mutual friend:

> Paula's a doll. She used to laugh and tell me that my linen suits were wrinkled. And I would say, "See, that's the beauty of linen. Linen gets wrinkled, and if it didn't, you'd know it was a poly blend." This is how I would wear wrinkled clothes and still feel chic.

Other clothes problems require the assistance of skilled professionals.

Then there's "dry cleaning." There's a reason for the phrase "She was taken to the cleaners." The Chinese were making, cleaning, preserving, and restoring beautiful silk garments thousands of years before dry cleaners. Among the most extraordinary fabrics ever made, these were never dry cleaned. How did they do it? Soap and water. Why the sudden need to dump petrochemicals on clothes to call them clean? Maybe the emergence of the need to use petrochemical by-products. We are victims of the marketplace in this regard. Designers make clothes too fragile to withstand washing, and we cart them off to be coated in toxins and call that "clean." As Feldon notes, the solvent most dry cleaners use, perchloroethylene, "fouls the air, causes cancer in animals, and has been classified by the U.S. Environmental Protection Agency as a probable human carcinogen."[33]

Given all this, some things must be dry cleaned. I took a sweater my grandma Sibby made to the cleaners. (It's the only thing I have that she made—she's been dead over thirty years.) It had candy stripes, and to my absolute delight, each button was sewn on with a different-colored wool. When I got the sweater back, the candy-stripe colors in the button holes had turned white. I didn't know cleaners removed and then replaced buttons for cleaning. I raged, then mourned. They refused to apologize, and soon went out of business.

Closet space

Can you answer "Yes!" to the following closet questions? "Is there enough room for everything you keep in it? Is everything easily seen? Is everything easy to get at?"[34]

Like many clothes-related pursuits, if you're interested in this, be discreet about whom you discuss it with. Some people just don't get it. Jeremy Stone comments:

> My friend Sylvia had a boyfriend who was very jealous of her relationship with me. One night when we went out to dinner with him and some friends, Sylvia did not want to go back to his house with him. She wanted to come over to my new apartment and see my new walk-in closets. He found that very suspect. He decided and then circulated the rumor that we were really lesbians. He could not believe that on a Friday night the woman he was dating would rather go over to a girlfriend's house to look at her two new walk-in closets and help organize them. His ego could not accept that.

I understand completely. This next section contains only common sense. I have to leave it in for my mother's sake.

Most of the effects of "designer" closets can be easily recreated with a few prudent shopping expeditions to the garage, the local hardware store, the lumber yard and a discount emporium. After you've cleaned out your closet and it's empty, naked of everything, look at it. Do you want to paint? What do you want to do structurally?

1. Add another shelf above? Add another clothes bar at waist height? Plumber's piping or wooden dowels work well.

2. Divide the shelf into cubicles? Plastic milk boxes turned on their sides work fine, as do clear plastic boxes with lids.

3. Get some sealable clothes storage? Regardless of where I live, something will happily eat my favorite wool garments. Moths are nature's great reminder that I can't just ignore problems until they go away.

4. Exchange folding doors for hinged flat doors that can be used for storage or to hang a mirror? Slatted doors allow for more air circulation.

5. Clearly label everything that's not in a clear container, so you can see what's there without having to go into the box?

6. Check out kitchen gadgets for storage alternatives? "Kitchen bins are ideal for hanging on the walls and the doors of your closet. A couple of kitchen towel racks, mounted on the walls or door of your closet, will serve as permanent holders for favorite slacks, sweaters, scarves and. . . jewelry."[35]

7. Move your drawer space into the closet?

8. Go to real estate open houses in rich neighborhoods and steal closet ideas? (New construction tends to have more interesting closets.)

9. Stop using wire hangers? They distort the clothes, leaving lines and ruining the drape of the garment.[36] Plastic are better, and they're cheap and colorful.[37] Wooden or stuffed hangers that simulate a natural shoulder (best for clothes) come cheap at thrift stores.

10. Use one hanger for each garment? The layered hanger means clothes will not be seen, and not be used. And when putting clothes back in your closet, hang all your spare hangers together for easy access.

11. Get an electric light so you can see your clothes? Some closets have a window built in. This can cause tragedy, as one shoulder of every garment soon develops a faded spot. If your closet has a window, put in a sun-blocking curtain.

Regardless of what you decide to do, eventually it becomes time to put clothes back in the closet. Some suggestions:

1. "Use your clothing closet just for clothes."[38]

2. "The clothes in your closet should be organized into categories that make it easy for you to see and choose what to wear."[39] Do you separate clothes by season? Hang skirts, blouses, etc. together? Hang outfits together?

3. All closets can achieve "the suitcase effect," whereby stored garments are transformed "into a mass of wrinkles a raisin could envy."[40] Give your garments space to hang freely. If they don't, throw out more or find more storage space.

Dressing

A lady friend may have said to Emerson: "The sense of being perfectly well-dressed gives a feeling of inward tranquility which religion is powerless to bestow."[41] Or perhaps it was the notorious Social Darwinist Herbert Spencer who wrote that "the consciousness of being perfectly dressed may bestow a peace such as religion cannot give."[42] In any event, how to attain this peace? "Clothes must fit you, they must fit the occasion, and they must fit together."[43] After you've faced your closet and put aside all the stuff that doesn't work, look and see how what works goes together.

Your closet's cleaned out and in order. Your clothes, hanging neatly or folded before you, are clean and ready to wear. You have a list of what's missing. Or do you? There's more to dressing than that.

Unless you're an actress or a model, dressing is an intimate and private act. Most days, if you work, dressing is done at home, in solitude, upon just waking or in a state of semi-sleep. In the winter it is done in the dark or semi-dark. Under these conditions, you are expected, finally, to apply all the self-knowledge you've acquired about dress.

Dress is a problem to be solved in that most people don't dress in a way that's self-consistent. Your face and body are a form of art, and your job is to see the beauty in yourself and choose things that enhance that.

How can you prepare for dressing so that your sleepy morning routine can have gorgeous results? Look at things you love in your closet and ask what's missing to complete the outfit. Then, form a picture of it in your mind's eye, and note it on your shopping list. The greatest difficulty some people have after closet-cleaning is how to deal with the new emptiness, the void as manifested in the closet, without running out and buying more stuff to fill it. Sit with the void. It's good training. If you feel a need to shop, take the metro to the nearest ocean and take a long walk. Remember, by letting go of clutter, you're "lightening up and opening up space for something new to happen."[44]

With the exception of completing outfits, you may not need to buy new stuff. Regarding the obvious gaps: Do you have emergency hose, in case your last pair ran away? Are there must-haves for your closet, for your well-being? When you're two from the bottom on panty hose, or some necessary wearable, note on your shopping list to buy more. You don't have to go to a department store to buy staples unless you want to. You can call the store, tell them the size and style, and they can mail it. It's often cheaper to pay for postage than to take the train or park the car.

Examine assembling outfits more closely. When you get dressed in the morning:

• Who do you want to be?
• Who do you need to be?
• What do you want to look like?

For most of us it's too early to think clearly. When you have made some time, pull out all your clothes and accessories (or if they're already out, leave them there) and play a little. Weiland and Wood suggest you make "scarecrows."

A "scarecrow" is a totally accessorized outfit placed on your bed as if it were on your body. Each season we create new looks from old clothes by scarecrowing. It also helps us to discover missing parts that would make an outfit complete.

While scarecrowing, think of "crossovers"—the things that can do double duty. Think of suits as separates. Can the jacket be teamed with a sweater and pants for casual wear? Will a favorite dress work in the office with a jacket and for evening with different accessories?[45]

Multiple-use coordination is another way women can drive themselves crazy. Every clothing book I've seen provides a list of what to buy, including how many shirts, separates, sweaters, and shoes, so that four garments can provide you with 756 outfits. Like the promise of a diet, these lists are haunting. "If only I could stick to it. . . . " Resist temptation. If you're caught up in that multi-purpose, multi-use trap, go back to your closet. Don't make yourself nuts trying to make everything into six different outfits. Fiedorek comments, "Ideally, each suit could function as well as separates, with the jacket and skirt leading independent lives. But don't expect this. Because of fabric and cut, some jackets simply won't translate well as blazers. Ditto for some skirts."[46] Look at what's really there and what you really need. Finish unfinished outfits you love. Satisfy yourself, not the coordinating dictators of some clothing consultancy. You may just need a white blouse.

Jean Patton and Jacqueline Brett note the difference between a really great wardrobe and a collection of clothes: a wardrobe provides you with complete outfits.[47] The emphasis on making outfits runs through all the dressing literature, as well as through the consultant interviews I did. My experience, and their emphasis, leads me to believe there may be something to it. It's not such a bad idea, having clothes that go with each other, having groups of things you can put on and rely on, knowing you look great.

Years ago, after seeing the uncoordinated minimalist experiment that was my wardrobe, Sharon Frederick lectured me on the coordinates concept, outlining a simple way to approach this (for beginners) for sportswear:

> I want as many alternatives as possible with my clothes, once I get my basics. If I were getting my basics in blue, I'd get a sweater or a jacket that matches the leggings, jeans, trousers, or skirt. Then I'd get a top in several different colors: magenta, red, yellow, or gold looks real good with these colors. [The colors relate to the navy pants we were looking at.]
>
> I then want to know what else I'm going to do with this. I look at what else the manufacturer made. I look for a cardigan. For example, a little cute jacket over this. The basics are cool; they're wonderful; they fit. But the outfit's not finished. I then ask: Are there scarves that I can add to it? Accessories?
>
> I want two things. I want color in here, and I want you to have a matching something. I want to use the word "suit." Call this cardigan and trousers a suit. Then you get to play with all these different tops. Don't panic when I say suit. I'm really after a jacket. If you got one set of walking shorts and a matching blouse, you've got one suit. If you then buy one skirt and jacket to match, right off the bat you'd have more outfits now than you have here. You'd cover a mood, fill the void.[48]

I understand what she's saying about the void. When I cleaned out my closet, there was so little there, I was startled. Once you learn to see how things coordinate, you advance to a more sophisticated level, where you see coordinating clothes outside the limits of the manufacturers' sets-for-sale in the racks. Byers notes:

> What makes expensive things expensive . . . is the ensembling—the look of belonging together—that takes thought, not talent. . . . You must think of your clothes as if they were people. You introduce them to each other. If there is no bond between them, they simply won't mix.[49]

Finish your outfits. An outfit, like a story, cries out for completion. What does a completed outfit mean to you? Everyone has different outfit rules. The trick is discovering and standing by your own. When an outfit works, then rules go out the window. When Mary Armentrout's got a great clothing ensemble going, "I can wear the wrong hat, all of my red earrings, or yellow socks and red shoes and it will just be another aspect of the outfit."

When figuring out outfits, you will discover the wide range of "goes with." In part, "goes with" has to do with function: Glow-in-the-dark stuff goes with night exercise, brightly colored stuff goes with day exercising—visibility is safer. Warmth goes with cold days (you don't have to open the window for a blast of cold air to check the weather. Touch the windowpane to find out the temperature.) Comfort in the practical sense includes having your physical needs met. One friend makes sure there are coins in her penny loafers for a phone call. Another always brings a warm sweater "just in case."

"Goes with" can be extended out into the environment. A best-selling etiquette book suggests: "On entering a room, try to select a chair or sofa that suits your height and figure."[50] "Goes with" also has to do with mood. Mary Armentrout comments:

> Dressing also gets into the realm where you don't feel like you're wearing a purple silk blouse. You're wearing an autumn day. Or you're wearing the feeling of sadness that you want to remember when X left or when X came back or whatever. Or you're embodying some concept of yourself or some emotion. You're embodying something other than mere fabric.

Play. Emily Cho suggests the following dress-up exercises:

1. For one week, try to project a different image each day, and observe the reactions of others. Every evening, decide whether that new image has had an effect on the events of the day or on your mood.

2. See if you can vary one outfit with accessories three different ways—different enough so you won't mind wearing that same basic dress.

3. If you tend to wear one color, try staying away from it totally for one whole week. Did you miss it?

4. If you wear heavy makeup, try less. If you don't wear makeup, try a little. Experiment.

5. Try concentrating on new ideas for your hair.

6. Try consciously to get three genuine compliments on your appearance.[51]

Roth suggests a different type of dress-up: "Tomorrow, when you wake up, dress as you would if you were expressing your power. Then walk through the day as a powerful woman would."[52] If you don't have the clothes, act as if you were wearing them. Get used to the idea by assuming the attitude first; it will ease your adjustment. Play helps. You can expect contradictory feelings about dressing.[53] It might be useful to write out your reactions or completions to the statement: "I don't like feeling well-dressed because . . ."[54] until you've worn out the phrase.

Armentrout, Cho and Roth all give different advice. I like it all.

Make note of your outfits

If a closet, as Jeremy Stone puts it, is a library, know before you enter its domain what you seek, unless you have time to browse. In a library you look through the card catalog or computerized database. In the film *Clueless*, Cher had her clothes on a computer program that assembled outfits. The rest of us can just keep a list of the components of each outfit we love thumbtacked to the closet door.

Write down outfits? It's embarrassing, you shouldn't have to do it, nobody else does it, it's weird, you should be able to figure it out, but write them down anyway. Every morning at 7 A.M. when I had to get dressed and go to work, I looked in my closet and found "nothing to wear." So one weekend—it only took forty minutes—I went into my closet and I counted the number of work outfits. I had twenty-four I liked, and only two of them needed hemming, sewing, or fixing.

Laurel Fenenga comments, "The key is keeping up with it and not forgetting that you did that once. You can do it again if you start feeling that first-thing-in-the-morning anxiety." Her fingers grabbing at her heart demonstrate that feeling: clutching, twitching, tweaking.

If you're unwilling to do that much planning, lay out your clothes the night before. If you're a little less orderly and don't want to lay out your clothes, you can do a quick visualization the night before. Kathryn Hoover comments: "When I go to sleep, I contemplate what to wear that will support me throughout that whole day." Even if you're a last-minute type, you can still indulge in pre-planning upon waking:

> Close your eyes and ask yourself, What kind of physical sensation do I have and how can I best satisfy it? Do I want to wear something soft or rough, warming or cooling? What do I want to be covered and what uncovered? Do I want to feel formal or informal, structured or unstructured? . . .[55]

Pre-planning is also helpful for dress-up for special occasions. The actress Sarah Bernhardt would wear the formal dress of her characters for weeks before the curtain went up on her performances so that she could appear completely at ease in the clothes. I'm not suggesting you dress as Napoleon and wear those clothes to your job. However, it's important to note the modern danger of always wearing casual clothes: one loses the sense of comfort available in more formal clothes, and perhaps loses the ability to wear them with grace. Dress-up is a kind of performance, which may warrant "dress rehearsals." As Bixler notes, it helps to wear "something you can trust if you already have something to be nervous about."[56]

Just before you leave the house

Test your outfits. Move around, walk, sit, stand, and maybe do the rhumba. Consider the sensations of your body in the clothes. Are your feet warm, cold, comfortable? What about your legs, torso, butt, arms, neck, head, face? Are they constrained, embraced, free?[57] And, finally . . . check the mirror, front, back, and sides. Move in front of it!

Then there's the "Blink Test." Larkey suggests that, once dressed, you stand at least five feet from a full-length mirror. Close your eyes. Count to three. Open your eyes and quickly shut them, glimpsing yourself in the mirror in a long blink. "Instantly: What do you see first? Do you and all the parts of your wardrobe look good together?"[58] By only getting a quick picture of how you look, you see broad outlines and general shapes. It becomes clear what you'd like to add or subtract. You may automatically notice what is missing. What would make this outfit complete? Does anything need to change? I do this to figure out accessories. Once I am fully clothed, I do the test, and my intuition will say, "Try dark beads, or the bright vest," and I'll keep adding and doing the test until it looks balanced. Usually it takes under a minute total.

This chapter contains a great many practical suggestions for getting your closet and mind in order so you have the equanimity to dress efficiently in the morning; these include how to get past obstacles to throwing out dreadful clothes, whom to pray to for help with maintenance, how to reorganize your closet to fit you, how to dress well while half asleep, and what quick checks to do before leaving the house.

There are still probably some gaps in your wardrobe. This means shopping. . . .

Notes:

1. Batterberry, Michael and Ariane Batterberry. *Mirror, Mirror.* Page 126.
2. Batterberry. Page 120.
3. Merriam, Eve. *Fig Leaf.* Page 30.
4. Goldsmith, Olivia and Amy Fine Collins. *Simple Isn't Easy.* Page 41.
5. Jackson, Carol. *Color Me Beautiful.* Page 185.
6. Fiedorek, Mary. *Executive Style.* Page 53.
7. Goldfein, Donna. *Everywoman's Guide to Time Management.* Page 34.
8. Laury, Jean Ray. *The Creative Woman's Getting-It-All-Together-At-Home Handbook.* Page 19.
9. Goday, Dale and Molly Cochran. *Dressing Thin.* Page 21.
10. Goday and Cochran. Page 17.
11. You can play with this idea of Whose-Clothes-Are-These-Anyway? Olivia Goldsmith and Amy Fine Collins suggest two partner exercises:

> If you still have nagging doubts about some of your remaining clothes, why not have a friend try on some of them so you can see how they look from a more objective perspective. Amy discovered through this method that some of her clothes that were almost right for her were actually perfect for her friend Miriam, who wears the same size and has a similar (but not identical) style. [Goldsmith and Collins. *Simple Isn't Easy.* Page 41]

> Also,

> Get together with a friend, and have her take pictures of you in different outfits . . . Talk, walk, move, sit, turn, bend, etc. Study the results. Again, decide what you like and what you don't, and analyze why. Always ask why. [Goldsmith and Collins. Page 57.]

12. Fiedorek. Page 7.
13. Thompson suggests you:

> separate all the "if only's" from the rest of the bunch. "If only I'd lost those ten pounds" . . . "If only I'd taken up the hem" . . . or, the most common, "If only I hadn't bought this thing in the first place." Be prepared for your "if only" pile to be quite substantial in size; that's usually the case in first-time closet cleaning. Console yourself with the knowledge that on your next shopping trip you'll be much wiser. [Thompson. Page 32.]

14. A young designer commented later, "I . . . think of a garment as something which becomes a part of the wearer, to be worn until it has completely worn out, physically or intellectually . . . over a certain period of time, it has exhausted the dialogue which existed between it and its wearer." [*Fashion: Poetry and Design Approaches to Creativity.* Page 57.]
15. Cho. Page 158.
16. Goldsmith. Page 121.
17. Fatt, Amelia. *Conservative Chic.* Page 134.

18. Roth, Geneen. *Breaking Free From Compulsive Eating*. Page 184.

19. Miller, Liz Leverett. *I Just Need More Time*. Page 171.

20. Barber. Page 247.

21. Lurie, Alison. *The Language of Clothes*. Page 13.

22. Wagenvoord, for example, has a whole chapter just on brushing clothes.

23. McJimsey, Harriet. *Art in Clothing Selection*. Page 41.

24. Beaton, Cecil. *The Glass of Fashion*. Page 222

25. McGill, Leonard. *Stylewise*. Page 164.

26. Brown, Helen Gurley. *The Late Show*. Page 322.

27. McGill. Page 163.

28. Feldon, Leah. *Dress Like a Million*. Page 64.

29. Batterberry. Page 71.

30. Cho. Page 168.

31. Wagenvoord, James and Fiona St. Aubyn. *ClothesCare*. Page 28.

32. Wagenvoord and St. Aubyn. Page 125.

33. Feldon, Leah. *Dress Like a Million*. Page 67.

34. Cho, Emily and Hermine Lueders. *Looking, Working, Living Terrific 24 Hours a Day*. Page 112.

35. Goldfein. Page 68.

36. Feldon. Page 167.

37. Miller. Page 171.

38. Miller. Page 169.

39. Cho and Grover. Page 168.

40. McGill. Page 164.

41. Advertisement for Oliver Peeples. *The New York Times Magazine*. October 24, 1993. Page 46.

42. Pierre, Clara. *Looking Good*. Page 53.

43. Woods, Vicki. "Working Girl." *Vogue*. November 1994. Page 327.

44. Dominguez, Joe and Vicki Robin. *Your Money or Your Life*. Page 26.

45. Weiland, Barbara and Leslie Wood. *Clothes Sense*. Pages 72-73.

46. Fiedorek. Page 56.

47. Patton. Page 99.

48. Sharon adds, "And do wear your clothes. It makes me very sad when customers say, 'Well, I've never worn that.' 'Why didn't you wear that?' 'I was saving it.' " I'm reminded of Jacob Koved's comment in Myerhoff: "Dress neatly and don't try to save your best clothes, because after you leave this world you won't need them anymore."

49. Byers, Margaretta with Consuelo Kamholz. *Designing Women*. Page 160.

50. Vanderbilt, Amy. *Amy Vanderbilt's Complete Book of Etiquette*. Page 204.

51. Cho and Grover. Page 92.

52. Roth, Geneen. *Breaking Free From Compulsive Eating*. Page 198.

53. Orbach, Susie. *Fat Is a Feminist Issue*. Page 82.

54. Based on an exercise from Geneen Roth's *Why Weight*. Page 94.

55. Based on an exercise from Susie Orbach's *Fat Is a Feminist Issue.* Page 120.
56. Bixler, Susan. *The Professional Image.* Page 44.
57. Inspired by an exercise in Geneen Roth's *Why Weight?* Page 62.
58. Larkey, Jan. *Flatter Your Figure.* Page 115.

Shopping:
Planning, Dealing with the Dressing Room Mirror, and Resisting the Bargain's Allure

Yearning makes the heart deep.

—St. Augustine of Hippo

Some Financial Questions

1. How would you characterize your spending habits?
   _____ If I want it I get it.
   _____ If I want it I get it and I'm still paying for it years later.
   _____ Clothes are so expensive that I don't shop.
   _____ I never spend more than $16.99 on a dress.

2. How do you pay for clothing?
   _____ I always pay cash.
   _____ I always use checks.
   _____ I always use credit cards and am shocked when the bill comes. Shocked.

3. How do you feel about spending money on clothes? Think back to purchases you made in the last year and remember the moment of purchase in detail. Do you have any regrets? What did the purchase mean to you at the time? What purchases satisfy you? Why?

4. Have you spent too much on your clothes considering the enjoyment you received from them? Where do you underspend on clothes that get a lot of use?

5. What proportion of your income do you spend on clothes?

6. What would be "enough" money to spend on clothes?

7. What "makes" you buy something? List the various influences, impulses, and rationalizations.

8. Does your budget limit you in any way? What would you purchase if your budget were larger? Smaller? Which would you prefer?

9. I often buy things because
   _____ They look good on someone else.
   _____ My mother would approve of it.
   _____ My mother would look good in it.
   _____ My mother would hate it.

10. What did you learn from your family about spending? Which learned spending habits support you?

Shopping can go awry because of emotional issues, inadequate planning, incomplete garment inspection, fascination with quality or designer labels, insufficient break time, the horror of the dressing room mirror, and financial self-delusions. After a thorough examination of your methods and anxieties, shopping can become more effective.

Our culture and emotional shopping

Many experience shopping as a problem. In *Accidental Empires*, Cringely describes what we lost during the shift in the American mind-set, in the last thirty years, to a consumerism-driven society:

Years ago, when you were a kid, and I was a kid, something changed in America. One moment we were players of baseball, voters, readers of books, makers of dinners, arguers. And a second later, and for every other second since then, we are all just shoppers. Shopping is what we do. It's entertainment. Consumers are what we are. We go shopping for fun. Nearly all our energy goes into buying, thinking about what we'd like to buy, or earning money to pay for what we have already bought.[1]

In a cannibalistic way, the society that created the shopper turns on her with feral savagery. We see this hostility in the stereotypes that accompany the idea of women who shop—for example, the Jewish American Princess. If, as a result of shopping, she doesn't meet the standard, then she is attacked as a Fashion Victim. Camille DePedrini comments on the paradox of the compulsive shopper: "There's somebody who just wants, wants, wants, and nothing's ever enough. And she's a retailer's dream."

Though the causes of this are societally based, the problem is experienced as deeply personal. Shopping lovers have to work to disentangle meeting their own needs from dealing with the internalized demands of our culture. Libby Granett comments:

Shopping doesn't seem to be the right kind of social indulgence. Talk about double whammies! Not only is it a self-indulgence, but it's not a correct self-indulgence. What would be correct? Taking a walk, reading. In this world which is falling apart left and right, consuming seems so petty and so wrong. I don't spend my life chastising myself for this, but there's definitely no pride in it. There's pride in "I have a good sense of style. I can wear interesting things, and that people like what I wear." But there's a little bit of shame in the fact that I'm so consumed by shopping or that I spend so much time at it.

The other side is, "My God, it's not like I hurt people in the process of doing this." Yet it feels embarrassing.

I also start to get anxious when I haven't been shopping. I don't know how much of that is connected to not having been alone, on my own, for a while, but I get kind of bitchy if I haven't had this time. So, I try to arrange time on a regular basis. Maybe once a month, I'll actually go on a shopping trip for more than four or five hours. When I'm on my way to do it, it just feels wonderful.

There is a moment of unease when I get to where I'm going and realize that I really don't need anything. That makes me feel bad and takes away from the adventure. So it's nice to have a purpose, like a pair of shoes or some kind of blouse. And as I'm saying this, I'm thinking, "Jeez Louise! What kind of nonsense is that, to need to have a purpose? I love this adventure." I would like to be able to just say, "This is just fun schmoozing around a mall. That's good. There's no other purpose."

Sneaking is just one way shopping-related anxiety is expressed by many who are troubled and fascinated by shopping. Because we're encouraged to shop recreationally, and our television sets bombard us with as many as an hour's worth of encouragements per hour, people who love shopping can falsely invest in the idea of dressing, the power to do wondrous things for them.[2] They don't know how to stop nurturing endless wanting.

Eileen Sullivan became very involved with shopping when she married a wealthy man. Her lifestyle changed dramatically from that of a typical working professional. There were expectations that she would dress a certain way:

I had to wear a lot of jewelry, hats, really become that totally together "look" of the idle wealthy. For example, at summer resorts where you have to dress in white, there's a look. In order to fit in, one has to have that. So I cultivated it.

But it was a time when personally I was going through a lot. I was overdressing and overfocused on clothes to disguise the inner feeling of impoverishment and the lack of solidness inside. The clothes wore me instead of me wearing them. I think that real fashion-plate look is something that people buy when they're feeling empty on the inside. It's an attempt to try to feel worthy, an unskillful way to try to get that. A lot of times people want to be wrapped in love. If we can't wrap ourselves in loving feelings through our partners, we can wrap ourselves in fine clothes.

Clothes can be a real armament, a real isolation. They can be a power statement, not true power, but power over, an affluence that sets one apart from the masses. For a person who's insecure, it creates a false sense of power.

A false sense of power as opposed to?

A genuine power that comes from being strong inside, feeling autonomous. Not feeling threatened by another person. Able to accept differences and able to accept one's own weaknesses and one's vulnerabilities. True power is knowing oneself and loving oneself, not putting on airs.

Eileen and her husband divorced. She's middle class again.

I was very upset at the dissolution of the marriage. It was, for both of us, the right thing to do, but I felt my life wasn't working out the way I wanted it to. So I began soul-searching and did a lot of meditation and psychotherapy. I realized I didn't want to be ever again in a lonely marriage. I didn't ever want to feel as alienated as I did then, and that I would go to the ends of the earth to find out how to heal that in me.

What supports that kind of process?

Telling the truth to oneself. Putting facts with feelings. It's about courage, having the courage to first feel the feelings so we know who we are, and then, secondly, having the courage to say who we are. To be so internally focused that we don't give a damn what it looks like on the outside.

It sounds like the "riches to rags" phase has actually been better.

By necessity, with my financial situation changing so much, I had to stay home and stop buying. But it also has been a real time to go inside. That stuff just doesn't have the allure that it used to have.

What kinds of things call to her now that the clothes don't?

Good friends, good communication, good times. I have such rich relationships and so much contact that all that other stuff doesn't hold a candle to my experience now. I feel much more solid as a person. My identity doesn't feel transient like it did then; I could change how I felt about myself by how I looked.

She points to her T-shirt. "I like this color. This matches with how I feel. I really like quality things so I have less, but what I have is really fine. It's more because it matches with how I think about myself and is not something to pump me up."

Often the people who love to shop are, paradoxically, the ones who don't feel satisfied with the results. Do you take unmet emotional needs shopping? Next time they cry out to go shopping, meet a need instead. Or if you feel an overpowering urge to shop, stop for a moment, take a breath, and figure out where you can be alone and not shop—the woods? An art museum? (Forget that, there's the gift shop.) Church? Walk around or meditate. Some people stop to listen to themselves and instead hear a pre-recorded litany.

I am so bad. No one will ever love me. I will never have a partner. I feel so ugly. I am so ugly. I am so unattractive. I am a dog: "Woof woof." I will never be happy in a job. I will never find a good job again. I will never find a job that's up to my skill level. I can't do anything fun. I am no fun. No one will ever love me. . . .

Listen to your endless tape. What does it say? Next time yours starts to play, pop it out and put in another tape you like better. If you don't have another tape, make one up or memorize some great poetry.

If shopping for you is a plunge into oblivion, find other oblivions that aren't so damaging.[3] Mine are reading, bathing, sewing patchwork, sorting through old letters, writing, going to the movies, and swimming.

Ask yourself the hard questions and write down the answers.

1. Why do you shop?

2. How do you feel about shopping?

3. Do you have enough physical affection, color, and quiet in your life? Do you have enough love and support in your life? If not, where do you need or want more?

4. If your shopping is out of control, specifically how is it out of control?

5. Think back on the last time you shopped. Did you have enough time to do it in a thorough way? Did you need clothes? What went wrong? Did you buy the "right" thing?

Come to intimate terms with your shopping compulsion, because, unlike drug addiction, you still have to do it after you recover, unless you get others to shop for you. Look carefully at your naked thoughts and feelings about this issue. If you obtain clarity about the emotional issues which involve you in your habit, it becomes easier to shop in a sane manner. This will take you closer to discerning your own uniqueness and pleasure in clothing.

Planning

Why plan ahead? If you insist on shopping "spontaneously," look in your closet to see where your spontaneity has brought you.

Boring Common-Sense To-Dos:

1. From previous chapters, you have a sense of the colors, textures, fabrics, styles, and even outfits you love. You also may have a sense of the issues that have clouded your judgment before, related to family, sexuality, fashion, etc. You have inklings, or perhaps a full description, of what makes you feel beautiful. Take a moment to jot down your shopping worldview, including your demons, history, and pleasures.

2. Make a shopping list. Weiland and Wood add, "Be specific! 'Pants' is not enough to help you avoid impulse purchases. Write down color, style, fabric, type, and the pieces you intend to wear with it."[4] It's like a grocery list for clothes. You wouldn't settle for liver when you want prime rib, would you?

3. Dress to shop so it's easy to change, in clothes that are easy to get out of. Wear underwear you can bear to see in a changing-room mirror.

4. If the garment you seek requires special accessories, underwear or shoes, or is needed to complete an outfit, bring or wear the other pieces. If a garment is too uncomfortable to wear or carry, why are you trying to get outfits from it?

5. Stores are usually quietest when they first open and at the dinner hour. Consider taking a morning off from work (OK, forget that). Consider letting the family fend for themselves one evening while you pack a snack and make an expedition. Shop when you have enough time, and when you're rested enough to do a good job. (Good luck.)

6. Don't shop tired. As soon as I got to England, I dragged my jet-lagged body out shopping. I quickly became fascinated by an oversized, unreturnable, bright green mohair sweater. When I got it home I realized I spent sixty dollars on a garment identical to my nightshirt—only in mohair. I was just trying to buy some sleep.

7. Prepare to shop for the size you are now. Sizing numbers are not an absolute authority. If you don't like the size number tag of a garment you buy, cut it out. According to *Vogue* patterns measurements I wear a size 16 top. I have made their patterns and they look wonderful. Yet in my closet I also have a Donna Karan size 2 blue silk jacket that fits well. Even within a group of garments that are all "the same," sizing is not reliable. As Procter notes, if you try on two of the same size garment you often find one fits better.[5] Some designers have discovered that if a woman can say, "Oooh, I'm a 4," she's more likely to buy it. Joan Vass has made wonderful cotton knit separates in sizes 1-2-3.

8. Practice the art of waiting. Marilyn Cooperman comments: "I think you should always wait until you absolutely love a thing and not make do. That's discipline."[6] Lex Eurich talks a little about serendipitous waiting. She points to a skirt:

> This I wear a lot. It's a sheer skirt with a little sheer liner underneath, and it's long and flowy and it's all the colors I love, very bright green and blue and pink and black patchwork pattern, mostly floral, but also with some geometric prints, and polka dots. My parents saw it in Virginia and they both said, That reminds us of Lex; and they sent it to me. Meanwhile I was out here in California contemplating buying a skirt just like this and thinking, "I can't do it," because the cheapest one I could find even at the flea market was like thirty-five to forty bucks. This skirt came from my parents, and it was totally free, free to me. I'm sure they spent a fortune on it, but it made them really happy to spend the money, and it makes me happy that I didn't have to spend any.

9. Before you go out of the house, deal with the "maybes" from the closet-cleaning. (Remember them from the last chapter?) If any need alterations, do them or have them done. (See the section on tailoring.) If you don't want them, get a sense of the mistakes you tend to make that are tricky.

Informational shopping

Use informational shopping to orient yourself to the stores which suit your style and price range. Leave your wallet at home. Just take enough money to pay for transportation or parking and to buy yourself a nice lunch (or pack one). If shopping is dangerous for you, pre-shop for information only as needed. The clothes start showing up in stores for spring/summer in March and for fall/winter in August. What's your reaction? "But I don't want to." "Is this really necessary?" "Without my wallet? Come on, I'm a grown-up." If the way you shop now works and trying something new never does, ignore this.

In the store, start with something wonderful, your response. Alice Koller discovered what she liked by noticing what she moved toward, smiling.[7] What are your body's signals for wanting, loving, needing? If you can't start there, start with knowing how shopping makes you feel: anxious, gleeful, restless, upset? What?

If shopping freaks you out, visualize. Imagine going into stores, even stores you don't dare go into. What happens? Imagine you have an unlimited amount of money to spend. Look, touch, sniff, try on. Buy as much as you want. Someone or someones will carry your parcels. You have plenty of time. Bring them home. How do you feel surrounded by all these clothes?[8]

Nancy Roberts asks, outraged about the difficulty of finding beautiful clothes, "What kind of madness has brought us to this situation where we have to hunt and search for things to wear?"[9] Shopping for clothes is a modern concern. Before ready-to-wear, there were no sizes. A garment was made, or a hand-me-down altered to fit a specific body. In the nineteenth century, merchants introduced the department store. The disorientation of this shopping experience begins before you enter the store, in its reflecting plate glass windows where you see your own reflection and the idealized, dressed-up dummy side by side. Upon entering their doorways you become the prisoner of their vision. The twentieth-century mall produces the same effect, multiplied. With no linear layouts and no windows to the outside, the disorientation is deliberately manufactured to get you into a state where buying seems like the right thing to do.

What are your expectations of the marketplace? You've left your home to come to the modern agora, which in the past was a place to meet with community, to socialize, to catch up on the news, to be a public person. Today its function has shifted. What does shopping mean to you?

You can use research day to learn about any aspect of clothing you need to. Compare garments from different departments and price brackets in a large department store. If possible, carry similar garments to different departments and compare directly. Once, on a whim, I went into Tiffany's to try on engagement rings. The stones in the rings looked small to me. I tried on the biggest one displayed. As I slid it on I noticed it cost $23,000. (I tried to pretend I was cool with this.) Later, in a costume jewelry shop I saw a nearly identical ring (to my eye) for $19.95. I bought it. Andrew reimbursed me. Je ne regrette rien.

Boutique and department stores aren't the ultimate answer. The perfect thing could be anywhere: I found my favorite scarf at a gardening supply outlet. I picked up four pair of Levi's at the thrift store for $1.75 a pair. Consider the discount store, the used clothing store. Consider the free bin, the flea market, the mail-order catalogue. But consider also the hazards of discount stores and bargains. Joseph Ettedgui, owner of the Joseph chain of clothing stores in London, observes:

> Going to buy . . . is like going to the market in the morning. The stalls are piled with ingredients, but even if some items are particularly attractive or astonishingly good value, if you do not need them for your menu, for the dishes you are going to make, then you do not buy them. It would be a waste, and it would confuse you, because you would start looking for ways to include them in your menu—and you would then find yourself buying other items to complement them. Your menu would be a mess and . . . your statement would be unclear.[10]

Some common-sense shopping advice:

1. For discount shopping to really work, you must know deeply that you're looking for a garment that makes you look beautiful, not a price tag that gives you a rush. Buying on sale can be a good thing, when you'll wear what you're buying until it begs to be used to wash the car. The real issue is love and utility, not price or brand.

2. There's something about a sale rack, a sale catalogue, a discount mall that gets the sale addict into a blind lathering heat. She becomes focused and hard, gets that look in her eye that means she won't be distracted, and comes home with a pile of stuff she doesn't really like that she can't return. If you're one of them, find another way.

3. Once I was traveling up to the sixteenth floor of an office building in the same elevator with the senior partner of the law firm I worked for. He said, as his gold cufflinks glittered in the soft light, "I never take anything for free that I wouldn't pay full price for." I glanced at his shirt pocket where his initials were embroidered in tiny letters and thought, "You never have to. . . . " I realized later that just because economy is necessary doesn't mean I should buy anything "so-so."

4. Where? Find out where the department stores dump their old merchandise, where the rich people give away their clothes, where the best discount shopping is. In department stores, know where the markdown racks are. Use the discount mega-mall if you have brand loyalty and you're willing to put up with zero atmosphere and shop-drunk nuts. (Your best buy may not be there. Department stores sell sixty to eighty percent of all merchandise on sale.[11]) (If a garment you've bought goes on sale, try to bring the receipt back for a price adjustment.)

5. Avoid shopping from Thanksgiving to mid-January—all the people who hate and are terrified of shopping converge on the stores for their once-a-year misery fest.

6. If a garment you love has a defect, ask politely for an additional discount. What have you got to lose?[12] Do not, like some people's mothers (you know who you are), deliberately injure a garment so you can attempt to save some money on it. Attempted murder is a crime.

7. Some manufacturers produce clothes with the same measurements more cheaply under a different brand name. Contact manufacturers of clothes you love to find out whether they do.

Once you find stores you like and the manufacturers who make clothes that you love, shopping can become almost painless. For those of us who like to linger in stores and try things, informational shopping can provide hours of entertainment at a very low cost.

Designers and quality

The best couturier in the world is love.

—Josephine Baker

Part of informational shopping may include scanning the fashion magazines. A study of 300 years of fashion revealed the six details to watch: 1) skirt length; 2) height of waistline; 3) depth of neckline; 4) width of skirt; 5) width of waist; 6) width of neckline.[13] When looking at clothes in magazines, what details do you see more than once, and of those, what do you like? Which would you like on you? Inventory and classify your preferences. Then there's the momentary pleasure of a fling with a trend. Trends have themes that can be followed very inexpensively—the sea, flowers, clear plastic, neon colors. How to find trends? Trends travel fastest on TV. Weiland and Wood suggest you

> read a magazine by flipping through the pages checking only one detail at a time. If you are interested in trends in hem lengths, look only at hems in all the ads and fashion pages. Look through the magazines again noting only shoulder widths and sleeve styles, then again only looking at collars and necklines.[14]

Once you observe, say, a print you love, where does it go on the body? Sharon Frederick observes, "It goes anywhere you want. You don't take it like it's presented in the picture. You take it and play with it, if you want to. In this particular instance [a wild Pucci print] it would be darling in tight little pants with a big top over it."

Then, Frederick continues, "you've got to see how it is finished." You observe accessories, socks, the earrings, hair, etc. "No matter what game you're going to play—nautical, the General, Southwest, etc.—you've got to stay with your theme."

If you see something you like, visualize yourself wearing it. Ask yourself: What works? What doesn't? Who likes you in it? Who doesn't? How do you behave that's different from how you behave normally? Whom do you meet? If your life is different, how is it different when you wear those clothes? The object is not to purchase the dreamed-of item, but 1) to understand its hold on you, and 2) find things that do work.

If there are things you admire in advertisements (bearing in mind some ads are prepared months ahead of publication for clothes that never make it to the stores), phone ahead: If the store gives you the runaround, call their publicity department. "Their whole reason for being is to get you to respond. So they'll respond to you."[15] It is important to go the distance for what you want. Feldon cites the example of a woman who did so:

> When she found a belt she liked, she called the manufacturer and asked if he could make her two belts a foot longer so she could loop them around twice and let them hang a bit. "You could never buy those belts in the store," says Gayle. "I invented it because I wanted that look and I had to make it for myself."[16]

Be gentle with the garments: someone spent hours constructing them. Try to survive the snobbism falsely built into the designer departments and stores (for more information, see the section on dealing with salesladies). If you go in educated and prepared for this nonsense, you are less likely to feel your self-esteem trickle out through the bottoms of your feet. Do you find yourself inventing excuses for other shoppers, for your mother? Do you find yourself imagining being interviewed by *Vogue* or Oprah? You're here to discover what suits you. Do you find luxury intimidating? Why? Does something in you purr, "I could get used to this"? Does the urge to steal come up?

Look at and inside the clothes and see if they are well made. Learn more about what "well made" means. As McDowell summarizes cynically, "One of the enduring myths that supports the designer scam is that you get what you pay for."[17]

A great many of the flashy designer things end up at Filene's Basement and other such places at five percent of the original price, somewhat soiled but still outrageous. If you find you have a secret hankering for such things even after trying them on and you can afford 'em, get 'em. If you don't have wealth, call and find out where your local luxury department store dumps their stuff after the season. Once the garment gets a brisk cleaning and a few sequins are restored, it's as good as new. You can even figure out who the designers are (if the labels have been removed) by checking the side-seam tag. The RN (registered number) or WPL (wool products labeling) number on the fiber content tag tells you who the designer is if you're willing to check that number against the RN and WPL directories from the Federal Trade Commission at your local library.[18]

When designers do make money on clothing, it's not on the outrageous stuff. McDowell, a former designer, wrote that designer profit from clothes comes from "the basics—an all-purpose jacket, a flattering skirt, an adaptable blouse and well-cut pants. Everything else is literally show biz. But, of course, they do not wish to be known for such banal items."[19] A dozen gorgeous black skirts and white silk blouses, one from each major designer, wouldn't fill the pages of *Vogue*.

Demystify the false status of designer goods. Many know that most "designer" clothing is usually mass-produced by a licensee, and may never have been seen by the designer. Unless you go to the designer's atelier in Paris (or wherever) for fittings for a garment made for you, you are buying a mass-produced garment, regardless of what the label means to you. One woman who let herself try on designer garments in a store commented, "In the magazines, they're presented as the pinnacle towards which you should aspire. I've always thought that I should want that stuff. When I put it on, I couldn't feel comfortable in it. I worried about spilling things. The clothes wore me." Molloy points out that "if [fashion designers] really worked for the public, they would design reasonably priced, durable garments with as little built-in obsolescence as possible."[20]

If the clothes are great, and the prices too outrageous to consider, look to copy them. Some other manufacturer has already produced knock-offs at a more affordable price. Some, when trying on designer clothes, even go as far as to trace a pattern in the fitting room. Needless to say, this is frowned upon by store personnel. They may be observing you with hidden cameras. Let them deal with it.

It's important to have a sense of humor about the labels. Designers can be endearingly clueless. For example, Ralph Lauren manufactures a lower-priced casual collection called "ralph" for the younger market, seemingly oblivious to the fact that to that generation, the word "ralph" is synonymous with "vomit." Our friend Jim Pettivan walked into a store in Korea that sold knock-off Louis Vuitton bags and men's suits. He pointed to the canvas fabric stamped with LVs, pointed to the suits, and made it clear he wanted a "Louis Vuitton" men's suit. After he convinced them, they made him a suit which he wears on Halloween in Japan "after I take it out and dust it." The Japanese go wild over it.

Before you get caught up in the experience of being swept off your feet by a brand name, remember, the clothes are supposed to enhance who you are right now, to support you in your life right now. Some of us achieve label-gasm, getting so excited by a garment's brand that we seize it, drag it home, and throw it on the bed. Then we open the bag, look at the wrinkled thing lying there, and wonder, "What was I thinking?"

How to crawl out of the trap? Imagine it without the label. Do you still like it? After you buy it, remove the label.[21] Do you want it without the label? What does the label give you that your life does not? The promise can be intoxicating. But the promise may be a lie. How do the clothes look on you? You might observe with Kennedy Fraser that "just as a decorator house looks decorated, so too a designer outfit looks designed."[22]

In a well-designed—as opposed to "designer"—garment, everything should work. If it has buttons, they should actually button something. If pockets are indicated, they should actually be there. Ask your tailor, or someone who knows clothes, to teach you. Or ask at a very good men's store. "Take ten minutes to examine the inside of an $80 suit, and then check a $300 suit the same way. You'll see the difference immediately."[23]

Quality is something to be educated about if you love clothes, but not something to use to drive yourself crazy. Camille DePedrini doesn't believe in a rigid adherence to the tyrant Quality: "There are things that are made so well that don't have very much charm. Some things of lesser quality are so fun. They can pass without being made so well." There's something to be said for an experience where all you're left with is tattered finery and a remembered pleasure. Figure out how important it is to you. One woman commented on the quality issue, "It is absolutely ridiculous to say that older people are more interested in quality than style. I am seventy-nine years old; I'm not going to make it to a hundred. And I should worry about durability?"[24]

Meditation shopping

If you're happy to drift through a store without goals, shopping can function as sort of a meditation or a social activity. As Cringely noted, it's odd how potential acquisition has this effect. Young describes the satisfactions of this for those who love it: "Often they walk out of the store after an hour of dressing up with no parcels at all; the pleasure was in the choosing, trying, and talking, a mundane shared fantasy."[25] Libby Granett, who talked earlier about the compulsive side of shopping, talks about the positive side:

> At good times, which is most of the time, browsing becomes meditative. I feel things when I look at colors and I imagine combinations and each area of a store is a new adventure. Clothing, jewelry, underwear, handbags, and shoes are all these little islands of adventure, and that's a treat.
>
> Having lunch in a department store brings me back to being with my mother as a child, going into New York to have lunch at Macy's. I thought of it as a kind of sophisticated thing adults do. I always have that sense of "being an adult" when I have lunch in a department store. I like having that feeling come back. It's a wonderful treat now to take my daughter. She's not always as fond of the shopping, but having lunch is fun.
>
> I don't have to buy something for myself. I don't even have to buy. The act of shopping, of browsing, of looking at things, feeling things, the idea of pulling together an outfit, is something that I find so appealing. Although it's definitely nice to actually then own something.
>
> I think again part of the gratification is that I almost always go shopping by myself these days, although I occasionally go with a good friend, but we separate and then decide to meet back in a couple of hours. So part of what's so gratifying is that it's just me. It feels so luxurious. Here I am with a certain amount of time that's just mine. I go into some kind of meditative trance.

Thrift store shopping

You can thrift-shop with the preparedness required to withstand the assault of regular retail shopping, but you can also do it with no list of things needed, and no sense of purpose or urgency. The dangers of accidental purchases are much less severe because the costs are negligible. Thrift store shopping can yield the perfect wardrobe, but it tends to captivate the dreamers and the easily amused among us. We tarry there awhile and regret having to leave.

When I learned about thrift shops—I was sixteen or seventeen—Ann Sheehan, an expert at this, said, "There're two things you need to know. One is, there's more than enough to go around. And the second thing is no one in here has the same taste you do." A sense of the abundance of the thrift store environment struck home. It still feels that way to me, though the type of stuff available changes because we are moving through time. Tom Hassett, a hard-core thrifter, comments on a positive aspect of thrift for us sensitive types:

I like things that are slightly damaged, but not very. It takes the edge off. If they're dinged a little bit, which being old and used helps fulfill right off the bat, I can actually be comfortable in it. It can even get ruined and I wouldn't be crushed. Which is important. I used to get crushed easily when things that I really loved got ruined.

Thrift stores are a way to special-order from history. The people involved in thrift store shopping often talk about an element of magic in it, different from just "going to the store." Tom says:

Whatever you pull out of there is a reflection of your tastes on a very idiosyncratic level, because it's such a potpourri. I also buy paintings in thrift stores for five to seven dollars. When I see some homemade thing that's wound up there that really touches me, I'll buy it. I have maybe fifteen paintings, a few up, most not, from thrift stores. It's not a statement. What it came down to was I couldn't leave it there. It was too touching, and the price was right.

How does he feel about the stigma attached to "used" clothes? Tom replies:

Well, it's essential that I don't notice on some level that they're used. There they are. They got here. Gosh, it's nice. The price, five dollars. But if I thought of them as "used," that they had spent part of their lives anywhere else really, then I don't . . . that's the essential illusion, I think.

Mary Armentrout describes how she thrift-shops:

If I'm in a shop that has a lot of potential, one that has men's and women's clothes, shoes, pots and pans and whatever, it's like rehearsal. I just go into this space, a part of me that opens up, and I'm waiting to see what will affect me in a good way.

Some things I find right away, and other things I really love I won't find until after I've tried on half of the jackets. Then there are things that I think right away I want to get. I carry them around for three hours, and then I realize that I don't want them.

And very often I go in thinking roughly of trying to find an X, and a Y, and probably a blue hat. And I come out with completely different things. I go through a period of having slightly preconceived notions of what I want and trying to match those with what's there. And then if I'm lucky and I stay long enough—at least for me, it takes a long time—I give that stuff up, and just start looking more.

Does this appeal to you? To find used clothing stores, look in the yellow pages, and at the classified ads in the local paper. Often, the better the neighborhood, the tonier the contributions. If a store is affiliated with a rich philanthropic organization, such as an elite private school or a symphony, you may find better stuff. But the old standbys, such as the Salvation Army and Goodwill, can also be terrific. Go prepared. If there are no dressing rooms, wear clothes that you can try on other clothes over. At consignment stores, it's OK to haggle gently.

In addition to the above-mentioned pleasures, there are a variety of advantages in buying used clothing. Your limits are usually marked by your taste, not your finances. You can get the pleasures of worn-in garments without the guilt of knowing the manufacturer has used toxic chemicals or strip-mined to create the worn-in effect. Alice Molloy adds, "With pre-worn clothing you know what to expect from washing them." The designers are all affordable. Donna Karan, Armani, Ungaro, and all of the Kleins were at one point hanging in my closet, obtained for a few dollars each at a thrift store. Department stores have an agenda, unlike thrift stores, which is to convince you to buy the current fashion. Thrift stores can't distract you with that nonsense.

Mary Armentrout says:

In the old days, it didn't matter so much. I could spend twenty dollars in a thrift shop and have a closet full of clothes.

I have a green dress I got in college. It was probably made in the 1950s or early 1960s, judging from the jacket. It's one of the best dresses I'll ever have. I have no idea what size it is. It doesn't matter. The shape is just perfect, and there's no question that I would ever want to return such a thing as that. You put it on and you know. It cost only two dollars. In a certain way, you can always take it back. It's clothing that's in circulation. If I don't give it back to the thrift store, I give it to my friends or whoever it looks good on who comes to the house. For whatever period of time, a garment holds me, or it expresses me, I wear it, and then I give it up.

Some things to look for before you buy: "Only buy things in relatively good condition (or that can be easily repaired). If the seat is shiny or beading is missing or there are perspiration stains give it a pass."[26] Thrift stores can be especially good for dress-up clothes, offering silk dresses for a fraction of what they originally cost. You need to check them over carefully, though. Sweat, food stains, and overwear kill a garment. Don't buy one in its death throes unless you have a very good reason. Does the idea of leaving the store without it make you frown?

Thrift store shopping can degenerate into something unpleasant. Some stores just smell bad. Also, the person shopping next to you may be completely out of his mind. Once I was breezing through the Goodwill men's department and I saw an astonishing blazer in red-and-white-tablecloth check. I said to the gentleman next to me, "Can you imagine who would wear that?" He screamed "Fuck you!" at me and ran out of the store.

Shopping break

Accompany yourself when you're shopping. Keep yourself amused and cared for. When you find yourself getting tired, take a break. This can't be emphasized enough: When you need to, go to the bathroom, go outside and get a breath of fresh air, go to a chair and sit down, go to a water fountain and drink. Take the kind of break you need.

Take a break especially when your insides scream, "I don't have time." Breaks are especially good for considering garments that have you in a tizzy. Have the merchant put them on "hold" and go away for a while. Take a premature break, before you're worn out. It can be invigorating to sit in a quiet place and watch the world go by for a few moments, free from the pressure to choose well, to express the meaning of life through a few shapeless garments. You may decide you'd rather go home.

Sitting on a couch or bench in a store is not enough. Leave the grip of the store's influence, its vision, its property. You can get caught up in the pressure of becoming "a whole new me" (basically whatever the tempo of that place is) regardless of the fact that the old you is quite wonderful. The best sorts of breaks involve thinking things over at your leisure. Take some time to check your notes, and make a few more about what you found. Jot down your emotions about the day, especially the hard ones. Did you feel embarrassed or awkward about anything? Why? Visualize yourself going through the scene again. What could you have said and done to emerge feeling good?

If you snack, have nothing that will make you feel groggy or guilty. Try Donna Karan's favorite, hot water with lemon, or try some fresh-squeezed juice. Do you have a hard-boiled egg in your purse? Eat something that doesn't bite back, so your shopping emotions aren't complicated by food feelings.

If you feel tense, try a few deep breaths or a brisk walk. If the garments have a chokehold on your mind, maybe you don't want to own garments that do this to you. Obsession is another distraction from presence. Let them go. Call up and ask to have them taken off hold. The salesperson will be shocked that someone had the courtesy to call.

Do you want to go back to shopping? If not, what would you rather do? If your need for clothes isn't urgent, quit for today, do less than what you planned, and see how that feels.

Mail order, infomercials, and other indirect forms of shopping

After you take a break, you may decide you never wish to shop in stores again. Mail order may seem like a viable option even though you can't touch the garment, look it over, or try it on until you get it home, by which point it will cost you money—in postage and handling fees—to return it. A catalog-induced meditation fantasy doesn't end even after you purchase the garment. When it arrives for your inspection, however, the fantasy often falls to earth with a thud. Despite this, mail order has its fans. (I used to be one of them.) In a recent year, over 10,000 mail-order companies mailed 13.5 billion catalogues. Fifty-five percent of the adult population spent $51.5 billion on mail-order goods.[27]

Mail order has its pleasures. You don't have to deal with a saleslady staring at you. You can shop naked. Graphic designer Jackie Thaw says about mail order, "It's good at 11 P.M. on a Thursday night when I'm thinking, 'I want to buy something now.' If it's not shipped by FedEx, I forget about it, and then, woo-hoo, I get a surprise a few days later." If you don't want to deal with a store, if you know exactly what you want, if you've found a catalog you really like, with clothes that fit, in a palette of colors that suit you, mail order can be bliss.

I tend to wander off into huge errors: I ordered a hooded sweatshirt in Mango once (Mango? Oxblood? Tuscan? Cadet? Atmosphere? Haven't they heard of Orange? Maroon? Tan? Blue- green?)

When it arrived, I wondered, "Who am I?" and sent it back. The catalogs, like the ads, pander to our emotions, not our need for clothes. Witness the phenomenal success of the catalogue (you can name it) where everyone's out sailing or doing other vacation activities on some Martha's Vineyard-like location, while slaves in foreign countries make the clothes.

Electronic shopping is worse. Though it generated around $900 million of sales in 1993, 40% of the merchandise was returned.[28] Why? Most of it is crap. The advertisers prey on the fact that most people who are dissatisfied are very unlikely to bother returning it. As the Sterns point out, the infomercials reap enormous profits even though "every on-the-level consumer report reveals that the same (or much better products) are available in stores at lower prices."[29] The scam is larger than one would want to believe. MTV sells some goods before they've been manufactured.[30]

I've heard good things about mail order from Hong Kong, as long as you ship to a reputable tailor. "The method most recommended by Hong Kong tailors is to send a well-fitting garment of the type you want to be copied. It will be returned unharmed with your completed order. . . . And you can specify any problem areas in the garment you send."[31] It seems simpler to find someone here to do it. But whatever floats your boat.

Some tips: Don't order unreturnable products. Phone order, find out the total cost, and check that it's still worth it once you include tax, postage, and handling and any other bizarre fees. It's worth trying the flea market line "Is this your best price?" when on the phone. Ask for the measurements of garments, and compare them to measurements of clothes you own and love. If after the garment arrives it doesn't work, face the biggest drag about mail order: returns. Some catalog companies will reimburse you for postage. Include a note requesting postage refund.

Look at your mail order expenses from last year, including return postage, and think about whether they are worth it. I did, and canceled all the catalogs. To be removed from mailing lists for all catalogs, you can contact the companies directly, or send one three-by-five-inch card with your name, as it appears on the mailing labels, requesting removal, to the Mail Preference Service Department of the Direct Marketing Association, 11 West 42nd Street, P.O. Box 3861, New York, NY 10163-3861. They will take your name off all mailing lists.

If there's one catalog you particularly love and can't live without, call their customer service department and ask them to cut down on the number of catalogs they send. Many can send you just two a year instead of one every few weeks. Think of the trees you'll save.

Of course, if you shop mail order or electronically, you don't have to face the dressing room.

The dressing room

No life is more interesting than any other life; everybody's life takes place in the same twenty-four hours of consciousness and sleep; we are all locked into our own subjectivity, and who is to say that the thoughts of a person gazing into the vertiginous depths of a volcano in Sumatra are more objectively interesting than those of a person trying on a dress at Bloomingdale's?

—Janet Malcolm[32]

It may seem that the point of the dressing room is humiliation of the shopper by making her face, under terrible light, the full extent of the fragility of corporality. Bixler points out, "The lighting in most store dressing rooms seems designed to make everyone, no matter what the hue of her skin, look like a freshly plucked chicken."[33] If you are shopping in a place that has dressing rooms, check out the available rooms and choose the best, preferably a large one with a chair, good light, and a three-way mirror. Remove the abandoned garments in it.

When you enter the room, hang up the clothes, sit down and rest for a moment. Experimentation requires the courage to try new things and discover what works and what doesn't, and the kindness to recognize that if the garment doesn't look right, the garment is at fault, not you. Take a moment to look in the mirror and find the self you like. If the person you like isn't there in the mirror before you try on clothes, she won't stride in as you're trying them on. Go home. Practice looking in the mirror until you can find your own steady reserve of self-esteem. You can't buy it, you can't shop for it, you can't find it in some garment.

As you try on garments, use different types of gazing to see the full picture. Morton suggests looking as an artist might, with half-closed eyes, to see "the essential pattern and to perceive shapes that jump out in a spotty fashion, destroying unity and rhythm, because they seem not to lie on the same surface."[34] The "Blink Test" can come in handy here, too. (You know never to leave your wallet in the fitting room when you go out.)

In the dressing room, try out your ideas about how color, style, pattern, etc. relate to your unique beauty. If you love some look from a magazine, you may have fused your ideal self with the "look" and left your real self behind. Trying on the fantasy object in the dressing room will teach you where your fantasy doesn't support your reality. Since you know to try on your real size and a size bigger, you may even enjoy this process. However, the dressing room can be a place where we fall right down to earth in a heap of shimmering finery. It was the place I acknowledged that Romeo Gigli's clothes look lovely even though I can't move my arms in them.

Many people have habitual "dressing room postures" that have nothing to do with how they hold and move their bodies in real life. How do you hold your jaw, your shoulders, your hips, your stomach, while looking in a dressing room mirror? How does that compare with the comfortable postures of your everyday life? By sucking in my stomach and expelling all breath, I can shrink three sizes in jeans. Of course I can't even zip them once I get home.

Your body will give you the essential clue about fit. Consultant Kathryn Hoover comments:

If you put something on and think, "Oh, God. I don't know if this is too weird for me or if it's too great. I'm a little afraid of it." Be in it for a few minutes and see if you feel more comfortable or less comfortable, and that's your answer. The clearest clue is fidgeting. I've never seen anyone looking good while they were fidgeting with their clothes. If you have to fidget with it to be in it, it's a "Not."

If a client is on the edge I will say, "You be in it for a few minutes. I'm going to run and get this and come back, and I'll ask you if you feel more comfortable in it or less comfortable in it after you've been in it for a while." By the time I get back, they know.

Until the garment fits the body correctly, it won't look right regardless of how fashionable the silhouette is. Buying too-tight clothes can be more tempting than buying too-loose ones for many. These clothes offer the pleasures of greater tartiness, and the experience of being held.

When I try on a garment that has a part that fits the upper body, I move my upper body in every direction it comfortably goes, in order to see if the garment will go with me and not look silly. Everything gets the elbow swing test to see if it puckers in front or constricts in back. Also, I put my hands on my hips and in the pockets to see what the garment does. I wiggle my shoulders to make sure I move freely in it. I bend over and see if my breasts make a run for it out the front. I lift my arms and move them about. If a top or dress is too tight, I know I'll get cranky wearing it. So I don't buy it.

This was and is my beef with shoulder pads: you lift your arms and you look increasingly silly, like some fashion football player. If the fashion dictates a close fit in the body, and I want something in fashion, I can always find a design which provides the illusion of the fashionable cut and still gives me free range of movement.

Wagenvoord points out the importance of the correct lingerie for tops: "Always try on dresses wearing the bra you intend to wear with that dress—a different bra may alter the position of the dress's bust darts and make them pucker."[35]

Regarding jackets, do the armholes have to be deep enough to hold sweaters? Fiedorek suggests, regarding the fit of the jacket, that if the garment doesn't fit well and lie flat across the shoulders, it's better not to get it.[36] Wagenvoord adds to the discussion, "Horizontal ripples across the back mean that it's too tight. A vertical crease down the back means that it's too loose, causing the lapels to sag in front."[37]

With skirts, trousers, and the bottom half of garments, I prefer waists with some give in them so I can sit down and not feel my organs reshuffled. Again, there's a difference between the size of your waist when you stand and when you sit. This isn't wrong or bad, it's just basic anatomy.

Sit for a while in any garment you intend to buy. When you stand, look at the crotch. Did it get "instant crotch wrinkle"? Unless the fabric is linen and you expect this, the quality of the fabric isn't high enough. Don't buy it. Jan Larkey suggests that if the garment binds across your legs as you sit or gets stuck on the tummy or hips when you stand, "try the next size."[38] Look for visible panty line.

Is the skirt wide enough at the bottom, or are the pants unconfining enough so that you can walk freely? I start to grit my teeth if I come up against confines before I've reached the full stretch of my walk. Life is hard enough—I don't need my clothes to struggle with me as well.

For years I told myself "I'm so fat" and proved it by the chafing caused by my thighs rubbing together. I never experimented with different kinds of trousers that would ease the stress of contact; rather I gloried in my misery and neglect. My body tells me if clothing really, rather than sort of, fits. After wearing it, if I see red lines along my waist or other body parts, the clothes don't fit.[39] If a garment is too small, the item is a metaphor for yearning, not an actual piece of clothing I can wear today. The hair shirt went out a long time ago.

A moment when you just know it's right? A friend said, "When I put the trousers on in the store, all of a sudden everything else I was wearing worked. It was as if my clothes were searching, waiting, on hold for these trousers." What are other signals something is right? Mary Armentrout comments:

A facet of yourself that you always knew was there but had never seen so clearly is suddenly there, and you don't want to let it go. It's not something you have to force, grasp after, or nip and tuck in and make be there.

Think of a garment you have that really works for you. What was your first response to it in the store? What did you see in the mirror when you tried it on? What are your signals that something is right? Clothes shopping is not a shallow activity. As with all things done fully and with heart, it can have importance, resonance, and deeply felt meaning.

And then of course there are people who wouldn't enter a dressing room for love or money. Our resident maverick, Stacey Lamiero, comments:

I went into Ann Taylor not too long ago, and I saw some silk blouses that I liked. I hate shopping so much that I don't even try my clothes on when I'm there. So I just went in and said, "I'll take the navy one, the pink one, and the beige one." If I see something I like, I'll buy multiple colors. I think that's kind of weird, but again, I don't like shopping enough to want to go out and look for that good color that I need.

Did it work? "Yes, it works great. I gave one to my mom because I felt a little guilty. Three was overkill. But I kept the pink and the blue one."

Buying clothes

> *If you see something that shrieks "buy me," then your instincts are probably right.*
> —Jane Procter, *Clothes Sense* [40]

> *Never trust to love at first sight in buying a costume. Since we're the kind of women who find
> clothes irresistible, we know the wisdom of being choosy rather than promiscuous.
> When a perfectly fascinating dress beckons from a shop window,
> consider it as seriously as if you were going to be married to it.*
> —Margaretta Byers, *Designing Women* [41]

Whether you information shop, meditation shop, or just plain shop, wisely deciding what to buy is a complex issue involving juggling emotions about spending and self-worth, relative financial balance, "investment dressing," and presence of mind at the moment of choosing.

If clothing is something you love, and you have very little income and no good clothes, consider whether your unwillingness to have wonderful clothes is "realistic" or rather a rigid pose to foster self-pity or evoke sympathy. As a result of financial limits, what games do you play that prevent you from having the life you want and the clothes you love? You have choices.

For the frugal fashion lovers among us, thrift stores and rummage sales can provide excellent clothes for as little as pennies. Volunteering at such places can provide clothes for free, as can asking friends whose wardrobes you admire to give you their unwanted garb. Charities or towns frequently sponsor "free bins." Invariably they have a few excellent things.

People often tightly limit their spending even if they have ample funds to buy clothes. Barbara Jay talked about the self-imposed spending rules she's heard from clients:

"I was raised in a retail family. We don't buy anything at retail." "It has to be on sale!" "In order for me to be politically correct within my family, I have to pay no more than $14 for a dress." Or, "My grandma always looked beautiful on a shoestring. I ought to be able to do it, too." Whatever . . .

I have people whose homes are like castles, and the amount of money they tell me they're going to spend on clothes disgusts me. I think, "What are you doing here? Do you cherish yourself or not? You don't need to be dressed from head to toe in Donna Karan, but if you can't even enjoy something that might make you look wonderful, where's the artistry in this?"

Do you have emotional issues that stand in the way of your buying clothes you are happy with? What are they? If you feel you don't deserve wonderful clothes, why? Who is involved? What would allow you to resolve this and move on? How about taking a small step now?

On the flip side, many women overspend, creating financial constraints and sometimes catastrophe, often without getting clothes that satisfy. They buy as if the spending itself proved something about the appropriateness or wonderfulness of the purchase, a central mistake in consumer culture. People spend grandiosely and grossly for many reasons. Have you ever misspent? What did you buy and why did you buy it? Did you keep it? How did you feel?

One woman I spoke with accumulated a five-figure clothing debt after leaving her husband when she got lost in a fantasy of who she could be, surrendering to the dark side of shopping. How did it start? "At the time, my wardrobe was modest. I could contain my clothes in one normal-sized closet." When she met the man who would later become her ex-husband, she thought she needed "good girl" clothes, "like the kind of dress you would wear to meet someone's mother." When they decided to get married, she thought the wedding trip required garments, "such as the cute, virginal, sweet-thing sundresses." She bats her great doe eyes like an ingenue. "I bought clothes that reflected an enthusiastic approach towards new beginnings." After they married, she did a lot of shopping. She wanted "good wife" clothes.

I needed, for example, a navy blazer. I went through my "Talbot's catalogue" period, where the message my clothes conveyed was, "We don't have to look attractive. We're intelligent." It was a clear demonstration of my attitudes about marriage, another identity.

When they relocated to New York, another aspect was added. The weather was quite different. She thought, "Professional work clothes for the good wife. Ooh, what does she wear?" She took it one step further.

She doesn't have any of those clothes anymore. When she left her husband, she literally left the clothes hanging in the closet. She did not want to bring them with her into her new life. She started her own business. Instead of stopping shopping then, she went to the next phase, the "young professional woman" look. This is where the debt started getting serious.

Silk shirt dresses, not too attractive, not sexual, but very professional and elegant. I left the Muffy Buffy little tweed suits behind, and was trying to look older, more sophisticated and interesting.

After that phase, she realized, "Well, I own my own business. It's creative. I can look fun." She walked through self-definitions by buying clothes. After she and her husband separated, she moved into an apartment she loved.

This apartment had the greatest closets in the world. Because it had such great closet space, I thought I could now really explore clothes.

I had this idea about becoming the husband I always wanted. I'd always had this fantasy that my husband would buy me lingerie, and it would be this romantic thing. That never happened in my marriage.

For Christmas she bought herself everything she really wanted a boyfriend or husband to buy her, starting with a leopard print bra and bikini underwear. She thought, "I'm not going to look to a man to do these things for me. I need to do this for myself."

After the divorce came through, she went on a vacation trip to Italy. "I thought I was going to see museums and galleries, but the woman I went with was really into clothes."

She went over with $500. After the first day, her companion assured her she could put anything she wanted on her companion's charge card. They'd work it out later in trade for her business services. In eleven days, she bought $11,000 worth of clothes. Her companion spent about $18,000. The difference was that her companion's husband was an investment banker, making $450,000 a year.

The more places they went—from Milan to Venice to Rome—the more her companion lost any pretense of being the slightest bit interested in museums and galleries. They just spent days shopping. They went to Maud Frizon. The shoes were seventy-five dollars a pair. "The value of the dollar was so incredible. I bought at least eight pairs of shoes, six purses, belts, scarves, evening pants, and at least four dresses, and blouses. I was totally out of my league. I was with a pro."

When she got home she organized her closet according to the really beautiful, expensive things she never wore because she worried about ruining them, and the inexpensive, comfortable, fun everyday clothes she would wear for work, so she didn't have to worry about spilling on them.

I would keep reorganizing and reorganizing where I would put things according to frequency of wear, and according to the function I'd wear them to, and the volume at this point was huge. For example, I had over one hundred pairs of shoes. I had fourteen coats, including five raincoats and three fur coats (of which two were Fendi). One I got from Bergdorf's was a full-length Fendi mink coat. I just charged it. It was marked down from $20,000 to $12,000. The monthly installments on this coat were $480. I could have been driving a Mercedes. There was no way in the world I could make the payments. . . .

After the trip I came back to my life, and instead of feeling like, "Okay, that was that," I continued to shop and spend. I got to a place financially where it was just disastrous. I had to cut up all my charge cards and basically go cold turkey because I had created a total monster.

And seven years later she is still paying off the debt. Poorer, but wiser.

Before shopping for clothes ask:

- What can I afford to spend?
- Do I need new clothes?
- Does my soul need new clothes?
- How do I make choices about clothes that are so perfect that I never waste money on things which don't suit me?

You may find you enjoy the practice of restraint. My friend Sarah cites the pleasant tension to financial limits, which people with few financial constraints never face. The question "Do I want this?" adds some weight because there is a real cost. Your opinion, your judgment, has value and consequences.

People's limits vary. Barbara Jay splurges on T-shirts. "For instance," she says while touching the T-shirt she's wearing. "This is my archetypal favorite. My life is a series of T-shirts."

"But that's more than just a T-shirt, though," I say. " That's fabulous."

"Well, it's an Italian T-shirt. $200," she replies.

I blanch. "That ain't no ordinary T-shirt."

"But you know," she continues, "I bought one on my lunch hour for $70. They don't all have to be so fancy."

Sometimes spending gets out of control. I have had my moments when I've set a bad example.

One day a few years ago, I was moving quickly through Macy's on my way back to the office at lunch hour. Walking through the bag department, I noticed a small brown purse behind the glass, and my gut response was, "That's sexy."

Unaccustomed to thinking of a purse as sexy, I decided to circle round for a second look. A fluttery Christmas-help saleswoman called over someone else to help me. I said, "Don't tell me the price."

I put the bag over my shoulder and liked it. I looked at the price—with tax, the bag would cost just over $600. Rent for a month and a half. I expected it to be around $250, but somehow $600 was so absurdly expensive, I had to go look at myself holding the bag again in a long mirror. It looked good. I asked the sensible, mom-like saleslady, "Do they ever go on sale?" She said, "No. These bags sell." I wondered to whom.

I took a breath and thought, "Do I want this bag?" I smiled in reply. I asked her, "Why is it so expensive?"

She said, "It's a Vecchi." This meant nothing to me. She continued, "I'm getting my couch reupholstered. I picked out the fabric, the couch is out of the house. I'm nervous. My husband asks me what I'm worried about. The fabric is beautiful. But it was such a small swatch, I couldn't see how it would look on the couch."

I decided to buy the bag. This surprised the fluttering person standing next to her. The woman who was reupholstering said, "You will love it. You will have it for the rest of your life."

I said, "I can't tell my mother how much it cost."

She said, "No, don't tell your mother." I gave her my credit card. She ran it through the machine. It was rejected.

"There's no reason for it to be rejected," I said, fighting embarrassment. I thought: The Universe knows I have no business buying the bag and is beeping, begging me to THINK. The saleslady told me to go up to the fourth floor to customer service. I said, "Don't sell the bag."

Customer service directed me to the pay phones. I called my credit card company. They extended my credit limit. I walked to the elevator. Thinking I was crazy, but that it felt right to do this, that I would feel sad if I walked away without it, that I can always return it, I bought the bag.

She put it in a little fabric pouch and in a Macy's bag. I just wanted to wear it out of the store. I walked back toward the office, passing homeless, hungry people and wondering what I had just done. I saw a dark green Jaguar caught in the intersection, and I thought, "A hundred purses would buy one of those. But the bag does less damage to the environment!" I bought a large white rose with pink edging around the petals a few blocks from the office. Then I stopped at the stand on Pine Street where the Polish woman makes smoothies. Her hair was a mass of blond curls.

"You got a perm," I said. "It looks great!"

"Thank you so much," she replied with a giggle. "It was very expensive, but it lasts forever."

I still love the purse. I rarely use it. Don't tell my mom.

With that contrary example in mind, let's discuss common sense.

1. "Investment dressing." That phrase doesn't mean budgeting, buying navy wool separates, or only wearing coordinates. The real issue is not the cost of the garment, it's the cost per wear. Kathryn Hoover comments that some clients only buy clothes on sale:

   > My perspective is, "Great, when you get a bargain, of course, who would argue with it?" But when you find something that's really you, you love it, and you buy it at whatever price, what it does for you inside is great. That's the thing people wear one hundred times in the first month they own it.

   Laurel Fenenga adds, "If your budget is limited, why not put the most money in the thing you wear every day? So you buy the best-fitting pants you find no matter what they cost." Or as Bixler puts it, "Doesn't it make sense to put your money where you put your time?"[42]

2. One friend distinguishes between the shopping questions she used to ask—"Can I stand to wear this? Is it going to be durable? Okay. Yes. I'll buy it"—and the questions she asks now—"Do I absolutely love it? Can I not live without it?" She comments, "Because if I want it, I'll buy it, I don't tempt myself unless I'm really in the mood to spend a lot of money."

3. At the point of purchase if you're not sure and you can't bear to leave without it, make sure you can return it. Before purchase, stop and ask yourself some questions. If you need privacy, go back to the dressing room and sit down, or put it on hold and leave the store. Ask:

   - Does this garment fit the real life I lead?
   - What makes me feel beautiful?
   - Does this item support that?
   - How will I feel if I leave the store with this?
   - Without it?
   - How will I feel looking at it every day in my closet?

   If it's the only one and it's flawed, ask the salesperson to call other stores to see if they have the perfect version. If she won't, you can use the store's free personal shopping service or call yourself.

4. Is the garment a risk? What kind? It's important to take risks, even make mistakes, so that, at the end, you don't look back upon your life wistfully wishing you had lived more fully and more generously. Nancy Roberts talks about risking the jeans quest:

   > On one of the first TV programs I ever did about finding clothes for big women, one of my "models" said she'd always wanted jeans but had never been able to find them. I came into the studio for our dress rehearsal with four or five different pairs

for her to try. The first three pairs were too big. "I thought you told me you couldn't find jeans," I asked her. "Well, I never really tried them on before," she admitted.[43]

If you feel the need to buy something just for the thrill, remember, as Dr. Alan Gelman once said sagely, "The thrill of buying is the same as the thrill of throwing things out. And just as transient." Go home and throw something out instead.

5. If you've got a special event and you want something new, but don't want to borrow or buy something to wear, consider renting a fabulous gown. It can cost a lot less than buying one. And consider something I don't understand, clothing rental for day-to-day clothes. A store called Changes in Boston, for a flat fee of ninety-nine dollars a month (this seems like a lot to me), offers women the opportunity to "check out" suits, dresses, separates, and accessories. Customers have access to as much as $7,000 worth of clothing each month.[44]

P.S. If you're buying something, be sure the salesperson keys in the amount correctly. Check your receipt. Make sure they remove any security tags. More than one friend has purchased a garment and brought it home only to find the security tag still attached.

After Shopping

It's important to set aside time to integrate a garment into your wardrobe when it gets home, even if that means trying it on with everything you own. This is playtime.

If you know you love it and you're going to keep it, feel free to cut tags. But save them just in case. If you get it home and you realize you hate it, so what? You're going to make mistakes. The idea of unerring judgment is a prison. As you practice, your mistakes will diminish. Mary Armentrout has a forgiving attitude toward shopping errors:

> I don't worry if I'm only succeeding seventy percent of the time, and thirty percent is for shit, doesn't work, it was stupid to buy it. If I'm really good, I will realize before I buy that the things I'm carrying around are not really what I want, but I can't always do that.

The only danger of making mistakes is spending beyond what you can afford on something you cannot or will not return. A little soul-searching is in order to prevent reoccurrence. If the mistake leaves you able to pay the rent and feed yourself and family, but rankles terribly anyway, remember that making mistakes is part of the democratic process of learning. See what you did wrong and stop yourself from repeating it the next time. Ask yourself, for example, as my girlfriend did: "Did I buy this because I liked this garment, *not* because I like me in it? Because I liked the way it looked although there's no way I could ever wear it?" While you were shopping, if some angel could have taken you aside for a little heart-to-heart, what would she have said to you? What was the clue that it was "off"? Talk with someone who understands this problem.

Don't eat your shame. If it's returnable, return it. You can even frequently get refunds on things such as "nonrefundable" airline tickets. If they ask what is wrong with it, tell them. The larger the business, the less this return means to them. For that reason, it's often easier to shop in department stores. In the eighties, many women would buy whole wardrobes, wear them a season, and then return them at the end of the season. For this reason, many stores have a no-returns policy on evening wear, but will accept anything else back. In the national chain I worked at in the mid-eighties, the policy was to take back anything, no questions asked. Our store once took back a bald automobile tire. None of the stores had ever sold automobile tires.

Once, for a party, I spent several hundred dollars on the most beautiful blue silk dress I have ever worn. I felt vibrant in that dress. However, just in case, I saved the receipt. After I wore the dress I noticed it was coming apart at the seams. I sent it back because I believed that I should get more wear for my money. I came to this conclusion after much inner debate about morality ("Do I have a right to return it?"); blame ("Is this my fault?"); and being nice ("I should take the loss, it's not nice to take advantage of them.") I decided that self-preservation mattered more—I needed the money or I needed a working dress. I had neither. I also rationalized that the store would prefer getting one return and having me as a good customer for life to my never setting foot in there again because of anger. However, I was sufficiently embarrassed that I mailed it back to Customer Returns. If my ship comes in, I may still mail them a check for the full amount.

Notes:

1. Cringely, Robert X. *Accidental Empires*. Page 3.

2. The same thing applies to thinness. See Susie Orbach's *Fat Is a Feminist Issue*. Page 83.

3. Geneen Roth suggests this in *Why Weight?* on page 55.

4. Weiland, Barbara and Leslie Wood. *Clothes Sense*. Page 69.

5. Procter, Jane. *Clothes Sense*. Page 13.

6. Leopold, Allison Kyle and Anne Marie Cloutier. *Short Chic*. Page 25.

7. Koller, Alice. *The Stations of Solitude*. Page 9

8. Susie Orbach, in *Fat Is a Feminist Issue*, page 143, suggests you do the same thing with "forbidden" foods.

9. Roberts, Nancy. *Breaking All the Rules*. Page 111.

10. Coleridge, Nicholas. *The Fashion Conspiracy*. Page 268.

11. Schniederman, Ira P. and Debra Gill. "A day in the life of a cross shopper." *Women's Wear Daily*. April 26, 1995. Page 2.

12. Feldon, Leah. *Dress Like a Million*. Page 125.

13. Barthes, Roland. *The Fashion System*. Page 295.

14. Weiland. Page 10.

15. Cho, Emily and Linda Grover. *Looking Terrific*. Page 179.

16. Feldon. Page 109.

17. McDowell, Colin. *The Designer Scam*. Page 75.

18. Weiland. Page 84.

19. McDowell. Page 93.

20. Molloy, John. *The Women's Dress for Success Book*. Page 20.

21. Bixler, Susan. *The Professional Image*. Page 44.

22. Fraser, Kennedy. *The Fashionable Mind*. Page 168.

23. Cho and Grover. Page 189.

24. Chapkis, Wendy. *Beauty Secrets*. Page 187.

25. Benstock, Shari and Suzanne Ferris, eds. *On Fashion*. Page 206.

26. Feldon. Page 127.

27. Brubach, Holly. "Mail-Order America." *New York Times Magazine*. November 21, 1993. Page 54.

28. McDowell. Page 100.

29. Stern, Jane and Michael Stern. *Encyclopedia of Pop Culture*. Page 242.

30. Strauss, Neil. "I want my MTV, and maybe a silk shirt." *New York Times*. December 4, 1994. Arts and Leisure. Page 37.

31. McGill, Leonard. *Stylewise*. Page 55.

32. Malcolm, Janet. "A House of One's Own." *The New Yorker*. June 5, 1995. Page 64.

33. Bixler. Page 60.

34. Morton, Grace Margaret. *The Arts of Costume and Personal Appearance*. Page 152.

35. Wagenvoord. *Clothes Care*. Page 20.
36. Fiedorek, Mary. *Executive Style*. Page 80.
37. Wagenvoord. Page 20.
38. Larkey, Jan. *Flatter Your Figure*. Page 95.
39. Goday. Page 27.
40. Procter. Page 21.
41. Byers, Margaretta with Consuelo Kamholz. *Designing Women*. Page 209.
42. Bixler. Page 41.
43. Roberts, Nancy. Page 144.
44. Norwich, William. "Fashion front." *Vogue*. December 1994. Page 100.

Seeking Help from Others . . .
How Humiliating

[W]hat if someone agrees to read and work on your stuff for you . . . and it turns out that he says things about your work, even in the nicest possible tone of voice, that are totally negative and destructive? . . . Would you stand for someone talking this way to your children—for instance, telling them that they are not very talented at painting and shouldn't even bother? Or that their poetry is not very interesting? Of course not. You'd want to go pay this person a little visit with your flamethrower. So why, if someone says something like this to you, would you want anything further to do with him?

—Anne Lamott, *Bird by Bird*[1]

Anne Lamott writes about a writing partner, but the same issues underlie one's choice of a shopping partner or tailor, be she a friend, a department store employee, or a hired hand. Given the risks involved, it might be better to dispense with these people altogether, especially as you train yourself to see in a new way. However, given the benefits involved, it might be essential to get help, especially as you refine your vision.

Friends

Debbie admits what we all know about shopping with friends: "Some friends would say it looked good no matter what because they don't want to hurt your feelings." They do this regardless of the chaos that may ensue later.

Sometimes you have to actively ignore the friends you take shopping with you. Lex shows me a wild Hawaiian men's sport coat. It's got this great tapa pattern on it in green, black, and brown with pineapples and abstract designs. It was five bucks at a church thrift store, and the friends who accompanied her "both were dying, making those gagging faces and sticking their fingers down their throats like they were going to throw up. But I just persevered because I knew it was really great, and I bought it." Now whenever she wears it (she wears it with a black tank top and jeans), "I am so cool and styling that when one of the people who was there when I bought it sees me, he says, 'You were right about that jacket. It's great.' "

Clothes lover Susan Zeidman admitted, "I once tried to talk a friend I was mad at into a garment that looked bad on her. I was unsuccessful, but could see the destructive potential there."

Leave men home. (Let that be a mantra.) Leave home whoever doesn't enjoy this as much as you do, whoever will silently sulk or vociferously whine. They don't want to be there and you don't want them there. Grow up and admit it. When I shop, I'm tired of seeing forlorn-looking men sitting awkwardly in department store chairs and children whose faces have turned to little inflamed raisins of misery. And it's your fault.

If you're going to go ahead and shop with another, consider carefully whom you choose and what your expectations are. Jennifer Robin suggests guidelines:

The most important quality you should look for in a shopping partner is an unshakable belief that you are beautiful and absolutely perfect the way you are.

The next most important characteristic your partner should have is a heartfelt desire for you to succeed.

The perfect person to take shopping wants to go with you and does not have to be coerced. She has plenty of time, and won't rush you while you make a decision, or worse yet, convince you something is "good enough" so the day can come to an end.[2]

Another essential quality in a shopping partner is an aesthetic sense that can put its own biases aside and tailor itself to your needs. A shopping buddy doesn't actually have to go shopping. I have friends with whom I talk deeply about shopping but very rarely shop with.

Jeremy Stone comments on the ups and downs of good shopping with friends:

I did an inordinate amount of shopping with my girlfriend Sylvia who was also a clotheshorse. This woman also lived on a budget. It became a really important part of our friendship and female bonding to go to the Neiman Marcus discount shop and hit the sales. When neither of us was dating, we would spend the whole day at I. Magnin—if there were a great sale—just shopping. We had the best time.

She was like an older sister who would always give me her most honest opinion, but she'd always focus on what I looked good in. I would pick out a dress, and when I looked in the mirror, I wouldn't see me. As you know, I would see a 5'8" flat-chested blonde with green eyes. I'm 5'1½", petite, brown hair, brown eyes. I am a small person. Some aspects of me can be larger or smaller depending on my weight, but basically I'm a small person. Anyway, she would always pick out dresses for me and say, "This is going to look great on you," and I would say, "Really?" Whatever I put on that she picked out would look incredible. She was really good at finding things for me, and I was really good at finding things for her. She used to say things to me like, "Can I be honest? I'm your friend."

I'd say, "Yes, what is it?"

She'd say, "No pleats. Never! You're too short. No pleats! This isn't your best look. You're small. Your best look is fitted. It's narrow." We had a lot of fun doing all of this together. She really got me into accessories. This was a woman who had fifteen different pairs of sunglasses. Every outfit had different things that went with it.

Remember what Anne Lamott wrote: If, despite your training, what they're saying in speech or gesture doesn't support you, let them go, cut them loose. Shop alone, or train another friend. Find a Sylvia.

Salespeople

Shopping Anxiety Checklist:

____ I don't belong here.

____ I'm not good enough.

____ Salespeople frighten me.

____ I frighten salespeople.

____ When shopping, I become obsessed with the idea that they think I'm shoplifting even though I've never stolen anything in my life.

____ Salespeople glance at me, say snide things about me I almost hear, and laugh. I'm never going shopping again.

In the worst-case scenario (a frequent occurrence), sales help can be really bad. If you think they're checking you out, you're right. If you've picked up the idea that you will more than likely be poorly served for ridiculous reasons, you're right. Debbie Epidendio comments:

We went shopping at Circuit City one day. I had jeans and a T-shirt on. Rich had just gotten off work. He was completely dirty from head to toe, in beat-up shoes. We walk in, and we were there twenty minutes. They're swarming with salespeople. I said, "How come nobody's come up to help us yet? Not one person's asked us." He said, "Debbie, look what we look like!" Eventually we got this man to come over and help us and we ended up buying a whole bunch of stuff from him. So we really laughed over that one.

Have you experienced painfully bad sales help? What do you expect? Sadly, it's unrealistic to expect well-informed helpful salespeople. Most salespeople are poorly paid. They have to dress as if they're not or risk losing their jobs. Their lousy jobs depend on your spending—whether they're on commission or not—not your happiness. Don't blame them. Sympathize with their plight and politely get them the hell out of your way unless they're very astute about clothes and you, and they're kind.

Forgo any attempt at the hauteur attitude (trying to mirror back what you're being sent) if you feel intimidated. This isn't high school. At the same time, recognize that if you're in a place where snobbery is the token of the realm, you may have to play to get results. Do you have a snob mask that you can wear with gentleness and humor if you need to?

Regarding salespeople behaving at their worst, revenge is possible and sweet. An old friend who has the voice and demeanor of God himself was recently shopping in a discount store. One clerk called out to another, "Hey faggot, get over here." At which point my friend called out in his booming godly voice, "As a gay person, I am offended by your using the word 'faggot.'" The rest of the store became quiet. Gazes turned toward the offending clerk. My friend then went to the manager and complained. The manager was last seen with murder on his face, running toward the department where the clerks were.

If you find yourself buying clothes because you feel sorry for the salesperson, buying something because they've been "so nice," or because you feel like you have to flee and you always buy something, because she says "it's you," because it's "polite" to buy something, you've got some issues to straighten out in your own head. You have other options. You can thank her and leave. Try practicing these comments at home so you can use them while shopping:

"No, thank you."
"Thanks for your help so far. I need to shop alone now."
"Please help another customer. I'm happy to shop alone."
"Oh my God, there's a fire in lingerie. Call 911!"

How do you find a good salesperson? Wallach suggests you look for one you think is well dressed. If you tell her what you need, what you have, and what you're willing to spend, she will be able to help you better. "Ask her how to put the clothes together. Tell them to call you when merchandise is going on sale and when new clothes come in."[3] Emily Cho suggests that after someone asks you the right questions, you see if she really listens to your answers. Someone who's just plodding through won't attend to what you say, and doesn't deserve your time and attention.[4]

What do you do when you find a great one? Feldon notes:

My friend Ronnie, an inveterate sales shopper who has gotten more great deals at sales than anybody else on the planet, has made buddies of a few select salespeople in many of her favorite stores by sharing shopping sources, bringing in little goodies like Batman pins for their kids, or treating them to an occasional cappuccino at coffee break time. Now they call her the minute there's a great sale. "I just do tiny little things so they don't forget me," she explains.[5]

Chandra Cho, a store owner and veteran saleswoman, comments about the other side of supporting customers:

A lot of people don't want you to know. If you show them what they like, they feel the thrill is gone. It's like you're infringing on their privacy. Their expression says, "Who are you to know?" Well, I only do this for a living.

How do customers develop a sense of what makes them look beautiful?

That's what I do. I mean, that's my job. I sort of tap into their energy and bring out what's good for them. And then they tell me their limitations. A woman comes in and says to me, "I only wear pants. I don't wear any skirts." Then my limitation is I have to put her into pants. Gradually, when I explain to her the theory of skirts, especially things like if you're wearing a full skirt, the wind can go between your legs and it feels good and all that stuff, then she might open up to that. Maybe she'll start wearing a skirt with some kind of pant underneath, which I may even suggest to her, which is totally outrageous.

Clothes can be a way for people to remind themselves of their inner strength, their inner being, their inner peace. It gets back to them saying, "I want something deeper." What they're saying is, "I want myself." If I can give a person a little bit of themselves . . . that's a tall order, yes, but that's the secret of selling—to give a person what they really want, what makes them feel beautiful.

If a department store's sales help doesn't satisfy you, check out the personal shopping department. The day before the most important party of my life, I realized I didn't have the perfect dress. While I was hyperventilating with panic, David Simons came by my office and ordered me to call Nordstrom's personal shopping department. I asked for a dark floral silk print dress, fitted at the waist, and on the long side, size eight or ten. When I showed up at the store a few hours later, the perfect dress was hanging in the dressing room. The service was free. If you hate to shop and know what you want, you can call in your size and requirements, and the clothes you love might be waiting in the dressing room.

Consultants

Consultants' services cost money. Friends, salesladies, and department stores' "personal shoppers" do not. Because you pay consultants, you risk rip-off. Many people feel the whole premise is a rip-off. Camille DePedrini comments about getting "colors done":

Color is very personal and so much a part of who I am that I have trouble understanding that someone wouldn't want to choose their own colors. You see a color and you want it. That's what you should wear. What you respond to is fine for wearing.

Consultants, in person or in book, are not all bad. The few who are genuine artists are really quite wonderful. However, it takes courage to seek help, and effort to find these people. Why this embarrassment over seeking paid help with appearance? Barbara Jay comments, "If you're really classy, wealthy, everything that this culture pushes, then it should be easy. It shouldn't be hard. And it shouldn't bring about any anxiety at all." Maybe in avoiding help when we want it, some of us are victims of this Marlboro-man myth of independence (the Marlboro man died of lung cancer), of doing it on one's own. In general I find that I cannot do it alone—live my life without intelligent caring support—and I enjoy hearing and understanding the opinions and ideas of others who have had reason to give a more thorough examination to a subject than I have.

The inner voices chorus: "Oh, please, what are they doing but preying on your insecurities? You're already obsessed enough with this as it is." "You're paying her what? You're kidding, right?" "You're fine as you are, you look fine. What is the problem?" "Excuse me, but aren't there more important things to deal with than how you look? Aren't we being a mite superficial here?" "Wouldn't you rather spend the time and money on something important?" "You need therapy to deal with your insecurity, not a wardrobe consultant." "You're crazy." "Getting dressed is such a basic activity. You can't pick out your own clothes? You're that helpless? What is wrong with you?"

Nothing, really.

Sure, there are a lot of good reasons not to seek help from impartial outsiders. Sometimes, however, a neutral pair of eyes can be helpful. The best consultants educate about dressing and shopping efficiently (they show how, not just what) so that by the end of your work together you have learned to have a realistic confidence in how you dress and shop.

What can a consultant do? I am sitting with Barbara Jay in her office on Sutter Street. I look at the tall windows with great creamy drapes of cascading canvas and chiffon. A pot of bright yellow chrysanthemums sits on the desk. It's a tiny office that feels spacious. Barbara, a tallish attractive woman with short dark hair, wears a black T-shirt and a long grey skirt. Her accessories are a wide belt with an interesting buckle, striped silver chunky earrings, and silver bracelets.

When she starts working with someone, she goes to their home and into their closet. She asks them to show her the clothes that they really love the most and to put them on.

Most people say, "You'll hate my closet. It's the worst. There's nothing in it. That's why I have to hire you, because I'm so stupid." And she always says, "You're probably exactly right, but just let me look. Let me see."

Barbara recalled a client who had a closet full of clothes and was very impatient for Barbara to look through those clothes and tell her just exactly what she needed.

But I couldn't. When I start with someone, I want to build from their strengths. I don't start by saying, "Well, that isn't right." I wait until I can find something in which I feel that they really look like themselves.

Barbara kept having her client try clothes on. Barbara didn't think the client looked at rest in anything. The client was becoming increasingly impatient with Barbara, saying, "Look, I'm paying you such and such an hour. We've got to get going here."

I couldn't think of anything to say except "Where'd you get that? What does that mean to you?" I couldn't figure it out.

Finally the client said, "Okay, here are my three fanciest dresses. These you're really going to like. I don't know what you're trying to do here. I can't understand, but these you'll have to have a reaction to." Barbara hadn't really given her much of a reaction. She pulled out the dresses. Barbara comments:

This was a woman who looked rather like me. She's very lean and dark, and her hair was short and straight, and she had sort of clear features. She was a basic classic person with a more or less lean, athletic type of body, and she was very straightforward as I am, very direct.

These dresses were fluffy organza. They were just bizarre.

Barbara looked at her and said, "Would you agree that you and I look alike? You and I are a similar type?" She said, "Yes." Barbara said, "Give me one of the dresses." Barbara comments:

I took this dress, which was pale yellow and white and had short, fluffy sleeves and a full skirt, and held it up to me on the hanger, and I said, "What do you think?" She burst into tears.

After Barbara worked with her over a period of about three years, she finally met the young woman's mother, who was a plump blonde lady "on whom organza and those colors would make some sense." She learned this young woman wasn't a very happy person. She had been an abused child, pretty badly knocked around. "She wasn't used to any kind of decent care."

One of the qualities people need to effectively choose clothes for themselves, the clothes in which they are happy, is a strong sense of caring about themselves. If they treat themselves tenderly and accept themselves, then they're going to have some ability to look in the mirror and say, "Well, here's what this body needs."

One of the things she likes to say to a new client is, "You and I both have the same job. We're both here to take care of you." One other statement follows: "You have an extra job, which is to be brutal." The client has to learn how to say "No."

If she can pull out of there three things in which the client looks lovely, then the client begins to see she simply needs help to go further down the road on which she's taken a few tentative steps.

I provide some real technical support . . . and if you can't love yourself, you're going to hire somebody who will, whose main promise is to love you. That sounds kind of funny, but that's what I'm saying when I say, "We both have the same job, and that is to take care of you."

The young woman that I spoke of had lost her instincts. I found one piece of clothing in her closet that she could wear, a black jumpsuit. It was minimalist and simple enough. Her little body didn't get lost in it. And everything else was much too heavy. You couldn't find her inside the clothes.

She adds:

I'm not selling clothes. What I want really is people waking up to themselves and to their clothes sense. I see people whose sense of themselves in other ways is better than mine. I just happen to have this thing that I'm good with clothes and I can open people up about that. People say to me, "You must love what you do. I just love to shop, and it would be so much fun." I don't really like shopping. What I'm interested in is defining style and seeing what works for people. I wish I could hand it over after that.

How to choose a consultant? Carefully.

1. Get referrals from people whose dress sense you respect.

2. Use the phone as a screening tool. If you feel uneasy after making an appointment, firmly and politely cancel it.

3. Check this person out. Before you put yourself in a consultant's hands, look at her own presentation, not what nature gave her but what she does with it. Meet with her for a brief interview. Are you comfortable with her? Or as comfortable as you can be considering you're offering yourself up to her scrutiny? Does she speak sense?

4. Clarify for yourself what you want from the encounter. "My life" is not sufficient. What parts of your wardrobe do you not choose well?

5. During the consultation, regularly check out how you feel. If she says something you do not understand or that is plain wrong, make her clarify her position. Don't let her rush you. You are buying an opinion, hopefully a well-informed one—not the absolute pure truth.

6. Tape the session; take notes. Identify what you agreed with and disagreed with, and what you are willing to try. If anything isn't clear, call her up and ask for a few moments of her time. She shouldn't bill you for a few minutes of clarification.

7. Then take the necessary steps. If you need clothes but don't get them, get them but don't wear them, wear them but only so no one can see, play down your strengths and play up your discomfort, or whatever your shtick is, only you can put a stop to it.

The results can be wonderful. Karen Kaufman says:

Major personal growth occurred for me with color and wardrobe and image. First, I had my colors done. I've had them done five times. When I had them done the first time, something just went click. A marriage occurred between my internal and external lives. I discovered my "surface" wasn't separate from who I was. When I looked in the mirror and saw myself wearing a color that really worked with my skin tone and my hair color and me, what I noticed was me. I don't look in the mirror and say, "Oh, what a nice color!" I shine through.

Whom do you trust to see you? Whom can you train? How do you maintain your inner balance and knowing while seeking guidance?

Finding Tailor Charming

Sewing needles 30,000 to 40,000 years old have been found.[6] The need for alterations is ancient and very much present as well. Today's "ready-to-wear" actually isn't for most people. Anthony Lane notes accurately that ready-to-wear only means "ready to wear if you have legs as long as the Eiffel

Tower."[7] A subtle alteration in such a garment can transform it from so-so to fabulous. However, people avoid tailoring for many reasons. Sometimes there's fear involved, fear of the garment looking homemade or simply fear of getting stabbed by a pin. Others worship at the shrine of designer labels, wanting to leave the garment "as is" even though "as is" looks bad.

Why bother to get the clothes to fit right? As Swift puts it, "wearing an outfit that fits properly makes you look thinner, better proportioned, cleaner, wealthier, healthier, and in general, more attractive."[8] Altering also makes economic sense; as Wagenvoord notes, wearing clothes that are too tight strain them, shortening their wearing life. Clothes too large will wrinkle and rumple, necessitating more ironing and pressing than they were designed to withstand.[9]

Some obvious tailor tips: Learn to put up a hem and sew on a button so you're not at the mercy of a tailor for your every alteration need. Don't bring your favorite garment to a tailor if you have never worked with him or her before. Before the tailor starts to pin or baste the alterations, put all the stuff you normally carry around into the pockets of your new garment.[10] Don't fake "correct" posture when the tailor is planning an alteration. Stand and move the way you usually do. After the work has been done, don't take it home or pay for it if it is wrong. Try it on there. "Fit," Goday reminds us, is an absolute word, like "pregnant."[11] Or is it? Boyer observes:

> Everyone wants clothes that "fit," but fit is really something of a nonsensical concept. If clothing did indeed conform to our body's shape we should most of us not look our best. The point of clothing is not to "fit" us in the sense of conforming to our individual shapes, but rather to help us conform to some ideal shape more or less culturally determined.

The tailor, Boyer continues, may have images other than our idealized vision for ourselves.

> He sees people in a certain way and will transform that vision into cloth at every turn. . . . The tailor who will produce the suit you want is the man who understands your view of yourself. He must have the same ideas, the same vision. . . .

Where to find such a magician? Ask a friend, whose clothes you admire, who her tailor is. Boyer suggests, "Never ask a stranger. My father used to say that anybody who will talk about his tailor in public probably has other nasty habits as well." If you try out a strange tailor, talk at length about what you want. If possible, show him or her the effect you're seeking in another garment you own that creates that effect.

> [Y]ou may assume that he wants to make you happy and will do his best for you—craftsmen are like that—but you must also understand that he does not know you, has no idea what image of yourself you are trying to present to the world through your wardrobe . . . one person's ideal man is another person's smarmy gigolo, for example.[12]

People make their own clothes or have them made for many reasons. Even if a garment is perfect for you, due to the vagaries of clothing production, when it wears out, you will probably not be able to replace it except by having a tailor copy it. For less than 1/1000 of one percent of the global population, haute couture tailoring is the way to go. For the rest of us, learning to sew and finding a good tailor can free us from the limits of fashion-bound department-store shopping. But it's important to keep the sense of sewing's promise within sane limits.

Kathy Upton describes one peril of sewing. As a freshman in college, she made money sewing hems and doing alterations for rich girls while she listened to lectures. She learned from looking at the insides of their garments how high-quality things are made. When she developed her skills and discovered that she could make things that other people had to pay tons of money to buy, hubris got her into trouble.

> I reached a point where I would not purchase an item of clothing. And that's crazy. I would go into stores, look at clothes, see the price, sniff, and say, "I could make that for a tenth of the price."

When her first husband got a job with an import company, the wives of the men he worked with were very well and expensively dressed, but they were in their forties and fifties. They wore Norman Norell coats they got at I. Magnin, "Well, I couldn't afford a $2,500 Norman Norell coat." So she went to Home Yardage and spent $129 on double-faced, tobacco-colored French wool, interfacing, underlining, and buttons.

> And I went to all the obsessive trouble that I always went through in preparing a pattern and cutting the thing out. I got that coat about maybe one-quarter made up, then all hell started breaking loose in my life. I put the unfinished coat in a box under my bed with the pattern envelope. (That was going to be my statement about how well I could do and how much better I could do it than all these rich women.)

The box remained under her bed—actually she changed beds twice, changed dwellings several times, and men—that unfinished coat was under her bed for twenty-three years. "I finally decided that I was never going to finish it, and I didn't care how much time I put into it or how much I paid for the fabric." She bundled it up and gave it to charity.

Personal help can come from within

It can be a joy to wear something you've made, clothed in your own creation. After a salesman helped me in Cody's bookstore, I complimented him on his shirt. The fabric pattern was iridescent orange palm trees, a ferris wheel, and fireworks exploding. When he replied, "Thank you. I call it 'Midnight in Balboa on the Fourth of July,'" I knew he was one of us, introduced myself, and asked for an interview. Russ introduced himself and agreed.

Russ is a big, attractive man with a long slight ponytail, more like a wisp of whimsy. For the interview he wore a shirt with toucans and tropical vegetation on it. Two silvery iridescent hoop earrings hang from his left earlobe. He was raised in Southern California, always at the beach, and he grew up in Hawaiian shirts: "It was always my comfortable style." When he started making his own money, he treated himself every year to what he considered a real Hawaiian shirt: something with an invisible pocket and wooden buttons, something well-made instead of a "KMart special." Then all of a sudden those shirts cost over $50 apiece, and he was having trouble making his $160 rent.

One day, he went into a fabric store to pick up some things for his girlfriend who was making a quilt. He saw bright red fabric with big blue dinosaurs, and said, "That is a shirt I have to own." The clerk found him a pattern. He carefully read the back and bought his three- and five-eighths yards of fabric and spool of red thread and wooden buttons. He went home, dumped it on the table, and said to his girlfriend, "Tonight, you teach me to sew."

Because he had helped her sew and had spent time working with fabrics, all she had to do was tell him how to cut the pattern out and how to thread the machine. They did that before dinner and at two o'clock that morning he sewed the last button on his shirt, hung it up, and went to bed. When she woke up in the morning, there was a bright red Hawaiian shirt with big blue dinosaurs hanging from the door.

He ordered fabric the next week and made another one. By the end of the year he had six, and was still wearing a coat and tie every day to the job. This affected him: "The more Hawaiian shirts I had, the less comfortable I was wearing grey and blue and herringbone."

When the opportunity came to stop working at a necktie sort of job, he stopped. Now he has about thirty shirts and wears nothing but. This being California, there are maybe two restaurants in the city where he cannot go in wearing a Hawaiian shirt. "I just don't go."

I looked up one day in the bookstore and standing in front of me is a guy I knew in high school. Now, he was the first person at our high school to grow a beard because they had just changed the dress code. I was the second person, so we kind of bonded. (Because there was probably nobody else who could grow a beard.) He's standing there in a gorgeous Hawaiian shirt with parrots all over it. I said, "Nice shirt." I looked closely. It's the same pattern I wear. This guy is balding and bearded (like I am) and from my hometown of Tustin, standing there in Burda pattern #4539, which is the pattern his wife had chosen as fitting him best, and she made all his shirts.

The process of making a shirt? "I got lucky. I stumbled across that specific Burda pattern which is exactly what I need. It hangs well. It's big enough. It's built the same way that I am." He spends a lot of time walking through fabric stores. And once he sees the right cotton, it's just a matter of saying, "This is the one I want. They jump off the rack as I walk by." Russ sees Hawaiian shirts in the fabric: "I see how it should lay out. I see what parts of the pattern I want to highlight, and it just falls together from there."

The important part for him is laying out the fabric and pattern. Everything has to match. The picture must continue across both pieces. The pocket virtually disappears against the fabric. It took a long time for him to learn how to do it accurately every time. He shows me a picture of a shirt he made for Earth Day where he just forgot, laid it out, cut it, and then realized that the whale ended here and the shark ended there. It's still fabulous. It's an ocean blue shirt covered with all kinds of marine creatures on a background of seaweed. It's his Earth Day shirt "because, after all, the health of the ocean is the health of the planet."

Once it's laid out, it takes about an hour to cut out a pattern and about four hours to sew the shirt on a sewing machine. It sounds like this Hawaiian shirt making is somewhat of a spiritual exercise for him.

It's true. You have to realize that I'm cluttered with way too much stuff, and despite what I tell you, I don't live this, but it has to do with an almost Zen attitude of surrounding myself with things that have a satisfaction and beauty beyond their utility. Not to mention the therapy involved in actually doing fine detail work, and the satisfaction of completing something that I consider art.

The act of assembling it, of knowing the quality, of knowing where every seam and every thread are, to be able to choose which corners I cut, or not, and the level of perfection I try to achieve in the act, that is satisfying.

After talking with Russ I began to feel guilty that I don't make all my clothes, that I didn't want to make my clothes. Then I snapped out of it. I like shopping. I'm allowed my pleasures. Sewing is a risk. Sometimes I enjoy taking it, other times not. Sewing is not fool- or addict-proof. People who sew risk the temptation of fabric stores, and the aforementioned dangers of hubris. Their cars tend to sport bumper stickers like "She who dies with the most fabric wins."

Case study: Kathryn Alexander's socks

> *The controlling metaphor for the power contained in the creative force of thought is that of weaving, as the spider spins a web which through its symmetry enthralls and constitutes a world in itself. This is a metaphor of being, of selfhood, and yet it is fundamentally one of social relations. . . .*[13]
> —Teresa McKenna and Flora Ortiz, *The Broken Web*

Some people I spoke with, like Kathryn Alexander, follow the production process in a more intimate way, joining it at an even earlier stage. When I first see her socks at an art co-op, I am amazed. In one sock she knits twelve colors and eight patterns. The price panics me, but I phone her anyway. On a cold foggy July day, I bike down to her studio in jeans, a T-shirt, and my green socks with little sheep on them (in her honor). Her studio is on the second floor in a converted red brick factory building. A bakery makes fragrant French bread down on the first floor. Kathryn greets me at the door wearing jeans and a long-sleeved shirt with a horse pattern on it. There's a silver bolero tie at her neck, multiple silver bracelets on each wrist, silver belt buckle, and brown leather boots. Her hair falls down her back to her thighs and is tied back in a ponytail.

Looking around her studio, I see sweaters and socks on the wall, framed like art. There's a hand carder, a loom, and barrels full of colorful fluff—hand-colored unspun wool.

She points to the diagonal checkerboard pattern on a sock. "This is my signature, it's called entrelac. Seven rows of it." It's red, hot pink, brown, caramel, dusty purple, and then red again. She says,

> I just work with it. I love it. It's like architecture within the piece because you can do really interesting things with the shaping. Entrelac naturally wants to flare out because of the way that the squares are put together, on the bias. I stick it in everything I make, even if it's someplace you don't really see.

Where does her fiber come from? "I used to tell everybody that these started in the barn with a rake and shovel, because they did. I raised all the animals, too. I had angora rabbits and llamas. First I had to take care of the animals." She points to llama fleece, naming the animals it came from— "That one's Darcy, that's Big Will, and that's R.C." (It's the color of cola.) She also uses other creatures for fleece, including her mother's Samoyed dog. "She was very pleased to give part of herself for my project." No fleecy creature seems to escape notice. Her brother raises Columbia sheep in Montana. Every year he handpicks six fleeces for her. She reaches into a sack—underneath the old wooden table supporting her carders are bags of wool fiber—and lifts out the unspun Columbian. The fibers are about four inches long, dark toward where they grow from the sheep, going to blond where they were touched by the sun. It has a very fine wave to it. "It's called crimp. And Columbias are known for it." She pulls on it, stretching out the curl. It bounces right back.

> See how that boings like that? That transfers right into your yarn. . . . It's a wonderful wool to spin and make wearable garments with like coats and socks because it's so springy. Your ribbing stays in place. It doesn't just stretch out. Usually a sock of commercially made yarn, for instance, after you wear it a few times, stretches out. But socks made with this wool boing right back. It's got so much life of its own.

She hands me some dark wool. I can feel the sticky lanolin. She continues, "I just love it. It's heaven to work with." Before dying, she washes the lanolin out (otherwise the dye takes unevenly because lanolin repels dye, plus lanolin stinks).

I don't quite understand why she doesn't just go to the store and buy yarn. She shows me the second pair of socks she knit, made from the best-quality yarn commercially available. It hangs from her hand limply, lacking the lustrousness and depth of color of the other socks. It feels rough and heavy. She says:

> I thought I could use some commercial yarn to give me more time, and it didn't work. Even good commercial yarn in a sock tends to pill, and it just doesn't stand up to my yarn. I realized I needed to be happy with less money and be totally happy with my product. That's fine. It pleases me to be able to come up with something like this.

Workshops taught her about blending different fibers together and about colors. We stand looking at fleece dyed burgundy, another dark peach one, and a light blue-green one. Like a chef with spices, she starts throwing fleece on the drum carder as she cranks the handle. She comes up with an incredible pink like dark watermelon. I say, "I need to lie down!" We laugh. She says:

Swooning from beauty! And I can't get the range of color that I want to do in commercial yarn. I'd be spending so much time going to yarn stores and picking it out. And then I'd have ten pounds of one color and think, "God, what am I going to do with that?" I don't spin a lot of each one of these colors of yarn, and I never duplicate colors.

She does something with color in socks I've never seen before, and I've watched clothes my whole life. She replies, "I tell people that I don't think I've ever had a completely original design in my entire life. I went to Diane Varney's workshop and I saw this sock." She points to a runty wool sock with brown and oatmeal stripes at the heel and a diagonal entrelac pattern.

Diane and her husband had taken a trip around the world on their bicycles. They were camped out one night in Tibet, and a shepherd saw their smoke from their campfire and came walking over. They didn't speak each other's language, but she pantomimed to him. He invited them over to his hut and made them yak butter tea, and they were talking as best they could. About halfway through the evening, he put his feet up on this stump in the center of the hut and his pants came up so she could see the top of his socks and she just snapped. She started saying, "Nice socks! Nice socks!" and pointing at his ankles and just smiling. Finally after quite a while of that, he said, "Why don't we trade socks?" She had on a little pair of those twelve-in-a-pack cotton athletic socks from JC Penney.

Kathryn took the idea and ran with it, adding stripes in the ribbing to spice them up, then stripes in the feet, then a little splash of color at the heel, then brighter, more vivid color, geometrics, etc. Who wears these socks?

The people I sell them to wear them. And my husband wears them. My mom wears them. I gave her a few. And I wear them on special occasions with Birkenstocks. I never put them in a boot or a shoe.

I make the yarn for socks wearable. By that, I mean I do a three-ply yarn, which is really durable. Plus, I'm always carrying the threads so they're like two thicknesses. The inside of this thing is just as beautiful as the outside. I think they're incredible. Every time I make a pair, I think, "Oh! I can't believe you made those!"

The neat thing from a spinner's and a knitter's perspective is, socks are a small project. Compared to a coat or large sweater, you're talking forty hours as opposed to four hundred. And they're little. You can carry them in a little bag. Sometimes, I knit nonstop. When I'm not here, I'm knitting in the morning at my house and I knit at night. And I take knitting with me everywhere. I just stick the whole thing in my pocket or I'll carry it in a sack. If we have to stand in line at a movie or something, I'll just pull it out and start knitting. I never feel that I'm just waiting for no reason and wasting time. I just whip my knitting out.

We're standing looking at the wall. Six different pairs of socks with the entrelac pattern in a whole bunch of different colors are push-pinned to the wall against a black ground. They're framed works of art.

She says, "They're neat in a group. I tell people, 'You should buy five pair.'" We laugh. I say, "Absolutely."

"Yes, they are happy together. A litter."

Who is ripped off when a $200 pair of socks is purchased? It takes about forty hours to knit a pair. She grows the wool, she washes, dyes, and spins it. For every project she spins the yarn differently. Then she knits in at least twelve colors per sock. From the barnyard to your sock drawer, and all she charges for is knitting time. At $5 an hour, she's a grossly underpaid artist. At $200 a pair, they're one of the last bargains left. She says, "They should be $500." And, agreeing, we laugh at the absurdity of it.

Consider learning to sew, knit, or weave for the pure pleasure of it, to deepen your understanding of wardrobe. In so doing, you become your own consultant. You can even reduce stress through sewing. One study showed heart rate dropped eight beats per minute for novice sewers as they worked, and eleven beats per minute for experienced sewers.[14] If you can't find the clothes you want in a store, and you're unwilling to make them or have them made, maybe what's wanted has nothing to do with clothing. Think about it. If you could have your heart's desire, what would it be?

Notes:

1. Lamott, Anne. *Bird by Bird*. Page 169.
2. Robin, Jennifer. *Clothe Your Spirit*. Page 129.
3. Wallach, Janet. *Looks That Work*. Page 206.
4. Cho, Emily. Page 194.
5. Feldon, Leah. *Dress Like a Million*. Page 124.
6. Sproles, George. *Fashion*. Page 25.
7. Lane, Anthony. "The Last Emperor." *The New Yorker*. November 7, 1994. Page 85.
8. Swift, Pat and Maggie Mulhearn. *Great Looks*. Page 28.
9. Wagenvoord, James and Fiona St. Aubyn. *Clothes Care*. Page 8.
10. Wagenvoord. Page 12.
11. Goday, Dale and Molly Cochran. *Dressing Thin*. Page 24.
12. Boyer, G. Bruce. *Elegance*. Pages 244-246.
13. McKenna, Teresa and Flora Ida Ortiz, eds. *The Broken Web*. Page i.
14. Gleason, Suzanne. "Body Works." *Harper's Bazaar*. October 1995. Page 112.

Conclusion: It's a Wrap

Clothing brings us joy.
　　　　　　　　　—Designer Issey Miyake[1]

Before I began working on this book I loved clothes, but something about my own presentation wasn't working. When I leafed through a fashion magazine, viewed mannequins in a shop window, or glanced at a beautifully dressed woman on the street, I could see how each outfit was assembled. However, I didn't understand how to relate that information to effective decision-making in clothing selection. I didn't understand that I brought complicating factors to the equation, that my unique face, body, proportions, preferences, and history mattered. Because of my confusion about clothing, I spent attention, time, and money inefficiently.

In my research I found that curmudgeons and experts suggested three main ways to dress relative to the beauty culture:

The first way was to ignore it and "do your own thing." Germaine Greer offers an alluring version of this when she talks about the body as something to look out from rather than something to adorn. She writes:

> I walk the same paths now that I walked twenty-five years ago, but now I am not aware of the figure I am cutting. I neither expect nor hope to be noticed. I am hoping only to take in what is happening around me even on the bleakest winter day, the blood-warm glow of the up-turned clods in the ploughland, the robin's greedy whistle, the glitter of the stubble against a dark sky. I want to be open to this, to be agog, spellbound.[2]

But for someone who loves clothes, looking out and taking in is not enough.

The second suggested way of dealing with the barrage of information was to ignore it by sticking to a specific clothing "equation" (like three skirts plus five blouses plus three jackets equals forty-five different outfits). The all-important issue is the "good taste" implicit in the classic type of outfit chosen. The inner life and distinctive qualities of the wearer have little or no impact.

The third way was to aspire to resemble some version of fashionable taste. This is fine if you have a lot of money, height, slenderness, and leisure, and a flamboyant streak the size of the Grand Canyon.

None of these options worked for me. My explorations kept pointing to a fourth way, to thoroughly study myself and my context so that my notions of beauty and comfort evolved from within.

I investigated the relationship between wardrobe and the big picture—how cultural constructs about sexuality, frivolity, family, death, fashion, and appropriateness influence clothing choice. By then using all my senses, not just sight, to discover what is beautiful to me, by broadening my appreciation to include all that has been considered beautiful, I discovered my place in the dance, the distinctive qualities that make me feel beautiful. From this place of power, I chose to shatter the false mirror society put before me, telling me that the fairest woman of all is a two-dimensional, hand-painted, carefully starved young girl.

After that, answering the question "What do I wear?" became a lot simpler. I used the inner and expressive fundamentals of the art of dress to define the kinds of clothes that work for me. I started to find the best clothes, which, as Wagenvoord notes, "finally fall apart rather than out of fashion."[3]

I also found something deeper: I rediscovered pleasure in the process. As I learned to take pleasure in what works for me, this educated passion imparted confidence. I learned to let criticism roll by. I also learned something more difficult for me: how to respond graciously to compliments.

Most people disagree with me when I compliment them, or take the compliment as an excuse to talk about how ugly they feel. This, in a sense, makes my praise unreceived, and makes me feel awful. I've gotten to the point where if I express my admiration about someone's presentation, I listen for a few seconds to their protest and then interrupt them to tell them to say "Thank you." This works for me. Since I felt uncomfortable with others' resistance to compliments, I thought that I also should start trying to say "Thank you," as appropriate.

I was walking down Bancroft Street one day after I first decided to make a practice of saying "Thank you" when receiving a compliment (so that we could move on from my mingled embarrassment and pleasure to something else), and a guy in rasta braids said to me as he biked by: "Scenery gettin' betta now." I laughed and said "Thank you" to his back. And he hollered, "You're welcome." When you're open to compliments, they come from all over the place. Stacey Lamiero has a different take on it:

> When somebody gives me a compliment about my clothes—"Gee, that's a lovely scarf" —
> I think the appropriate answer's supposed to be, "Oh, thank you." But I say, "Oh, yeah. I
> love it, too, and the best thing is I got it on sale. It was only five bucks." I don't have this
> attitude. I've gotten really lucky lately in my life and I just tell people. Instead of putting a
> mystique behind it—"Aren't I so wonderful? And this is so hot. . . . "—I say, "Yeah, can you
> believe it? I can't believe it." No mystique. My mom said, "God, can you exercise some
> decorum?" I said, "No, that's not me."

We've each figured out ways of responding to nice words that work for us. There's no one answer, just questions that lead closer to the self and clothing happiness.

Sure, there are still mornings when I look in my closet and want to howl. I can't claim perfection. On one of those dark days, Mary Armentrout came over and told me kindly:

> Clothes are a great tool for transformation, for pursuing yourself. And you have to not be too
> hard on yourself about it. You have to get dressed every day. You can't always be perfect. You
> can't always be the most beautiful thing you ever saw. And things change. You can't always be
> perfect in that one dress either. Things change.

She also brought several hats with her for me to try on. This was very cheering, as trying on hats is one of my favorite activities.

Sure, there's more to life than "just" clothes, but in my discussions, research, and day-to-day experience I find clothes contribute such pleasure, comfort, and interesting complexity that I feel encouraged to continue to look more deeply. Clothing is one of my needs and joys, so I pursue it. I do it for its own sake, and I do it out of altruism. If it makes me happy, so much the better because my happiness, in little ways, seems to influence others' happiness as well. (For instance, I'm less likely to snap at the nice lady who works at the copy place.) I also do it because my interest and enthusiasm make a contribution. Thank you for accompanying me on this way. I encourage you to continue on. The world needs your beauty and your joy.

Notes:

1. Dowd, Maureen. "The Hat and the Cat Walk." *New York Times Magazine.* January 15, 1995. Page 45.
2. Greer, Germaine. *The Change.* Page 381.
3. Wagenvoord, James and Fiona St. Aubyn. *Clothes Care.* Page 8.

Open and Clothed

Acknowledgments

I am grateful to the following people for their generous participation in in-depth interviews for this project: Kathryn Alexander, Mary Armentrout, Melissa C. Batchelder, Chandra Cho, Nick Debs, Camille DePedrini, Debbie Epidendio, Lex Eurich, Laurel Fenenga Parker, Sharon Frederick, Libby Granett, Lisa Graves, David M. Grossman, Russell B. Harvey, Tom Hassett, Kathryn Hoover, Barbara Jay, Sarah H. Jurick, Karen L. Kaufman, Stacey Lamiero, Sherlee Land, Ed Perry, Rhonda A. Pretlow, Barton A. Shulman, Beau Simon, David B. Simons, Joan M. Songer, Daphne Stannard, Heather M. Stone, Jeremy Stone, Eileen Sullivan, Naomi R. Tickle, Kathy Upton, Elliot Wenger, and those who preferred to remain anonymous.

Thanks to the many wonderful people, named and anonymous, who contributed their wisdom and humor to this project, especially for their patience and insights during the interview process.

Thanks also to my fabulous grandma, Ruth Stone, without whose continuous generosity this book would have never happened. Thanks also to Mom and Andrew for support. Thanks to my sister Alicia and my brother Matthew for their love.

Thanks to Cheryl Reinhardt for brilliant teaching. Thanks also to Dorothy Edlin and Larry Klein.

Thanks to Wendy Ellen Ledger for terrific transcription. Thanks to the readers: Kirsten Burge, Andrew Gelman, Jane Gelman, and Shea Godwin.

Danika Lew and Sarah Jurick provided the daily good sense and humor that make life wonderful. Thanks to Carol Adler, Alan Gelman, Bob Gelman, Maureen Murphy, Audrey Jarach, Sarah Wong, Seth Roberts, Hilary Macht, Renée Passy Zale, David Rosenmon-Talb, Tom Siegel, Julia Priest, Marion Sorenson, and Jackie Thaw for help along the way. Thanks to Oriane Stender for the encouraging first glance and spell check, as well as long-distance research. Thanks to Malcolm Margolin for his graciousness to the curious writer next door (especially for suggesting the scissors-and-tape editing method when the manuscript was 1600 pages and growing). Thanks to Carol Sanoff for asking about the "next book," not realizing the question conceived it. Thanks to Susan Jones for the Photoshop rescue, and Julie Murkette for her graceful, good work.

Thanks to the generous and intelligent reference librarians throughout the San Francisco Bay Area and New York City, especially those at the Fashion Institute in San Francisco and the Fashion Institute of Technology in New York City. Thanks to Erin Overbey. Thanks to Lenore Benson, archivist at the Fashion Group for her intelligence and generosity with their remarkable archive.

Thanks to the Brussels Scribblers Group, especially Jeni Redfern and Stephanie Gardner. Thanks to Jennifer Bilek, Laura Greenberg, Judith Lucero, Natalie Rogers, Jenny Sward and Andy Scheinman.

Thanks to Roberta Cairney and Emily Miller for the wise and helpful guidance which no Belgian chocolate in the world can repay. . . . Thanks also to Tom Nathan, Steve Purcell, Ned Rosenthal, and Ron Urbach.

Thanks to the companies producing post-consumer waste recycled paper products.

Illustration Acknowledgments

Cover
Woman handing dress to young girl with curls
Archive Photos, N.Y.

Chapter 1
Christian Dior with model in gown
The Archives of the Fashion Group International, N.Y.

Chapter 2
Women look unfavorably at topless mannequin
Express Newspapers/Archive Photos, N.Y.

Chapter 3
Sweater girl
SuperStock, Inc., N.Y.

Chapter 4
Woman handing dress to young girl with curls
Archive Photos, N.Y.

Chapter 5
Angel at a fashion show
The Archives of the Fashion Group International, N.Y.

Chapter 6
The fabulous Mrs. Gertrude Shilling dresses for Ascot
Express Newspapers/Archive Photos, N.Y.

Chapter 7
Lounging pajamas
SuperStock, Inc., N.Y.

Chapter 8
Woman sitting in mud bath
Archive Photos, N.Y.

Chapter 9
Figure of Bodhidharma
The Metropolitan Museum of Art, N.Y.
Gift of Mrs. Winthrop W. Aldrich, Mrs. Arnold Whitridge, and Mrs. Sheldon Whitehouse,
1963 (63.176)

Chapter 10
Hat: Chandra Cho, Berkeley, CA
Model: Ananda Zen Tzu Cho
Photographer: Mirjam Einsiedler

Chapter 11
Woman riding a camel on the Sahara, Egypt
Archive photos, N.Y.

Chapter 12
Model wearing only a big handbag and bracelets
The Archives of the Fashion Group International, N.Y.

Chapter 13
Woman holding up dress in attic
SuperStock, Inc., N.Y.

Chapter 14
Lady in street holding bags
Photographer: Bill Cunningham
The Archives of the Fashion Group International, N.Y.

Chapter 15
Madame Grès with gown
The Archives of the Fashion Group International, N.Y.

Conclusion
Gianfranco Ferré Show
The Archives of the Fashion Group International, N.Y.

Author photo
by Jennifer Bilek

Grateful acknowledgment is made to the Fashion Group International's archive which consists of photographic records of European and American fashion collections and fashion industry history dating from 1930 to the present. They are located at 597 Fifth Avenue, New York (phone: (212) 593-1715, website URL: www.fgi.org).

Text Acknowledgments

From *Elegance: A Guide to Quality in Menswear* by G. Bruce Boyer. Copyright © 1985 by G. Bruce Boyer. Reprinted by permission of W. W. Norton & Company, Inc.

From *Beauty Secrets: Women and the Politics of Appearance* by Wendy Chapkis. Copyright © 1986 by Wendy Chapkis. Reprinted by permission of South End Press.

From *Looking Terrific* by Emily Cho and Linda Grover. Published by G.P. Putnam's Sons. Copyright © 1978 by Emily Cho and Linda Grover. Reprinted by permission of McIntosh and Otis, Inc.

From *Looking, Working, Living Terrific 24 Hours a Day* by Emily Cho. Published by Putnam. Copyright © 1982 by Emily Cho. Reprinted by permission of McIntosh and Otis, Inc. "Widely acknowledged as a founder and leader of the image consulting field, Emily Cho is available for private consultations, lectures and seminars: Emily Cho, 17 Daniel Drive, Englewood, NJ 07631. (201) 816-8530"

From *Dress Like a Million (on Considerably Less): A trend-proof guide to real fashion* by Leah Feldon. New York: Villard Books, 1993. Reprinted by permission of Random House.

From *Dressing Rich: A Guide to Classic Chic for Women with More Taste than Money* by Leah Feldon. Copyright © 1982 by Leah Feldon. Published by G.P. Putnam's Sons. Reprinted by permission of Leah Feldon.

From *The Psychology of Clothes* by J. C. Flügel. Published by the Hogarth Press. Reprinted by permission of Random House UK Limited.

From *From Room to Room* by Jane Kenyon. Copyright © 1978 by Jane Kenyon. Reprinted by permission of Alicejamesbooks.

From *The Language of Clothes* by Alison Lurie. Copyright © 1981 by Alison Lurie. Reprinted by permission of Melanie Jackson Agency.

From *The Triumph of Individual Style* by Carla Mason Mathis and Helen Villa Connor. Copyright © 1993 by Carla Mason Mathis and Helen Villa Connor. Reprinted by permission of Timeless Editions. For more information on the book or their approach, write Timeless Editions at 219 Sycamore Street, San Carlos, California 94070. (415) 593-5288. Email: ConnorVil@aol.com.

From *Fat Is a Feminist Issue*. Copyright © Susie Orbach 1978 Berkeley Publishing Group. Reprinted by permission of Susie Orbach.

From *Fat Is a Feminist Issue II.* Copyright © Susie Orbach 1982 Berkeley Publishing Group. Reprinted by permission of Susie Orbach.

From *Breaking All the Rules* by Nancy Roberts. Copyright ©1985, 1986 by Nancy Roberts. Used by permission of Viking Penguin, a division of Penguin Books USA Inc.

From *Clothe Your Spirit: Dressing for Self-Expression* by Jennifer Robin. Copyright © 1987 Spirit Press. Reprinted by permission of Jennifer Robin. For more information on the book or her approach, write Clothe Your Spirit, 222 Redding Way, San Rafael, California 94901.

From *Breaking Free From Compulsive Eating* by Geneen Roth. New York: Signet, 1986. For more information on her books or her approach, write Breaking Free, P.O. Box 2852, Santa Cruz, California 95063. (408) 685-8601.

From *Home: A Short History of an Idea* by Witold Rybczynski. Copyright © 1986 by Witold Rybczynski. Used by permission of Viking Penguin, a division of Penguin Books USA Inc.

From *Looks That Work* by Janet Wallach. Reprinted by permission of Janet Wallach.

From *Working Wardrobe* by Janet Wallach. Reprinted by permission of Janet Wallach.

From *Looking Good* (previously entitled *Clothes Sense: Straight Talk About Wardrobe Planning*) by Barbara Weiland and Leslie Wood. Portland, Oregon: Palmer/Pletsch Associates, 1984.

From *The Beauty Myth* by Naomi Wolf. Copyright ©1991 by Naomi Wolf. By permission of William Morrow & Co., Inc.

From *The Beauty Myth* by Naomi Wolf. Copyright ©1991 by Naomi Wolf. Reprinted by permission of Random House of Canada Limited.

From *Elle* Magazine. Published by Hachette Filipacchi Magazines. Reprinted by permission of *Elle* Magazine.

Selected Resources

Fashion: Poetry and Design. Milan: Domus Academy Edizioni, 1990.

Alexander, Christopher. *The Timeless Way of Building*. New York: Oxford University Press, 1979.

Anderson, Doris. *Simplified Systems of Sewing and Styling Lesson 10*. Chicago: Neely Printing Co., 1946.

Angeloglou, Maggie. *A History of Make-up*. New York: The Macmillan Company, 1970.

Angelou, Maya. *Wouldn't Take Nothing for My Journey Now*. New York: Random House, 1993.

Anspach, Karlyne. *The Why of Fashion*. Ames, Iowa: The Iowa State University Press, 1967.

Avery, James with Karen Jackson. *The Right Jewelry For You*. Austin, Texas: Eakin Press, 1988.

Bailey, Adrian. *The Passion for Fashion*. Great Britain: Dragon's World, 1988.

Baker, Nancy C. *The Beauty Trap Exploring Woman's Greatest Obsession*. New York/Toronto: Franklin Watts, 1984.

Balmain, Pierre. *My Years and Seasons*. New York: Doubleday, 1965.

Barber, Elizabeth Wayland. *Women's Work, The First 20,000 Years*. New York: W. W. Norton & Co., 1994.

Barbizon International. *Barbizon Models Handbook*. New York: Barbizon International, Inc. 1984.

Barthes, Roland. *The Fashion System*. Translated by Matthew Ward and Richard Howard. Berkeley: University of California Press, 1990.

Batterberry, Michael and Ariane Batterberry. *Mirror Mirror, A Social History of Fashion*. New York: Holt, Rinehart and Winston, 1977.

Beaton, Cecil. *The Glass of Fashion*. Garden City, New York: Doubleday, 1954.

Bell, Quentin. *On Human Finery*. New York: Schocken Books, 1978.

Benstock, Shari and Ferriss, Suzanne, eds. *On Fashion*. New Brunswick, New Jersey: Rutgers University Press, 1994.

Bixler, Susan. *The Professional Image*. New York: Putnam, 1984.

Boyer, G. Bruce. *Elegance*. New York: W.W. Norton & Co., 1985.

Braithwaite, Brian. *Women's Magazines, The First 300 Years*. London: Peter Owen, 1995.

Brill, Dianne. *Boobs, Boys, and High Heels or How to Get Dressed in Just under Six Hours*. New York: Penguin Books, 1992.

Brooke, Iris. *Footwear, A Short History of European and American Shoes.* New York: Theatre Art Books, 1971.

Brown, Helen Gurley. *The Late Show.* New York: Morrow, 1993.

Burbank, Emily. *Woman as Decoration.* New York: Dodd, Mead and Company, Inc., 1920.

Byers, Margaretta with Consuelo Kamholz. *Designing Women, The Art, Technique, and Cost of Being Beautiful.* New York: Simon & Schuster, 1938.

Carlyle, Thomas. *Sartor Resartus.* London: James Nisbet & Co., Limited, 1903.

Chapkis, Wendy. *Beauty Secrets, Women and the Politics of Appearance.* Boston: South End Press, 1986.

Chase, Linda and Laura Cerwinske. *In Your Own Style.* New York: Thames and Hudson, 1994.

Cho, Emily and Neila Fisher with Hermine Lueders. *It's You! Looking Terrific, Whatever Your Type.* New York: Villard Books, 1986.

Cho, Emily and Grover, Linda. *Looking Terrific.* New York: G.P. Putnam's Sons, 1978.

Cho, Emily and Hermine Lueders. *Looking, Working, Living Terrific 24 Hours a Day.* New York: Putnam, 1982.

Coffey, Barbara and the editors of *Glamour. Glamour's Success Book.* New York: Simon & Schuster, 1979.

Coleman, Jonathan. *Exit the Rainmaker.* New York: Atheneum, 1989.

Coleridge, Nicholas. *The Fashion Conspiracy, The Dazzling Inside Story of the Glamorous World of International High Fashion.* New York: Harper & Row, 1988.

Crawford, Morris De Camp. *The Heritage of Cotton.* New York and London: Putnam, 1924.

Cringely, Robert. *Accidental Empires—How the Boys of Silicon Valley Make Their Millions, Battle Foreign Competition, and Still Can't Get A Date.* Reading, Mass.: Addison Wesley, 1992.

Daria, Irene. *The Fashion Cycle.* New York: Simon & Schuster, 1990.

Davis, Fred. *Fashion, Culture, and Identity.* Chicago: University of Chicago Press, 1992.

Dobson, Terry. *It's a Lot like Dancing . . . An Aikido Journey.* Edited by Riki Moss and Photographs by Jan E. Watson. Berkeley, California: Frog Ltd. 1993.

Dominguez, Joe and Vicki Robin. *Your Money or Your Life.* New York: Penguin books, 1992.

Doyle, Sir Arthur Conan. *The Complete Sherlock Holmes.* Garden City, New York: Doubleday, 1930.

Druesedow, Jean L. *In Style, Celebrating Fifty Years of the Costume Institute*. New York: Metropolitan Museum of Art, 1993.

Duffy, Mary. *The H-O-A-X Fashion Formula*. Tucson, Arizona: The Body Press, 1987.

Ehrlich, Gretel. *The Solace of Open Spaces*. New York: Viking, 1985.

Ephron, Nora. *Wallflower at the Orgy*. New York: Ace Books, 1973.

Ewen, Stuart. *All Consuming Images, The Politics of Style in Contemporary Culture*. New York: Basic Books, 1988.

Fairchild, John. *Chic Savages*. New York: Simon & Schuster, 1989.

The Fashion Group, 597 Fifth Avenue, 8th Floor, New York, New York 10017 (212) 593-1715 (www.fgi.org).

Fatt, Amelia. *Conservative Chic*. New York: Times Books, 1983.

Feldenkrais, Moshe. *Awareness Through Movement*. New York: Harper & Row, 1972.

Feldon, Leah. *Dress Like a Million (on Considerably Less)* New York: Villard Books, 1993.

Feldon, Leah. *Dressing Rich*. New York: G.P. Putnam's Sons, 1982.

Fiedorek, Mary B. *Executive Style*. Piscataway, New Jersey: New Century Publishers, Inc., 1983.

Finklestein, Joanne. *The Fashioned Self*. Philadelphia: Temple University Press, 1991.

Flügel, J. C. *The Psychology of Clothes*. Great Britain: The Hogarth Press, 1950.

Fraser, Kennedy. *The Fashionable Mind*. Boston: David R. Godine, 1982.

Friedman, Lenore. *Meetings with Remarkable Women*. Boston: Shambhala, 1987.

Gaines, Janet and Charlotte Herzog, Eds. *Fabrications*. New York: Routledge, 1990.

Garber, Marjorie. *Vested Interests*. New York: Routledge, 1992.

Garland, Madge. *Fashion*. Middlesex, England: Penguin, 1962.

Gilday, Katherine. *The Famine Within*. A documentary film produced by Kandor Production in association with Studio D of the National Film Board of Canada and TV Ontario. Distributed by Direct Cinema, Los Angeles, 1990.

Glynn, Prudence. *Skin to Skin, Eroticism in Dress*. New York: Oxford University Press, 1982.

Goday, Dale with Molly Cochran. *Dressing Thin*. New York: A Fireside Book, Simon & Schuster, 1980.

Goldberg, Benjamin. *The Mirror and Man*. Charlottesville: University Press of Virginia, 1985.

Goldberg, Natalie. *Long Quiet Highway*. New York: Bantam, 1993.

Goldberg, Natalie. *Writing Down the Bones*. Boston: Shambhala, 1986.

Goldfein, Donna. *Everywoman's Guide To Time Management*. Millbrae, California: Les Femmes Publishing, 1977.

Goldsmith, Olivia. *Fashionably Late*. New York: Harper Collins, 1994.

Goldsmith, Olivia and Collins, Amy Fine. *Simple Isn't Easy*. New York: Harper Paperbacks, 1995.

Greer, Germaine. *The Change, Women, Aging and the Menopause*. New York: Alfred A. Knopf, 1992.

Griffin, Marius. *Take Back Our Bodies*. A flyer by the Body Image Task Force, P.O. Box 934, Santa Cruz, CA 95061-0934. (408) 457-4838.

Gross, Michael. *Model, The Ugly Business of Beautiful Women*. New York: Morrow, 1995.

Hawthorne, Rosemary. *Knickers, An Intimate Appraisal*. London: Souvenir Press, 1991.

Hauser, Gayelord. *Mirror, Mirror on the Wall, Invitation to Beauty*. New York: Farrar, Straus and Cudahy, 1961.

Heilbrun, Carolyn G. *Writing a Woman's Life*. New York: Ballantine Books, 1989.

The World Almanac and Book of Facts 1993. Mark Hoffman, ed. New York: World Almanac, 1993.

Hollander, Anne. *Seeing Through Clothes*. New York: Avon, 1978.

Ive, Josephine. *By Jeeves!* Melbourne, Australia: Josephine Ive, 1992.

Jackson, Carole. *Color Me Beautiful*. Washington D.C.: Acropolis Books Ltd., 1980.

Kelly, Katie. *The Wonderful World of Women's Wear Daily*. New York: Saturday Review Press, 1972.

Kentner, Bernice. *A Rainbow in Your Eyes*. Concord, California: Kenkra Publishers, 1981.

Kentner, Bernice. *Tie Me Up With Rainbows*. Concord, California: Kenkra Publishers, 1984.

Kenyon, Jane. *From Room to Room*. Farmington, Maine: Alicejamesbooks, 1978.

Kidwell, Claudia Brush and Valerie Steele, eds. *Men and Women, Dressing the Part*. Washington, D.C.: Smithsonian Institution Press, 1989.

Kingsolver, Barbara. *Animal Dreams*. New York: Harper & Row, 1990.

Kolander, Cheryl. *A Silk Worker's Notebook*. Loveland, Colorado: Interweave Press, Inc., 1985.

Koller, Alice. *The Stations of Solitude*. New York: Morrow, 1990.

Lamott, Anne. *Bird by Bird*. New York: Pantheon Books, 1994.

Langer, Lawrence. *The Importance of Wearing Clothes*. New York: Hastings House, 1959.

Larkey, Jan. *Flatter Your Figure*. London: Souvenir Press, 1991.

Latzke, Alpha and Beth Quinlan. *Clothing*. Chicago and Philadelphia: J.B. Lippincott Company, 1935.

Laury, Jean Ray. *The Creative Woman's Getting-It-All-Together-at-Home Handbook*. New York: Van Nostrand Reinhold Company, 1977.

Laver, James. *Costume and Fashion*. New York: Thames and Hudson, 1985.

Laver, James. *Modesty in Dress*. Boston: Houghton Mifflin Company, 1969.

Leggett, William Ferguson. *The Story of Wool*. Brooklyn: Chemical Publishing, 1947.

Lencek, Lena and Gideon Bosker. *Making Waves*. San Francisco: Chronicle Books, 1989.

Leopold, Allison Kyle and Anne Marie Cloutier. *Short Chic*. New York: Rawson, Wade Publishers, Inc., 1981.

LeShan, Lawrence. *Cancer as a Turning Point*. New York: Dutton, 1989.

Lipovetsky, Gilles. *The Empire of Fashion*. (Translated by Catherine Porter) New Jersey: Princeton University Press, 1994.

London, Liz E. and Anne H. Adams. *Color Right Dress Right*. New York: Crown Publishers, Inc., 1985.

Lurie, Alison. *The Language of Clothes*. New York: Random House, 1981.

Lurie, Alison. *The Language of Clothes*. New York: Vintage, 1981.

Lynes, Russell. *The Tastemakers*. New York: Grosset & Dunlap, 1954.

Madsen, Axel. *A Woman of Her Own*. New York: Henry Holt & Co., 1990.

Magnin, Cyril and Cynthia Robins. *Call Me Cyril*. New York: McGraw Hill, 1981.

Marcus, Stanley. *Quest for the Best*. New York: The Viking Press, 1979.

Mathis, Carla Mason and Helen Villa Connor. *The Triumph of Individual Style*. Menlo Park, California: Timeless Editions, 1993. For more information on the book or their approach write Timeless Editions, 219 Sycamore Street, San Carlos, California 94070. (415) 593-5288

McDowell, Colin. *The Designer Scam*. London: Hutchinson, 1994.

McGill, Leonard. *Stylewise*. New York: G.P. Putnam's Sons, 1983.

McJimsey, Harriet. *Art in Clothing Selection*. New York: Harper & Row, 1963.

McKenna, Teresa and Flora Ida Ortiz, eds. *The Broken Web.* Berkeley, California: Floricanto Press, 1988.

Merriam, Eve. *Figleaf.* Philadelphia and New York: J.B. Lippincott Company, 1960.

Milbank, Caroline Rennolds. *Couture.* New York: Stewart, Tabori & Chang, Inc., 1985.

Milbank, Caroline Rennolds. *New York Fashion.* New York: Harry N. Abrams, 1989.

Miller, Liz Leverett. *I Just Need More Time.* Wichita Falls, Texas: Woman Time Management, 1984.

Molloy, John T. *The Woman's Dress For Success Book.* Chicago: Follet Publishing Company, 1977.

Moncur, Susan. *They Still Shoot Models My Age.* London England: Serpent's Tail, 1991.

Montez, Madame Lola. *The Arts of Beauty or Secrets of a Lady's Toilet.* New York: The Ecco Press, 1978.

Morris, Bernadine. *The Fashion Makers, An Inside Look at America's Leading Designers.* New York: Random House, 1978.

Morris, Suzie Woodward. *Suzie Woodward Morris' Wardrobe Strategy.* San Francisco: Morris Publishing Company, 1984.

Morton, Grace Margaret. *The Arts of Costume and Personal Appearance.* 3d. ed. New York: John Wiley and Sons, Inc., 1964.

Myerhoff, Barbara. *Number Our Days.* New York: Touchstone, 1978.

Norman, Scott. *How to Buy Great Shoes That Fit.* New York: Prince Paperbacks/Crown Publishers, Inc., 1988.

Orbach, Susie. *Fat Is a Feminist Issue.* New York: Berkley Publishing Group, 1978.

Orbach, Susie. *Fat Is a Feminist Issue II.* New York: Berkley Publishing Group, 1982.

Patton, Jean E. with Jacqueline Cantey Brett. *Color to Color; The Black Woman's Guide to a Rainbow of Fashion and Beauty.* New York: Fireside, Simon & Shuster, 1991.

Phizacklea, Annie. *Unpacking The Fashion Industry.* New York: Routledge, 1990.

Pierre, Clara. *Looking Good, How Women See Themselves and How the Image is Packaged.* New York: Reader's Digest Press, 1976.

Poiret, Paul. *King of Fashion, The Autobiography of Paul Poiret.* Translated by Stephen Haden Guest. Philadelphia: J.B. Lippincott Company, 1931.

Pooser, Doris. *Secrets of Style.* Los Altos, California: Crisp Publications, 1992.

Procter, Jane. *Clothes Sense, Dressing Your Best for Your Figure and Your Lifestyle*. New York: Doubleday, 1984.

Quennell, Peter, ed. *Affairs of the Mind*. Washington, D.C.: New Republic Books, 1980.

Redman, Alvin, ed. *The Wit and Humor of Oscar Wilde*. New York: Dover Publications, Inc.

Revson, Lyn. *Lyn Revson's World of Style.* New York: Wyden Books, 1977.

Ribiero, Aileen. *Dress and Morality*. New York: Holmes & Meier, 1986.

Roberts, Jane. *The Education of Oversoul 7.* Englewood Cliffs, New Jersey: Prentice Hall, 1973.

Roberts, Nancy. *Breaking All The Rules, Feeling Good and Looking Great, No Matter What Your Size.* New York: Viking Press, 1985.

Robin, Jennifer. *Clothe Your Spirit*. San Francisco: Spirit Press, 1987. For more information on the book or her approach, write Clothe Your Spirit, 222 Redding Way, San Raphael, California 94901.

Rodin, Judith. *Body Traps*. New York: Morrow, 1992.

Rosenkrantz, Mary Lou. *Clothing Concepts*. New York: Macmillan, 1972.

Roth, Geneen. *Breaking Free From Compulsive Eating*. New York: Signet, 1986. For more information on her books or her approach, write Breaking Free, P.O. Box 2852, Santa Cruz, California 95063 (408) 685-8601.

Roth, Geneen. *Feeding the Hungry Heart, The Experience of Compulsive Eating.* New York: Signet, 1983.

Roth, Geneen. *Why Weight? A Guide to Ending Compulsive Eating.* New York: Plume Books, 1989.

Ryan, Mary Shaw. *Clothing, A Study in Human Behavior.* New York: Holt, Reinhart and Winston, 1966.

Rybczynski, Witold. *Home, A Short History of an Idea.* New York: Penguin, 1987.

Satran, Pamela Redmond. *Dressing Smart, The Thinking Woman's Guide to Style.* New York: Doubleday, 1990.

Scavullo, Francesco. *Scavullo on Beauty*. New York: Random House, 1976.

Sennett, Richard. *Flesh and Stone: The Body and the City in Western Civilization.* New York: W.W. Norton & Co., 1994.

Sproles, George B. *Fashion, Consumer Behavior Toward Dress*. Minneapolis, Minnesota: Burgess Publishing Company, 1979.

Stern, Jane and Michael. *Encyclopedia of Pop Culture*. New York: HarperPerennial, 1992.

Stout, Carol. *Weavers of the Jade Needle, Textiles of Highland Guatemala*. Albuquerque, New Mexico: Maxwell Museum of Anthropology, 1976.

Suares, J.C. and Susan Osborn. *Real Clothes*. New York: Quill, 1984.

Swift, Pat and Maggie Mulhern. *Great Looks*. New York: Doubleday, 1982.
Tarrant, Naomi. *The Development of Costume*. London: Routledge, 1994.

Temple, Norman J. and Burkitt, Denis. *Western Diseases*. Totowa, New Jersey: Humana Press, 1994.

Thompson, Jacqueline, Ed. *Image Impact, The Aspiring Woman's Personal Packaging Program.* New York: A & W Publishers, Inc., 1981.

Vanderbilt, Amy. *Amy Vanderbilt's Complete Book of Etiquette*. New York: Doubleday, 1958.

Vertes, Marcel. *Art and Fashion*. New York and London: The Studio Publications Inc., 1944.

Vlahos, Olivia. *Body—The Ultimate Symbol.* New York: Lippincott, 1979.

Vreeland, Diana. *DV.* New York: Alfred A. Knopf, 1984.

Wagenvoord, James and Fiona St. Aubyn. *ClothesCare.* New York: Pocket Books, 1985.

Walas, Kathleen. *Real Beauty . . . Real Woman.* New York: Mastermedia, 1992.

Wallach, Janet. *Looks That Work*. New York: Viking, 1986.

Wallach, Janet. *Working Wardrobe*. Washington, D.C.: Acropolis Books Ltd., 1981.

Weiland, Barbara and Leslie Wood. *Clothes Sense.* Portland, Oregon: Palmer/Pletsch Associates, 1984. (It is now called *Looking Good.*)

Wolf, Naomi. *The Beauty Myth*. New York: Morrow, 1991.

Woodforde, John. *The History of Vanity*. New York: St. Martin's Press, 1992.

John W. Wright, ed. *The Universal Almanac 1990.* Kansas City, Missouri: Andrews and McMeel, 1989.

With the exception of St. Augustine and Josephine Baker, the sources cited without footnotes were interviewed by the author.

To order additional copies of *Open and Clothed: For the Passionate Clothes Lover*,
send a check or money order for $24.00
plus $4.00 postage and handling
plus $1.98 sales tax (New York residents only) to:

Agapanthus Books,
P.O. Box 770103,
Woodside, New York 11377.

Thank you.

Prolific textile artist Andrea Siegel writes about topics close to her heart. While working with clients and colleagues in the fashion industry, Siegel discovered how integrity and individual experience relate intimately to effective selection of beautiful clothing. *Open and Clothed* presents her findings.

Siegel's martial arts practice led to her last book, *Women in Aikido* (North Atlantic Press), which explores the issues of power, heart and common sense in discussions with female black belts. She is currently at work on a book about her late father.

A graduate of the University of California at Berkeley, Siegel lives in New York City and visits California often. Her passion for clothing began at age fifteen: She left her heart in Rome where she saw the most gorgeous pair of leather boots.